MW01452073

THE LAW OF ARMED CONFLICT

Global Interdisciplinary Studies Series

Series Editor: Sai Felicia Krishna-Hensel
Interdisciplinary Global Studies Research Initiative,
Center for Business and Economic Development,
Auburn University, Montgomery, USA

The Global Interdisciplinary Studies Series reflects a recognition that globalization is leading to fundamental changes in the world order, creating new imperatives and requiring new ways of understanding the international system. It is increasingly clear that the next century will be characterized by issues that transcend national and cultural boundaries, shaped by competitive forces and features of economic globalization yet to be fully evaluated and understood.

Comparative and comprehensive in concept, this series explores the relationship between transnational and regional issues through the lens of widely applicable interdisciplinary methodologies and analytic models. The series consists of innovative monographs and collections of essays representing the best of contemporary research, designed to transcend disciplinary boundaries in seeking to better understand a globalizing world.

Also in the series

The United States and Europe: Policy Imperatives in a Globalizing World
Edited by Howard M. Hensel
ISBN 0 7546 3319 5

Conflict and Security in the Former Soviet Union
The Role of the OSCE
Maria Raquel Freire
ISBN 0 7546 3526 0

Sovereignty and the Global Community
The Quest for Order in the International System
Edited by Howard M. Hensel
ISBN 0 7546 4199 6

The New Security Environment
The Impact on Russia, Central and Eastern Europe
Edited by Roger E. Kanet
ISBN 0 7546 4330 1

The Law of Armed Conflict
Constraints on the Contemporary Use of Military Force

Edited by
HOWARD M. HENSEL
Air War College, USA

ASHGATE

© Howard M. Hensel 2005

All rights reserved. No part of this publication may be reproduced, stored in a retrieval system, or transmitted in any form or by any means, electronic, mechanical, photocopying, recording or otherwise without the prior permission of the publisher.

Howard M. Hensel has asserted his right under the Copyright, Designs and Patents Act, 1988, to be identified as the editor of this work.

Published by
Ashgate Publishing Limited
Gower House
Croft Road
Aldershot
Hampshire GU11 3HR
England

Ashgate Publishing Company
Suite 420
101 Cherry Street
Burlington, VT 05401-4405
USA

Ashgate website: http://www.ashgate.com

British Library Cataloguing in Publication Data
The law of armed conflict : constraints on the contemporary
   use of military force. - (Global interdisciplinary studies
   series)
   1. War - Moral and ethical aspects 2. War (International law)
   3. Just war doctrine
   I. Hensel, Howard M.
   172.4'2

Library of Congress Cataloging-in-Publication Data
The law of armed conflict : constraints on the contemporary use of military force / edited by Howard M. Hensel.
       p. cm. -- (Global interdisciplinary studies series)
   Includes index.
   ISBN 0-7546-4543-6
   1.War (International law) 2. Prisoners of war--Legal status, laws, etc. 3. War victims--Legal status, laws, etc. 4. War on Terrorism, 2001- I. Hensel, Howard M. II. Series.

KZ6385.L39 2005
341.6--dc22
                                                                                          2005014420
ISBN 07546 4543 6

Printed and bound in Great Britain by MPG Books Ltd. Bodmin, Cornwall

Contents

List of Contributors		*vii*
Introduction		*ix*
1	Military Necessity and the War Against Global Terrorism *Gregory A. Raymond*	1
2	Targeting Regime Leaders During Armed Hostilities: An Effective Way to Achieve Regime Change? *Catherine Lotrionte*	21
3	The Protection of Cultural Objects During Armed Conflicts *Howard M. Hensel*	39
4	The Principle of Civilian Protection and Contemporary Armed Conflict *Mika Nishimura Hayashi*	105
5	Detention, the 'War on Terror' and International Law *Françoise J. Hampson*	131
6	The Impact of the War on Terror on the Accountability of Armed Groups *George J. Andreopoulos*	171
7	The War on Terrorism: Time for a New 'Wise War' Framework? *April Morgan*	193
8	Conclusion: Amid Normative and Conceptual Crisis *Richard Falk*	241
Index		*247*

List of Contributors

George J. Andreopoulos, Associate Professor, John Jay College of Criminal Justice and the Graduate Center, City University of New York, United States.

Richard Falk, Albert G. Milbank Professor of International Law and Practice, Emeritus, Princeton University and, since 2002, Visiting Professor, Global Studies, University of California at Santa Barbara, United States.

Françoise J. Hampson, Professor of Law, University of Essex, United Kingdom.

Mika Nishimura Hayashi, Associate Professor, International Law, Graduate School of International Cooperation Studies, Kobe University, Japan.

Howard M. Hensel, Professor of Politico-Military Affairs, Air War College, United States.

Catherine Lotrionte, Adjunct Professor, School of Foreign Service and the Law Center, Georgetown University, United States.

April Morgan, Assistant Professor of Political Science, University of Tennessee, United States.

Gregory A. Raymond, Frank Church Professor of International Relations, Boise State University, United States.

Introduction

Howard M. Hensel

Throughout the ages men have debated whether it is ever appropriate to resort to the use of armed force as an instrument of policy in the process of conflict resolution. If answered in the affirmative, under what circumstances should armed force be used? In addition, what, if any, normative standards should govern the conduct of armed conflict and, if such standards exist, should they be applied universally or selectively?

In an effort to address these questions, Western philosophers and theologians developed criteria for just and unjust wars. These criteria had their origin in the writings of St. Ambrose (339-397) and St. Augustine (354-430) and were further developed by St. Thomas Aquinas (1225-1274), Francisco de Vitoria (c. 1480-1546), Francisco Suarez (1548-1617), Alberico Gentili (1552-1608), Hugo Grotius (1583-1645), Samuel Pufendorf (1632-1694), Christian Wolff (1676-1756), Cornelius van Bynkershoek (1673-1743), and Emerich de Vattel (1714-1767).[1] These and other scholars agreed that "just wars" are those that "are waged to redress a wrong suffered". Hence, "wars must always be preceded by an injury," consisting "either in the neglect of a state to suppress crimes committed by its subjects, or in attacks upon the rights of others".[2] As Joachim von Elbe observed,

> Punishment and measure of damages are determined by the purpose of the just war; its aim is not primarily victory, but the establishment of peace, *viz.*, a state of *"tranqullitas ordinis"* or the ordered harmony where all things have their allotted place. Thus, the concept of the just peace is from the outset closely associated with the ideal of the just war. No specific rules, however, are as yet laid down with respect to the content of the peace; it must, in general, restore the injured rights and lead to a well-ordered concord among men.[3]

Based upon this central proposition, a series of principles for *jus ad bellum*, the conditions for justly resorting to war, have emerged. (1) Legitimacy: only legitimate, sovereign authorities can authorize the resort of armed conflict. (2) Just Cause: force may be used only to secure just goals. (3) Proportionality: the positive benefits created by a better peace following the conclusion of the armed conflict must outweigh negative costs in human lives, damage to property, and societal dislocation incurred as a result of the armed conflict. (4) Right Motives: the motivation for resorting to the use of armed force must be to promote good or avoid evil. (5) Last Resort: all other reasonable efforts to resolve the dispute peacefully must have been taken before resorting to armed hostilities. (6) Prospect of Victory: except in situations involving self-defense, there must be a reasonable prospect for the attainment of the just objectives sought. (7) Declaration: the legitimate authorities must issue an explicit statement declaring the commencement of armed hostilities. Finally, (8) Relative Justice of Cause: often, various antagonists engaged in hostilities pursue causes that are based upon relative degrees of justness.[4]

Once the decision had been taken to resort to the use of force, the principles of *jus in bello*, the just conduct of war, were said to govern the actual use of armed force. Two principles have emerged as paramount. (1) Discrimination: a distinction must be made between combatants and objects used for military purposes versus non-combatants and properties that are not used for military purposes. Only the former may legitimately constitute the object of military operations. (2) Proportionality: the cost of military operations in terms of casualties and amount of collateral damage to civilian property must not be excessive or disproportionate compared to the military advantages gained by the partial or total destruction or neutralization of the contested military objectives.[5] In addition to these broad principles, implicitly and/or explicitly agreed upon normative standards for the conduct of warfare, usually adhered to among similar belligerents, as well as codes of chivalry, contractual arrangements, and, eventually, a body of customary and conventional laws governing warfare all contributed to the patrimony of guidelines regarding the use of force in armed conflicts.[6]

During the 20th century, the Covenant of the League of Nations and, later, the Charter of the United Nations delineated the conditions under which states or the international community collectively could legitimately use military force as an instrument of policy. In doing so, the focus shifted from unjust versus just wars to aggressive versus defensive wars.[7] According to Article 2, paragraph 4 of the Charter of the United Nations, "All Members shall refrain in their international relations from the threat or use of force against the territorial integrity or political independence of any state or in any other manner inconsistent with the Purposes of the United Nations". Article 51, however, states, "Nothing in the present Charter shall impair the inherent right of individual or collective self-defense if an armed attack occurs against a Member of the United Nations, until the Security Council has taken measures necessary to maintain international peace and security". In addition, Article 39 provides that, "The Security Council shall determine the existence of any threat to the peace, breach of the peace, or act of aggression, and shall make recommendations, or decide what measures shall be taken in accordance with Articles 41 and 42 to maintain or restore international peace and security". While Article 41 suggests possible measures short of the application of military force that the Security Council could take, Article 42 states, "Should the Security Council consider that measures provided for in Article 41 would be inadequate or have proved to be inadequate, it may take such action by air, sea or land forces as may be necessary to maintain or restore international peace and security".[8] In short, as embodied in the U.N. Charter, the international community established that the use of armed force is legitimate only as an act of self-defense by the individual states or in actions authorized by the Security Council designed to "maintain or restore international peace and security".

As throughout human history, the objectives pursued in contemporary armed conflicts range from limited to unlimited goals. Moreover, while armed clashes between states continue to characterize modern warfare, many contemporary manifestations of armed conflict involve civil strife, secessionist movements, popular resistance movements, and movements of national liberation, The forms of contemporary warfare extend along the spectrum of conflict from total war, to wars that are, in various degrees of gradation, limited in scope, nature, intensity, and duration, to low-intensity conflicts. While many contemporary wars continue to be fought by traditional armies composed of clearly identifiable soldiers, modern armed conflicts are also often waged by guerrilla or partisan fighters whose identities are easily confused with non-combatants. Indeed, tragically, modern warfare very often fails to distinguish between combatants and non-combatants, as well as between legitimate military objectives and civilian objects.

Terrorism is increasingly a characteristic manifestation of contemporary armed conflict. Similarly, modern weaponry ranges from nuclear, radiological, chemical, and biological weapons of mass destruction, through precision guided munitions and conventional weaponry, to less sophisticated, but very lethal, home-made explosive devices. Indeed, as the world saw on September 11, 2001, vehicles not normally considered to be weapons can, under certain circumstances, be transformed into deadly instruments of large-scale destruction. In this context, questions arise as to the circumstances, degree, and criteria that must be satisfactorily met to determine whether an imminent, unambiguous threat exists, thereby arguably justifying the preemptive use of force against the perpetuator of the threat under the individual self-defense or collective security provisions of the U.N. Charter. Alternatively, if the threat is neither imminent nor unambiguous, does the prospect of massive, catastrophic devastation ever justify a preventative war against a possible future threat to an individual state or the general peace and security of the international community? Moreover, what standards should be applied in calculating proportionality of response to these types of threat?[9]

In conjunction with this transformation of virtually all aspects of contemporary warfare, there has been an analogous transformation in important aspects of military strategies employed by contemporary belligerents in pursuit of their objectives. Indeed, such concepts as the targeting of enemy leaders have been increasingly incorporated into military strategies. Similarly, many have sought to redefine such concepts as military necessity, collateral damage, the definitions of combatants and non-combatants, and the status of prisoners-of-war and detainees. Finally, in view of the diverse nature of contemporary challenges, fundamental questions have been raised concerning the universality versus selective applicability of conventional and even customary norms governing the conduct of armed conflict. In short, the transformation of modern warfare and the resultant changes in military strategies pursued by various state and non-state belligerents have often raised controversial and vexing questions concerning the interpretation and applicability of many of the concepts and principles incorporated not only in traditional ideas regarding *jus ad bellum* and *jus in bello*, but also in international legal accords, as well as many of the tenets of customary and conventional law of armed conflict as they have developed during the past century and a half.

This volume presents a diversity of scholarly opinion as it seeks to assess some of the contemporary normative and legal challenges and problems associated with the application of customary and conventional normative standards and laws governing the use of armed force in the context of 21st century armed conflicts.[10] In chapter 1, Gregory Raymond examines the general principle of military necessity and critically assesses its application within the context of the contemporary doctrine "anticipatory self-defense". Chapter 2, by Catherine Lotrionte, analyzes the legal basis and policy implications associated with the increasingly discussed strategic option of targeting enemy regime leaders during periods of armed hostilities. Chapter 3 provides a comprehensive historical review and assessment of the concept of protecting cultural objects during periods of armed hostilities, as reflected both in the conduct of 20th century armed conflicts, as well as in various draft and enacted international treaties and agreements since the mid 19th century. The chapter concludes with a review of the 1999 Second Protocol to the 1954 Hague Convention for the Protection on Cultural Property in the Event of Armed Conflict. In chapter 4, Mika Nishimura Hayashi analyzes alternative perspectives adopted by legal scholars concerning the principle of civilian protection during armed hostilities. Her chapter, however, has implications for similar alternative viewpoints concerning the concept of protecting cultural objects discussed in the previous chapter. Chapter 5 by Françoise Hampson analyzes contemporary issues concerning the status of prisoners-of-war and detainees during periods of armed conflict. In Chapter 6, George Andreopoulos examines and assesses the implications of the broader question of the status and accountability of armed groups under the provisions of the law of armed conflict. In Chapter 7, April Morgan returns the focus of discussion to the topic of just war theory raised in the Introduction and relates that criteria to the types of conflicts confronting the global community at the outset of the 21st century. She concludes by suggesting that a "holistic" approach might prove particularly useful in providing insights in assessing ambiguous threats directed against extremely valuable, but highly vulnerable populations and societal assets, as well as in formulating an appropriate policy response to these types of threats. Lastly, in the final chapter, Richard Falk draws a series of conclusions that provide a valuable perspective on the application of the laws of armed conflict within the contemporary global security environment.

I would like to thank Ashgate Publishing Ltd., especially Kirstin Howgate and Maureen Mansell-Ward, whose invaluable support and cooperation helped to make this book possible, as well as my wife and daughter for their immense help and encouragement in preparing this volume. Hopefully, the book will contribute to the global community's understanding of the nature, complexity, and applicability of the principles and tenets of customary and conventional normative standards and laws governing the contemporary use of armed force. As such, it is hoped that scholars, statesmen, military leaders, international policy analysts, and any within the global community who seek to understand the relationship between global normative values and the use of military instruments of power in the 21st century will find this work both illuminating and thought provoking.

Notes

[1] Elbe, 1939, pp. 665-688; Nussbaum, 1954, pp. 35-174; Taylor, 1979, pp. 245-258.
[2] Elbe, 1939, p. 668.
[3] Elbe, 1939, p. 669.
[4] Elbe, 1939, pp. 669-683; Nussbaum, 1954, pp. 35-174; Bailey, 1972, pp. 4-16; Taylor, 1979, pp. 245-258; Miller, 1991, pp. 13-15; Howard, 1994, pp. 2-3; Fixdal and Smith, 1998, pp. 286, 290-305. See also Walzer, 1977.
[5] Bailey 1972, pp. 12-16; Bothe, Partsch, and Solf, 1982, pp. 309-311, 323-326, 360-369. Miller, 1991, pp. 13-15; Howard, 1994, p. 3; Rogers, 1996, pp. 7-24; Fixdal and Smith 1998, p. 286. See also Walzer, 1977.
[6] Howard, Andreopoulos, and Shulman, 1994.
[7] Taylor, 1979, p. 255.
[8] Charter of the United Nations, cited in Claude, 1964, pp. 419, 427-429.
[9] Kegley and Raymond, 2003, pp. 385-394.
[10] The opinions, conclusions, and/or recommendations expressed or implied within this book are solely those of the authors who are entirely responsible for the contents of their works and do not necessarily represent the views of any academic institution, the Air University, the United States Air Force, the U.S. Department of Defense, any U.S. government agency, any other government, multinational agency, or non-governmental organization.

References

Bailey, Sydney B. *Prohibitions and Restraints in War* (Oxford: Oxford University Press, 1972).
Bothe, Michael, Partsch Karl Josef, and Solf, Waldemar A. *New Rules for Victims of Armed Conflicts* (The Hague: Martinus Nijhoff Publishers, 1982).
Claude, Inis, L. *Swords into Plowshares* (New York: Random House, 1964).
Elbe, Joachim von, "The Evolution of the Concept of the Just War in International Law," *The American Journal of International Law*, Volume #33 (1939), pp. 665-688.
Fixdal, Mona and Smith, Dan "Humanitarian Intervention and Just War", *Mershon International Studies Review*, #42 (1998), pp. 283-312.
Howard, Michael "Constraints on Warfare", in Michael Howard, George J. Andreopoulos, and Mark R. Shulman (eds), *The Laws of War: Constraints on Warfare in the Western World* (New Haven: Yale University Press, 1994).
Howard, Michael, Andreopoulos, George J. and Shulman, Mark R. (eds), *The Laws of War: Constraints on Warfare in the Western World* (New Haven: Yale University Press, 1994).
Kegley, Charles W. and Raymond, Gregory A. "Preventive War and Permissive Normative Order", *International Studies Perspectives* #4 (2003), pp. 385-394.

Miller, Richard B. *Interpretations of Conflict, Ethics, Pacifism, and the Just War Tradition* (Chicago: University of Chicago Press, 1991).

Nussbaum, Arthur *A Concise History of the Law of Nations* (New York: Macmillan, 1954).

Rogers, A.P.V. *Law on the Battlefield* (Manchester: Manchester University Press, 1996).

Taylor, Telford "Just and Unjust Wars", in Malham M. Wakin, *War, Morality and the Military Profession* (Boulder: Westview Press, 1979), pp. 245-258.

Walzer, Michael *Just and Unjust Wars* (New York: Basic Books, 1977).

Chapter 1

Military Necessity and the War Against Global Terrorism

Gregory A. Raymond

Throughout history, political leaders have appealed to strategic necessities as a justification for violating international law. Pleas of necessity challenge the wrongfulness of an act on the basis that it was the only means of safeguarding a vital interest against a grave danger. Of all the areas of world affairs covered by international law, the laws of war are considered the most 'subject to corruption by the rude pressures of necessity'.[1] As expressed in the ancient aphorism, *Inter arma silent leges* (In times of war the law is silent), statesmen and commanders in the field have long been tempted to waive legal prohibitions on the use of force to gain momentary advantages. Despite complaints that 'military necessity' is an 'elusive blanket phrase'[2] and an 'utter juridicial nullity',[3] appeals to its alleged demands continue to be a common feature of national security debates.

In the wake Al Qaeda's September 11, 2001 attacks on the World Trade Center and the Pentagon, the concept of necessity has been employed by various members of the Bush administration to justify preemptive uses of military force against terrorists and the states that harbor them. Old security doctrines emphasizing deterrence and containment must be reassessed in the light of the attacks on New York and Washington, declared U.S. Secretary of Defense Donald Rumsfeld. 'You cannot defend against terrorism', he continued. 'You can't defend at every place at every time against every technique. You just can't do it, because they just keep changing techniques and time, and you have to go after them. And you have to take it to them, and that means you have to preempt them'.[4]

The Bush administration's new doctrine of preemptive warfare, as formally presented in the September 2002 *National Security Strategy of the United States of America*, has been characterized as a 'profound strategic innovation'.[5] Among its most innovative aspects is the conflation of preemption with preventive military action. A *preemptive* attack entails the use of force to quell or mitigate an impending strike by an adversary. *Preventive* action entails the use of force to eliminate any possible future strike, even when there is no reason to believe that aggression is planned or the capability to launch such a strike is operational.[6]

Whereas the grounds for preemption lie in evidence of a credible, imminent threat, the basis for prevention rests on the suspicion of an incipient, contingent threat. Israel's June 5, 1967 surprise attack against Egypt is as a classic example of military preemption. On the other hand, its June 7, 1981 raid on Iraq's Osirak nuclear facility exemplifies the preventive use of military force. In the first case, Israeli leaders had evidence that an invasion was forthcoming and believed the costs would be devastating if Egypt landed the first blow. In the second case, they concluded that using force before Iraq fabricated nuclear weapons was preferable to risking war under less favorable conditions later.

Although the Bush administration describes its new security strategy with the language of preemption, the president and his foreign policy advisors have disclosed that it contains elements of prevention. The United States, they insist, will not wait for the final proof of an impending strike.[7] Strategic necessity counsels using America's unparalleled military strength against emerging threats *before* they are fully formed, even if Washington has to act unilaterally. As Deputy Secretary of Defense Paul Wolfowitz bluntly put it: 'Anyone who believes that we can wait until we have certain knowledge that attacks are imminent has failed to connect the dots that led to September 11'.[8] Preventive intervention against what the administration calls 'gathering' (as opposed to imminent) dangers is a strategic imperative. In the words of President George W. Bush, 'We must take the battle to the enemy and confront the worst threats before they emerge'.[9]

During certain historical periods, prevailing international norms have accepted appeals to military necessity; at other times they have restricted its use. Given the dominant position of the United States in the world, an American policy of preventive intervention could exert enormous pressure to expand the notion of 'inherent right' of self-defense contained in Article 51 of the United Nations Charter, pushing international norms toward a more permissive interpretation of military necessity.[10] The purpose of this study is to examine the formation and decay of those international legal norms that justify acts of violence through appeals to military necessity. After defining the concept of military necessity, it will trace the evolution of international norms pertaining to its use, and then analyze the impact that the Bush national security strategy will likely have on the prescriptions and proscriptions contained in those norms.

Necessity and the War Convention

Political interaction among nation-states occurs within an anarchic setting. Although states vary in putative strength, they are juridicial equals whose sovereignty is not superseded by any higher authority. Nevertheless, even in the absence of such an authority, their behavior is circumscribed by a structure of acknowledged normative standards. Those standards that guide the conduct of belligerents are what Michael Walzer calls the 'war convention'.[11]

The substance of the war convention is grounded in the international community's expectations about armed combat, expectations that are most explicitly set forth in prevailing legal norms. International norms are generalized standards of conduct that delineate the scope of a state's entitlements, the extent of its obligations, and the range of its jurisdiction by prescribing certain actions but proscribing others.[12] Rather than simply being modal forms of state practice, they embody collective expectations about the proper activities of states.

To conceptualize international norms in this way is to see them as a medium through which generally held beliefs about acceptable forms of behavior are transmitted to members of the state system. The specific subset of norms that concern us here are the legal precepts that comprise the war convention. Reduced to their essence, these norms are 'a form of communication' that is 'stored in memories that include treaty collections, statute books . . . and treatises on international law'.[13] They contain interrelated linguistic symbols arranged in propositional form that provide generic perceptual categories through which events are given meaning. How we interpret right and wrong conduct in war is through the perceptual categories furnished by international norms. They supply a shared frame of reference on the way states should or should not behave in specific military situations.

The aim of the war convention is to place normative restraints upon the conduct of war by delineating when it is legitimate for states to use deadly force, how it should be used, and against whom it may be applied. Periodically, attempts are made to circumvent these restraints by citing the exigencies of necessity. Appeals to necessity challenge the wrongfulness of an act on the basis that it was the only means of safeguarding an essential interest against a grave and imminent peril. It was this meaning of necessity U.S. Secretary of State John Quincy Adams conveyed when he defended American military actions in Spanish Western Florida during 1818. His sentiments were echoed a century later by British Secretary of State for War Lord Kitchener, who insisted: 'We must make war as we must; not as we should like'.[14]

In order to sidestep normative limitations on the use of force, the doctrine of military necessity has been invoked by political and military leaders alike. Chancellor von Bethmann-Hollweg of Germany, President McKinley of the United States, as well as such famous commanders in the field as Napoleon and Sheridan are among those who have drawn upon the logic of military necessity to justify their actions. References to the doctrine have appeared in international treaties (e.g., Article 23 [g] of the *Hague Convention IV*), the judgments of international tribunals (e.g., the Hardman incident of 1910 [*Great Britain v. the United States*]), military field manuals (e.g., *Kriegsbrauch im Landkriege*, General Staff of the German Army, 1902), and diplomatic notes (e.g., letter of September 6, 1814 from U.S. Secretary of State Monroe to British Vice-Admiral Cochrane regarding the burning of the village of Newark in Upper Canada). Since they may absolve a state from the nonobservance of international obligations, pleas of military necessity have been advanced to excuse behavior ranging from belligerent measures taken against an enemy to egregious breaches of neutral rights. For example, military necessity was invoked in 1854 by the United States to defend the bombardment of Greytown, Nicaragua; it was employed by Prussia to excuse the sinking of British colliers in the Seine during the Franco-Prussian War; it was used by Great Britain to justify mining the North Sea during World War I; and it was conjured up by Germany to excuse the devastation of the Somme region during the retreat of 1917.[15] In each of these episodes the defense that was mounted represented a variant of the maxim, *Necessitas non subditur legi* (Necessity is not subject to the law).

Traditionally, those invoking necessity to excuse the nonobservance of international obligations have claimed that national self-preservation justified their actions. Although many legal scholars consider the doctrine of self-preservation 'overdue for elimination from the vocabulary of the international lawyer',[16] those who argue from defensive necessity claim that 'no other obligation ought to outweigh . . . [one's] own safety').[17] In the *Nitisara*, for example, the ancient Hindu writer Sukra maintains that for reasons of self-preservation a leader may have to wage a treacherous war (*Kuta Yudha*), where ordinary limits on the conduct of hostilities do not apply.[18] According to Sukra and virtually all subsequent members of the realist school of thought, political leaders are agents of the state charged with the responsibility of guaranteeing its survival; hence they cannot be judged by the same standards that apply in an ordinary citizen's private life.

Typical expressions of the argument from necessity have the form 'Circumstances required that I do X.' The rhetorical strategy behind this form of argument is to frame situations of circumscribed options as situations where no alternatives exist. This creates an opportunity to bypass moral considerations as the discourse is moved from the *conditional* ('My choices are limited to options X, Y, and Z.') to the *categorical* ('I have no alternative but to do X.'). In effect, the strategy attempts to blur the difference between expediency and real necessity.[19] Whereas the former involves doing what is advantageous based on considerations of utility, the latter implies that one cannot help but act in a certain way in order to survive. By shifting the discourse in this manner, an effort is made to relieve the actor of responsibility. Once expedient actions are masked as being unavoidable, the actor is insulated from criticism so long as others accept the proposition that he or she is not accountable for acts performed under compulsion. 'Praise and blame are accorded to voluntary acts', noted Aristotle in a famous expression of this view, 'but involuntary acts are accorded pardon, and at times pity'.[20]

Of course, not everyone is persuaded by efforts to cloak expedience as a strategic necessity. In particular, people who subscribe to deontological ethics do not accept necessity as a license for violating restrictions on how wars should be fought. Moral duty, from their perspective, imposes an absolute injunction that is independent of any advantage gained by ignoring restrictions on battlefield practices. Take, for instance, the behavior of Gaius Fabricius, the Roman consul, who on the eve of a battle in 278 BCE with King Pyrrhus of Epirus, turned down an offer from a Greek deserter to poison the king. Waging war by devious means is morally wrong, contend deontologists, even if such tactics can guarantee a victory against overwhelming odds. It would be preferable, observes Cicero, to lose with honor, rather than to triumph without it.[21]

Whereas deontologists hold that certain inherent features of a military action make it right or wrong, whatever its ultimate results on the battlefield, political leaders are deeply interested in policy outcomes and thus tend to gravitate toward the consequentialism of the argument from necessity. From their standpoint, foreign policy is crafted in 'a realm of moral approximations, tentative compromises, and, occasionally, choices among lesser evils'.[22] Leaders responsible for national security, they contend, cannot always abide by a set of Marquis of Queensberry rules; violations of humanitarian restrictions on the excesses of war may be unavoidable. For those who accept this Hobbesian image of states being in a 'posture of gladiators' struggling for survival, the lure of the argument from necessity is powerful. In fact, it is so enticing some people complain that 'governments seem universally tempted to invoke this excuse at the drop of a hat, to use it as a pretext for committing all sorts of unconscionable acts'.[23]

Normative Support for Appeals to Necessity

In order to determine when the necessity defense was accepted as an integral part of the war convention, we need a way to trace changes over time in the degree of support that appeals to military necessity have received from international legal norms.

To say that relations between belligerents are tempered by a web of norms grounded in the international community's expectations about combat is to say there is a normative structure to the state system that is intersubjectively shared. This structure is not composed of objective, materially-based entities that can be measured in a straightforward manner, like one might do when counting the number of great powers to determine the size of a multipolar system. Reproducible evidence on the content of international norms is difficult to acquire because the expectations that were held at different points in history about the right way for states to behave are not amenable to direct visual inspection. Nonetheless, evidence may be obtained indirectly by examining what publicists from these periods reported about prevailing norms.

Publicists have long sought to communicate what legal norms held sway in their lifetime when they wrote their treatises on international law. Indeed, some of them have had their works 'quoted and requoted almost as if they were oracular pronouncements'.[24] Although the role of publicists in actual law-making may be nominal, their writings have traditionally been accepted by judicial tribunals as a subsidiary means of determining the content of prevailing legal norms (see *Paquete*

Habana, Lola, 175 U.S. 677 [1900]; and Article 38 [1][d] of the Statute of the International Court of Justice). Moreover, they continue to be recognized for their role in revealing the content of international legal norms.[25] It is shortsighted to dismiss the value of publicists, writes legal scholar Malcolm Shaw. 'States in the presentation of their claims, national law officials in their opinions to their governments, the various international judicial and arbitral bodies in considering their decisions, and the judges of municipal courts when the need arises, all consult and quote the writings of leading juristic authorities'.[26] As the only professional group dedicated to monitoring and summarizing changes in international legal norms, their descriptions can be considered an information source from which data on the changing content of international legal norms can be made. 'If we turn to the most eminent publicists, and look for common agreement between them on some specific rule', recommends Ingrid Detter Delupis, 'we will find considerable guidance as to the contents of international law on a specific problem'.[27] Publicists, in other words, may be thought of as members of an 'international guild whose bread and butter comes from expounding . . . what the law at any given moment actually is rather than what it ought to be or could have been'.[28]

Since our concern here is with the extent to which legal norms during different historical periods admitted appeals to military necessity as a justification for violating generally held restrictions on how war should be fought, a content analysis of what eminent publicists from those periods reported would provide a way to gauge the degree of support for the necessity defense.

Content analysis is a data-making procedure that may be performed on virtually any communication, from constitutions to comic strips. Devised for the study of social artifacts, it has proven extremely useful in longitudinal research designs for examining the values and ideas of inaccessible subjects. Legal treatises are artifacts that document the commonly held expectations for state behavior that existed in their day. When these works are subjected to content analysis, the publicists are considered expert witnesses whose descriptions constitute observations that may be coded to make quantitative data on the directives contained in prevailing international legal norms.

The major drawback of this procedure is that content analysis only deals with what explicitly appears in a document – its manifest, outward message. It does not reveal any deeper meaning that may be implied 'between the lines' of the text. Fortunately, this liability does not invalidate the limited purpose for which content analysis is being used here: namely, to extract information on generally held expectations about state behavior from a physical record of communication written for that very reason. While the memoirs of statesmen can also furnish this kind of information, these documents suffer from more drawbacks than legal treatises. Whereas treatises are comprehensive, systematic records that often go through multiple editions to reflect changes in norms, memoirs are produced episodically and may not directly address the topic of international norms. In short, treatises provide running historical record that is readily amenable to coding and offers a reasonable empirical proxy for measuring the content of international legal norms.

To trace the changes over time in the degree of support for the necessity defense, 275 legal treatises were content analyzed under the auspices of the Transnational Rules Indicators Project (TRIP). Because not all treatises are equally relevant for data-making purposes, some reproducible method is required for identifying those authoritative texts written by the most eminent publicists. The criteria used by TRIP was whether a work had gone through multiple revised editions or had been identified as authoritative by either independent scholarship (e.g., listed in the Association of Law Schools' bibliography of international law texts), or by a recognized legal body such as the International Court of Justice. Because the TRIP project is described in detail elsewhere,[29] the presentation here will focus on the specific procedure used for measuring changes in those norms pertaining to military necessity.

Index Construction

A spectrum of views can be identified on what conduct is justified by military necessity. At one extreme lies a *maximalist* position that argues whatever justifies resorting to war in the first place justifies employing the means required for achieving one's objectives.[30] As suggested in the written works of such military thinkers as Bissing, Blüme, Disfurth, Goltz, Hindenburg, and Moltke, any acts of violence are acceptable if they are deemed necessary to ensure victory. Indeed, sharp practices that shorten wars are claimed to be humane. The fate of Duke Hsiang of Sung is occasionally used by maximalists to illustrate how failing to circumvent generally acknowledged rules of warfare in an emergency can be dangerous. In 638 BCE, the duke refused to attack an army from the rival state of Ch'u while it was crossing the Hung River, even though his forces were outnumbered and would probably be vanquished if their adversaries made it to the other side. Believing that such an attack would be immoral, the duke waited until the army from Ch'u had forded the river. By not doing what was militarily necessary, maximalists blame him for the terrible defeat suffered by Sung.

At the opposite extreme are *minimalists* who see appeals to necessity as a subterfuge for illegal acts. Rejecting the aphorism *Kriegsraison geht vor Kriegsmanier* (Necessity in war overrules the manner of warfare), they insist that the so-called necessities of war have already been sufficiently observed in drawing up the laws of war, and thus military necessity can only be invoked in those situations where international legal norms have in advance given express sanction for its use.[31] Necessity cannot be used as a defense for violating norms that specify absolute prohibitions. As articulated by Francis Lieber in United States Army General Orders No. 100 (1862), military necessity consists of 'those measures which are indispensable for securing the ends of war, and which are lawful according to the modern law and usages of war.' To adopt the doctrine of

Kriegsraison, according to Paul Pradier-Fodéré, Elihu Root, and other minimalists, would be tantamount to abandoning international law. As the legal scholar C.H.M. Waldock summarized this view, 'The doctrine of necessity is a rejection of international law'.[32]

Finally, located between these polar extremes are advocates of a *limitationist* position whose roots lie in the Grotian interpretation of necessity.[33] Whereas Grotius accepted the doctrine of military necessity, he argued that it should be subject to guidelines. Among those proposed by contemporary exponents of the limitationist position are legitimacy (just cause), immediacy (imminent danger), indispensability (no practical alternative), discrimination (respect for the principle of noncombatant immunity), proportionality (damage must not exceed the importance of the objective), and responsibility (the decision must be made by a competent authority who is accountable to judicial review). In essence, the British adopted the limitationist position when they defended their 1807 bombardment of Copenhagen by claiming that the danger they faced 'was certain, urgent and extreme, as to create a case of urgent, paramount necessity, leaving his Majesty's ministers no choice'.[34] Another example can be found in the *Caroline* incident of 1837, during which U.S. Secretary of State Daniel Webster conceptualized necessity in terms of being 'instant, overwhelming, leaving no choice of means and no moment for deliberation.'

When movement occurs from a maximalist to a minimalist position, the conception of military necessity gradually shifts from permissive to prohibitive. At any given point in time, the climate of opinion within the state system may be said to reside somewhere between these polar extremes. As a result, each of the 275 treatises was coded on a five point scale that measured the degree to which prevailing norms were perceived by the author of the treatise as supporting a permissive definition of military necessity. Once every treatise in a particular half-decade was coded, the mean value was calculated for each successive recording period. The resulting index ranged from 5.00 (maximalist conception of military necessity) to 1.00 (minimalist conception), with intermediate positions arrayed in between indicating various shades of limitationism. The higher the score on the index, the more prevailing legal norms supported a permissive interpretation of necessity; the lower the score, the more they restricted appeals to military necessity.

Historical Trends in Support for Military Necessity

Figure 1.1 shows the evolution of support for the necessity defense during the nineteenth and twentieth centuries. As the plot of the values of the necessity norm index over the past two centuries reveals, support for a permissive conception of military necessity was strong during the early decades of the nineteenth century. The French Revolutionary and Napoleonic Wars had battered Europe for almost a quarter century, leaving over two and a half million combatants dead. With the Congress of Vienna, the Treaty of the Holy Alliance, and the Quadruple Alliance, which followed in succession between 1815 and 1818, the major continental powers of the period forged a security regime that envisioned preventive military intervention as a strategic necessity whenever liberal threats to monarchical legitimacy surfaced. At the Congress of Aix-la-Chapelle in 1818, Tsar Alexander I of Russia proposed an alliance to intervene on behalf of rulers who were threatened by revolutionary insurrection. A few years later, revolts in Spain and Naples led Russia, Austria, and Prussia to agree at the Congress of Troppau that force could be used against states 'which have undergone in their internal structure an alteration brought on by revolt, whose consequences may be dangerous to other states'.[35] Two months later at the Congress of Laibach, the conservative continental powers backed Austria's intervention into Naples and Piedmont to suppress liberal revolts. Furthermore, during the following year at Verona, they agreed to a French proposal to crush Spanish rebels. In the ensuing years, liberal revolutions were suppressed in Palma (1831) and Portugal (1846-1847).

Figure 1.1 Three Eras in the Evolution of Necessity Norms, 1820-1999

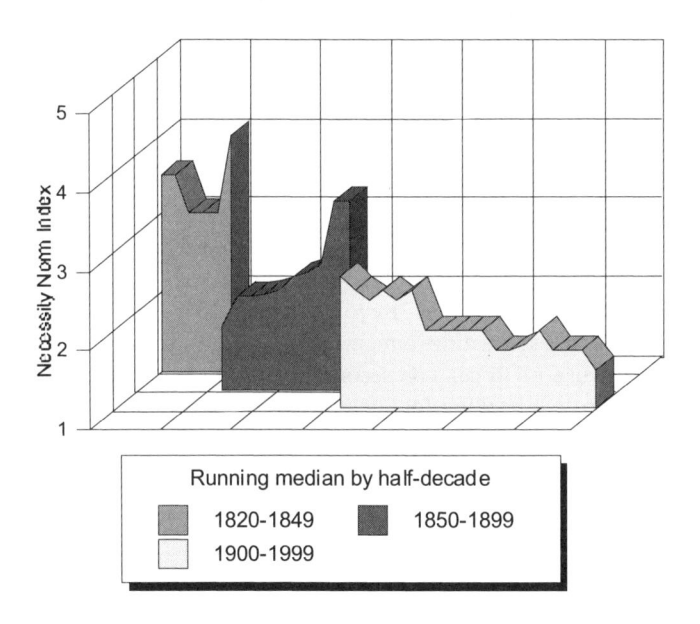

The revolutions that swept through Europe in 1848 eroded the rules of international conduct these monarchies had advocated. Normative support for a permissive conception of necessity plummeted. As military historian Geoffrey Best observes, this was the 'golden decade' of restraints on warfare.[36] Concern over the plight of soldiers at Solferino during the Franco-Austrian War of 1859, which led to the Geneva Red Cross Conferences of 1864 and 1868, ushered in a more restrictive conception of military necessity. In addition, conferences were held in St. Petersburg (1868) and Brussels (1874) to regulate weapons that aggravated suffering on the battlefield. Despite these efforts to codify international humanitarian law, support for a permissive definition of necessity returned during the last quarter of the century, as the military establishments of various countries (e.g., Spain, 1882; Britain, 1884; France, 1884; Portugal, 1890; Russia, 1895; and Italy, 1896) began drafting field manuals which reaffirmed the necessity defense.

Normative support for the necessity defense underwent a steady decline in the twentieth century. From the Hague Congresses (1899, 1907) onward, the situations under which appeals to military necessity would be accepted by the international community gradually diminished. The positions taken in the Geneva Protocol of 1925, the Nuremberg and Tokyo war crimes trials, the Geneva Convention of 1949 and Protocols of 1977, as well as in several United Nations documents (e.g., GA Doc. A/7720, November 20, 1969 and GA Doc. A/8052, September 18, 1970) testify to the growing restrictiveness of international legal norms. To be sure, this did not mean states refrained from using the argument from necessity; it simply indicates that military necessity was less likely to be accepted by the international community as a legitimate defense for violations of the war convention.

Military Necessity and Asymmetric Warfare

The prescriptions and proscriptions within the war convention are not static; international norms pertaining to the use of military force change over time. As Figure 1.1 reveals, normative support for the necessity defense has evolved through three phases since the end of the Napoleonic Wars. During the first phase, roughly from the Congress of Vienna to the Revolutions of 1848, prevailing norms countenanced appeals to extenuating circumstances as an excuse for violating accepted limits on the use of force. The second phase, though beginning in mid-century with little normative backing for such pleas, ended fifty years later with a renewed acceptance of their legitimacy. Finally, in the third phase, which extended over the entire twentieth century, normative support for the necessity defense underwent a gradual, long-term decline.

Calls for a more permissive conception of the necessity defense have recently arisen within the Bush administration, prompted by American military operations against the Taliban regime in Afghanistan and Saddam Hussein's Iraq. An example can be found in a March 2003 classified report on prisoner interrogation prepared for Secretary of Defense Rumsfeld. As described in *The Wall Street Journal*,[37] Bush administration lawyers argued that defensive necessity justified interrogation methods that violated the literal language of international law when they were undertaken to prevent further terrorist attacks on the United States. Terrorism, administration spokespeople insisted, posed a unique threat that necessitated extraordinary countermeasures.

Political terrorism entails the deliberate use or threat of violence against noncombatants, calculated to instill fear, alarm, and ultimately a feeling of helplessness in an audience beyond the immediate victims.[38] Because the perpetrators of terrorism often strike symbolic targets in a horrific manner, the psychological impact of an attack can exceed the physical damage. A mixture of drama and dread, it presents people with a danger that seems ubiquitous, unavoidable, and unpredictable.

What makes the necessity defense seem so compelling to U.S. national security policy makers today is the prospect that terrorists with global reach will eventually gain access to weapons of mass destruction. When a catastrophic terrorist attack seems inevitable, the urge to launch a preventive strike can feel overwhelming, especially since detecting the imminent use of such weapons by clandestine organizations is more difficult than observing the military buildup by a neighboring state prior to a conventional assault. Moreover, when an adversary possesses a 'warrior' ethos and flouts the code of conduct observed by disciplined professional soldiers, it is easy to conclude that unilaterally adhering to the restrictions contained in the war convention may be disadvantageous.[39] Believing the laws of war are the 'least codified' part of international law,[40] and that what has been compiled is largely irrelevant for addressing the new security threats posed by global terrorism, American policy makers have appealed to strategic necessities as a justification for subsuming preventive military action under the guise of anticipatory self-defense.

Bellum Versus Guerra

The strategic logic behind current thinking about preventive military action can be traced to the ancient Greek and Roman preference for fighting decisive engagements, meeting adversaries head on in the hope that a looming threat could be eliminated with a single blow.[41] Additionally, the argument that no tactics should be barred when fighting enemies who show little concern for legal niceties has roots in the double standard Romans adopted when dealing with different kinds of adversaries. Unlike in the Hellenistic world, where the Romans faced what they defined as 'civilized' states, elsewhere they encountered 'barbarian' tribes, which were fought on other terms.[42] Between 150 and 130 BCE, for example, Roman leaders saw the inhabitants of the Iberian Peninsula as treacherous foes. Strategic necessity, they asserted, required Rome to be as brutal and duplicitous as their barbarian enemies.[43] Similar claims were made during the ferocious campaign of 15-16 CE led by Germanicus Caesar against Arminius, chief of the Cherusci and the architect of the massacre of three legions under the command of Publius Quintilius Varus in the Teutoburg Forest.[44] Simply put, Romans distinguished between two distinct forms of warfare: *bellum* was conducted against states according to rudimentary laws of warfare; *guerra* was waged with few restraints against nonstate actors, including the irregular armed forces of barbarian tribes as well as marauding bands of pirates and brigands.[45]

Rome's *guerra* strategy represented an early approach to conducting asymmetric warfare. In brief, asymmetric war is organized violence conducted between international actors of vastly unequal military capability, where the weaker side generally relies on relatively unconventional means to attack its more powerful opponent. The belligerents may be states, or they may involve some combination of state and nonstate actors. According to various legal scholars, applying the term 'war' to the use of military force against nonstate actors is problematic. International law has traditionally defined war as an armed conflict between states, and some people view the bloodshed perpetrated by transnational terrorist groups as crimes against humanity that should be prosecuted by law enforcement agencies and punished in national courts. Since 9/11, however, the concept of 'armed attack' has been generally acknowledged to include acts of terrorism by nonstate actors that, taken singly or collectively, occur on a significant scale. From this perspective, small, isolated incursions across national frontiers do not pass the gravity threshold; conversely, massive assaults, as well as a pattern of smaller strikes that comprises a wider campaign of violence, tend to be seen as armed attacks covered by Article 51 of the UN Charter.[46] What remains controversial is whether the necessity defense can be invoked to legitimize preventive military actions as part of a twenty-first-century *guerra* strategy aimed at destroying transnational terrorist organizations such as Al Qaeda.

When Osama bin Laden announced his 1996 'Declaration of War Against Americans Occupying the Land of the Two Holy Places' and issued a *fatwa* (religious ruling) two year later calling for Americans to be killed anywhere in the world, he laid the rhetorical foundation for an asymmetric war against the United States – the infidel state he blamed for propping up corrupt, apostate Arab regimes. Prior to 9/11, bin Laden had sponsored a series of vicious attacks by Al Qaeda operatives against U.S. citizens and facilities, including suicide truck bombings of the Khobar Towers military housing complex in 1996 near Dhahran, Saudi Arabia, and the American embassies in Nairobi, Kenya and Dar es Salaam, Tanzania in 1998. Pointing to the withdrawal of U.S. forces from Lebanon following the 1983 bombing of the Marine barracks in Beruit, and their withdrawal from Somalia a decade later after losses were sustained while fighting in Mogadishu, bin Laden apparently concluded that terror was an unconventional but effective instrument in his asymmetric armed conflict with the United States. Just as the mujahadeen evicted the Soviets from Afghanistan through a combination of resourcefulness, resolve, and unrelenting pressure, so too, he believed, a new group of holy warriors would oust Americans from the Middle East.

How can the United States thwart shadowy terrorist networks that engage in indiscriminant, suicidal attacks against noncombatants? Does the barbaric nature of these attacks excuse countermeasures that would otherwise violate the war convention? What are the ramifications of reversing the twentieth-century trend shown in Figure 1.1, which increasingly restricted the legitimacy of appeals to strategic necessities?

The Normative Consequences of a Permissive Conception of Military Necessity

The policy debate over how the United States should conduct its so-called 'war on global terrorism' has raised anew timeless questions about the use of preventive military action in the name of defensive necessity. Throughout history, the behavior of the powerful has exerted a major impact on whether prevailing international norms were permissive or restrictive. Thus the way in which Washington responds to global terrorism will have an enormous influence on the behavior of others. When the reigning hegemon justifies certain behavior, it alters the frame of reference for virtually everyone else. In the anarchic, horizontal normative order of international affairs, what the strongest do eventually shapes what others do, and when that practice becomes common, it tends to take on an aura of obligation. As Stanley Hoffmann has observed, rules *of* behavior tend to become rules *for* behavior.[47]

If American appeals to the exigencies of necessity entitle Washington to engage in preventive self-defense under an expanded interpretation of Article 51 of the UN Charter, a dangerous precedent will be available for other states to follow. While preemption is justifiable whenever an attack is truly imminent, a normative order that sanctions preventive military action gives every truculent, egoistic ruler a pretext for launching premeditated, forestalling strikes against prospective adversaries.

In addition to weakening restraints on *when* states are allowed to use force, a return to a more permissive interpretation of military necessity will also weaken restraints on *how* they use force. Adhering to the longstanding *jus in bello* principle of discrimination and gauging proportionality are difficult in a preventive war. Any state acting in a discretionary, preventive manner must make a subjective assessment about how much force is needed to ensure a reasonable chance of success. Faced with uncertainties, reliance upon a worst-case analysis is likely. Yet the devastation wrought by an unbridled first strike emanating from worst-case assumptions might outweigh whatever benefits the initiator hoped to achieve. The immediate gain from neutralizing a possible threat could be eclipsed by the protracted international rancor resulting from a disproportionate use of military might.

Since the dawn of the modern state system, the international legal community has sought to establish a code of conduct that would mitigate war's horrors. Although some observers assert that this code has focused upon 'procedural minutiae and superficial issues',[48] others see it as an important force reducing the cruelty of warfare. 'Violated or ignored as they are', notes Telford Taylor, 'enough of the rules are observed enough of the time so that mankind is very much better off with them than without them'.[49]

As important as these rules may be, appeals to military necessity have long been used to nullify their proscriptions. War has been called 'a tyrant' lording 'over all law'[50] and necessity the tyrant's plea for superseding legal norms.[51] Like Shakespeare's Richard II, many statesmen and military commanders envision themselves as 'sworn brother' to 'grim Necessity.' Insisting that they cannot be judged by the same standards as those that pertain to everyone else, they demand the latitude to do whatever must be done to advance state interests, even if their actions contravene moral sensibilities. War, as General Sherman told the citizens of Atlanta, 'is cruel and you cannot refine it'.[52]

Still, efforts to reconcile humanitarian aspirations with military necessity were undertaken throughout the twentieth century, motivated by an aspiration articulated in the Preamble to the 1907 *Declaration of St. Petersburg*: 'the progress of civilization should have the effect of alleviating as much as possible the calamities of war'. Unfortunately, the recent emergence of terrorism as an existential security threat may reverse the century-long trend toward a more restrictive interpretation of the necessity defense. The new U.S. national security strategy unveiled by the Bush administration in the wake of the 9/11 attacks argues for an interpretation of anticipatory self-defense that supports preventive military action on the grounds of strategic necessity. From the president down, administration officials have insisted that they have no choice. They face an enemy who cannot be deterred, cannot be contained, and cannot be expected to adhere to humanitarian limits on the use of force. Under these circumstances, it is not surprising that they have sought to broaden the legal scope of Article 51 of the UN Charter, even if it sets an inauspicious precedent that may generate new security problems in the years ahead. 'Law is mighty', Goethe reminds us, but 'necessity is mightier'.

Notes

[1] Nardin, 1983, p. 291. Also see Draper, 1973.
[2] Delupis, 1987, p. 333.
[3] Laurent Basile Hautefeuille, cited in Neff, 1996, p. 55.
[4] Cited in Woodward, 2004, p. 34.
[5] Daalder and Lindsay, 2003, p. 125.
[6] Kegley and Raymond, 2004; 2003.
[7] See, for example, the speech delivered by Vice President Richard B. Cheney at the 103rd national convention of the Veterans of Foreign Wars. A similar argument was previously made by former U.S. Secretary of State George Shultz, in which he insisted that American leaders should 'prevent acts of terror through intelligence that enables . . . [U.S. forces] to preempt and ultimately eliminate' terrorists with global reach. 'We have a war to win', he proclaimed. 'Every tool available must be used aggressively'. Cheney, 2002; Shultz, 2002.
[8] Cited in Brzezinski, 2004, p. 36.
[9] Bush, 2002.
[10] According to Article 51, 'Nothing in the present Charter shall impair the inherent right of individual or collective self-defense if an armed attack occurs against a Member of the

United Nations, until the Security Council has taken the measures necessary to maintain international peace and security'.

[11] Walzer, 1977, p. 44. For a summary and critique of the social science literature on international norms, see Raymond, 1997. An analysis of the empirical findings on the impact of international norms on war is presented in Raymond, 2000.

[12] Any effort to define international norms raises important conceptual issues since some scholars differentiate among principles, norms, and rules, while other scholars use these terms interchangeably. In this study, the term 'principle' will refer to those beliefs of rectitude that legitimize the purposes members of the state system are expected to pursue, 'norm' will refer to generalized standards of conduct that specify rights and obligations, and 'rule' will refer to relatively specific injunctions. The following example illustrates how these terms will be employed. International law has focused considerable attention on armed hostility between states. The laws of war have been influenced by the *principle* of humanity, which prohibits any military force not required for defeating an enemy. An international *norm* based on this principle is the admonition against weapons that cause superfluous injury and needless suffering. Finally, one of the many *rules* anchored in this norm is the specific prohibition of dumdum bullets. See the *Hague Declaration Concerning Expanding Bullets* (1899) and the *Annex to the Hague Convention No. IV Respecting the Laws and Customs of War on Land* (1907).

[13] Gould and Barkun, 1970, p. 136.

[14] Cited in Howard, 1991, p. 31.

[15] Botti, 1969; Hazan, 1949; Rodick, 1928.

[16] Schwarzenberger, 1955, p. 346.

[17] von Pufendorf, 1749, p. 200.

[18] Sastry, 1966, p. 570; Chacko, 1958, p. 132.

[19] Raymond, 1998-1999.

[20] Aristotle, 1963, p. 316.

[21] Cicero, 1991, pp. 132-33. In contrast to Fabricius, Themistocles, the wily Athenian general who engineered an unexpected naval victory by a combined Greek fleet over the Persians at Salamis in 480 BCE exemplifies consequentialist ethics. According to Plutarch, Themistocles was brilliant and manipulative; he was an Odyssian leader willing to do whatever was expedient in order to be successful, even if it contravened moral scruples. Plutarch, 1864.

[22] Coll, 1993, pp. 3-4; Giesen, 1993, p. 325.

[23] Little, 1991, p. 11.

[24] Onuf, 1982, p. 21.

[25] Rosenne, 1984, p. 119.

[26] Shaw, 1991, pp. 92-93.

[27] Delupis, 1994, p. 152.

[28] Best, 1994b, p. 406.

[29] Kegley and Raymond, 1990, pp. 76-116.

[30] Garner, 1920, p. 281. Also see Strupp, 1920; Rivier, 1896; Lueder, 1898; and von Hartmann, 1877.

[31] Castrén, 1954, p. 66. Also see Jones, 1979; Dunbar, 1953.

[32] Waldock, 1952, p. 462.

[33] Rhyne, 1971; O'Brien, 1957.

[34] Taoka, 1978, p. 39.

[35] Great Britain, the other major power of this period, generally resisted the argument that

strategic necessities sanctioned intervention to regulate other states' domestic affairs. For example, Foreign Minister Castlereagh rejected the Protocol of Troppau, and the influential writer and philosopher John Stuart Mill condemned the use of military intervention to promote political change abroad.

[36] Best, 1994a, p. 266.

[37] June 7, 2004, p. A17.

[38] Raymond, 2003, pp. 72-74.

[39] Kaplan, 2002, pp. 118-19, 128; Peters, 1996.

[40] U.S. Department of Defense, 1992, p. 616.

[41] The ancient Greeks excelled at a style of warfare based on the hoplite phalanx. A formation of massed heavy infantry, soldiers aligned shoulder-to-shoulder and weighted down with some 70 pounds of weapons and armor, sprinted forward to overwhelm the enemy in a short, terrifying clash. In contrast, Roman legions during the Republican period fought in a checkerboard fashion to allow for greater movement than was possible in a tight phalanx. Attacking in a series of waves, troops from the rear of the formation would rotate with those on the front line throughout the course of the battle. Both styles of warfare shared an emphasis on shock combat. Their legacy can be seen in the premium Western military strategists place on reducing an enemy's offensive capability with a single decisive stroke. Dawson, 1996.

[42] Badian, 1968, pp. 4-11. Among the most important international norms influencing the use of force are those norms of inclusion/exclusion that enumerate what constitutes a 'civilized' nation and how its members can treat 'uncivilized' outsiders. Such norms frequently cast outsiders as unscrupulous adversaries against whom all necessary military means must be used. The philosopher David Hume, for example, argued that if a 'civilized nation' was in a conflict with barbarians 'who observed no rules even of war, the former must also suspend their observance of them . . . and must render every action . . . as bloody as possible'. Hume, 1948, p. 188.

[43] Appian, 2000; Frank, 1914. For an alternative interpretation of the rationale for Rome's brutality in Spain, see Schulten, 1914.

[44] Carr, 2003, pp. 38-42. Not all Romans accepted the necessity defense. The philosopher Lucius Annaeus Seneca, for example, observed that political leaders sometimes used the argument from necessity to frame policies based on expediency as if they were addressing supreme emergencies.

[45] Worley, 2003, p. 1. Also see Cicero, 1991, pp. 15-16, 141-142.

[46] Watkins, 2004, pp. 2-6; Stahn, 2003, pp. 45-46.

[47] Hoffmann, 1971.

[48] Vaux, 192, p. 30.

[49] Taylor, 1970, p. 40. The importance of a code of conduct in warfare has been recognized for millennia. The *Ilioupersis*, a lost epic poem on the sack of Troy, is said by other ancient sources to describe the atrocities committed by some Achaian warriors. Divine retribution, as exemplified in the narrative on Ajax the Lesser's drowning by Poseidon in book 4 of the *Odyssey*, signified that there were right and wrong ways to wage war, and those culpable for wrongdoing would be punished.

[50] Ayala, 1912, p. vii.

[51] Lord Stowell, cited in Weidenbaum, 1984, p. 120.

[52] Cited in Gutmann and Thompson, 1990, p. 3.

References

Appian (2000), *Wars of the Romans in Iberia*, translated and edited by John S. Richardson, Oxford: Aris & Phillips.
Aristotle (1963), *The Nicomachean Ethics*, translated by A.E. Wardman and edited by Renford Bambrough, New York: New American Library.
Ayala, Balthazar (1912), *De Jure et Officiis Bellicis et Disciplina Militari*, translated by J. Bate, Washington, DC: Carnegie.
Badian, E. (1968), *Roman Imperialism in the Late Republic*, 2nd edn., Ithaca: Cornell University Press.
Best, Geoffrey (1994a), 'Restraints on Land War', in Lawrence Freedman (ed.), *War*, New York: Oxford University Press, pp. 266-270.
Best, Geoffrey (1994b), *War and Law Since 1945*, Oxford: Clarendon Press, 1994.
Botti, Giannantonio (1969), *Lo 'stato di necessita,' nel diritto internazionale*, Ferrara: Universita di Ferrara, Facolta di Giurisprudenza.
Brzezinski, Zbigniew (2004), *The Choice: Global Domination or Global Leadership*, New York: Basic Books.
Bush, George W. (2002), 'West Point Speech', accessed at <www.whitehouse.gov/news/releases/2002/06/print/20020601-3.html>.
Carr, Caleb (2003), *The Lessons of Terror*, New York: Random House.
Castrén, Erik (1954), *The Present Law of War and Neutrality*, Helsinki: Suomalaisen Kirjallisuuden Seuran Kirjapainon Oy.
Chacko, C. Joseph (1958), 'India's Contribution to the Field of International Law Concepts', *Recueil des Cours*, no. 1, pp. 195-383.
Cheney, Richard B. (2002), 'Veterans of Foreign Wars Speech', accessed at <www.whitehouse.gov/news/releases/2002/08/print/20020826.html>.
Cicero, Marcus Tullius (1991), *On Duties*, translated by Margaret Atkins and edited by M.T. Griffin and Margaret Atkins, Cambridge: Cambridge University Press.
Coll, Alberto R. (1993), 'Prudence and Foreign Policy', in Michael Cromartie (ed.), *Might and Right After the Cold War: Can Foreign Policy Be Moral?* Washington, D.C.: Ethics and Public Policy Center, pp. 3-28.
Daalder, Ivo H. and James M. Lindsay (2003), *America Unbound: The Bush Revolution in Foreign Policy*, Washington, DC: Brookings Institution Press.
Dawson, Doyne (1996), *The Origins of Western Warfare: Militarism and Morality in the Ancient World*, Boulder: Westview Press.
Detter Delupis, Ingrid (1994), *The International Legal Order*, Aldershot: Dartmouth.
Detter Delupis, Ingrid (1987), *The Law of War*, Cambridge: Cambridge University Press.
Draper, G. (1973), 'Military Necessity and Humanitarian Imperatives', *Revue de droit pénal militaire et de droit de la guerre*, vol. 12, pp. 129-142.

Dunbar, N.C.H. (1953), 'Military Necessity in the War Crimes Trials', *The British Year Book of International Law*, London: Oxford University Press, pp. 442-452.

Frank, Tenney (1914), *Roman Imperialism*, New York: Macmillan.

Garner, James Wilford (1920), *International Law and the World War*, 2 vols,. London: Longmans, Green & Co.

Giesen, Klaus-Gerd (1993), 'Corporatisme paradigmatique, théories déontologiques et nouvel ordre mondial', *Études Internationales*, vol. 24, pp. 315-29.

Gould, Wesley L. and Michael Barkun (1970), *International Law and the Social Sciences*, Princeton: Princeton University Press.

Gutmann, Amy and Dennis Thompson, eds. (1990), *Ethics and Politics: Cases and Comments*, 2nd edn., Chicago: Nelson-Hall.

Hartmann, Julius von (1877), 'Militätische Notwendigkeit und Humanität', *Deutsche Rundschau*, vol. 13 , pp. 111-28, 450-71.

Hazan, Edouard (1949), *L'Etat de necessité en droit pénal interétatique et international*, Paris: Pedone.

Hoffmann, Stanley (1971), 'International Systems and the Control of Force', in Karl Deutsch and Stanley Hoffmann (eds.), *The Relevance of International Law*, Garden City, NY: Doubleday-Anchor, pp. 34-66.

Howard, Michael (1991), 'British Grand Strategy in World War I', in Paul Kennedy (ed.), *Grand Strategy in War and Peace*, New Haven: Yale University Press, pp. 31-41.

Hume, David (1948), *A Treatise on Human Nature*, New York: Hafner.

Jones, Roy E. (1979), *Principles of Foreign Policy*, New York: St. Martin's Press.

Kaplan, Robert D. (2002), *Warrior Politics: Why Leadership Demands a Pagan Ethos*, New York: Vintage.

Kegley, Charles W., Jr. and Gregory A. Raymond (2004), 'Global Terrorism and Military Preemption: Policy Problems and Normative Perils', *International Politics*, vol. 41, pp. 37-49.

Kegley, Charles W., Jr. and Gregory A. Raymond (2003), 'Preventive War and Permissive Normative Order', *International Studies Perspectives*, vol. 4, pp. 385-394.

Kegley, Charles W., Jr. and Gregory A. Raymond (1990), *When Trust Breaks Down: Alliance Norms and World Politics*, Columbia: University of South Carolina Press.

Little, David (1991), 'Morality and National Security', in Kenneth M. Jensen and Elizabeth P. Faulkner (eds.), *Morality and Foreign Policy: Realpolitik Revisited*, Washington, DC: United States Institute of Peace, pp. 1-19.

Lueder, Carl (1898), *Voelkerrecht* , Freiburg: Mohr.

Nardin, Terry (1983), *Law, Morality and the Relations of Nations*, Princeton: Princeton University Press.

Neff, Stephen C. (1996), 'The Prerogatives of Violence–In Search of the Conceptual Foundations of Belligerents' Rights', *German Yearbook of International Law*, vol. 38, pp. 41-72.

O'Brien, William V. (1957), 'The Meaning of Military Necessity in International Law', *World Polity*, vol. 1, pp. 61-176.

Onuf, Nicholas Greenwood (1982), 'Global Law-Making and Legal Thought', in Nicholas Greenwood Onuf (ed.), *Lawmaking in the Global Community*, Durham: Carolina Academic Press, pp. 1-81.

Peters, Ralph (1996), 'Winning Against Warriors', *Strategic Review*, vol. 24, pp. 12-21.

Pufendorf, Samuel von (1749), *The Law of Nature and Nations*, 5th edn., translated by Basil Kennet, London: Bonwicke.

Plutarch (1864), *The Lives of the Noble Grecians and Romans*, translated by John Dryden and revised by Arthur Hugh Clough, New York: Modern Library.

Raymond, Gregory A. (2003), 'The Evolving Strategies of Political Terrorism', in Charles W. Kegley, Jr. (ed.), *The New Global Terrorism: Characteristics, Causes, Controls*, Upper Saddle River, NJ: Prentice-Hall, pp. 71-83.

Raymond, Gregory A (2000), 'Normative Orders and Peace', in John A. Vasqez (ed.), *What Do We Know About War?* Lanham, MD: Rowman & Littlefield, pp. 281-297.

Raymond, Gregory A. (1998-1999), 'Necessity in Foreign Policy', *Political Science Quarterly*, vol. 113, pp. 673-688.

Raymond, Gregory A. (1997), 'Problems and Prospects in the Study of International Norms', *Mershon International Studies Review*, vol. 41, pp. 205-245

Rhyne, Charles S. (1971), *International Law*, Washington, DC: CLB Publishers.

Rivier, Alphonse (1896), *Principes du droit des gens*, Paris: Rosseau.

Rodick, Burleigh Cushing (1928), *The Doctrine of Necessity in International Law*, New York: Columbia University Press.

Rosenne, Shabtai (1984), *Practice and Methods of International Law*, London: Oceana.

Sastry, K.R.R. (1966), 'Hinduism and International Law', *Recueil des Cours*, no. 1, pp. 507-615.

Schulten, Adolf (1914), *Die Keltiberer und ihre Kriege mit Rom*, Munich: F. Bruckmann.

Schwarzenberger, Georg (1955), 'The Fundamental Principles of International Law', *Recueil des Cours*, no. 1, pp. 195-383.

Shaw, Malcolm N. (1991), *International Law*, 3rd edn., Cambridge: Cambridge University Press.

Shultz, George P. (2002), 'National Foreign Affairs Training Center Speech', accessed at <www..state.gov/secretary/rm/2002/10564pf.htm>.

Stahn, Carsten (2003), 'Terrorist Acts as 'Armed Attack': The Right to Self-Defense, Article 51½ of the UN Charter, and International Terrorism', *The Fletcher Forum of World Affairs*, vol. 27, pp. 35-54.

Strupp, Karl (1920), *Das Volkerrechtliche Delikt*, Stuttgart: Kohlhammer.
Taoka, Ryoichi (1978), *The Right of Self-Defense in International Law*, Osaka: Institute of Legal Study Research Series, Osaka University of Economics and Law.
Taylor, Telford (1970), *Nuremberg and Vietnam: An American Tragedy*, New York: Bantam.
U.S. Department of Defense (1992), *Conduct of the Persian Gulf War: Final Report to Congress*, Washington, DC: Department of Defense.
Vaux, Kenneth L. (1992), *Ethics and the Gulf War: Religion, Rhetoric, and Righteousness*, Boulder: Westview.
Waldock, C.H.M. (1952), 'The Regulation of the Use of Force by Individual States in International Law', *Recueil des Cours*, no. 2, pp. 455-515.
Walzer, Michael (1977), *Just and Unjust Wars: A Moral Argument with Historical Illustrations*, New York: Basic Books.
Watkins, Kenneth (2004), 'Controlling the Use of Force: A Role for Human Rights Norms in Contemporary Armed Conflict', *American Journal of International Law*, vol. 98, pp. 1-34.
Weidenbaum, Paul (1984), 'Necessity in International Law', *Transactions of the Grotius Society*, vol. 24, pp. 105-132.
Woodward, Bob (2004), *Plan of Attack*, New York: Simon & Schuster.
Worley, D. Robert (2003), *Waging Ancient War: Limits on Preemptive Force*, Carlisle, PA: Strategic Studies Institute, U.S. Army War College.

Chapter 2

Targeting Regime Leaders During Armed Hostilities: An Effective Way to Achieve Regime Change?

Catherine Lotrionte[1]

Introduction

According to US officials, ensuring the safety of the United States and its allies from the use of weapons of mass destruction by Iraq would require the dismantling of the very regime that called for the development and use of those weapons in the first place. In December 2002, the President released his National Strategy to Combat Weapons of Mass Destruction that stated:

> Because deterrence may not succeed, and because of the potentially devastating consequences of WMD use against our forces and civilian population, U.S. military forces and appropriate civilian agencies must have the capability to defend against WMD-armed adversaries, including in appropriate cases through preemptive measures.[2]

As long as a regime that developed and harbored such weapons remained in power there would be no possibility of ensuring that those weapons were not be used.

Policymakers bear the burden of weighing the practical, ethical and legal advantages and disadvantages, among other implications, of all possible options, in light of the particular goal. With regime change as the stated policy goal of war in Iraq, targeting regime leaders has once again become a moral, legal, and practical debate worthy of serious consideration. As an instrument of a national security strategy to combat weapons of mass destruction and unilaterally act in self-defense, killing regime leaders might not only be fair game, but in a variety of circumstances outlined here, it might be the best alternative. So in examining the advantages and disadvantages of killing a regime leader what criteria could policymakers consider for the lawfulness and overall appropriateness of such action?

History of Targeting Regime Leaders

Ethical concerns have historically tended to bar the killing of heads of state as a policy option. In the United States, both for practical reasons and on moral grounds, the killing of foreign leaders as an instrument of foreign has been condemned. The United States is the only state – through executive order – that has enacted a clear declaratory policy renouncing assassination. And US officials publicly deny that targeting foreign leaders would be part of any US foreign policy objective. Indeed, in 1990 Air Force Chief of Staff General Michael Dugan stated that if war were to erupt between the United States and Iraq, US military planes would probably target Saddam, his family, and his mistress. When Secretary of Defense Richard Cheney learned of Dugan's statement, he immediately fired General Dugan.[3] In 1991 President Bush, in responding to questions about whether the US military had targeted Saddam Hussein, President Bush responded, "[w]e're not in the business of targeting Saddam Hussein."[4]

In the mid-1970s much public attention was given to the topic of killing foreign leaders when the US Congress investigated alleged CIA improprieties in conducting intelligence activities, including plots to assassination state leaders. The most comprehensive investigation was conducted by the Church Committee and its results were published in a report entitled "Alleged Assassination Plots Involving Foreign Leaders."[5] The Church Committee opposed the use of assassinations because it "violates moral precepts fundamental to our way of life . . . [and] traditional American notions of fair play."[6]

The Church Committee specifically questioned the Central Intelligence Agency's role in the deaths or attempted killings of five world leaders: Fidel Castro (premier of Cuba); Patrice Lumumba (leaders of the Congo); Rafael Trujillo (the Dominican Republic leader); Ngo Dinh Diem (president of South Vietnam); and Rene Schneider (commander-in-chief of the Chilean Army who opposed a military coup against Salvador Allende). Each of these leaders other than Castro was killed in connection with a coup. The Church Committee made the following conclusions:

(1) Officials of the United States Government initiated plots to assassinate Fidel Castro and Patrice Lumumba, apparently believing such activities were lawful and authorized;
(2) American officials encouraged or knew about the coup plots that resulted in the deaths of Trujillo, Diem, and Schneider;
(3) No foreign leaders were killed as a result of assassination plots initiated by officials of the United States;
(4) The plots occurred in a cold war atmosphere perceived to be of crisis proportions; and
(5) Assassinations should not be characterized as a legitimate method of foreign policy because the act of assassination is "incompatible with American principle, international order, and morality."[7]

The public outcry stemming from these investigations led President Gerald R. Ford to issue Executive Order 11905 prohibiting U.S. involvement in assassination plots.[8] Both President Jimmy Carter and President Ronald Reagan issued subsequent Executive Orders banning assassination.[9]

Yet in light of recent US foreign policy actions overseas – like Kosovo, Somalia, the first Gulf War and responses to terrorist attacks against the United States – there has been increased public debate about the prohibition against assassinations. From this debate there have been an increasing number of calls from the US Congress and commentators to rescind any legal ban within an executive order or otherwise on the use of assassinations as a foreign policy tool.[10] The American public's views on the use of assassination reveal that the American public may be more receptive to the use of assassination in many cases.[11] During the first Gulf War, a poll revealed that 65 percent of the American public favored "covert assassination of Hussein to end the war quickly."[12]

In discussing the killing of foreign leaders some have highlighted the "ethical disconnect" between prohibiting the assassination of a tyrannical ruler while allowing casualties from a bombing war to claim the lives of thousands of civilians and soldiers.[13] Their reasoning collectively conveys that when considering the alternatives to killing regime leaders – full-scale war, massive causalities, and devastating diplomatic and economic sanctions – killing the regime leader appears more humane then some of the alternatives.

When Killing Regime Leaders is Legal

Defining the term assassination under the relevant U.S. domestic and international laws is the first significant challenge in order to be able to identify any legal or practical limitations to killing regime leaders. According to Black's Law Dictionary "assassination" is an "act of deliberately killing someone, esp. a public figure, usu. for hire or for political reasons."[14] In addition, the 1980 Oxford Companion to Law states, assassination is "the murder of a person by lying in wait for him and then killing him, particularly the murder of prominent people from political motives, e.g., the assassination of President Kennedy."[15] Killing regime leaders in self-defense in order to ensure international security is not analogous to murdering someone for his political or religious beliefs. As for US laws related to assassination as a foreign policy tool; there are none. Furthermore, within the US Constitution, article II, articulating the foreign affairs powers of the President, including the President's authority as Command-in-Chief, to commit US armed forces in armed hostilities; there is no mention of assassination. The legality of killing regime leaders can be gleaned from a collective analysis of several presidential executive orders establishing guidelines for US intelligence activities and from numerous international legal conventions and principles, where explicit guidelines for assassination can be found.

US Domestic Law

Nowhere in President Ford's, President Carter's or President Reagan's executive orders banning assassination does one find a definition for the term "assassination." Whether this absence of a definition for "assassination" was the result of an oversight in drafting or – more likely – an intentional effort to grant the President flexibility in interpreting the applicability of his order, the Congressional hearings that lead President Ford to sign the first intelligence executive order can shed light on the intent of the original executive order.

The Presidential prohibitions against assassinations were intended to prohibit the killing of foreign political leaders when the US was not engaged in armed conflict with those countries.[16] And nothing in President Reagan's executive order indicates that the intent of the order was to replace any aspect of the legal framework of the law of armed conflict with something that is more restrictive. In fact, the executive order was meant to control the activities of the intelligence community at a time of peace and not the military or the intelligence community at times of armed conflict. The Church Committee examined five cases of alleged assassination plots. Two (Castro and Lumumba) were plots to kill political leaders as ends in themselves, in the absence of any boarder political-military effort to overthrow a regime. The remaining plots (Diem, Trujillo, Schneider) involved killings incident to coups. The Church committee distinguished between "targeted assassinations instigated by the United States" in the absence of any military conflict and "support for dissidents seeking to overthrow local governments."[17] The Committee recommended that "targeted assassination" be prohibited but it did not recommend any restrictions on the US support for coups, whether though military or other support, even though the Committee recognized that "the death of a foreign leader is a risk foreseeable in any coup attempt."[18] Indeed, the Reagan administration's own interpretation of Executive Order 12333 specifically "exempted death incidental to a military action."[19] During a time of armed hostilities the United States Government operates under the laws of war and not any executive order ban.

In its Final Report, the Church Committee endorsed President Ford's Order.[20] At the time President Ford issued his executive order there was a pending Senate anti-assassination bill. President Ford did not endorse the Senate bill when he issued his Executive Order, although he agreed to support "legislation making it a crime to assassinate or attempt to conspire to assassinate a foreign official in peacetime."[21] In the 1970s and early 1980s there continued to be a number of proposals to pass legislation by Congress that would create a flat ban against assassinations. None of the proposals were ever successfully enacted into US law.[22] A number of commentators writing at the time of the Church Committee investigations have offered various explanations for Congress' failure to legislate a ban on assassinations. Some explanations cited include the public's apparent lack of support,[23] Congress' unwillingness to fight with the intelligence community,[24] and difficulties involved in getting sufficient information from the intelligence community.[25] Ultimately, the ambiguity that has exists since the issuing of Ford's executive order surrounding the meaning of assassination and how it relates to activities by US military or US civilian organizations involved in activities like coup d'etats and insurgencies may be the real reason why there has been no US legislation on the issue.

Reagan's Executive Order 12333 is the only legal prohibition to the intelligence agencies' assassination plots of the 1950s and 1960s. Based upon Congress' and the Executive Branch's understanding of the prohibition at the time of Ford's Executive Order the ban on assassination was not meant to extend to actions taken during the execution of lawfully authorized military hostilities. The prohibition applies to peacetime killings of specifically targeted officials for political purposes and was never intended to apply to all circumstances where there may be loss of life of a leader. Under the circumstances when the United States is engaged in armed hostilities with another country, the US acts in accordance with the laws of war as developed under international law.

International Law

Under international law there are two elements that deal with the use of force; *jus ad bellum*, the rules related to when a state can use force and *jus in bello*, the rules related to how a state, when engaged in the use of force, must conduct the hostilities. These international rules that guide states in the conduct against other states are based upon both the practice and behavior of states and the rules codified in international conventions or agreements between states. In using force and engaging in armed hostilities the United States acts within these international rules.

Jus Ad Bellum

During peacetime, international law restricts the circumstances under which a nation can use force against another nation. According to the UN Charter, there are only two specific circumstances when a state legally can resort to the use of force: in self-defense when the nation has suffered from an "armed attack"[26] or when the Security Council has authorized such action.[27] Before the UN Charter came into existence there was customary international law that recognized a state's right to anticipatory self-defense. Based upon this principle, a state could initiate force in self-defense if that use of force was necessary and proportionate to the existing threat. Under these circumstances international law recognizes the right of a nation to take pre-emptive action in order to prevent a threat from coming to fruition. This article does not address the question of when the recourse to the use of force is lawful; rather, it addresses the specific issue of whether a state should engage in killing regime leaders when they are engaged in armed conflict. Nevertheless, the international legal principles derived from this area of international law are useful in developing pertinent criteria when considering the killing of a regime leader when a state is engaged in armed conflict.

Jus in Bello

Under international law, during peacetime, citizens of a nation are entitled to immunity from international acts of violence or uses of force by citizens or military forces of other nations under the United Nations Charter. During a time of armed hostilities, however, the same protection does not exist. Throughout history, the rules of the law of armed conflict, *jus in bello*, has recognized killing the enemy, whether lawful combatants or unprivileged belligerents, as legitimate. These principles of the Laws of War are codified in the Hague Convention on the Laws and Customs of War of 1907 and the Geneva Conventions of 1947.[28] The United States has been a party to the Hague Convention since 1956 and the Geneva Convention since 1949.

According to principles of the Laws of War, when the US is engaged in a state of armed hostilities, whether as a result of congressional declaration or presidential initiative,[29] the killing of enemy combatants is considered a legitimate act. Such enemy combatants may include regime leaders. While no international laws, including the Hague and Geneva conventions ban "assassinations" per se the Laws of War recognize that the rights of combatants "to adopt means of injuring the enemy is not unlimited." The Hague and Geneva conventions have codified specific prohibitions against certain types of killings during combat as well as limitations on the means used to kill in combat. These prohibitions would apply to any legitimate targets like enemy combatants and would also apply to regime leaders.

According to Article 23(b) of the regulations annexed to the Hague Convention: "It is especially forbidden to kill or wound treacherously individuals belonging to the hostile nation or army."[30] In referring to "treacherous" behavior the convention refers to fighting, killing or wounding an enemy in a deceitful way. For example, the convention prohibits fighting under false pretenses that would include flying the enemy's flag or wearing the enemy's uniform to lure him to his death. This prohibition has been reiterated in Article 37 of Protocol 1 to the Geneva Convention.[31] The Hague Convention also outlaws the killing by means that would cause "unnecessary suffering."

Discrimination

There is precedent in US military history of targeting regime leaders during a time of war conflict. In 1986 the US Air Force and Navy planes bombed Libya after a Libyan terrorist attack against a nightclub frequented by American soldiers in Berlin. One of the targets was Muammar Qaddafi's tent. During Desert Storm in 1991, the US military bombed Saddam Hussein's official residences and command bunkers. In 1998 the United States launched cruise missile attacks against Osama bin Laden's al Qaeda bases in Afghanistan after he was linked to the attacks against U.S. embassies in Kenya and Tanzania. In 2001 the United States military attacked Afghanistan bombing al Qaeda camps after al Qaeda was linked to the attacks against the United States on September 11, 2001. Under international law, all of these actions were legitimate acts of self-defense against an on-going threat. It is irrelevant, for purposes of the law, as whether an individual, including a regime leader, was a target also. Under international law, if the U.S. had known that these attacks were going to take place before they actually had, the US could have acted in self-defense before the attack occurred, preventing the actual attack. If killing the regime leader was part of this act of self-defense that would also have been legitimate under international law as long as the action did not violate any of the prohibited means of killing within the Laws of War.

According to international law and US domestic law, the United States President, in executing his constitutional authorities as commander in chief of the US Armed Forces, may legally order the killing of a regime leader as part of an armed conflict as long as it is not a "treacherous" killing, an indiscrimination killing and it does not cause "unnecessary pain and suffering." As commander-in-chief the President alone is responsible for directly the use of force by the Armed Forces and he alone must determine the appropriate, most effective, means in which to bring the conflict to a conclusion. If the President were to determine that the most effective way to bring the armed conflict to a successful conclusion, minimizing loss to life while accomplishing the objective of the conflict, is to eliminate the enemy state leader, he has the legal authority to do so.

Consequences

Both scholars and policymakers alike seem to indicate that changes in the contemporary security environment seriously undermine the continued applicability of any prohibition on targeted killings of regime leaders. One scholar, Ward Thomas, discusses the weakening of the "international norm against assassination," highlighting two structural changes in the post-World War II international system that undermines the norm.[32] The first is the increasing prevalence of unconventional violence, including guerrilla warfare and terrorism.[33] The second structural change that Ward identifies as threatening the norm against assassination is the destructive and brutal nature of modern warfare, including, but not limited to, the advent of nuclear weapons. Indeed, the prevalence of concern regarding such asymmetric threats as weapons of mass destruction in US security considerations is unmistakable. It may be that from the end of the Cold War to challenges to state sovereignty, the challenging and changing nature of the international political order has prompted re-examination of the assassination ban.

In order to address the issue of killing regime leaders in a clear and precise fashion and deal with all of the complex legal, moral and practical considerations involved in such an issue, an evaluation of the consequences of the action is necessary. Depending upon the circumstances of the specific case, there will be particular costs and benefits involved. In order to evaluate the action these advantages and disadvantages should be carefully analyzed first. Described below are a few of the advantages and disadvantages of a policy to kill regime leaders:

Assassination may preclude greater atrocities. Is it possible that the killing of a regime leader is justified from a moral point of view? If the killing of a leader would prevent the death, torture, serious injury or continued suffering of many innocent people, then, at least according to some, it would seem that removing the responsible individual or regime would be the best possible choice among the alternatives. Indeed, one argument that has been made to support the use of killing a regime leader is that some of the alternatives options such as full-scale armed conflict with potentially thousands of deaths and casualties and diplomatic and economic sanctions that are crippling to a civilian population are less humane then the elimination of a regime leader and those that are integral to his regime; particularly when removing those individuals will help accomplish the policy objective.[34] These alternatives harm the very individuals who have already suffered at the hands of the dictator. If the laws and moral principles allow states and individuals to use deadly force in self-defense the same principles provide for the use of deadly force in defense of others. If an Adolf Hitler or a Slobadon Milosevic had been assassinated millions of lives would have been saved from genocide. When other policy alternatives are found to be ineffective then states may reserve the ability to take action, including removing a leader by deadly force, in order to prevent further loss of life.

Assassination may produce fewer military causalities then a full-scale war. In terms of the number of deaths as the result of conventional warfare, an assassination of a regime leader and potentially those immediately surrounding the leader and in charge of the control and command results in far fewer deaths. In the face of such dramatic differences in the numbers of deaths some have come to criticize any notion that there would be any ethical restrictions to such actions. "While it was acceptable to bomb those divisions of hapless conscripts, it was unthinkable to announce and carry out a threat to kill Saddam Hussein, although he bore overwhelming guilt for the entire war ad its atrocities. . . . Where is the ethical logic in this?"[35]

Assassination may prevent fewer innocent victims from becoming the collateral damage of an armed conflict. Even with precision-guided weapons being used in armed conflict inevitably there will be innocent victims. While these victims may never have been targeted in the during conflict ultimately that will matter little, other then providing legal protections for war fighters, as these victims still suffer the consequences. Modern warfare is destructive. And the consequences of such wars may continue far longer then the actual armed conflict itself. Particularly in a world where nuclear weapons are no longer the anomaly and weapons of mass destruction are too readily available to both state and non-state actors willing to use them. What is the sense of prohibiting the killing of one individual while allowing the deaths of thousands of innocent people? For some like Michael Walzer, the military codes, principles of norms that control behavior in armed conflict must "first be morally plausibility" and "must correspond to our sense of what is right."[36] Only then can such principles, codes or norms constrain behavior in conflict.

As in surgery when the procedure is to remove the malignant tumor without destroying the healthy tissues so too the objective is to remove the regime leader without decimating the people or country. In going directly to the source of the problem and eliminating it you not only reduce the total amount of suffering but you also hold open the possibility of peace and the resumption of pre war activities in the country devoid of the threats. If by eliminating a regime leader and the regime that supports that individual one limits the harm to civilians and thereby avoiding the dangers of provoking reprisals and bitterness because of conduct that could be considered unnecessary or brutal, then the overall benefits may outweigh any costs that accompany such a policy.

Assassination of certain leaders may effectively disrupt the brutal activities of the leader and his regime more then a conventional conflict would. Strategically removing a tyrannical regime leader may impair followers' ability to operate and carry out any command and control decisions. If the leader is a charismatic individual who cannot be replaced easily, the loss of the leader will likely cause confusion and disarray. Especially in authoritarian regimes, where a single individual is often in power for many years, their elimination is apt to lead to a lack of direction at the topic level. If there are multiple potential successors there may be a struggle for control that further exacerbates the disarray. If there is doubt about who is responsible for the killing the leader this may cause speculation about an inside traitor and cause further deterioration on the top levels. The cumulative result of the confusion and disruption may lead to the interruption of operational effectiveness. Even if this is a temporary disruption, it may give the opposing side enough time to implement other elements of the policy effectuating a complete regime change. In contemplating the possibility of a second level of leaders that may be able and ready to take over in the absence of the regime leader one option to keep in mind is the need to eliminate or neutralize these other potential leaders.

Assassination leaves no prisoners to become causes for reprisal or blackmail scenarios. If a regime leader is eliminated he will not be sitting in a jail. He will not stand jail before a court of justice. The elimination of the leader avoids the potential for acts of reprisal or retribution against the state that holds the leader as a prisoner. It also prevents the leader from becoming a talisman for his followers or seeking sovereign immunity for his action while he was a head of state. Furthermore, if the leader remains at large or in criminal custody there remains the potential for the leader to communicate and to direct and control, albeit to some limited degree, certain operations. Depending on the circumstances of the case, there may be the potential for the leader to seek asylum outside the country. This scenario may be a satisfactory resolution to the extent that the objectives of the armed conflict can still be accomplished. Indeed, the objectives can be accomplished at a potentially lower cost then if assassination was a necessary option.

Assassination or total disruption of the command and control may prevent the use of WMD. After the Cold War, with the introduction of weapons of mass destruction and their proliferation into the international community, the past standard of maintaining international world order was brought into question. In the past the superpowers shared a common interest in maintaining minimum world order. This common interest was effective in neutralizing any threats that could trigger a nuclear war. Today, in a world where non-superpowers develop and proliferate WMD there is no such common interest in maintaining world order. Regime leaders who develop WMD in violation of international commitments and defy any calls from the international community to act lawfully do not share those same common interests. By killing such regime leaders the threat from these weapons is eliminated once and for all. Destroying only the weapons will only incite the same regime leader to amass his followers once again to develop the weapons. Destroying the root of the cause of the problem will ultimately be the way to kill the tree.

One of the factors that made the ethical and moral prohibition against killing leaders a strongly supported principle was the concentration of any such devastating weapons – like nuclear weapons – in the hands of states that felt subject to common interests and principles of reciprocity and retaliation under international law. But for those states that do not share in those common interests and are not subject to the same principles their possession of these devastating weapons is a threat to the entire international community. Under these circumstances, the previous prohibition against the killing of regime leaders is not applicable.

Using the element of surprise in killing the regime leader, before there is an opportunity to use the weapons, would be an act of self-defense, albeit a pre-emptive act. It would be an act of self-defense on behalf of the state taking the action and also on behalf of all of the lives of countless innocent civilians that would have died at the hands of the regime leader. In addition by killing the leader and avoiding the potential use of WMD in an armed conflict scenario, the civilian population will possess fewer feelings of bitterness against any outsiders who will try to bring lasting settlement to the country. With fewer feeling of bitterness to dwell on and more shared interests to build on there is a lesser likelihood that hostilities will re-ignite and encourage acts of reprisals.

Few observers would probably deny that some of these advantages are quite attractive. But national security planners also must consider the disadvantages to be weighed against these advantages. Depending upon the specific facts of a situation some of these advantages and disadvantages may be different or non existent. In addition, based upon other factors that may come into play, the weighted balance between the advantages also may be change. Nevertheless, considering some of the disadvantages that may accompany any policy is crucial. After considering both the advantages and disadvantages related to the specific policy then security planners can formulate a general criteria for evaluating any future policy plan.

Assassination is morally questionable. The position taken in 1976 by the Church Committee was that assassinations conducted with the authority of the US Federal Government were not in line with American values of justice and fairness. The committee concluded that assassination "violates moral precepts fundamental to out way of life ... traditional American notions of fair play," and that assassination is not an acceptable foreign policy tool.[37] Furthermore, within the international community there has been a long standing consensus that the killing of foreign leaders is an inappropriate means of conducting foreign policy. It is often these ethical concerns that place assassinations off the table as legitimate policy options.

As far back as 1598 international scholars like Alberico Gentili condemned the killing of foreign leaders on moral grounds, calling it a "shameful" and "wicked" practice, and arguing that objectives of war should be achieved by valorous means.[38] Irrespective of any other legitimate policy or ethical argument that can be made in support of such action there still will remain those that oppose the policy on moral grounds. Even in light of some recent support from certain Congressional leaders to rescind the ban on assassination within the executive order, there still could be a significant outcry from Congress and the international community if the US President were to formally authorize the killing of a foreign leader.

Assassinations could cause a loss of domestic and international legitimacy for the United States. If such a policy to kill a regime leader – with Presidential authorization – were publicly disclosed it would likely cause a fraction in any international support the President had created for the current military engagement at issue. This loss of legitimacy and any damage to the US President's reputation could also have further long-term political implications both domestically and internationally. The President could lose public Congressional support even from those that silently supported the policy. This could negatively affect any campaign for a re-election. In addition, the President's ability to gain international support on future issues unrelated to the current conflict – for instance trade agreements and security procedures – may be severely damaged resulting in long-term effects for the United States. In addition, international organizations like the United Nations may also be unwilling to support the US in any effort after the military conflict in efforts to carry out the overall objectives of the policy.

Assassinations could cause retaliatory assassination attempts. There are also some short-term consequences that would be harmful to the interests of the leaders of a state that engages in assassination plots and to the interests of the state itself. In the first instance, the killing of an enemy leader will ultimately create hostile feelings by the successors or followers of the regime leader against the perpetrators of the assassination. If the involvement of a state was acknowledged or disclosed to the world feelings of hostilities would likely spur acts of vindication or revenge against the individual leaders that authorized the assassination. This would create a dangerous situation for any President. Particularly, within a political system that is open to the public, such as a democracy, leaders are more vulnerable to such retaliatory assassination attempts. One way to minimize this danger is if a state had a policy of never acknowledging the authorization or involvement in any activity to conduct assassinations. In the world of covert foreign affairs it is easier for nations to yield to or accept the terms of a secret rather than a public threat.

Assassinations may cause international/regional instability. In the second instance, for those nations that engage in assassinations, one negative effect is to diminish the safety and security of the nation itself. Such acts may cause instability and unpredictability in the region. In considering various means to minimize this risk a nation would incorporate any assassination plan within a comprehensive package that would deal with measures that would include working in a cooperative fashion with any successors, legitimate followers of the former regime leader and neighboring states in the region. Efforts to establish and maintain stability in the region would go far to ensure that any potential negative impact from assassination attempts may be countered to the extent possible. Such efforts could include humanitarian efforts and assistance to the domestic efforts to establish legitimate institutions.

Assassinations may be difficult to accomplish. Targeting a regime leader and killing him may not be that easy. In fact, the United States does not have a good record of success in this area, particularly during a time of peace. According to the Church Committee investigations, the U.S. made numerous attempts to kill Fidel Castro of Cuba but failed repeatedly. Spy planes, bombers and tanks can be quite effective in destroying an enemy's infrastructure. However, the targeted killing of a single or a few individuals is much more difficult. With conventional weapons it is quit easy to kill a lot of people and difficult to kill just one moving target. The ability to locate, track and target an individual will depend on accurate and timely information. At a time of armed conflict this may not be easy to accomplish.

Conclusion

When a containment policy fails, diplomacy is ineffective and a full-scale war is too costly, killing a regime leader may be an option a state may seriously consider. In the international community states have always maintained the right to use force in order to maintain world order and preserve its own defense. In a world transformed into one where states will amass weapons of mass destruction, unlawfully invade their neighbors and threaten other's national and international security, national security experts may need to re-examine their policy choices including killing regime leaders. The issue is not necessarily the lawfulness of such an action during the time of military conflict. Rather, the issue is the effectiveness and general viability of a policy of targeting regime leaders. If the international system and legal regime were more adept at preventing threats to the peace of other nations or if system were more effective in using enforcement means to deter or punish such actions, a discussion about the legality, morality and utility of killing regime leaders would not be necessary. In the absence of an effective collective security system, in a world with more dangerous weapons and in the hands of actors willing to use them, killing regime leaders, however regrettably, may been an appropriate policy option.

In the process of considering some of the complex consequences to such a policy, policymakers may want to consider satisfying the following criteria:

(1) **The Target** The killing itself should be limited to the greatest extent possible to the persons within the regime that are responsible for the threats.
(2) **A Level of Certainty** Access to accurate and reliable intelligence information that provides a high level of certainty of the identity of the individuals responsible for the threats.
(3) **A Likelihood of Success** Founded on a strong likelihood that the attempt to eliminate the reader will be successful and the leaders' elimination will remedy the problem and do less harm to civilian populations then another form of action would.
(4) **A Necessary Action** There is no other feasible, reasonable, less extreme way of stopping the regime leader's actions.
(5) **A Proportionate Action** The killing of the regime leader is proportionate to the threat posed by that leader and the consequences of killing of the regime leader is less destructive then the use of conventional warfare to resolve the threat.
(6) **A Discriminate Action** Targeting the responsible individuals will avoid the deaths of innocent victims.

These determinations could be exceedingly difficult, and might, individually or collectively, be founded upon erroneous information or assumptions. However, the only alternative to such difficult determinations within international law is a general renunciation of killing regime leaders as part of an act of self-defense during a lawful armed conflict or a general reliance upon more aggressive uses of force, like a full-scale war. The alternative of a general ban on killing regime leaders could ultimately result in thousands of innocent victims. The second alternative of full-scale war would represent a far costlier means of ensuring international peace and security and self-defense both in terms of money required to support such a war, human lives lost in a war and physical devastation of a war. Recognizing the costs of these alternatives, policymakers should not dismiss outright the targeted killings of regime leaders without contemplating a criteria under which to take such action and considering all of the consequences that may result.

Notes

[1] Catherine Lotrionte is an Adjunct Professor in the School of Foreign Service and the Law Center at Georgetown University, as well as a senior fellow in the Institute for International Law and Politics at Georgetown University. She currently is the General Counsel for the President's Foreign Intelligence Advisory Board at the White House. She previously served as an Assistant General Counsel at the Central Intelligence Agency. The opinions, conclusions, and/or recommendations expressed or implied within this chapter are solely those of the author and do not necessarily represent the views of the United States government or any US government department or agency.

[2] NATIONAL STRATEGY TO COMBAT WEAPONS OF MASS DESTRUCTION 3 (Dec. 2002), available at http://www.dtic.mil/doctrine/jel/other_pubs-nssr.99.pdf.

[3] Church, 1990, p. 29.

[4] Chase, 1991, p. 16.

[5] Prados, 1986. See also Select Senate Committee to Study Governmental Operations with Respect to Intelligence Activities, 1975 [herein referred to as the church Committee Report].

[6] Select Senate Committee to Study Governmental Operations with Respect to Intelligence Activities, 1975, pp. 257 and 259.

[7] Select Senate Committee to Study Governmental Operations with Respect to Intelligence Activities, 1975, pp. 257 and 259.

[8] President Ford, 1976. The ban against assassination states, "No employee of the United States Government shall engage in, or conspire to engage in political assassination." Id. at 101.

[9] President Ford, 1976; President Reagan, 1981.

[10] Richter, 1998, p. A6; Stephanopoloulos, 1997, p. 34; Bueno de Mesquita, 1989, p. A23.

[11] Jenkins, 1986, p. A2; Miller, 1993, p. A6 (During the Persian Gulf War, a poll revealed that 65 percent of the American public favored "the covert assassination of Hussein to end the war quickly.").

[12] Jenkins, 1986, p. A2.

[13] Peters, 1996, pp. 102-108.

[14] Black 1999.

[15] Walker, 1980.

[16] Select Senate Committee to Study Governmental Operations with Respect to Intelligence Activities, 1975, pp. 4-5. The Church Committee investigated the United States' involvement in plots targeting Patrice Lumumba of the Congo, Fidel Castro of Cuba, Rafael Trujillo of the Dominican Republic, General Rene Schneider of Chile and Ngo Dinh Diem of South Vietnam.

[17] Select Committee to Study Governmental Operations with Respect to Intelligence Activities, 1975.

[18] Select Committee to Study Governmental Operations with Respect to Intelligence Activities, 1975, pp. 256-258.

[19] Schorr, 2001, pp. 1-2.

[20] Select Committee to Study Governmental Operations With Respect to Intelligence Activities. 1976.

[21] President Ford, 1976, p. 2.

[22] McClory, 1976, section 9(1).

[23] Horrock, 1976, p. A20.

[24] Gelb, 1976, p. A20.

[25] Gelb, 1976, p. A20.

[26] United Nations, 1945, article 51.
[27] United Nations, 1945, article 39.
[28] Parties to the Hague Convention on the Laws and Customs of War on Land, 1907, article 23, e.
[29] The U.S. Air Force, 1976, pp. 110-31.
[30] Parties to the Hague Convention, 1907, articles 22 and 23(b).
[31] The United States is not a party to this particular Protocol of the Convention.
[32] Thomas, 2001, pp. 80-83.
[33] Jackson, 1999, p. 669; Pickard, 2001; Wingfield, 1999, p. 669.
[34] Pierce, 1996, pp. 99-113; Mueller and Mueller, 1999, pp. 43-53.
[35] Peter, 1996, pp. 102-108; Stephanopoulos, 1997, p. 34.
[36] Walzer, 1991, p. 133.
[37] Select Senate Committee to Study Governmental Operations with Respect to Intelligence Activities, 1975, p. 257.
[38] Gentili, 1612, p. 166.

References

Black's Law Dictionary 109 (7th ed. 1999).
Bueno de Mesquita, Newman and Bruce *Repeal Order 12,333, Legalize 007*, NEW YORK TIMES, January 26, 1989, p. A23.
Church, George J. *Saddam in the Cross Hairs*, TIME, Oct. 8, 1990, at 29.
Chase, Eric L. *Should We Kill Saddam*, NEWSWEEK, Feb. 18, 1991, at 16.
Executive Order No. 11,905, 5(g), 3 C.F.R. 90 (1976). The ban against assassination states, "No employee of the United States Government shall engage in, or conspire to engage in political assassination."
Executive Order No. 12,036, 3 C.F.R. 112 (1978); Executive Order 12,333, 3 C.F.R. 200 (1981).
Ford, Gerald *Special Message to the Congress Proposing Legislation to Reform the United States Foreign intelligence Community*, Vol. I Public Papers of Gerald R. Ford 362 at 2 (Feb. 18, 1976).
Gelb, Leslie *Spy Inquiries Begun Amid Public Outrage, End in Indifference*, N.Y. TIMES, May 12, 1976, at A20.
Gentili, Alberico *De Jure Belli Libri Tres* (1612), reprinted in the *The Classics of International Law*, trans. John C. Rolfe (Oxford: Clarendon Press, 1933), p. 166.
Horrock, Nicholas *The Meaning of Congressional Intelligence Inquiries*, N.Y. TIMES, April 30, 1976, at A20.
Jackson, Jamie Melissa "Legality of Assassination of Independent Terrorist Leaders: An Examination of National and International Implications," 24 *North Carolina Journal of International Law and Commercial Regulation* 669 (1999).
Jenkins, Brian *Assassination: Should We Stay the Good Guys?* LOS ANGELES TIMES, November 16, 1986, p. A2.
McClory, Representative Robert, H.R. 15542, 94th Cong., 2nd Sess., section 9(1) (1976).

Miller, Allan C. *Americans Favor Killing Saddam Hussein*, LOS ANGELES TIMES, June 29, 1993, p. A6 (During the Persian Gulf War, a poll revealed that 65 percent of the American public favored "the covert assassination of Hussein to end the war quickly.").

Mueller, John and Karl "Sanctions of Mass Destruction," *Foreign Affairs*, Vol. 78, No. 3 (May/June 1999), pp. 43-53.

Peters, Ralph "A Revolution in Military Ethics?", *Parameters: The Journal of the Army War College*, Vol. 26, No. 2 (Summer 1996), pp. 102-108, at p. 104.

Pickard, Daniel P. "Legalizing Assassination: Terrorism, the Central Intelligence Agency and International Law," 30 *Georgia Journal of International and Comparative Law*, 1, (2001).

Pierce, Albert "Just War Principles and Economic Sanctions," *Ethics and International Affairs*, Vol. 10 (1996), pp. 99-113.

Prados, John *Presidents' Secret Wars: CIA and Pentagon Covert Operations Since World War II* 334 (1986).

Richter, Paul *Congress Ponders Whether the US Should Ease Ban on Assassinations*, LOS ANGELES TIMES, September 18, 1998.

Schorr, Daniel, *Stop Winking at the Ban*, CHRISTIAN SCIENCE MONITOR, Sept. 20, 2001 at 1-2.

Stephanopoloulos, George, *Why We Should Kill Saddam*, NEWSWEEK, December 1, 1997, p. 34.

The United Nations Charter.

The Hague Convention on the Laws and Customs of War on Land, with Annex of Regulations, Oct. 18, 1907, 36 Stat. 2277, T.S. No. 539, 1 Bevans 631, Annex, art. 23, e.

Thomas, Ward "International Assassination: 'An Infamous and Execrable Practice'" in *Ethics of Destruction* (Ithaca, New York: Cornell University Press, 2001), pp. 80-83.

U.S. Government, Select Senate Committee to Study Governmental Operations with Respect to Intelligence Activities, *Alleged Assassination Plots Involving Foreign Leaders*, S. Rep. No. 94-465, at 1 and app. A, 1118(e) (2), at 289 (1975) (Washington, D.C.: U.S. Government Printing Office, 1975) [hereinafter Church Committee Report]. The Church Committee investigated the United States' involvement in plots targeting Patrice Lumumba of the Congo, Fidel Castro of Cuba, Rafael Trujillo of the Dominican Republic, General Rene Schneider of Chile and Ngo Dinh Diem of South Vietnam.

U.S. Government, *National Strategy to Combat Weapons of Mass Destruction* 3 (Dec. 2002), available at http://www.dtic.mil/doctrine/jel/other_pubs-nssr.99.pdf.

U.S. Government, *Foreign and Military Intelligence: Final Report of the Select Committee to Study Governmental Operations With Respect to Intelligence Activities*. S. Rep. No. 755, 94th Cong., 2d Sess. 448 n. 29 (1976).

U.S. Air Force, "International Law: The Conduct of Armed Conflict and Air Operations," AFP 110-31, November 19, 1976.

U.S. Government, *Interim Report of the Select Committee to Study Governmental Operations with Respect to Intelligence Activities*, S. Rep. No. 465, 258 94th Cong., 1st Sess. (1975).

Walker, David, M. *David M. Walker Oxford Companion to Law* 84 (1980).
Walzer, Michael *Just and Unjust Wars,* rev. ed. (New York: Basic Books, 1991), p. 133.
Wingfield, Thomas, C. "The Legality of Assassination of Independent Terrorist Leaders: An Examination of National and International Implications," 24 *North Carolina Journal of International Law and Commercial Regulations*, 669, (1999).

Chapter 3

The Protection of Cultural Objects During Armed Conflicts

Howard M. Hensel[1]

Philosophers and statesmen have long debated whether armed conflict within and between various organized communities constitutes an inevitable aspect of the human condition. Irrespective of one's viewpoint concerning this discussion, all would agree that armed conflicts are always costly in both human life and property. As such, throughout history, efforts have been made to limit these costs. The primary focus of these efforts has been to protect non-combatants, but efforts have also been made to protect mankind's cultural patrimony from wartime loss, damage, or destruction. Prior to the mid 19th century, these efforts were largely based upon customary norms and often took the form of contractual arrangements among belligerents. During the past century and a half, however, the members of the international community built upon these customary norms and enacted a number of conventions designed to limit the scope and intensity of armed conflicts. One aspect of these efforts has been the adoption of provisions designed to better ensure the protection of cultural property during armed hostilities.

The purpose of this chapter is to analyze, assess, and evaluate the international community's efforts to protect cultural property during hostilities. The chapter will begin by framing this examination within the larger context of questions concerning the degree to which the normative standards governing the conduct of armed conflicts are universally applicable or should be dependent upon such situational considerations as the nature of the conflict and the relationship between the belligerents. It will also examine alternative ways in which cultural properties are perceived and the implications of these dichotomous viewpoints for the protection of cultural property during periods of armed conflict. The chapter will then chronologically examine the international community's various conventional efforts during the past century and a half to better ensure wartime protection for cultural property. Finally, the chapter will conclude by assessing the current status of contemporary customary and conventional laws for the protection of cultural property during armed conflicts, as well as by evaluating the degree to which these elements of the law of armed conflict are likely to succeed in protecting cultural properties during the various forms of hostilities that the global community is likely to experience as it enters the 21st century.

Types of Armed Conflicts and Perspectives on Cultural Property

Throughout human history, Western and non-Western, primitive and advanced organized communities have often distinguished between conflicts involving similar peoples, with common cultural bonds, versus conflicts involving alien peoples. This distinction, in turn, served to condition their perspective concerning what was permissible in the conduct of warfare. For example, drawing upon the heritage of Greco-Roman, Medieval, Renaissance, and Baroque warfare, Western attitudes toward armed conflict traditionally distinguished between wars among European sovereign authorities and armed conflicts between those authorities and alien peoples. Thus, in conflicts between Christian sovereigns and alien peoples, the rules of war were often suspended and, as *guerre mortelle* or *bellum romanum*, indiscriminate destruction and slaughter were permitted. Indeed, this type of warfare was usually directed against non-Christians, including the indigenous peoples of the New World and other colonial areas. Conversely, under *bellum hostile*, conflicts between European sovereign authorities were usually governed by basic customary rules of warfare. Even in conflicts among the European powers, however, the injection of religion, ideology, chauvinist rivalries and/or ethnic hostilities often led to the suspension of the rules of warfare, as was seen during the Religious Wars between the mid 16th and mid 17th centuries, the ideological struggle between Nazi Germany and the Soviet Union during the Second World War, and, most recently, the ethnic conflicts that accompanied the breakup of Yugoslavia at the end of the 20th century. Moreover, when wars were fought for total objectives, even those states that had heretofore subscribed to the rules of armed conflict have often been tempted to suspend those rules if that appeared to be the only option that promised to ensure survival. Finally, the rules of warfare that governed wars between European sovereigns were also often suspended in civil conflicts within their respective states.[2]

Alternatively, however, throughout history, reservations have often been expressed concerning the legitimacy of these dichotomous views concerning the conduct of warfare. Many have argued that all human beings are members of a universal brotherhood of mankind and, furthermore, each human is endowed with basic human rights. As such, basic norms of human decency should underpin all armed conflicts, irrespective of the ethnic or national identity, ideological beliefs, or religious convictions of the antagonists. These convictions were often grounded in the context of the Greco-Roman and Medieval natural law tradition in Western philosophy.[3] They were expressed in writings such as those of Francisco de Vitoria in the early 16th century with respect to the Spanish conquest of the New World. Moreover, even during the religious conflicts between the mid 16th and mid 17th centuries, many believed that the various antagonists should adhere to minimal standards of human decency, at least with respect to conflicts between Christian sovereigns, irrespective of religious conviction.[4] Similarly, a century ago, the famous Martens Clause in the 1899 and 1907 Hague Conventions on Land Warfare suggested a universalist perspective.[5] Finally, the actions taken by the international tribunals held at the conclusion of World War II, combined with a large number of declarations and covenants adopted by the members of the United Nations, have served not only as crucial pillars supporting the growing body of human rights law, they have further reinforced the enduring conviction that the conduct of international and non-international armed conflicts between all peoples must be governed by basic norms, universally adhered to at all times.

Parallel to the controversy concerning the universal versus selective application of the rules of armed conflict is a seemingly separate, but in certain respects, partly coinciding debate concerning the status of cultural property. In the most basic sense, everyone involved in discussions concerning cultural property would agree with John Merryman that cultural properties represent products of the human mind and human society that, in turn, helps us to "define us to ourselves, give us cultural identity, enrich our lives and extend our experience".[6]

Beyond recognition of the significance of cultural property, however, controversy revolves around the precise scope and definition of cultural property.[7] Indeed, in a larger sense, some reject the applicability of the legal concept of property itself in reference the tangible and intangible components of culture.[8] Finally, many of those committed to the preservation of society's cultural heritage are divided into an internationalist, cosmopolitan camp that emphasizes the global community of mankind versus a nationalist camp that centers on the state sovereignty.[9] The division revolves around whether cultural objects should be viewed as "components of a common human culture, whatever their places of origin or present location, independent of property rights or national jurisdiction" or as "part of a national cultural heritage". The nationalist perspective "attributes" a "national character" and identity to those tangible and intangible cultural objects and customs located on or originating from within a nation's territory. Thus, they maintain that nations have "a special interest" in these properties and customs, irrespective of their present "location or ownership". Alternatively, adherents to a cosmopolitan, internationalist perspective disagree, and, as Patrick Boylan has stated, "humanity's culture and patrimony cannot be defined in narrow nationalistic, religious, linguistic or ethnic terms". Indeed, as "members of the same species sharing a common genetic ancestry," the members of the global community possess "a common culture and patrimony . . . in which the loss of the physical or spiritual cultural heritage of one people is a loss for the whole of humanity".[10] Given the current state-centric character of the contemporary international system, it has been suggested that the individual states should regard themselves as custodians, but not owners in the traditional sense of the term, of those cultural sites and objects belonging to mankind's universal heritage that are located within their borders. Thus, all states have a mutual obligation to protect and preserve their common cultural heritage.[11]

The cultural cosmopolitan, internationalist perspective versus the cultural nationalist perspective often serves to frame the context for discussions concerning the peacetime international market for cultural objects.[12] In addition, however, these dichotomous perspectives concerning cultural property also, to some degree, coincide with the aforementioned discussion concerning whether the norms and laws that govern armed conflicts are universal or situational and depend on such considerations as the nature of the belligerents, their mutual relationship, and their respective objectives during periods of armed conflict.

As observed earlier, the multiplying forces of rival ideologies, religions, ethnic hostilities, and chauvinist rivalries, often serve to motivate belligerents to pursue unlimited political objectives and amplify the scope and intensity of domestic and international armed violence, so as to stretch the norms governing the conduct of armed conflict beyond their limit. As such, in these types of armed conflicts, in circumstances where belligerents fail to acknowledge and appreciate that the movable and immovable, tangible and intangible cultural properties located on enemy soil are part of the global community's common cultural heritage, but, instead, view them from a culturally nationalist perspective that attributes national identity to these cultural properties, the result is often the destruction of the defeated enemy's tangible and even intangible national culture. Indeed, the international community has witnessed a great many tragic examples of the conscious, state sponsored destruction of an alien enemy's cultural properties and, indeed, the attempted eradication of a defeated enemy's entire cultural heritage.

Even in less extreme cases of international and non-international armed conflict, however, where the various belligerents attempt to conduct military operations in conformity with the rules of warfare, the damage to cultural property can be quite significant. Cultural properties are not only vulnerable to collateral damage, they are also often at risk due to an application of the doctrine of military necessity, as well as from vandalism and looting.

In short, irreplaceable cultural properties are always vulnerable during periods of armed conflict. The degree of risk is greatly enhanced, however, during those armed conflicts that are comparatively unlimited in scope and intensity, involving alien peoples, each seeking unlimited political objectives, and impelled by the multiplying forces of religion, ideology, chauvinist rivalries, and/or ethnic hostilities. But, while cultural property is endangered during all types of armed conflicts, the inherent risks can be reduced if belligerents adopt an attitude of mutual respect for each other's cultural objects. While the attribution of national identity to cultural objects certainly does not preclude mutual respect for these objects during hostilities, it does require the various belligerents to project outside their own national cultural bounds and recognize and appreciate the value and immunity of the enemy's cultural objects. Such empathy with the enemy and what is perceived to be his national cultural heritage is often difficult under the best of circumstances. Even in limited wars, situations arise involving close judgment calls in which collateral or incidental damage to enemy cultural objects may occur depending upon a belligerent's course of action. A belligerent may find it easier to justify actions that risk damage to these cultural objects if the belligerent identifies these objects with the enemy, not himself. Obviously, even this degree of restraint is unlikely during the aforementioned mentioned conflicts that are comparatively unlimited in scope and intensity, involving alien peoples, each seeking unlimited political objectives, and impelled by the multiplying forces cited earlier. Alternatively, however, if the components of culture, including those of the enemy, are perceived to be part of mankind's common cultural heritage, any destruction of these cultural objects, including those under enemy control, implies a personal loss, not simply one associated with the enemy. Hence, insofar as the belligerents identify with all components of mankind's cultural heritage, including those located on enemy soil, mutual respect for and protection of these objects becomes a norm more readily identified with and more likely to be mutually adhered to.

Early Attempts to Preserve Cultural Property in Armed Conflicts

The destruction and plunder of cultural objects during times of war has been a matter of concern since antiquity. First, with respect to combat operations, from earliest times, customary norms governing the conduct of warfare between similar antagonists in Western and non-Western societies often extended protective immunity to certain cultural properties, especially religious buildings and ceremonial sites.[13] Alternatively, however, in warfare between alien societies, very often wartime protection for cultural objects considered sacred by an alien enemy was neither recognized nor honored.[14]

Many cultural objects, of course, have traditionally been located in towns, which, in turn, have often been the focus of military operations. In addition to strategic and operational considerations,[15] customary norms of siegecraft influenced the terms and conditions for the surrender of a town or the conditions under which it was bombarded, assaulted, or pillaged.[16] These circumstances, in turn, had a direct impact on whether or not cultural objects located within the urban center survived intact. In addition, during bombardments and assaults, civilian casualties and damage to civilian objects, including cultural objects were often the result of collateral damage or a failure by belligerents to distinguish between these objects and legitimate military targets. Moreover, irrespective of the degree of destruction associated with the fall of a particular city or town, often the conquering belligerent seized cultural objects because of their inherent value or as trophies of conquest.[17] Furthermore, in many cases, the intentional destruction or defacement of enemy monuments and buildings often accompanied the seizure of enemy urban centers. Even more extreme are numerous examples throughout history of conquering powers that sought to systematically exterminate a defeated enemy's society and eradicate the tangible objects associated with defeated enemy's cultural identity, such as the destruction of Carthage by the Romans, the attempted destruction of the Hindu civilization in South Asia by the Muslims, and the destruction of the pre-Columbian civilizations in America by the Spanish.[18]

Just as throughout history, damage, destruction, and the seizure of cultural objects have often characterized armed conflict, alternatively, there have been voices that have called for the wartime protection of cultural objects and restrictions against the removal of these objects from subjugated peoples. One of the first, known advocates for restraint was the late 3rd, early 2nd century B.C. Greek historian, Polybius.[19] Similarly, writing at the end of the 16th century, Alberico Gentili condemned the wartime pillage of art, while Hugo Grotius, writing at the outset of the 17th century, argued against indiscriminate devastation.[20] One of the most articulate proponents of protecting cultural property in times of armed conflict, however, was Emerich de Vattel (1714-1769). He argued for a clear distinction between legitimate objects against which military force should be directed[21] and objects that belligerents should respect and protect. Indeed, arguing that some forms of warfare were impermissible and certain elements of society should be protected from hostilities, Vattel hinted that cultural property was part of mankind's common heritage. Thus, all belligerents should respect the wartime immunity of these objects, unless dictated by overwhelming necessities of war.[22] In short, counterbalancing the tendency for cultural properties to fall victim to armed conflict, were both voices advocating restraint, as well as customary norms, applicable, at least, to wars involving similar peoples, designed to partly ameliorate the destructive potential of warfare. But, while there are many examples of moderation, unfortunately, too often belligerents heeded neither the voices of restraint, nor the customary norms of warfare.

Societies, however, often appear to make their greatest progress in advancing efforts to ameliorate hostilities in the aftermath of tremendously destructive wars. For example, in the wake of the devastation of the Thirty Years War (1618-1648), the period between 1648 and the French Revolution in 1789 was characterized by limited wars fought for limited objectives, in which customary norms limiting armed conflict were more generally observed.[23] Similarly, after 1815, following the wars of the French Revolution and the Napoleonic Era, there was renewed resolve by the international community to place limits on the conduct of warfare.[24]

19th and Early 20th Century Efforts to Protect Cultural Objects in Wartime

General Order No. 100, entitled "Instructions for the Government of the Armies of the United States in the Field," prepared under the direction of Professor Francis Lieber of Columbia College and promulgated by President Abraham Lincoln on April 24, 1863, constituted the first modern attempt by an individual state to codify the law of armed conflict.[25] After establishing in Article 21 that a citizen of a hostile power should be considered as "an enemy, . . . and as such is subjected to the hardships of the war,"[26] Article 22 stated,

> Nevertheless, as civilization has advanced during the last centuries, so has likewise steadily advanced, especially in war on land, the distinction between the private individual belonging to a hostile country and the hostile country itself, with its men in arms. The principle has been more and more acknowledged that the unarmed citizen is to be spared in person, property, and honor as much as the exigencies of war will admit.[27]

With respect to the bombardment, Article 19 stated,

> Commanders, whenever admissible, inform the enemy of their intentions to bombard a place, so that the noncombatants, and especially the women and children, may be removed before the bombardment commences. But it is no infraction of the common

law of war to omit thus to inform the enemy. Surprise may be a necessity.[28]

Articles 34, 35, and 36 explicitly addressed the status of cultural property in periods of armed conflict. They stated:

> Art. 34. As a general rule, the property belonging to churches, to hospitals, or other establishments of an exclusively charitable character, to establishments of education, or foundations for the promotion of knowledge, whether public schools, universities, academies of learning or observatories, museums of the fine arts, or of a scientific character – such property is not to be considered public property . . .
>
> Art. 35. Classical works of art, libraries, scientific collections, or precious instruments, such as astronomical telescopes, as well as hospitals, must be secured against all avoidable injury, even when they are contained in fortified places whilst besieged or bombarded.
>
> Art. 36. If such works of art, libraries, collections, or instruments belonging to a hostile nation or government, can be removed without injury, the ruler of the conquering state or nation may order them to be seized and removed for the benefit of the said nation. The ultimate ownership is to be settled by the ensuing treaty of peace. In no case shall they be sold or given away, if captured by the armies of the United States, nor shall they ever be privately appropriated, or wantonly destroyed or injured.[29]

Reinforcing these points, Article 44 prohibited, among other crimes, "all destruction of property not commanded by the authorized officer" and stated that this prohibition was "under the penalty of death, or such other severe punishment as may seem adequate for the gravity of the offense".[30] But notwithstanding these constraints, the Lieber Code provided for the concept of "military necessity", defined in Article 14 as "those measures which are indispensable for securing the ends of war, and which are lawful according to the modern law and usages of war".[31] Elaborating, Article 15 stated, "Military necessity admits of all direct destruction of life or limb of armed enemies, and of other persons whose destruction is incidentally unavoidable in the armed contest of the war; . . . it allows of all destruction of property, . . ."[32] In short, within the context of its broader effort to delineate the law of war, the Lieber Code established that, in wartime, cultural objects should normally be both respected and safeguarded, except in extenuating situations involving the principle of military necessity. Indeed, the Lieber Code served as a model for several subsequent unilateral and multilateral efforts to codify the law of armed conflict.[33]

The Declaration of Brussels, signed by delegates from fifteen states on August 27, 1874, contained the first major reference to the wartime protection of cultural objects in a multilateral effort designed to codify the law of armed conflict in modern times.[34] Article 8 of the Declaration stated,

> The property of municipalities, that of institutions dedicated to religion, charity and education, the arts and sciences even when State property, shall be treated as private property. All seizure or destruction of, or willful damage to, institutions of this

character, historic monuments, works of art and science should be made the subject of legal proceedings by the competent authorities.[35]

Article 12 delineated the general and often subsequently repeated principle of the law of armed conflict: "The laws of war do not recognize in belligerents an unlimited power in the adoption of means of injuring the enemy".[36] The next article, Article 13, specifically stated that, "according to this principle are especially forbidden . . . (g) Any destruction or seizure of the enemy's property that is not imperatively demanded by the necessity of war".[37] With specific reference to sieges and bombardments, Articles 15, 16, 17, and 18 stated,

> Art. 15. Fortified places are alone liable to be besieged. Open towns, agglomerations of dwellings, or villages which are not defended can neither be attacked nor bombarded.
>
> Art. 16. But if a town or fortress, agglomeration of dwellings, or village, is defended, the officer in command of the attacking force must, before commencing a bombardment, except in assault, do all in his power to warn the authorities.
>
> Art. 17. In such cases all necessary steps must be taken to spare, as far as possible, buildings dedicated to art, science, or charitable purposes, hospitals, and places where the sick and wounded are collected provided that they are not being used at the time for military purposes. It is the duty of the besieged to indicate the presence of such buildings by distinctive and visible signs to be communicated to the enemy beforehand.
>
> Art. 18. A town taken by assault ought not be given over to pillage by the victorious troops.[38]

Finally, Article 38 stated that "private property cannot be confiscated".[39] Unfortunately, however, the Brussels Declaration did not come into force.[40]

Building upon the Brussels Declaration, the Oxford Manual on the Laws of War on Land, adopted by the Institute of International Law on September 9, 1880, represented a further attempt to codify the rules governing warfare.[41] With reference to the protection of cultural objects, Articles 32, 33, and 34 stated,

> Art. 32. It is forbidden: (a) to pillage, even towns taken by assault; (b) to destroy public or private property, if this destruction is not demanded by an imperative necessity of war; (c) to attack and to bombard undefended places.
>
> Art. 33. The commander of an attacking force, save in cases of open assault, shall before undertaking a bombardment, make every effort to give notice thereof to the local authorities.
>
> Art. 34. In case of bombardment all necessary steps must be taken to spare, if it can be done, buildings dedicated to religion, art, science and charitable purposes, hospitals and places where the sick and wounded are gathered on the condition that they are not being utilized at the time, directly or indirectly, for defense. . . .[42]

Moreover, Articles 43 and 53 were relevant to the status of cultural property with respect to the occupation of enemy territory. They stated,

> Art. 43. The occupant should take all due and needful measures to restore and ensure public order and public safety.

> Art. 53. The property of municipalities, and that of institutions devoted to religion, charity, education, art and science, cannot be seized. All destruction or willful damage to institutions of this character, historic monuments, archives, works of art, or science, is formally forbidden, save when urgently demanded by military necessity.[43]

As with the Brussels Declaration, the Oxford Manual proved to be very influential in future international efforts to codify the law of armed conflict.[44]

In 1899, for the first time in history, the members of the international community successfully concluded a multilateral convention at The Hague delineating the provisions of the law of armed conflict as agreed upon at the time. The 1899 Conference was followed in 1907 by a second Hague Conference, at which these provisions were further refined and developed. From the perspective of the protection of cultural property, the 1899 Convention (II) with Respect to the Laws and Customs of War on Land, signed on July 29, 1899 and which entered into force on September 4, 1900, the 1907 Convention (IV) Respecting the Laws and Customs of War on Land, signed on October 18, 1907 and which entered into force on January 26, 1910, and the 1907 Convention (IX) Concerning Bombardment by Naval Forces in Time of War, also signed on October 18, 1907 and which entered into force on January 26, 1910, were the most significant.[45] Indeed, these Conventions collectively constitute the first of what are now the four most significant enactments adopted by the members of the international community to protect cultural property in wartime.

In the Regulations Respecting the Laws and Customs of War on Land annexed to the Conventions, Article 22 of both the 1899 Convention II and the 1907 Convention IV reaffirmed Article 12 of the Brussels Declaration and Article 4 of the Oxford Manual by stating that, "The right of belligerents to adopt means of injuring the enemy is not unlimited". Developing this, Article 23 of both Conventions stated that, "it is especially prohibited" (the 1907 Convention used the word "forbidden") "(g) To destroy or seize the enemy's property, unless such destruction or seizure be imperatively demanded by the necessities of war".[46]

The provisions concerning bombardments of towns and cities delineated in the 1899 and 1907 Conventions II and IV, respectively, were somewhat different than the provisions set forth in the 1907 Convention IX concerning naval bombardments.[47] With respect to the 1899 and 1907 Conventions II and IV concerning bombardments from land, respectively, Article 25 of the 1899 Convention II stated, "The bombardment of towns, villages, habitations or buildings which are not defended, is prohibited". In response to the prospect of the future use of new technologies in bombardment, the 1907 version of Article 25 contained in Convention IV inserted the words, "by whatever means," thus revising the article to read, "The attack or bombardment, by whatever means, of towns, villages, dwellings, or buildings which are undefended is prohibited".[48]

Article 26 of both Conventions required that the attacker "do all in his power" to provide warning "before commencing a bombardment, except in cases of assault".[49] With specific reference to protected sites, Article 27 of 1899 Convention II stated,

> In sieges and bombardments all necessary steps should be taken to spare as far as possible edifices devoted to religion, art, science, and charity, hospitals, and places where the sick and wounded are collected, provided that they are not used at the same time for military purposes. The besieged should indicate these buildings or places by some particular and visible signs, which should previously be notified to the assailants.[50]

In addition to stylistically rewording the text, Article 27 of the 1907 Convention IV added "historic monuments" to the list of protected sites.[51] Neither the 1899 nor 1907 Conventions II or IV on land warfare, respectively, however, prescribed the nature or design of the "signs" indicating the protected sites. By contrast, the 1907 Convention IX Concerning Bombardment by Naval Forces did prescribe a design for the signs.[52] Finally, Article 28 in both Conventions stated that, "the pillage of a town or place, even when taken by assault, is prohibited".[53]

The 1907 Hague Convention IX stated in Article 1 that, "The bombardment by naval forces of undefended ports, towns, villages, dwellings, or buildings is forbidden". Article 2 qualifies this, however, by stating,

> Military works, military or naval establishments, depots of arms or war material, workshops or plant which could be utilized for the needs of the hostile fleet or army, and the ships of war in the harbour, are not, however, included in this prohibition. The commander of a naval force may destroy them with artillery, after a summons followed by a reasonable time of waiting, if all other means are impossible, and when the local authorities have not themselves destroyed them within the time fixed. He incurs no responsibility for any unavoidable damage which may be caused by a bombardment under such circumstances. If for military reasons immediate action is necessary, and no delay can be allowed the enemy, it is understood that the prohibition to bombard the undefended town holds good, as in the case given in paragraph 1, and that the commander shall take all due measures in order that the town may suffer as little harm as possible.[54]

With respect to cultural objects, Article 5 stated,

> In bombardments by naval forces all the necessary measures must be taken by the commander to spare as far as possible sacred edifices, buildings used for artistic, scientific, or charitable purposes, historic monuments, hospitals, and places where the sick or wounded are collected, on the understanding that they are not used at the same time for military purposes. It is the duty of the inhabitants to indicate such monuments, edifices, or places by visible signs, which shall consist of large, stiff rectangular panels divided diagonally into two coloured triangular portions, the upper portion black, the lower portion white.[55]

Article 6 stated that, "if the military situation permits, the commander of the attacking naval force, before commencing the bombardment, must do his utmost to warn the authorities". Finally, Article 7 stated that, "a town or place, even when taken by storm, may not be pillaged".[56]

Comparing the 1907 Conventions IV and IX, Tami Davis Biddle argued that the list of legitimate targets delineated in Article 2 of Convention IX, implied that "lawful targets can include industrial installations of value to the enemy war effort". Thus, she maintained that, in contrast to the provisions set forth in Convention IV, "the Naval Convention acknowledged that bombing was related to the military significance of the target rather than whether a city or town in which the target was located was defended, and it conferred permission to attack legitimate military targets wherever located." This provision, in turn, would have enormous future implications for the future of aerial bombardment.[57]

Articles 43, 46, 47, and 56 of the 1899 Convention II and the 1907 Convention IV were the most relevant in delineating the protections accorded to cultural property during periods of military occupation.[58] As worded in the 1907 Convention,[59] they stated,

> Art. 43. The authority of the legitimate power having in fact passed into the hands of the occupant, the latter shall take all the measures in his power to restore, and ensure, as far as possible, public order and safety, while respecting, unless absolutely prevented, the laws in force in the country.
>
> Art. 46. Family honour and rights, the lives of persons, and private property, as well as religious convictions and practice, must be respected. Private property cannot be confiscated.
>
> Art. 47. Pillage is formally forbidden.
>
> Art. 56. The property of municipalities, that of institutions dedicated to religion, charity and education, the arts and sciences, even when State property, shall be treated as private property. All seizure of, destruction or willful damage done to institutions of this character, historic monuments, works of art and science, is forbidden, and should be made the subject of legal proceedings.[60]

Finally, the 1899 and 1907 Conventions recognized that the regulations annexed to the respective Conventions were incomplete and, in the words of the 1907 Convention, did not cover "all the circumstances which arise in practice". They went on to state, however, that the Parties to the Conventions "clearly do not intend that unforeseen cases, in the absence of a written understanding, be left to the arbitrary judgment of military commanders".[61] Hence, the Martens Clause was inserted into the Preambles to emphasize that the laws of war delineated in the Conventions were "to be supplemented by rules applied in the interests of humanity and civilization, even when these are not expressed in treaty form".[62]

In short, irrespective of the relationship between the Parties to the Conventions, the objectives pursued, or, the nature and scope of the conflict, the 1899 and 1907 Hague Conventions clearly established that, unless "imperatively demanded by the necessities of war" and assuming that the prescribed cultural properties were not being used for "military purposes," belligerents were obligated to "take all the necessary measures" to, "as far as possible," protect cultural objects from "willful" damage, destruction, expropriation, or theft during military hostilities, as well as during periods of occupation. As affirmed at the Nuremberg Tribunal in 1946 and reaffirmed at the Tribunal for the Far East in 1948, by 1939, the provisions of the 1907 Hague Convention IV concerning land warfare, in particular, were considered to be universally applicable customary rules of international law. Thus, the provisions of these Conventions were considered binding on all states, including those that were "not formally parties to them".[63]

The World Wars and the Interwar Period: 1914-1945

The international community's hopes that the progress made prior to 1914 in placing legal limits on the conduct of warfare would serve to limit the severity of war were dashed by the experience of World War I. Significant increases in the range of artillery, combined with the emerging technologies associated with air bombardment,[64] within the larger context of the total mobilization of national resources for war, offered unprecedented prospects for the destruction of enemy military-industrial and infrastructure assets within the interior of the enemy country. Unfortunately, however, bombardments deep within enemy territory significantly complicated the goal of protecting cultural properties. As James W. Garner wrote immediately following World War II, "Among the most regrettable violations of international law during the recent war – one for which adequate reparation in many cases was impossible – was the destruction on a large scale of buildings which fell within the category of historic monuments and of institutions devoted to science, art, education, religion, and charity".[65] Often collateral damage to cultural property was the result of inaccuracy of weapons used in bombardments, especially the extreme inaccuracy of aerial bombardment, as well as the proximity of cultural sites to legitimate military targets. In addition, the use of various corrosive gases during the war increased the risks to cultural objects. Moreover, damage to cultural sites was also the result of allegations that these sites were being used for military purposes, as well as justifications of military necessity and reprisal.[66] Indeed, as Professor Garner observed, "many buildings and historic monuments whose sanctity and immunity are well established by the customs of civilized warfare as well as by the Hague Conventions were seriously damaged and in some cases destroyed, either wantonly or as an unavoidable incident of military operations".[67] Especially egregious examples of the destruction of cultural property in France and Belgium included, the burning of the University of Louvain in September, 1914, including the library and its large collection of rare volumes, manuscripts, scientific objects, and works of art, by the Germans,[68] the German bombardment and significant damage to Rheims Cathedral,[69] the destruction of Cloth Hall in Ypres by the Germans in October 1914,[70] as well as damage to or the destruction of numerous other cathedrals and cultural sites.[71] Similar examples of destruction occurred in Italy, especially in Venice, as a result of Austro-Hungarian air bombardments.[72] Finally, as Professor Garner noted, "in Italy as in Belgium and

France the invaders were charged with committing spoliations upon both public and private art collections and with carrying off to Vienna, Budapest, and Berlin numerous masterpieces as well as the contents of churches and museums".[73] Indeed, the damage to European cultural objects was unparalleled since the end of the Thirty Years War in 1648.[74]

Throughout the war there were a number of proposals designed to help ensure the safety of cultural properties during hostilities,[75] including one that called for the establishment of an "International Bureau for the Protection of Monuments and Works of Art in Time of War," to be headquartered in Bern, Switzerland. Unfortunately, however, neither that proposal, nor other similar ideas were implemented.[76] In 1918, the Netherlands Archaeological Society prepared a report not only examining the need for improved protection of cultural sites during wartime, but also the need for contingency plans and preparations to be made for the protection of cultural properties in peacetime. The report suggested that this might be best facilitated through the coordinating efforts of an international organization which, among other things, would "draw up a statement of inventory, which would be made public, of buildings to be spared by enemy forces on condition that they would at no time be assigned to military purposes". In addition, the report raised the possibility that "a few historic centers of very special interest (Brussels, Florence, Nuremberg, Oxford, the City of Paris, Rome, Rothenburg, and Venice)" be "completely demilitarized throughout their entire extent, entailing a state of neutrality". Finally, the report recommended that peacetime preparations be made for the establishment of a list of individuals who would be willing to serve as neutral observers during wartime. These observers would certify that specifically enumerated cultural buildings and sites were not being used for military purposes. While not acted upon immediately, these suggestions influenced subsequent discussions concerning the wartime protection of cultural objects.[77]

During the interwar period, the international community made a variety of efforts designed to further regulate the conduct of warfare.[78] The international community was, however, unsuccessful in its efforts to reach agreement concerning a convention governing the wartime employment of aircraft. Between December, 1922 and February, 1923, a Commission of Jurists met in The Hague in an effort to formulate a body rules governing aerial warfare. Their efforts resulted in the 1923 Hague Rules of Air Warfare.[79] Eliminating the distinction made in the 1899 and 1907 Hague Conventions on Land Warfare between defended versus undefended towns, Articles 22 and 24 used the nature of the objective, even those located in the interior of the enemy's territory, as the criteria in defining what constituted legitimate targets for aerial bombardment.[80] Articles 22 and 24 stated,

> Art. 22. Aerial bombardment for the purpose of terrorizing the civilian population, of destroying or damaging private property not of military character, or of injuring non-combatants is prohibited.
>
> Art. 24.
> (1) Aerial bombardment is legitimate only when directed at a military objective, that is to say, an object of which the destruction or injury would constitute a distinct

military advantage to the belligerent.
(2) Such bombardment is legitimate only when directed exclusively at the following objectives: military forces; military works, military establishments or depots; factories constituting important and well-known centers engaged in the manufacture of arms, ammunition or distinctively military supplies; lines of communication or transportation used for military purposes.
(3) The bombardment of cities, towns, villages, dwellings or buildings not in the immediate neighbourhood of the operations of land forces is prohibited. In cases where the objectives specified in paragraph (2) are so situated, that they cannot be bombarded without the indiscriminate bombardment of the civilian population, the aircraft must abstain from bombardment.
(4) In the immediate neighbourhood of the operations of land forces, the bombardment of cities, towns, villages, dwellings or buildings is legitimate provided that there exists a reasonable presumption that the military concentration is sufficiently important to justify such bombardment, having regard to the danger thus caused to the civilian population.
(5) A belligerent state is liable to pay compensation for injuries to persons or to property caused by the violation by any of its officers or forces of the provisions of this article.

In short, the proposed rules for aerial bombardment were designed to provide maximum protection for civilians and civilian objects.[81] With specific reference to protection accorded to cultural objects, Articles 25 and 26 stated,

Art. 25. In bombardment by aircraft, all necessary steps must be taken by the commander to spare as far as possible buildings dedicated to public worship, art, science, or charitable purposes, historic monuments, hospital ships, hospitals and other places where the sick and wounded are collected, provided such buildings, objects or places are not at the time used for military purposes. Such buildings, objects and places must by day be indicated by marks visible to aircraft. The use of marks to indicate other buildings objects, or places than those specified above is to be deemed an act of perfidy. The marks used as aforesaid shall be in the case of buildings protected under the Geneva Convention the red cross of a white ground, and in the case of other protected buildings a large rectangular panel divided diagonally into two pointed triangular portions, one black and the other white. A belligerent who desires to secure by night the protection for the hospitals and other privileged buildings above mentioned must take the necessary measures to render the special signs referred to sufficiently visible.

Art. 26. The following special rules are adopted for the purpose of enabling states to obtain more efficient protection for important historic monuments situated within their territory, provided that they are willing to refrain from the use of such monuments and a surrounding zone for military purposes, and to accept a special regime for their inspection.
(1) A state shall be entitled, if its sees fit, to establish a zone or protection round such monuments situated in its territory. Such a zone shall in time of war enjoy immunity from bombardment.
(2) The monuments round which a zone is to be established shall be notified to other Powers in peace time through the diplomatic channel; the notification shall also indicate the limits of the zones. The notification may not be

withdrawn in time of war.
(3) The zone of protection may include, in addition to the area actually occupied by the monument or group of monuments, an outer zone, not exceeding 500 metres in width, measured from the circumference of the said area.
(4) Marks clearly visible from aircraft either by day or by night will be employed for the purpose of ensuring the identification by belligerent airmen of the limits of the zones.
(5) The marks on the monuments themselves will be those defined in Article 25. The marks employed for indicating the surrounding zones will be fixed by each state adopting the provisions of this article, and will be notified to other Powers at the same time as the monuments and zones are notified.
(6) Any abusive use of the marks indicating the zones referred to in paragraph 5 will be regarded as an act of perfidy.
(7) A state adopting the provisions of this article must abstain from using the monument and the surrounding zone for military purposes, or for the benefit in any way whatever of its military organization, or from committing within such monument or zone any act with a military purpose in view.
(8) An inspection committee consisting of three neutral representatives accredited to the state adopting the provisions of this article, or their delegates, shall be appointed for the purpose of ensuring that no violation is committed of the provisions of paragraph 7. One of the members of the committee of inspection shall be the representative (or his delegate) of the state to which has been entrusted the interests of the opposing belligerent.[82]

The influence of earlier efforts to delineate the rules of warfare and protect cultural objects in time of war, were apparent in the provisions of the 1923 Hague Rules of Air Warfare. Moreover, the Rules further clarified the principle of discrimination and developed the principle of proportionality, especially in Article 24, paragraph 4. While the Rules were never adopted, they exerted a significant influence on subsequent efforts to codify the rules of armed conflict, including the protection of cultural objects.[83]

Notwithstanding the failure of the states to adopt the 1923 Hague Rules of Air Warfare, additional attempts were made throughout the 1930s to abolish or, at least, place limits on air warfare.[84] Meanwhile, on April 15, 1935, twenty-one states of the Western Hemisphere signed the Treaty on the Protection of Artistic and Scientific Institutions and Historic Monuments in Washington D.C., also known as the Washington Pact or the Roerich Pact, in honor of Professor Nicholas Roerich who was the treaty's principal promoter. This treaty was the first international pact dedicated exclusively to the protection of cultural property and entered into force on August 26, 1935.[85] Consistent with the 1899 and 1907 Hague Conventions, Articles 1, 2, and 5 of the Roerich Pact stated,

Art. 1. The historic monuments, museums, scientific, artistic, educational and cultural institutions shall be considered as neutral and as such respected and protected by belligerents. The same respect and protection shall be due to the personnel of the institutions mentioned above. The same respect and protection shall be accorded to the historical monuments, museums, scientific, artistic, educational and cultural institutions in time of peace as well as in war.

Art. 2. The neutrality of, and protection and respect due to, the monuments and institutions mentioned in the preceding Article, shall be recognized in the entire expanse of territories subject to the sovereignty of each of the Signatory and Acceding States, without any discrimination as to the State allegiance of said monuments and institutions. The respective Governments agree to adopt measures of internal legislation to insure said protection and respect.

Art. 5. The monuments and institutions mentioned in Article 1 shall cease to enjoy the privileges recognized in the present Treaty in case they are made use of for military purposes.[86]

In contrast to the design prescribed in Article 5 of the 1907 Hague Convention IX, however, Article 3 of the Roerich Pact prescribed that a "distinctive flag" consisting of a "red circle with a triple red sphere in the circle on a white background," should be used "to identify" protected institutions and monuments.[87]

Meanwhile, as the prospects for another European war increased, a number of efforts were made to limit the scope and intensity of the impending conflict. On June 21, 1938, the British Prime Minister, Neville Chamberlain, presented three rules that, he maintained, should govern aerial bombardment. They were,

1. It is against international law to bomb civilians as such and to make deliberate attacks upon civilian populations.
2. Targets which are aimed at from the air must be legitimate military objectives and must be capable of identification.
3. Reasonable care must be taken in attacking those military objectives so that by carelessness a civilian population in the neighborhood is not bombed.[88]

In addition, the international community drafted, but failed to adopt, two major international conventions designed to provide wartime protection to civilians and civilian objects. In 1938, the International Law Association approved a Draft Convention for the Protection of Civilian Populations Against New Engines of War.[89] In addition, building upon the Roerich Pact and in the wake of the destruction of cultural objects during the Spanish Civil War, the International Museums Office formed a commission to prepare a draft convention containing safeguards for cultural properties. In 1938, the completed draft was submitted to the League of Nations and a conference was to be organized to discuss the document, but the outbreak of the Second World War in Europe overtook the planned conference.[90] Given this, in 1939, in an effort to place constraints on the scope and intensity of hostilities, the International Museums Office issued a ten-article declaration generally conforming to the draft convention, but even this effort was overtaken by the course of the war.[91] The Preliminary Draft International Convention for the Protection of Historic Buildings and Works of Art in Time of War adopted a cosmopolitan, internationalist perspective regarding cultural objects stating, "the destruction of a masterpiece, whatever nation may have produced it, is a spiritual impoverishment for the entire international community". Article 1 summarized the draft's focus: the Parties deemed it to be "incumbent upon every Government to organize the defense of historic buildings and works of art against the foreseeable effects of war, and undertake. . . to prepare that defense in time of peace".[92] Toward that end, Article 4 stated,

1. The High Contracting Parties undertake to refrain from any act of hostility directed against any refuge that a High Contracting Party may have designated in his territory to shelter in time of war works of art or of historic interest that may be threatened by military operations.
2. The number of such refuges shall be limited; they may take the form either of buildings erected for the purpose or of existing historic buildings or groups of buildings.
3. To secure immunity, refuges must: (a) be situated at a distance of not less than 20 kilometres from the most likely theatres of military operations, from any military objective, from any main line of communication, and from any large industrial center (this distance may be reduced in certain cases in countries with a very dense population and small area); (b) have already been notified in time of peace; (c) not be used directly or indirectly for purposes of national defence; (d) be open to international inspection during hostilities.
4. The military authorities shall have access to the refuges at any time for the purpose of satisfying themselves that they are not being used in any way contrary to the present Convention.[93]

With reference to cultural sites in general, Article 5 stated,

1. The High Contracting Parties, acknowledging it to be their joint and several duty to respect and protect all monuments of artistic or historic interest in time of war, agree to take all possible precautions to spare such monuments during operations and to ensure that their use or situation shall not expose them to attack.
2. Special protection shall be given to monuments or groups of monuments which: (a) are isolated from any military objective within a radius of 500 metres; (b) are not directly or indirectly used for purposes of national defence; (c) have already been notified in time of peace; (d) are open to international inspection during hostilities.[94]

Article 6 allowed the various states to individually conclude reciprocal agreements "extending the immunity" to properties that failed to "satisfy conditions laid down in Article 4". Article 7 described a "mark" for protected properties as "a light blue triangle inscribed in a white disk". It also stated that, "monuments and museums shall be brought to the notice of the civil population, who shall be requested to protect them, and of occupying troops, who shall be informed that they are dealing with buildings the preservation of which is the concern of the entire international community". Article 8 prohibited reprisals against "historic buildings and works of art". Articles 9 and 10 provided for the wartime transfer of cultural objects to and their temporary shelter in other countries. Article 11 provided for International Commissions of Inspection to "satisfy themselves while military operations are proceeding that no breach of the provisions of this Convention is committed" or to document any breaches that were found. Finally, Article 12 provided for general conferences, as well as the appointment of a Standing Committee and a Secretariat. In addition, a series of regulations were added to the draft convention for its implementation.[95] Thus, although the Convention was never adopted, like its predecessors, it further developed both the concept and details associated with the wartime protection of cultural objects.[96]

Meanwhile, on September 3, 1939, war erupted in Europe. On September 1, two days prior to the outbreak of hostilities, U.S. President Franklin D. Roosevelt sent a message to the governments of Germany, Great Britain, France, and Poland asking the authorities in each of these states to "affirm publicly its determination to not proceed, in any case or circumstance, to an aerial bombing of civil populations or undefended towns, being understood that the same rules shall be scrupulously observed by all their adversaries".[97] Each of the four powers replied affirmatively to President Roosevelt's request, stating that they would confine bombardments exclusively to military targets, provided that similar enemy restraint was shown.[98]

Despite these assurances, however, with the commencement of hostilities, many felt that Germany had indiscriminately engaged in the air bombardment of Warsaw and Rotterdam. Yet, at the outset of the war, the British Royal Air Force (RAF) exclusively focused its efforts on German military targets. On August 24, 1940, during the Battle of Britain, however, German bombers inadvertently dropped bombs on London. This, in turn, led to an RAF retaliatory strike against Berlin the following night. Notwithstanding this escalation, the British continued to focus on German military-industrial targets. Given the vulnerability of bombers, however, the RAF opted for night air operations, thereby further reducing the already poor accuracy of aerial bombardment and increasing the likelihood of collateral damage. Finally, in early 1942, RAF Bomber Command was directed to "focus 'on the morale of the enemy civilian population and in particular, of the industrial workers'". Henceforth, Bomber Command's emphasis would be on the destruction of enemy cities. In late March, 1943, under the direction of its new commander, Arthur Harris, Bomber Command further escalated the air war by intentionally igniting a firestorm in the historic German city of Lubeck. Germany retaliated with air raids against Britain's own historic cathedral towns, first Exeter, and then over the following three weeks against York, Norwich, and Canterbury. Under Harris' leadership, Bomber Command continued its unrestrained, counter-city raids designed to break the morale of the German people throughout the remainder of the war. Indeed, among the most dramatic examples of this aerial bombing campaign were the four RAF raids on Hamburg in late July and early August, 1943, the second of which "ignited the world's first great firestorm" and led to the death of an estimated 42,000 civilians.[99] By contrast, upon entry into the European war and continuing throughout its duration, despite heavy losses, the U.S. Army Air Corps remained committed to daylight, high altitude, formation, aerial bombardment directed exclusively at military-industrial targets. From Germany's perspective, however, the Anglo-American Combined Bomber Offensive entailed air raids by the Americans, directed at military-industrial targets, during daylight hours and RAF nighttime raids, directed at urban areas.[100] Finally, the European air war reached its terrible culmination with the highly inaccurate and indiscriminate German V-2 rocket attacks against British cities, beginning on September 8, 1944, and the infamous Dresden firestorm on February

13-14, 1945. In the end, most German cities, as well as significant portions of many British and other European cities, lay in ruins. Among those ruins were the damaged and destroyed remains of European civilization's cultural heritage.[101] On the other hand, it should be pointed out that Anglo-American efforts to identify and avoid damaging or destroying cultural properties during air bombardments did yield some dividends. For example, while it was estimated that "at least 95 percent of the damage inflicted to major monuments" in northern France, the Netherlands, Luxembourg, and Belgium were "caused by air bombardment," with the exception of "Rouen, the great Gothic monuments of France . . . escaped comparatively lightly".[102]

Meanwhile, initially during the war against Japan, the U.S. Army Air Corps attempted to implement its high altitude, formation, daylight bombing strategy in an effort to destroy Japanese military-industrial assets. Lack of success, however, led the United States to alter its approach to aerial bombardment and adopt night, low altitude, incendiary air strikes against Japan's cities. The result was indiscriminate firestorm infernos and massive devastation in sixty-six of Japan's urban centers. Indeed, over 80,000 people reportedly died in the Tokyo firestorm of March 9-10, 1945 alone. Finally, the dramatic culmination came in early August 1945 with the atomic bomb strikes against Hiroshima and Nagasaki.[103]

In addition to the tremendous destruction associated with aerial bombardment, ground operations during the German-Soviet war on Europe's Eastern Front, as well as German policies within occupied Soviet territory, were even more destructive. It was here that the Nazis pursued *guerre mortelle* in the modern industrial age: an ideologically inspired 20th century war of annihilation and extermination directed against Nazi Germany's political arch-enemy, the Soviet Union, and, more generally, against what the Nazis viewed as the inferior Slavic peoples. While the battle of Stalingrad epitomizes large-scale urban combat, the siege of Leningrad is the ultimate example of a prolonged bombardment by ground forces. But in addition to the tremendous destruction sustained at these two Soviet cities, Odessa, Kiev, Sevastopol, Minsk, Smolensk, Pskov, Novgorod, Kharkov, Orel, Rostov-on-Don, and Voronezh, among others, also suffered enormous devastation. In the broader sense, there were at least 25 million Soviet citizens killed, tens of millions of civilians injured, an estimated 25 million people were rendered homeless, and there was incalculable property damage and destruction in approximately 1,710 cities and over 70,000 villages throughout the vast area the western USSR. It was estimated that more than six million buildings were destroyed or badly damaged. Accompanying this devastation was the conscious damage or destruction of countless, priceless cultural objects and properties. Clearly, in terms of scope, intensity, degree of devastation, and loss of human life, the Soviet-German War was the largest, most destructive war in human history.[104]

With respect to occupation polices, the Nazis intended to totally eradicate a number of enemy urban centers. For example, as stated in an official memorandum from the Chief of the German Naval Staff, "The Fuhrer has decided to erase from the face of the earth St. Petersburg. The existence of this large city will have no further interest after Soviet Russia is destroyed". Similarly, Warsaw and the cultural treasures located therein were virtually eradicated by the conclusion of the war.[105] Finally, in blatant violation of the 1899 and 1907 Hague Conventions II and IV, respectively, the Nazis engaged in the systematic, organized, plunder of cultural objects throughout occupied Europe on an unprecedented scale.[106]

By contrast, insofar as possible, the Anglo-Americans attempted to respect and protect cultural properties in ground operations in Europe. Emphasizing the importance that the Allied High Command placed upon the need to respect and protect cultural properties, on December 29, 1943, the Allied Supreme Commander in Europe, General Dwight Eisenhower, issued the following directive:

> Today we are fighting in a country [Italy] which has contributed a great deal to our cultural inheritance, a country rich in monuments which by their creation helped and now in their old age illustrate the growth of the civilization which is ours. We are bound to respect those monuments so far as war allows. If we have to choose between destroying a famous building and sacrificing our own men, then our men's lives count infinitely more and the building must go. But the choice is not always so clear-cut as that. Nothing can stand against the argument of military necessity. That is an accepted principle. But the phrase 'military necessity' is sometimes used where it would be more truthful to speak of military convenience or even personal convenience. I do not want it to cloak slackness or indifference. It is a responsibility of high commanders to determine through AMC Officers the locations of historical monuments whether they be immediately ahead of our front lines or in areas occupied by us. This information passed to lower echelons through normal channels places the responsibility on all commanders of complying with the spirit of this letter.[107]

Similarly, on May 26, 1944, as the Allies prepared for the Normandy operation, General Eisenhower issued the following statement:

> Shortly we will be fighting our way across the Continent of Europe in battles designed to preserve our civilization. Inevitably, in the path of our advance will be found historical monuments and cultural centers which symbolize to the world all that we are fighting to preserve. It is the responsibility of every commander to protect and respect these symbols whenever possible. In some circumstances the success of the military operation may be prejudiced in our reluctance to destroy these revered objects. Then, as at Cassino, where the enemy relied on our emotional attachments to shield his defense, the lives of our men are paramount. So, where military necessity dictates, commanders may order the required action even though it involves destruction to some honored site. But there are many circumstances in which damage and destruction are not necessary and cannot be justified. In such cases, through the exercise of restraint and discipline, commanders will preserve centers and objects of historical and cultural significance. Civil Affairs Staffs at higher echelons will advise commanders of the locations of historical monuments of this type, both in advance of the front lines and in occupied areas. This information, together with the necessary instruction, will be passed down through command channels to all echelons.[108]

Finally, in order to facilitate implementation of these directives, Monuments, Fine Arts and Archives Officers were assigned to U.S., British, and French forces. Many of these officers were leading archaeologists, museum curators, and art historians.[109] Yet, notwithstanding the high degree of emphasis that the allied leadership placed on the protection of cultural objects in combat zones, however, many cultural properties were nevertheless seriously damaged or destroyed.[110]

Thus, by the end of World War II, among the rubble that now composed much of tangible portion of mankind's cultural heritage, also lay the hopes of many members of the global community that warfare could be successfully regulated.

Post World War II Efforts Preserve Cultural Objects During Period of Armed Conflicts

While World War II was still underway, on January 5, 1943, the United States, Great Britain, the Soviet Union, and fifteen other powers issued the Declaration of London in which they stated that they reserved "their rights to declare invalid" the pillaged or otherwise transferred property, located in territories under Axis occupation.[111] Following the end of the war in 1945, the victorious Allies began the lengthy process of repatriating moveable cultural objects, as well as addressing the difficult issue of compensating owners of destroyed objects.[112]

Meanwhile, at the Nuremberg tribunal, various Nazi leaders were held personally responsible for crimes, including those involving the looting of cultural property, which they had committed while acting on behalf of the German government.[113] The tribunal did not, however, directly address or attempt to delineate the limits of aerial bombardment. As pointed out by Telford Taylor, the Chief Counsel for War Crimes at Nuremberg, "If the first badly bombed cities – Warsaw, Rotterdam, Belgrade, and London – suffered at the hands of the Germans and not the allies, nonetheless the ruins of German and Japanese cities were the results not of reprisals but of deliberate policy, and bore witness that aerial bombardment of cities and factories has become a recognized part of modern warfare as carried on by all nations".[114] But with respect to other critical areas of the law of war and human rights law, the Nuremberg verdicts established that there were basic normative standards, universally applicable to all people and states, against which the actions of all would be judged, and against which they would be held accountable.[115] In so asserting, the members of the international community implicitly declared *guerre mortelle* to be an unacceptable form of warfare.

Following the post-war tribunals, the members of the international community amplified and expanded upon the assertion that there were minimal standards governing the conduct of war through the adoption of a series of declarations and conventions, beginning with the 1948 Universal Declaration of Human Rights, the 1948 Genocide Convention, and the 1949 Geneva Conventions. Of these three documents, the first two were said to be universally applicable in peacetime, as well as in times of domestic or international armed conflict. The 1949 Geneva Conventions were applicable not only to situations involving "declared war or any other armed conflict which may arise between two or more of the High Contracting Parties," but also to cases involving "armed conflict not of an international character occurring in the territory of one of the High Contracting Parties".[116]

60   *The Law of Armed Conflict*

Meanwhile, soon after the conclusion of the war, the members of the international community, under the auspices of UNESCO, undertook efforts to strengthen those provisions of the law of armed conflict designed to protect cultural properties during military hostilities and periods of occupation. These efforts culminated in an intergovernmental conference, attended by representatives from fifty-six states, held at The Hague between April 21 and May 14, 1954. At its closing session, in addition to enacting its Final Act, the conference produced the Convention for the Protection of Cultural Property in the Event of Armed Conflict, Regulations for the Implementation of the Convention, as well as a separate Protocol for the Protection of Cultural Property in the Event of Armed Conflict. The 1954 Hague Convention entered into force on August 7, 1956.[117] The 1954 Hague Convention constitutes the second of the four most significant components of the contemporary law of armed conflict designed to protect cultural properties during periods of armed hostilities. As such, it is important to review the provisions of the 1954 Hague Convention in some detail.

The Preamble to the 1954 Hague Convention began by stating that, since "damage to cultural property belonging to any people whatsoever means damage to the cultural heritage of all mankind, since each people makes its contribution to the culture of the world . . . the preservation of the cultural heritage is of great importance for all peoples of the world and that it is important that this heritage should receive international protection".[118] This cosmopolitan, internationalist perspective was reminiscent of the perspective adopted in the 1938 Preliminary Draft International Convention for the Protection of Historic Buildings and Works of Art in Times of War.[119] As Sharon Williams observed,

> The Convention is emphatic that a nation's artistic treasures are important not only to that nation but to the entire world and in this respect each state is a custodian of its treasures for the world at large. There is the clear implication that although a state is sovereign within its territory, in relation to cultural property certain minimum standards are expected by the world community.[120]

As John Merryman noted, in framing the 1954 Hague Convention in cosmopolitan, internationalist terms, it became "a charter for cultural internationalism".[121]

Article 1 defined "cultural property, . . . irrespective of ownership" as,

(a) movable or immovable property of great importance to the cultural heritage of every people, such as monuments of architecture, art or history, whether religious or secular; archaeological sites; groups of buildings which, as a whole, are of historical or artistic interest; works of art; manuscripts, books and other objects of artistic, historical or archaeological interest; as well as scientific collections and important collections of books or archives or of reproductions of the property defined above;
(b) buildings whose main and effective purpose is to preserve or exhibit the movable cultural property defined in sub-paragraph (a) such as museums, large libraries and depositories or archives, and refuges intended to shelter, in the event of armed conflict, the movable cultural property defined in subparagraph (a)
(c) centres containing a large amount of cultural property as defined in sub-paragraphs

(a) and (b), to be known as 'centers containing monuments'.[122]

Articles 18 and 19, paragraphs 1 and 2 delineated the scope of the Convention. They stated,

> Art. 18.
> 1. Apart from the provisions which shall take effect in time of peace, the present Convention shall apply in the event of declared war or any other armed conflict which may arise between two or more of the High Contracting Parties, even if the state of war is not recognized by one or more of them.
> 2. The Convention shall also apply to all cases of partial or total occupation of the territory of a High Contacting Party, even if the said occupation meets with no armed resistance.
> 3. If one of the Powers in the conflict is not a Party to the present Convention, the Powers which are Parties thereto shall nevertheless remain bound by it in their mutual relations. They shall furthermore be bound by the Convention, in relation to the said Power, if the latter has declared that it accepts the provisions thereof and so long as it applies them.
>
> Art. 19.
> 1. In the event of an armed conflict not of an international character occurring within the territory of one of the High Contacting Parties, each party to the conflict shall be bound to apply, as a minimum, the provisions of the present Convention which relate to respect for cultural property.
> 2. The parties to the Conflict shall endeavour to bring into force, by means of special agreements, all or part of the other provisions of the present Convention.[123]

Chapter I delineated "General Provisions" regarding the protection of cultural property. Article 2 stated that, "the protection of cultural property shall comprise of the safeguarding of and respect for such property".[124] The emphasis on peacetime preparation was reminiscent of Article 1 of the 1938 Draft International Convention.[125] As such, Articles 3 stated,

> The High Contracting Parties undertake to prepare in time of peace for the safeguarding of cultural property situated within their own territory against the foreseeable effects of an armed conflict, by taking such measures as they consider appropriate.[126]

Article 4 focused on respect for cultural property, but, like Article 8, in doing so, introduced the controversial provision of "military necessity".[127]

> 1. The High Contracting Parties undertake to respect cultural property situated within their own territory as well as within the territory of other High Contracting Parties by refraining from any use of the property and its immediate surroundings or of the appliances in use for its protection for purposes which are likely to expose it to destruction or damage in the event of armed conflict; and by refraining from any act of hostility directed against such property.[128]
> 2. The obligations mentioned in paragraph 1 of the present Article may be waived only in cases where military necessity imperatively requires such a waiver.
> 3. The High Contracting Parties further undertake to prohibit, prevent and, if

necessary, put a stop to any form of theft, pillage or misappropriation of, and any acts of vandalism directed against, cultural property. They shall, refrain from requisitioning movable cultural property situated in the territory of another High Contracting Party.
4. No High Contracting Party may evade the obligations incumbent upon it under the present Article, in respect of another High Contracting Party, by reason of the fact that the latter has not applied the measures of safeguard referred to in Article 3.[129]

Article 5 delineated provisions concerning the occupation of enemy territory.

1. Any High Contracting Party in occupation of the whole or part of the territory of another High Contracting Party shall as far as possible support the competent national authorities of the occupied country in safeguarding and preserving its cultural property.
2. Should it prove necessary to take measures to preserve cultural property situated in occupied territory and damaged by military operations, and should the competent national authorities be unable to take such measures, the Occupying Power shall, as far as possible, and in close co-operation with such authorities, take the most necessary measures of preservation.
3. Any High Contracting Party whose government is considered their legitimate government by members of a resistance movement, shall, if possible, draw their attention to the obligation to comply with those provisions of the Conventions dealing with respect for cultural property. [130]

Reminiscent of Article 4 of the 1938 Preliminary Draft Convention,[131] Chapter II of the 1954 Hague Convention provided for "special protection" for specifically designated cultural properties. Article 8 stated,

1. There may be placed under special protection a limited number of refuges intended to shelter movable cultural property in the event of armed conflict, of centers containing monuments and other immovable cultural property of very great importance, provided that they: (a) are situation at an adequate distance from any large industrial center or from any important military objective constituting a vulnerable point, such as, for example, an aerodrome, broadcasting station, establishment engaged upon work of national defence, a port or railway station of relative importance or a main line of communication; (b) are not used for military purposes.
2. A refuge for movable cultural property may also be placed under special protection, whatever its location, if it is so constructed that, in all probability, it will not be damaged by bombs.
3. A center containing monuments shall be deemed to be used for military purposes whenever it is used for the movement of military personnel or material, even in transit. The same shall apply whenever activities directly connected with military operations, the stationing of military personnel, or the production of war material are carried on within the center.
4. The guarding of cultural property mentioned in paragraph 1 above by armed custodians specifically empowered to do so, or the presence, in the vicinity of such cultural property, of police forces normally responsible for the maintenance of public order, shall not be deemed to be used for military purposes.

5. If any cultural property mentioned in paragraph 1 of the present Article is situated near an important military objective as defined in the said paragraph, it may nevertheless be placed under special protection if the High Contracting Party asking for that protection undertakes, in the event of armed conflict, to make no use of the objective and particularly, in the case of a port, railway station or aerodrome, to divert all traffic therefrom. In that event, such diversion shall be prepared in time of peace.
6. Special protection is granted to cultural property by its entry in the 'International Register of Cultural Property under Special Protection'. This entry shall only be made, in accordance with the provisions of the present Convention and under the conditions provided for in the Regulations for the execution of the Convention.[132]

Article 9 established the immunity of cultural property under special protection, stating, "The High Contracting Parties undertake to ensure the immunity of cultural property under special protection by refraining, from the time of entry in the International Register, from any act of hostility directed against such property and, except for the cases provided in paragraph 5 of Article 8, from any use of such property or its surroundings for military purposes".[133] Article 11 went on to delineate the conditions under which special protection immunity may be withdrawn. It stated,

1. If one of the High Contracting Parties commits, in respect of any item of cultural property under special protection, a violation of the obligations under Article 9, the opposing Party shall, so long as their violation persists, be released from the obligation to ensure the immunity of the property concerned. Nevertheless, whenever possible, the latter party shall first request the cessation of such violation within a reasonable time.
2. Apart from the case provided for in paragraph 1 of the present Article, immunity shall be withdrawn from cultural property under special protection only in exceptional cases of unavoidable military necessity, and only for such time as that necessity continued. Such necessity can be established only by the officer commanding a force the equivalent of a division in size or larger. Whenever circumstances permit, the opposing Party shall be notified, a reasonable time in advance, of the decision to withdraw immunity.
3. The Party withdrawing immunity shall, as soon as possible, so inform the Commissioner-General for cultural property provided for in the Regulations for the execution of the Convention, in writing, stating the reasons.[134]

Recalling provisions set forth in the 1938 Preliminary Draft International Convention,[135] Chapter III focused on the transport of cultural property under special protection. Articles 12, 13, and 14 stated,

Art. 12.
1. Transport exclusively engaged in the transfer of cultural property, whether within a territory or to another territory, may, at the request of the High Contracting Party concerned, take place under special protection in accordance with the conditions specified in the Regulations for the execution of the Convention.
2. Transport under special protection shall take place under the international

supervision provided for in the aforesaid Regulations and shall display the distinctive emblem described in Article 16.
3. The High Contracting Parties shall refrain from any act of hostility directed against transport under special protection.

Art. 13.
1. If a High Contacting Party considers that the safety of certain cultural property requires its transfer and that the matter is of such urgency that the procedure laid down in Article 12 cannot be followed, especially at the beginning of an armed conflict, the transport may display the distinctive emblem described in Article 16, provided that an application for immunity referred to in Article 12 has not already been made and refused. As far as possible, notification of transfer should be made to the opposing Parties. Nevertheless, transport conveying cultural property to the territory of another country may not display the distinctive emblem unless immunity has been expressly granted to it.
2. The High Contracting Parties shall take, so far as possible, the necessary precautions to avoid acts of hostility directed against the transport described in paragraph 1 of the present Article and displaying the distinctive emblem.

Art. 14.
1. Immunity from seizure, placing in prize, or capture shall be granted to: (a) cultural property enjoying protection provided for in Article 12 or that provided for in Article 13; (b) the means of transport exclusively engaged in the transfer of such cultural property.
2. Nothing in the present Article shall limit the right to visit and search.[136]

Article 15 dealt with the status of "personnel engaged in the protection of cultural property".[137] Articles 16 and 17 of Chapter V provided for a "distinctive emblem" designed to indicate protected cultural property. Describing the emblem and the conditions under which it was to be used, Articles 16 and 17 stated,

Art. 16.
1. The distinctive emblem of the Convention shall take the form of a shield, pointed below, per saltire blue and white (a shield consisting of a royal-blue square, one of the angles of which forms the point of the shield, and of a royal-blue triangle above the square, the space on either side being taken up by a white triangle).
2. The emblem shall be used alone, or repeated three times in a triangular formation (one shield below), under the conditions provided for in Article 17.

Art. 17.
1. The distinctive emblem repeated three times may be used only as a means of identification of: (a) immovable property under special protection; (b) the transport of cultural property under the conditions provided for in Articles 12 and 13; (c) improvised refuges, under the conditions provided for in the Regulations for the execution of the Convention.
2. The distinctive emblem may be used only as a means of identification of: (a) cultural property not under special protection; (b) the persons responsible for the duties of control in accordance with the Regulations for the execution of the Convention; (c) the personnel engaged in the protection of cultural property; (d) the

identity cards mentioned in the Regulations for the execution of the Convention.
3. During an armed conflict, the use of the distinctive emblem in any other cases than those mentioned in the preceding paragraphs of the present Article, and the use for any purpose whatever of a sign resembling the distinctive emblem, shall be forbidden.
4. The distinctive emblem may not be placed on any immovable cultural property unless at the same time there is displayed an authorization duly dated and signed by the competent authority of the High Contracting Party.[138]

Article 36 noted that, with respect to those powers that are bound by the terms of the 1899 and 1907 Hague Conventions IV and IX, as well as those bound by the 1935 Roerich Pact, the terms of the 1954 Convention were "supplementary to the aforementioned" Conventions, except that the emblem designated in Article 16 of the 1954 Hague Convention should substitute for the emblems described in Article 5 of the 1907 Hague Convention IX and Article 3 of the Roerich Pact.[139]

Under Article 7, the Parties undertook to incorporate into their respective "military regulations" provisions designed to "ensure observance of the present Convention, and to foster in the members of their armed forces a spirit of respect for the culture and cultural property of all peoples". The Parties were also to "plan or establish . . . services or specialist personnel" within their respective armed forces "whose purpose will be to secure respect for cultural property and to cooperate with the civilian authorities responsible for safeguarding it".[140]

Regarding violations, Article 28 stated, "The High Contracting Parties undertake to take, within the framework of their ordinary criminal jurisdiction, all necessary steps to prosecute and impose penal or disciplinary sanctions upon those persons, of whatever nationality, who commit or order to be committed a breach of the present Convention".[141] As Patrick Boylan observed, however, "bearing in mind the importance of measures of enforcement, and indeed the Nuremberg War Crimes Tribunal rulings, the provisions for enforcement action and sanctions were remarkably weak and rather vague".[142]

Article 20 of the 1954 Hague Convention provided for a series of "Regulations for the Execution of the Convention", which are designated as integrally part of the Convention itself. The Regulations established detailed procedures for the implementation of the provisions set forth in the 1954 Hague Convention, including the designation of a number of officials and authorities with various levels of oversight responsibilities.[143] In addition, the 1954 Hague Conference also adopted a separate Protocol designed to "prevent the exportation of cultural property" during periods of armed conflict, as well as during periods of occupation, and "to provide for the restitution of illegally exported objects".[144]

Two years after the conclusion of the 1954 Hague Convention, the International Committee of the Red Cross (ICRC) drafted a series of rules designed to afford the civilian population greater protection than had been provided heretofore in earlier conventions. These Draft Rules for the Limitation of the Dangers Incurred by the Civilian Populations in Time of War were approved at the 1957 Conference of the Red Cross held in New Delhi, India. According to Dietrich Schindler and Jiri Toman, "to a large extent, its provisions correspond to customary international law". Several members of the international community, however, reacted negatively the Draft Rules, apparently, in part, because Article 14 "prohibited" the use of "weapons whose harmful effects – resulting in particular from the dissemination of incendiary, chemical, bacteriological, radioactive, or other agents – could spread to an unforeseen degree or escape, either in space or in time, from the control of those who employ them, thus endangering the civilian population". Consequently, no further action was taken at that time. The ICRC Draft Rules, did, however, influence subsequent efforts to further safeguard civilians and civilian objects during international and non-international armed conflicts.[145]

Between the mid 1960s and the outset of the 1970s, a number of organizations issued resolutions and declarations calling for greater protection for civilians and civilian property during all types of armed conflicts.[146] Finally, after several years of preparation by the ICRC, a Diplomatic Conference was convened in Geneva and, on June 8, 1977, it adopted two Protocols Additional to the 1949 Geneva Conventions: Protocol I dealing with international armed conflicts and Protocol II dealing with armed conflicts not of an international character. Both Protocols I and II entered into force on December 7, 1978. Although much shorter than Protocol I, Protocol II contained many of the provisions delineated in Protocol I concerning the protection of civilians and civilian objects. Although it did not, however, contain the provisions set forth in Protocol I concerning means and methods of armed combat. Finally, both Protocols contained controversial provisions and, as a result, a number of powers have refrained from ratifying them.[147]

Protocol I drew upon, further developed, and clarified various principles developed in earlier conventions, especially those of discrimination and proportionality set forth in the 1923 Hague Rules of Air Warfare. Similarly, from the perspective of the protection of civilian objects generally, and cultural property specifically, Protocol I delineated a number of provisions that reaffirmed, clarified, or further developed principles of customary and conventional law of armed conflict. As such, Protocol I constitutes the third of the four most significant components of the contemporary law of armed conflict pertaining to the protection of cultural properties during periods of armed hostilities. Consequently, the relevant provisions will be cited in detail.

In addition to reiterating in Article 35 two of the most basic principles of the law of armed conflict, that "in any armed conflict, the right of the Parties to the conflict to choose methods or means of warfare is not unlimited," and "it is prohibited to employ weapons, projectiles and material and methods of warfare of a nature to cause superfluous injury or unnecessary suffering,"[148] Protocol I went on to delineate the principle of discrimination. Article 48 stated,

> In order to ensure respect for and protection of the civilian populations and civilian objects, the Parties to the conflict shall at all times distinguish between the civilian population and combatants and between civilian objects and military objectives and accordingly shall direct their operations only against military objectives.[149]

Defining military objectives, Article 52 (2) stated,

> In so far as objects are concerned, military objectives are limited to those objects which by their nature, location, purpose of use make an effective contribution to military action and whose total or partial destruction, capture or neutralization, in the circumstances ruling at the time, offers a definite military advantage.[150]

Thus, according to the provisions of Protocol I, an object must satisfy a "two-pronged test" to qualify as a military objective: it must "make an effective contribution to military action," and its "total or partial destruction, capture or neutralization" must offer "a definite military advantage".[151] These conditions must be satisfied "in the circumstances ruling at the time," not at some possible future time.[152] Furthermore, Article 57 (cited in full below), stated that if, as a result of an attack on a military objective, "incidental . . . damage to civilian objects" and/or civilian casualties are "expected," the damage must not "be excessive in relation to the concrete and direct military advantage anticipated".[153] Protocol I went on to define who are protected persons;[154] the provisions for the protection of certain specified areas; provisions for the general protection of civilian objects[155] and for specially protected objects.[156]

Article 59 delineated the provisions for the special protection of non-defended localities.[157] Paragraphs 1 and 2 stated,

> 1. It is prohibited for the Parties to the conflict to attack, by any means whatsoever, non-defended localities.
> 2. The appropriate authorities of a Party to the conflict may declare as a non-defended locality any inhabited place near or in a zone where armed forces are in contact which is open for occupation by an adverse Party. Such a locality shall fulfil the following conditions: (a) all combatants, as well as mobile weapons and mobile military equipment must have been evacuated; (b) no hostile use shall be made of fixed military installations or establishments; (c) no acts of hostility shall be committed by the authorities or by the population; and (d) no activities in support of military operations shall be undertaken.[158]

Paragraph 5 provided for the establishment of non-defended localities by mutual arrangement between the belligerents, even in those situations where the localities failed to satisfy the conditions delineated in paragraph 2. Finally, paragraph 7 stated that, "a locality loses its status as a non-defended locality when it ceases to fulfill the conditions laid down in paragraph 2 or in the agreement referred to in paragraph 5". But, "in such an eventuality, the locality shall continue to enjoy the protection provided by the other provisions of this Protocol and the other rules of international law applicable in armed conflict".[159]

In contrast to non-defended localities, demilitarized zones, described in Article 60,[160] are located in areas distant from the immediate area of ground combat and, hence, cannot be immediately occupied. Paragraph 1 stated that, "it is prohibited for the Parties to the conflict to extend their military operations to zones on which they have conferred by agreement the status of demilitarized zone". Paragraph 3 delineated the same first three conditions for the establishment of a demilitarized zone as were delineated with respect to non-defended localities as set forth in Article 59, paragraph 2. But in place of the fourth condition set forth in Article 59, Article 60 stated that it is normally a condition for the establishment of a demilitarized zone that, "any activity linked to the military effort must have ceased". Paragraph 5 provided for markers indicating a demilitarized zone and paragraph 6 provided that, "if the fighting draws near to a demilitarized zone, and if the Parties to the conflict have so agreed, none of them may use the zone for purposes related to the conduct of military operations or unilaterally revoke its status". Finally, as with Article 59, in the event of a violation of the conditions under which the demilitarized zone was established, Article 60 provided that "the other Party shall be released from its obligations," although, the zone would "continue to enjoy the protection provided by the other provisions" of Protocol I, as well as "the other rules of international law applicable in armed conflict".[161]

Regarding "the other provisions" of Protocol I mentioned in Articles 59 and 60, Article 52 delineated the provisions for the "general protection of civilian objects". Paragraphs 1 and 3 of Article 52 stated,

1. Civilian objects shall not be the object of attack or of reprisals. Civilian objects are all objects which are not military objectives . . .
3. In case of doubt whether an object which is normally dedicated to civilian purposes, such as a place of worship, a house or other dwelling or a school, is being used to make an effective contribution to military action, it shall be presumed not to be so used.[162]

Protocol I, however, also provided certain "cultural objects and places of worship," with special protection, in addition to the general protection provided to all civilian objects in Article 52.[163] Article 53 stated,

Without prejudice to the provisions of the Hague Convention for the Protection of Cultural Property in the Event of Armed Conflict of 14 May 1954, and of other relevant international instruments, it is prohibited: (a) to commit any acts of hostility directed against the historic monuments, works of art or places of worship which constitute the cultural or spiritual heritage of peoples; (b) to use such objects in support of the military effort; (c) to make such objects the object of reprisals".[164]

Commenting on Protocol I, Michael Bothe, Karl Partsch, and Waldemar Solf argued that Article 52 pertained only to those cultural objects and places of worship that "would qualify for special protection under Art. 8 of the Hague Convention of 1954 without, however, imposing a requirement for the procedural measures required by that Convention to effect such special protection".[165] This interpretation was said to be supported by Article 85, paragraph 4,[166] which stated,

. . . the following shall be regarded as grave breaches of this Protocol, when committed willfully and in violation of the Conventions or the Protocol: . . . (d) making the clearly recognized historic monuments, works of art or places of worship which constitute the cultural or spiritual heritage of peoples and to which special protection has been given by special arrangement, for example, within the framework of a competent international organization, the object of attack, causing as a result extensive destruction thereof, where there is no evidence of the violation by the adverse Party of Article 53, sub-paragraph (b), and when such historic monuments, works of art and places of worship are not located in the immediate proximity of military objectives.[167]

In short, they argued that Article 85 refers only to "certain civilian objects – highly privileged objects" that "are 'clearly recognized historic monuments, works of art or places or worship' which fulfill certain requirements, i.e. (1) they 'constitute the cultural or spiritual heritage of peoples;' and (2) 'to which special protection has been given by special arrangement'".[168] Finally, while it should be noted that Article 53 does not explicitly address the conditions under which protection would be withdrawn from the protected objects, Michael Bothe, Karl Partsch, and Waldemar Solf pointed out that the reference to the 1954 Hague Convention was sufficient to justify actions "which may be undertaken if the protected property is used to support the military effort". They further maintained that this view was reinforced by the provisions of Article 85 (4) (d), which justified an attack against specially protected cultural, religious and historic objects "if the objects have been apparently used in support of the military effort . . . or when such objects are located in the immediate proximity of military objectives," thereby covering "the problem of collateral damage". They added, however, that, "all activity in support of the military effort does not necessarily meet the two-pronged test for military objectives under Art. 52. This test must be met before an attack can be justified".[169]

With respect to the customary requirement of verification, Article 57 (2) required that "the following precautions shall be taken: (a) those who plan or decide upon an attack shall: (i) do everything feasible to verify that the objectives to be attacked are neither civilian nor civilian objects and are not subject to special protection but are military objectives within the meaning of paragraph 2 of Article 52 and that it is not prohibited by the provisions of this Protocol to attack them". The qualifier "feasible" suggested that commanders and planners are to do that which is reasonably possible under the circumstances that prevail at the time.[170]

Once verification has occurred, Article 48 reaffirmed the customary principle that "the Parties to the conflict shall at all times . . . direct their operations only against military targets". Elaborating, Article 51 stated, "1. The civilian population and individual civilians shall enjoy protection against dangers arising from military operations. . . . 2. The civilian population as such, as well as individual civilians, shall not be the object of attack". Similarly, Article 52 stated, "1. Civilian objects shall not be the object of attack or reprisals. . . . 2. Attacks shall be limited strictly to military objectives". Finally, Article 57 stated, "1. In the conduct of military operations, constant care shall be taken to spare the civilian population, civilians and civilian objects". Paragraphs 2 (b), and 4 reinforced this admonition.[171]

In this context, in conjunction with provisions for the "protection of the civilian population," paragraphs 4 and 5 of Article 51 defined "indiscriminate attacks":

4. Indiscriminate attacks are prohibited. Indiscriminate attacks are: (a) those which are not directed at a specific military objective; (b) those which employ a method or means of combat which cannot be directed at a specific military objective; or (c)

> those which employ a method or means of combat the effects of which cannot be limited as required by this Protocol; and consequently, in each case, are of a nature to strike military objectives and civilians or civilian objects without distinction.
>
> 5. Among others, the following types of attacks are to be considered indiscriminate: (a) an attack by bombardment by any methods or means which treats as a single military objective a number of clearly separated and distinct military objectives located in a city, town, village or other area containing a similar concentration of civilians or civilian objects; and (b) an attack which may be expected to cause incidental loss of civilian life, injury to civilians, damage to civilian objects, or a combination thereof, which would be excessive in relation to the concrete and direct military advantage anticipated.[172]

Protocol I acknowledged that, unfortunately, combat operations often produce collateral damage to civilians and civilian objects. Indeed, this was implied in the choice of words used in Article 51 (2) and 52 (1) that civilians and civilian objects "shall not be the object of attack". It has been also been suggested that the use of the words "as such" in Article 51 (2) "implies that there can be no assurance that attacks against combatants and other military objectives will not result in civilian casualties with respect to civilians in or near such objects".[173]

The goal, of course, is to avoid or, at least, minimize collateral injury and damage. Toward that end, in Article 57 built upon the principle of proportionality suggested in Article 51 (5) (b) and codified rules requiring belligerents to minimize, or, if possible eliminate incidental and collateral destruction and injury to civilians and civilian objects.[174] In delineating the precautionary measures that must be followed in the attack, Article 57, paragraphs 2-4, stated,

> 2. With respect to attacks, the following precautions shall be taken: (a) those who plan or decide upon an attack shall: . . . (ii) take all feasible precautions in the choice of means and methods of attack with a view to avoiding, and in any event to minimizing, incidental loss to civilian life, injury to civilians and damage to civilian objects; (iii) refrain from deciding to launch any attack which may be expected to cause incidental loss to civilian life, injury to civilians, damage to civilian objects, or a combination thereof, which would be excessive in relation to the concrete and direct military advantage anticipated; (b) an attack shall be cancelled or suspended if it becomes apparent that the objective is not a military one or is subject to special protection or that the attack may be expected to cause incidental loss to civilian life, injury to civilians, damage to civilian objects, or a combination thereof, which would be excessive in relation to the concrete and direct military advantage anticipated; (c) effective advance warning shall be given of attacks which may affect the civilian populations, unless circumstances do not permit.
> 3. When a choice is possible between several military objectives for obtaining a similar military advantage, the objective selected shall be that the attack on which may be expected to cause the least danger to civilian lives and to civilian objects.
> 4. In the conduct of military operations at sea or in the air, each Party to the conflict shall, in conformity with its rights and duties under the rules of international law applicable in armed conflict, take all reasonable precautions to avoid losses of civilian lives and damage to civilian objects.[175]

It should be noted that there were several qualifiers inserted into the text of Article 57. First, it required that the attacker take "feasible precautions" or "reasonable precautions".[176] Second, as noted earlier, in situations where incidental or collateral injury or damage was anticipated, the scope and degree of damage and injury must not be "excessive in relation to the concrete and direct military advantage anticipated".[177] Third, "effective" warning must be provided, "unless circumstances do not permit".[178] But, notwithstanding these qualifiers, Article 51, paragraph 8 stated in conjunction with the protection of civilians, that, "any violation of these prohibitions shall not release the Parties to the conflict from their legal obligations with respect to the civilian population and civilians, including the obligation to take the precautionary measures provided for in Article 57".[179]

Article 85, paragraph 3 a-d defined what actions, when taken by a belligerent in the attack, would be considered "grave breaches" of Protocol I. It stated,

> . . . the following acts shall be regarded as grave breaches of this Protocol, when committed willfully, in violation of the relevant provisions of this Protocol, and causing death or serious injury to body or health: (a) making the civilian population or individual civilians the object of attack; (b) launching an indiscriminate attack affecting the civilian population or civilian objects in the knowledge that such attack will cause excessive loss of life, injury to civilians or damage to civilian objects, as defined in Article 57, paragraph 2 (a) (iii); (c) launching an attack against works or installations containing dangerous forces in the knowledge that such attack will cause excessive loss of life, injury to civilians or damage to civilian objects, as defend in Article 57, paragraph 2 (a) (iii); (d) making non-defended localities and demilitarized zones the object of attack;[180]

It should be noted that these acts must have been "committed willfully" and must cause "death or serious injury to body or health" to qualify as "grave breaches". Furthermore, with respect to subparagraphs b and c, the act must also have been taken "in the knowledge" that such actions would cause the effects described. Finally, as noted by Michael Bothe, Karl Partsch, and Waldemar Solf, the reference to the principle of proportionality as delineated in Article 57, paragraph 2 (a) (iii) suggested that, while any violation of Article 57 that was expected to cause excessive injury and damage would be considered illegitimate, under Article 85, a grave breach "presupposes more: the knowledge (not only the presumption) that such attack will cause excessive losses in kind". Excessive losses were defined in Article 57, paragraph 2 (iii) as "incidental loss of civilian life, injury to civilians, damage to civilian objects, or a combination thereof, which would be excessive in relation to the concrete and direct military advantage anticipated". Thus, Article 85, paragraph 3 (b) and (c) required "a higher degree of intention than Art. 57".[181]

Finally, Protocol I delineated the responsibilities of the defender, not just those of the attacker, to safeguard civilians and civilian objects from collateral or incidental injury, death, damage, or destruction.[182] As such Article 58 stated,

> The Parties to the conflict shall, to the maximum extent feasible: (a) without prejudice to Article 49 of the Fourth Convention, endeavour to remove the civilian population,

individual civilians and civilian objects under their control from the vicinity of military objectives; (b) avoid locating military objectives within or near densely populated areas; (c) take the other necessary precautions to protect the civilian population, individual civilians and civilian objects under their control against the dangers resulting from military operations.[183]

In a related manner, Article 51, paragraph 7 stated that,

> The presence or movements of the civilian population or individual civilians shall not be used to render certain points or areas immune from military operations, in particular in attempts to shield military objectives from attacks or to shield, favour or impede military operations. The Parties to the conflict shall not direct the movement of the civilian population or individual civilians in order to attempt to shield military objectives from attacks or to shield military operations.[184]

In addition, as noted earlier, Article 53, prohibited the use of "historic monuments, works of art, or places of worship which constitute the cultural or spiritual heritage of peoples . . . in support of the military effort".[185]

Although many of the provisions of the two 1977 Protocols, especially those codified in Protocol I, remain controversial, they represent valuable efforts by the international community to further delineate and refine the scope and applicability of such key components of the customary and conventional international law as the protection of civilians and civilian objects during all periods of armed conflict, as well as the principles of discrimination and proportionality. Since 1977, the international community has continued its efforts to further broaden and refine the codified provisions of the law of armed conflict.[186]

Meanwhile, during the early 1970s, two other international conventions relating to the status of cultural property came into force. While these two conventions did not directly address the protection of cultural objects during periods of armed conflict, they did further develop both the definition of cultural property, as well as the way that cultural property is perceived and preserved.

The first of these was the Convention on the Means of Prohibiting and Preventing the Illicit Import, Export and Transfer of Ownership of Cultural Property, adopted by the General Conference of UNESCO on November 14, 1970, and entered into force on April 24, 1972. This Convention constituted the first successful international effort to provide peacetime protection to cultural objects.[187] In doing so, it adopted a more culturally nationalistic perspective than that adopted by the 1954 Hague Convention.[188] The Preamble to the Convention began by noting that "the interchange of cultural property among nations for scientific, cultural and educational purposes increases the knowledge of the civilization of Man, enriches the cultural life of all peoples and inspires mutual respect and appreciation among nations". It then went on to observe that "cultural property constitutes one of the basic elements of civilization and national culture, and that its true value can be appreciated only in relation to the fullest possible information regarding its origin, history and traditional setting". Accordingly, "it is incumbent upon every State to protect the cultural property existing within its territory against the dangers of theft, clandestine excavation, and illicit export," and that "to avert these dangers, it is essential for every State to become increasingly alive to the moral obligations to respect its own cultural heritage and that of all nations".[189] Article 1 defined "cultural property" more comprehensively than had heretofore been the case in previous conventions.[190] It stated,

> For the purposes of this Convention, the term 'cultural property' means property which, on religious or secular grounds, is specifically designated by each State as being of importance for archaeology, prehistory, history, literature, art or science and which belongs to the following categories: (a) Rare collections and specimens of fauna, flora, minerals and anatomy, and objects of palaeontological interest; (b) property relating to history, including the history of science and technology and military and social history, to the life of national leaders, thinkers, scientists and artists and to events of national importance; (c) products of archaeological excavations (including regular and clandestine) or of archaeological discoveries; (d) elements of artistic or historical monuments or archaeological sites which have been dismembered; (e) antiquities more than one hundred years old, such as inscriptions, coins and engraved seals; (f) objects of ethnological interest; (g) property of artistic interest, such as: (i) pictures, paintings and drawings produced entirely by hand on any support and in any material (excluding industrial designs and manufactured articles decorated by hand); (ii) original works of statuary art and sculpture in any material; (iii) original engravings, prints and lithographs; (iv) original artistic assemblages and montages in any material; (h) rare manuscripts and incunabula, old books, documents and publications of special interest (historical, artistic, scientific, literary, etc.) singly or in collections; (i) postage, revenue and similar stamps, singly or in collections; (j) archives, including sound, photographic and cinematographic archives; (k) articles of furniture more than one hundred years old and old musical instruments.[191]

After defining the term cultural property, Article 3 of the Convention declared that "the import, export or transfer of ownership of cultural property effected contrary to the provisions adopted under this Convention by the States Parties thereto, shall be illicit". In subsequent articles, the Convention delineated these provisions.[192]

The other major enactment was the Convention Concerning the Protection of the World Cultural and National Heritage, adopted on November 16, 1972 by the General Conference of UNESCO and entered into force on December 17, 1975.[193] In contrast to the 1970 UNESCO Convention, the 1972 World Heritage Convention adopted a cosmopolitan, internationalist emphasis similar to the 1954 Hague Convention.[194] The Preamble to the 1972 Convention stated,

> . . . the deterioration or disappearance of any item of the cultural or national heritage constitutes a harmful impoverishment of the heritage of all the nations of the world, . . . that the protection of this heritage at the national level often remains incomplete because of the scale of the resources which it requires and of the insufficient economic, scientific and technical resources of the country where the property to be protected is situated, . . . that the existing international conventions, recommendations and resolutions concerning cultural and natural property demonstrate the importance, for all the peoples of the world, of safeguarding this unique and irreplaceable property, to whatever people it may belong, . . . [and] that the parts of the cultural or natural heritage are of outstanding

interest and therefore need to be preserved as part of the world heritage of mankind as a whole, . . .[195]

Article 1 of the Convention broadly defined the term "cultural heritage,"[196] stating,

> For the purposes of this Convention, the following shall be considered as 'cultural heritage': monuments: architectural works, works of monumental sculpture and painting, elements or structures of an archaeological nature, inscriptions, cave dwellings and combinations of features, which are of outstanding universal value from the point of view of history, art or science; groups of buildings: groups of separate or connected buildings which, because of their architecture, their homogeneity or their place in the landscape are of outstanding universal value from the point of view of history, art or science; sites: works of man or the combined works of nature and of man, and areas including archaeological sites which are of outstanding universal value from the historical, aesthetic, ethnological or anthropological points of view.[197]

Article 3 of the Convention then stated that, Parties to the Convention were "to identify and delineate the different properties situated on its territory" that would be considered part of mankind's cultural or natural heritage.[198] The remainder of the Convention delineated provisions for international and national protection of the natural and cultural heritage, and the establishment of a "World Heritage Committee". According to Article 11, "Every State Party to this Convention shall, in so far as possible, submit to the World Heritage Committee an inventory of property forming part of the cultural and natural heritage, situated in its territory and suitable for inclusion" on a "World Heritage List". The World Heritage Committee was then to establish such a List, composed "of properties forming part of the cultural heritage and natural heritage . . . which it considers as having outstanding universal value in terms of such criteria as it shall have established," drawn, in turn, from the State compiled inventories. The Committee was also to establish "a list of the property appearing in the World Heritage List for the conservation of which major operations are necessary and for which assistance has been requested under this Convention". Finally, the Convention established a "World Heritage Fund," delineated "conditions and arrangements for international assistance," as well as provided for "educational programs" and periodic reports.[199]

Notwithstanding the various international efforts to protect cultural properties during periods of armed conflict, however, during the final decade of the 20th century, the world community witnessed a number of armed conflicts that endangered cultural property. Of these conflicts, two serve to illustrate the continuing vulnerability of cultural objects during periods of armed conflict.

The Gulf War of 1990-1991 occurred in a geographic region extraordinarily rich in cultural properties.[200] Several international conventions were, of course, applicable to the belligerents with respect to protection for these properties. The 1907 Hague Conventions, which are considered part of customary international law, are binding upon all states. While the general principle of protection of cultural property in periods of armed conflict and during periods of occupation, upon which the provisions delineated in the 1954 Hague Convention are based, is also part of customary law, the specific provisions of the 1954 Convention are not part of customary law.[201] Several key belligerents were, however, Parties to the 1954 Convention, including Iraq, Egypt, Kuwait, Saudi Arabia, and France. The United States, Great Britain, and Canada, however, were not Parties to the Convention, although "the armed forces of each receive training on its provisions, and the treaty was followed by all Coalition forces in the Persian Gulf War". Moreover, although Protocol I, like the 1954 Hague Convention, contained many general principles inherent in customary law, neither Iraq, nor key Coalition members, including the United States, France, and Great Britain, were Parties to Protocol I and, thus, were not bound by its specific provisions.[202]

Accordingly, as stated in the January 19, 1993 DOD Panel Report to the U.S. Congress on International Policies and Procedures Regarding the Protection of Natural and Cultural Resources During Times of War, the U.S. considered "the obligations to protect natural, civilian, and cultural property to be customary international law." Therefore, in operations during the Persian Gulf War, the U.S. held that "like any civilian object, cultural property is protected from intentional attack so long as it is not used for military purposes, or to shield military objectives from attack". Hence, "the U.S. and its Coalition partners . . . took extraordinary measures to minimize damage to cultural property".[203] Reinforcing this conclusion, the *Department of Defense Report on the Conduct of the Persian Gulf War* stated,

> Targeting policies . . . scrupulously avoided damage to mosques, religious shrines, and archaeological sites, as well as to civilian facilities and the civilian population. To help strike planners, CENTCOM target intelligence analysts, in close cooperation with the national intelligence agencies and the State Department, produced a joint no-fire target list. This list was a compilation of historical, archaeological, economic, religious and politically sensitive installations in Iraq and Kuwait that could not be targeted. Additionally, target intelligence analysts were tasked to look in a six-mile area around each master attack list target for schools, hospitals, and mosques to identify targets where extreme care was required in planning. . . . When targeting officers calculated the probability of collateral damage as too high, the target was not attacked. Only when a target satisfied the criteria was it placed on the target list, and eventually attacked based on its relative priority compared with other targets and on the availability of attack assets.[204]

By contrast, the DOD Report charged that the Iraqi government, "in callous disregard of its law of war obligations and the safety of its own civilians and Kuwaiti civilians," moved "military objects into populated areas in Iraq and Kuwait to shield them from attack".[205] In addition, the Report stated that,

> Similar actions were taken by the Government of Iraq to use cultural property to protect legitimate targets from attack; a classic example was the positioning of two fighter aircraft adjacent to the ancient temple of Ur . . . on the theory that Coalition respect for the protection of cultural property would preclude the attack of those aircraft. While the law of war permits the attack of the two fighter aircraft, with Iraq bearing responsibility for any damage to the temple, the Commander-in-Chief, Central Command (CINCCENT) elected not to attack the aircraft on the basis of respect for cultural

property and the belief that position of the aircraft adjacent to Ur (without servicing equipment or a runway nearby) effectively had placed each out of action, thereby limiting the value of their destruction by Coalition air forces when weighed against the risk of damage to the temple. Other cultural property similarly remained on the Coalition no-attack list, despite Iraqi placement of valuable military equipment in or near those sites.[206]

Consequently, notwithstanding the inherent vulnerability of these and other Iraqi and Kuwaiti cultural properties, compounded by the actions of the Iraqi authorities that only served to increase that vulnerability, damage to these properties was successfully minimized as a result of the careful efforts by the Coalition forces to adhere to customary and conventional safeguards.[207]

By contrast, the upheavals within the territory of the former Yugoslavia illustrated the relative failure to protect cultural property from damage and destruction. While numerous examples of deliberate damage and destruction of cultural objects can be cited, such as those in Mostar and Vukovar, one of the most notorious examples was the completely unjustifiable bombardment of the undefended Old City of Dubrovnik, in November and December 1991 and in May and June 1992. In addition to the protection afforded by customary international law, Yugoslavia was a Party to the 1954 Hague Convention, the 1977 Protocols to the 1949 Geneva Conventions, and the 1972 World Heritage Convention. Indeed, the Old City of Dubrovnik is listed as a World Heritage Site.[208]

In response to concerns over damage to Dubrovnik and many other cultural properties during the armed conflicts in the former Yugoslavia and elsewhere, there emerged a growing feeling among many states that the provisions of the 1954 Hague Convention were insufficient to meet the challenges of the 21st century. Among the concerns were: the Convention's degree of applicability in non-international armed conflicts; difficulties encountered regarding several of the Convention's specific provisions for implementation; its weak provisions for sanctions; and its relationship to other international conventions and institutions adopted or created since 1954, including Protocols I and II, the establishment of *ad hoc* international tribunals for crimes committed in Rwanda and the former Yugoslavia, and the 1998 adoption of the Statute of the International Criminal Court.[209] Consequently, after several years of preparation, a Diplomatic Conference was held in The Hague from March 15-26, 1999, and on March 26th the Conference adopted the Second Protocol to the Hague Convention of 1954 for the Protection of Cultural Property in the Event of Armed Conflict.[210] The Second Protocol is an optional supplement to the 1954 Hague Convention which continues to constitute the 'basic text'. Consequently, ratification of the 1954 Hague Convention is a prerequisite to become a Party to the Second Protocol.[211] Despite its supplemental relationship to the 1954 Hague Convention, the 1999 Second Protocol constitutes the fourth of the four most significant components of the contemporary law of armed conflict designed to protect cultural properties during armed hostilities. As such, the provisions of the 1999 Second Protocol must be examined in detail.

Notwithstanding the various definitions of cultural property delineated in the 1970 UNESCO Convention, the 1972 World Heritage Convention, and elsewhere, the Second Protocol continued to use the definition of cultural property originally delineated in the 1954 Convention.[212] As with the 1954 Hague Convention, the Second Protocol applied to international armed conflicts between Parties to the Protocol or the occupation of all or part of the territory of a Party to the Protocol. Article 3, paragraph 2 noted that, "when one of the parties to an armed conflict is not bound by this Protocol, the Parties to this Protocol shall remain bound by it in their mutual relations". Furthermore, they shall "be bound by this Protocol in relation to a State party to the conflict which is not bound by it, if the latter accepts the provisions of this Protocol and so long as it applies them". Moreover, as with the 1954 Convention, several of the provisions of the Second Protocol applied in peacetime. With respect to non-international armed conflicts, Article 19 of the 1954 Hague Convention had stated that, in conflicts occurring on the territory of a Party to the Convention, each of the belligerents "shall be bound to apply, as a minimum, the provisions of the present Convention which relate to respect for cultural property". In addition, "the parties to the conflict shall endeavour to bring into force, by means of special agreements, all or part of the other provisions of the present Convention". By contrast, Article 22, paragraphs 1 and 2 of the Second Protocol stated that: "1. This Protocol shall apply in the event of an armed conflict not of an international character, occurring within the territory of one of the Parties. 2. This Protocol shall not apply to situations of internal disturbances and tensions, such as riots, isolated and sporadic acts of violence and other acts of a similar nature". Paragraph 5 went on to clarify that, "nothing in this Protocol shall be invoked as a justification for intervening, directly or indirectly, for any reason whatever, in the armed conflict or in the internal or external affairs of the Party in the territory of which that conflict occurs".[213] Critically assessing the assertion made in Article 22 that the provisions of the Second Protocol apply "as a whole and without any further agreement of the parties to non-international armed conflicts,"[214] Thomas Desch observed,

> The attempt . . . to declare basically all the provisions of an international law treaty to be binding also upon actors who are neither subjects of international law nor parties to that treaty, ignores some of the most basic and still existing concepts of international law. Unless having been treated as insurgents and accepted by other states as belligerents, non-state actors in a non-international armed conflict are not, by the mere fact of rebellion or insurgency, subjects of international law. Although customary international law has developed rules to govern non-international armed conflicts, covering also the protection or cultural property, only a number of rules and principles governing international armed conflict have gradually been extended to apply to non-international armed conflicts, and this extension has not taken place in the form of a full and mechanical transplant of those rules to internal conflicts. State practice has shown that, beyond a set of minimum rules reflecting 'elementary considerations of humanity' applicable under customary international law to any armed conflict, the rules of international humanitarian law governing international armed conflicts, and in particular those enshrined in treaty law, need either the commitment in the form of an agreement

or at least the unilateral commitment by non-state Parties to a non-international armed conflict to become binding upon them. This practice corresponds with the general principle of international law, according to which a treaty does not create either obligations or rights for a third party without its consent.[215]

Chapter 2 of the Protocol delineated a series of "general provisions" for the protection of cultural property. Article 5 focused on "safeguarding" cultural objects during peacetime, including, ". . . as appropriate, the preparation of inventories, the planning of emergency measures for the protection against fire or structural collapse, the preparation for the removal of movable cultural property or the provision for adequate *in situ* protection of such property, and the designation of competent authorities responsible for the safeguarding of cultural property".[216]

As reviewed earlier, Article 52, paragraph 2 of 1977 Protocol I stated that, "in so far as objects are concerned, military objectives are limited to those objects which by their nature, location, purpose or use make an effective contribution to military action and whose total or partial destruction, capture or neutralization, in the circumstances ruling at the time, offers a definite military advantage". Moreover, both the 1954 Hague Convention and 1977 Protocol I provided for the application of the principle of "military necessity" in the context of provisions for the protection of cultural property.[217] Discussing this, Thomas Desch observed,

> In contrast to the 1954 Convention, where both the attacking and the defending sides could avail themselves to the waiver on the basis of imperative military necessity, the defending side under Protocol I was in a worse position in comparison with the attacking side, since it could not avail itself of any exception to the obligation not to use cultural property in support of military action. The attacking side, however, was privileged by Protocol I in comparison with the 1954 Convention insofar as it could legitimately attack cultural property which has become a military objective in the sense of Article 52 (2) of Protocol I without any further proof that military necessity imperatively required it to do so. This discrepancy between Protocol I and the 1954 Convention was obviously recognized during the negotiations on Protocol I but was not satisfactorily resolved: Protocol I merely states that its prohibitions with regard to the protection of cultural property shall be 'without prejudice to the provisions of' the 1954 Convention.[218]

Article 6, 7, and 8 represented an effort to reconcile the 1954 Hague Convention with the 1977 Protocol I and, specifically, to clarify the principle of military necessity, as applied to cultural property.[219] These Articles stated,

> Article 6. With the goal of ensuring respect for cultural property in accordance with Article 4 of the Convention: a waiver on the basis of imperative military necessity pursuant to Article 4 paragraph 2 of the Convention may only be invoked to direct an act of hostility against cultural property when and for so long as: i. that cultural property has, by its function, been made into a military objective; and ii. there is no feasible alternative available to obtain a similar military advantage to that offered by directing an act of hostility against that objective; b. a waiver on the basis of imperative military necessity pursuant to Article 4 paragraph 2 of the Convention may only be invoked to use cultural property for purposes which are likely to expose it to destruction or damage

when and for as long as no choice is possible between such use of the cultural property and another feasible method for obtaining a similar military advantage; c. the decision to invoke imperative military necessity shall only be taken by an officer commanding a force the equivalent of a battalion in size or larger, or a force smaller in size where circumstances do not permit otherwise; d. in case of an attack based on a decision taken in accordance with sub-paragraph (a), an effective advance warning shall be given whenever circumstances permit.

Article 7. Without prejudice to other precautions required by international humanitarian law in the conduct of military operations, each Party to the conflict shall: a. do everything feasible to verify that the objectives to be attacked are not cultural property protected under Article 4 of the Convention; b. take all feasible precautions in the choice of means and methods of attack with a view to avoiding, and in any event to minimizing, incidental damage to cultural property protected under Article 4 of the Convention; c. refrain from deciding to launch any attack which may be expected to cause incidental damage to cultural property protected under Article 4 of the Convention which would be excessive in relation to the concrete and direct military advantage anticipated; and d. cancel or suspend an attack if it becomes apparent: i. that the objective is cultural property protected under Article 4 of the Convention; ii. that the attack may be expected to cause incidental damage to cultural property protected under Article 4 of the Convention which would be excessive in relation to the concrete and direct military advantage anticipated.

Article 8. Parties to the conflict shall, to the maximum extent feasible: a. remove movable cultural property from the vicinity of military objectives or provide for adequate *in situ* protection; b. avoid locating military objectives near cultural property[220]

Article 9 focused on protecting cultural property in occupied territory, stating,

1. Without prejudice to the provisions of Articles 4 and 5 of the Convention, a Party in occupation of the whole or part of the territory of another Party shall prohibit and prevent in relation to the occupied territory: a. any illicit export, other removal or transfer of ownership of cultural property; b. any archaeological excavation, save where this is strictly required to safeguard, record or preserve cultural property; c. any alteration to, or change of use of, cultural property which is intended to conceal or destroy cultural, historical or scientific evidence.
2. Any archaeological excavation of, alteration to, or change of use of, cultural property in occupied territory shall, unless circumstances do not permit, be carried out in close co-operation with the competent national authorities of the occupied territory.[221]

In view of the extremely limited use of the provisions for "special protection" of cultural property as delineated in the 1954 Convention, the Second Protocol created a new category of protection, – "enhanced protection". Chapter 3 delineated the terms and conditions of this new category.[222] Article 10 stated,

Cultural property may be placed under enhanced protection provided that it meets the following three conditions: a. it is cultural heritage of the greatest importance for humanity; b. it is protected by adequate domestic legal and administrative measures recognizing its exceptional cultural and historic value and ensuring the highest level of protection; c. it is not used for military purposes or to shield military sites and a declaration has been made by the Party which has control over the cultural property, confirming that it will not be so used.[223]

Article 11 delineated the procedures for granting enhanced protection. Under its provisions, each of the Parties should submit an inventory of cultural properties that it intends to propose as candidates for "enhanced protection" status to a Committee for the Protection of Cultural Property in the Event of Armed Conflict, established under the provisions of Article 24. In addition, "the Committee may invite a Party to request that cultural property be included" on the "International List of Cultural Property under Enhanced Protection" provided for in Article 27, paragraph 1 (b). Moreover, other Parties, as well as appropriate non-governmental organizations, "may recommend specific cultural property to the Committee" and, based upon that recommendation, the latter may invite a Party to request that the cultural property be included on the List. Following a request for inclusion on the List, the Committee shall decide whether to include the property on the List, taking into consideration representations from other Parties to the Protocol and "the advice of governmental and non-governmental organizations, as well as of individual experts". Paragraphs 8 and 9 delineated exceptional situations and emergency exceptions to the normal procedures for the inclusion of cultural properties on the Enhanced Protection List.[224]

Article 12 established that "the Parties to a conflict shall ensure the immunity of cultural property under enhanced protection by refraining from making such property the object of attack or from any use of the property or its immediate surroundings in support of military action".[225] Addressing the conditions under which enhanced protection status would be lost, Article 13 stated,

1. Cultural property under enhanced protection shall only lose such protection: a. if such protection is suspended or cancelled in accordance with Article 14; or b. if, and for as long as, the property has, by its use, become a military objective.
2. In the circumstances of sub-paragraph 1 (b), such property may only be the object of attack if: a. the attack is the only feasible means of terminating the use of the property referred to in sub-paragraph 1 (b); b. all feasible precautions are taken in the choice of means and methods of attack, with a view to terminating such use and avoiding, or in any event minimizing, damage to the cultural property; c. unless circumstances do not permit, due to requirements of immediate self defense: i. the attack is ordered at the highest operational level; ii. effective advance warning is issued to the opposing forces requiring the termination of the use referred to in sub-paragraph 1 (b); and iii. reasonable time is given to the opposing forces to redress the situation.[226]

Article 14 addressed the conditions under which enhanced protection status might be cancelled or suspended. The Second Protocol did not, however, designate the design of an emblem signifying that a property has enhanced protection status.[227]

The Second Protocol strengthened the enforcement mechanism for violations to the Convention and the Protocol.[228] Article 15 defined "serious violations," stating,

1. Any person commits an offence within the meaning of this Protocol if that person intentionally and in violation of the Convention or this Protocol commits any of the following acts: a. making cultural property under enhanced protection the object of attack; b. using cultural property under enhanced protection or its immediate surroundings in support of military action; c. extensive destruction or appropriation of cultural property protected under the Convention and this Protocol; d. making cultural property protected under the Convention and this Protocol the object of attack; e. theft, pillage or misappropriation of, or acts of vandalism directed against cultural property protected under the Convention.
2. Each Party shall adopt such measures as may be necessary to establish as criminal offences under its domestic law the offences set forth in this Article and to make such offences punishable by appropriate penalties. When doing so, Parties shall comply with general principles of law and international law, including the rules extending individual criminal responsibility to persons other than those who directly commit the act.[229]

Articles 16-21 delineated provisions regarding jurisdiction, extradition, and prosecution, etc, of those alleged to have violated the provisions set forth in Article 15.[230] Analyzing the jurisdictional provisions of the Second Protocol, Jean-Marie Henckaerts observed that, the first three categories of violations delineated in Article 15, paragraph 1 (a), (b), and (c) corresponded "to what are called 'grave breaches' under the Geneva Conventions and Additional Protocol I. . . . States have a duty to try or extradite anyone charged with having committed any of these violations on the basis of universal jurisdiction". Elaborating on this, he stated that this means that the States "have to establish jurisdiction not only when the offence is committed in the territory of the State or when the alleged offender is a national of the State, but also when the offence is committed abroad by a non-national". Thus, "the principle of mandatory universal jurisdiction for grave breaches, . . . implies that all States have to establish jurisdiction to try or extradite non-nationals for war crimes committed abroad who are present in their territory". Comparing the first two serious violations, (a) and (b), directed against properties under enhanced protection, with grave breaches as defined under Protocol I, under the former, "both an attack on and the use of such property are established as serious violations," whereas under the latter, "only an attack on such property is defined as a grave breach and only in so far as it causes extensive destruction". Thus, the Second Protocol "establishes a balance between the criminal responsibility of both the attacker and the defender."[231] Regarding the last two violations delineated in Article 15, paragraph 1 (d) and (e), Jean-Marie Henckaerts stated,

> These two serious violations amount to war crimes, but States only have the obligation to repress them by criminal sanctions using the most common grounds for jurisdiction, namely when the offence is committed in the territory of the State or when the alleged offender is a national of the State. There is no obligation to establish jurisdiction over cases where the alleged offence was committed abroad by a non-national, although States *may* exercise such jurisdiction. This reflects the principle of permissive universal jurisdiction for war crimes, according to which all States have jurisdiction to try non-nationals for war crimes committed abroad but are under no obligation to do so if the

crimes do not amount to grave breaches.[232]

Chapters 6 and 7 addressed "institutional issues" and the "dissemination of information and international assistance". In addition to providing for meetings and the establishment of the Committee for the Protection of Cultural Property in the Event of Armed Conflict, Article 29 provided for the establishment of a "Fund for the Protection of Cultural Property in the Event of Armed Conflict". The Fund is designed to finance peacetime preparations for the protection of cultural property and to provide "financial or other assistance in relation to emergency provisional or other measures to be taken in order to protect cultural property during periods of armed conflict or of immediate recovery after the end of hostilities". The Fund is based on voluntary contributions and is disbursed by the Committee.[233]

In short, the Second Protocol updated the Hague Convention making it more compatible with international legal developments since 1954. It provided greater clarity concerning the applicability of the principle of military necessity to cultural property, as well as for a new, more functional category of cultural property under enhanced protection. It improved the mechanism for the enforcement of the provisions of the Protocol and the Convention by better defining those actions that constituted serious violations and establishing jurisdictional guidelines and, finally, it asserted its scope of application to include non-international armed conflicts.[234]

Conclusion

As has been discussed in the preceding sections, cultural objects have always been and are likely to remain vulnerable during combat operations, especially during the bombardment and assault of urban areas, as well as the result of individual and/or organized, state sponsored looting and punitive actions taken against defeated enemies. Recognizing these wartime dangers to cultural properties, there have been many individuals throughout history who have appealed for moderation and restraint in the conduct of armed hostilities. Moreover, customary norms governing military operations have evolved and these, directly or indirectly, often had an impact upon the security of cultural properties. Finally, during the past century and a half, against the backdrop of warfare of unprecedented scale and intensity, the world community has built upon these concerns and customary restraints to develop a considerable body of conventional law designed to ensure the wartime protection of cultural properties. Especially significant are the 1899 and 1907 Hague Conventions, the 1954 Hague Convention for the Protection of Cultural Property in the Event of Armed Conflict, the 1977 Protocol I Additional to the 1949 Geneva Conventions, and the 1999 Second Protocol to the 1954 Hague Convention. In short, the effort to protect cultural property during periods of armed conflict is a story that ranges from soaring hopes to the depths of despair, reflecting human beings at their best and at their worst.

Notwithstanding inconsistencies in the definitions used in various declarations and conventions concerning the definition of cultural property,[235] it is clear that the international community has long agreed that it is illegitimate to intentionally damage or destroy cultural property during periods of armed conflict, unless the enemy is currently utilizing that property for military purposes and/or the principle of military necessity in invoked. Indeed, the 1954 Hague Convention stated that immunity for protected cultural property could be waived only in situations "where military necessity imperatively requires such a waiver". Moreover, the introduction of special categories of protection for selected cultural properties containing objects of particular importance to mankind's cultural heritage further enhanced the protection accorded to certain cultural properties. Thus, the threshold for the withdrawal of immunity for cultural properties granted special protection status was even higher than that otherwise delineated; immunity for property under special protection could be withdrawn "only in exceptional cases of unavoidable military necessity". Even in situations where the principle of military necessity has been invoked and/or where the enemy is currently utilizing a cultural property for military purposes, however, consistent with the terms of the Second Protocol to the 1954 Hague Convention and 1977 Protocol I Additional to the 1949 Geneva Conventions, belligerents are expected to refrain from launching an attack upon cultural property if the attack could possibly be avoided or if a similar, definite military advantage could be obtained by attacking another objective. Moreover, the attacker is required to select methods and means of attack that are least likely to damage the cultural property in question. In addition, the attacker is expected to refrain from or suspend the attack upon a cultural property if the expected damage to the property is considered to be excessive compared to the "concrete and direct military advantage anticipated". Conversely, the defender is expected to refrain from using cultural properties for military purposes or locating potential military targets near cultural properties. Insofar as possible, the defender is also expected to take appropriate precautions to safeguard those cultural properties under the defender's control. Finally, an occupying power is expected to respect and safeguard cultural properties located within the territory under occupation and prevent any misappropriation, theft, or vandalism directed against such properties. This is particularly important during the breakdown of law and order that often accompanies the collapse or withdrawal of enemy authority over a territory, but prior to the complete establishment of the occupation regime.

The 1954 Hague Convention and the 1999 Second Protocol to that Convention provided for the establishment of an International Register of Cultural Property under Special Protection and a List of Cultural Properties under Enhanced Protection. Similarly, the 1972 World Heritage Convention provided for a World Heritage Site List and the List of World Heritage in Danger. Although many properties designated as World Heritage Sites would not be eligible for enhanced or special protection status, a large number of cultural properties on the World Heritage List could be so designated. Consequently, insofar as possible, the lists of cultural properties under special or enhanced protection should be synchronized and made compatible with the lists maintained by the World Heritage Committee. Moreover, in order to promote more widespread recognition of the emblems indicating protected properties by both civilians and the military, the prescribed emblems indicating cultural properties should be more prominently displayed. Specifically, the distinctive emblem prescribed in the 1954 Hague Convention to indicate cultural property protected under international law should be prominently displayed, at least at those World Heritage Sites that satisfy the definition of cultural property used in the 1954 Hague Convention, but that failed to satisfy the requirements for special or enhanced protection. Moreover, the appropriate emblems indicating cultural properties under special or enhanced protection should also be displayed prominently at those sites that have been listed on the International Register of Cultural Property under Special Protection and a List of Cultural Properties under Enhanced Protection.[236]

Notwithstanding all the customary and conventional provisions embodied in international law designed to protect various cultural properties during periods of armed conflict, however, in the final analysis, the fate of cultural properties largely depends upon how these objects are perceived and the value placed upon these objects by the respective belligerents. Sometimes military commanders and planners are confronted with dilemmas that are extremely stark and difficult, as in situations where the safety and, indeed, lives of their own troops are endangered unless a particular militarized cultural property is seized from enemy military control. This dilemma is punctuated by juxtaposing the views of two analysts. One view was cited by Professor T. R. Fehrenbach, who observed,

> To Americans, flesh and blood have always been more precious than sticks and stones, however assembled. An American commander, faced with taking the Louvre from a defending enemy, unquestionably would blow it apart or burn it down without hesitation if such would save the life of one of his men. And he would be in complete accord with American ideals and ethics in doing so. . . . If bombing and artillery would save lives, even through they destroyed sites of beauty and history, saving lives obviously had preference.[237]

As John Merryman noted, however, "a military necessity equation that routinely values the possibility of loss of life higher than the certainty of destruction of cultural property necessarily" results in "enormous damage to irreplaceable works".[238] By contrast, the British author and diplomat, Harold Nicholson, wrote,

> I am not among those who feel that religious sites are as such, of more importance than human lives, since religion is not concerned with material or temporal things; nor should I hesitate, were I a military commander, to reduce some purely historical building to rubble if I felt that by doing I could gain a tactical advantage or diminish the danger to which my men were exposed. Works of major artistic value fall, however, into a completely different category. It is to my mind absolutely desirable that such works should be preserved from destruction, even if their preservation entails the sacrifice of human lives. I should assuredly be prepared to be shot against a wall if I were certain that by such a sacrifice I could preserve the Giotto frescoes; nor should I hesitate for an instant (were such a decision ever open to me) to save St. Mark's even if I were aware that by so doing I should bring death to my sons. I should know that in a hundred years from now it would matter not at all if I or my children had survived; whereas it would matter seriously and permanently if the Piazza at Venice had been reduced to dust and

ashes ... The irreplaceable is more important than the replaceable, and the loss of even the most valued human life is ultimately less disastrous than the loss of something which in no circumstances can ever be created again.[239]

Obviously, these dichotomous viewpoints raise vexing, but fundamental questions concerning basic values and norms of behavior among civilized human beings. In a larger sense, however, with respect to the general principle of military necessity, many people ask why "should a great cultural monument be legally sacrificed to the ends of war? What does it say about our scale of values when we place military objectives above the preservation of irreplaceable cultural monuments"?[240]

As long as violence and armed conflict remain inherent in relations between individuals, organized groups, communities, and states, cultural objects will continue to be vulnerable to damage, destruction, and looting. While the increasing availability of precision guided munitions will, in certain situations, help to reduce collateral damage to these objects, they will, at least to some degree, remain endangered. Moreover, as in past conflicts, it unfortunately remains likely that, in certain cases, belligerents will utilize cultural objects for military purposes. Finally, perhaps in the future, the international community will deem it both desirable and appropriate to eliminate altogether the applicability of the principle of military necessity with respect to some or all categories of cultural properties. For the present and the foreseeable future, however, both customary and conventional international law provides for the invocation of the principle of military necessity to justify unavoidable damage and possible destruction of cultural properties.

Consequently, as throughout history, individual military commanders and planners must ultimately determine for themselves the relative value that they place on the lives of human beings; the timely, successful attainment of military objectives; and the protection of irreplaceable cultural properties. As John Merryman observed, "where the cultural property in question belongs to the enemy, the equation tilts ... against preservation".[241] If, however, in adopting a nationalistic perspective toward cultural property, a normative commitment to respect the cultural heritage of other peoples is maintained, the enemy's cultural property may yet be safeguarded. If such a commitment is absent, however, as was the case with the Spanish *vis-à-vis* the culture of the pre-Columbian civilizations of the New World or the Nazis toward non-Aryan peoples during the Second World War, then the cultural properties belonging to the alien peoples are quite likely to be destroyed. By contrast, however, if a cosmopolitan, internationalist perspective on the cultural property is adopted, cultural properties under enemy control, like the cultural objects under one's own control, are perceived to be part of the common heritage of all human beings. In that case, all cultural objects, including those under enemy control, will be approached carefully and with sensitivity based upon a normative commitment to preserve that which is of great value and which belongs to everyone, including one's own community and, indeed, one's self.

In short, the various declarations and conventions adopted by the members of the international community during the past century and a half designed to ensure the protection of cultural property are, in themselves, extremely valuable contributions in helping to control the scope and intensity of modern warfare. Indeed, efforts should be redoubled to achieve universal acceptance of the key conventions designed to protect cultural property during all periods of armed conflict.[242] But at least equally important are broad-based international educational efforts designed to instill a commitment to place limits on armed violence. As the international community confronts an increasing number of armed conflicts, particularly those of a non-international character, as well as acts of violence by terrorist individuals and groups, it is imperative that all peoples within the global community adopt and adhere to a high level of commitment to preserve and protect the manifestations of man's common cultural heritage.[243] There must be a global commitment by all peoples to uphold the conviction that *guerre mortelle* constitutes an illegitimate form of warfare in the 21st century. Therefore, in order to help ensure the preservation of those objects that are part of mankind's cultural heritage, probably the most important single action that could be taken by the members of the global community, is to inculcate in all peoples and in all societies throughout the world, a strong, internationalist commitment to do everything possible both in peacetime and during armed conflicts to protect mankind's common cultural heritage for themselves, their communities, and for posterity.

Notes

[1] The opinions, conclusions, and/or recommendations expressed or implied within this chapter are solely those of the author and do not necessarily represent the views of the Air University, the United States Air Force, the Department of Defense, or any other U.S. government agency.

[2] Howard, 1979, pp. 5-6; Howard, 1994, pp. 3, 5, 8; Ober, 1994, pp. 13, 14, 18; Stacey, 1994, pp. 28-34, 38-39; Parker, 1994, pp. 41-43, 47, 52, 54-57; Selesky, 1994, pp. 59-74; Rothenberg, 1994, pp. 87-89, 94-97; Roberts, 1994, pp. 119, 126, 129-133, 136; Kennedy and Andreopoulos, 1994, p. 215.

[3] Hensel, 2004, pp. 1-53.

[4] Brierly, 1955, p. 26; Howard, 1994, p. 3; Parker, pp. 52, 54, 56.

[5] Schindler and Toman, 1981, p. 64; see also Bailey, 1972, p. 63; Howard, 1994, pp. 7-8.

[6] Merryman, 1983, p. 757. Similarly, as Sharon Williams stated, "Works of art and sculpture, artifacts, great monuments and temples have been prized throughout history as being of significant importance. This has been so, not only because of their aesthetic worth, but also because they represent the talent and endurance of man and the history of diverse civilizations. The contributions made to this universal collection since time began have produced a store which comprises man's cultural heritage. This heritage is a compendium of the sufferings and the genius of mankind. It must be well-preserved to ensure that future generations can see and marvel at the accomplishments of their own epoch and those that came before". Williams, 1978, p. 52.

[7] Merryman, 1986, p. 831. Some define cultural property to include only tangible movable and immovable objects, such as objects and sites of architectural, "artistic, archeological, ethnological or historical interest". Others, however, not only broadly interpret the aforementioned definition, they also expand that definition to include other tangibles, such as "natural sites" that various peoples have in the past held or continue to hold to be endowed with religious and/or ceremonial significance. Some expand the definition even

further to include "intangibles," such as "the ideas on which new skills, techniques and knowledge are build," as well as "other traditional aspects of cultural life," such as "ceremonies where tradition may be handed on in song, dance or spoken words". Prott and O'Keefe, 1992, pp. 307-309.

[8] Some scholars maintain that, the central focus of property law is protection of the owner's rights and, as such, "implies control by the owner expressed by his ability to alienate, to exploit and the exclude others from the object or site in question". They assert that ownership is commonly perceived "as being the right to do what one wishes with what one owns". This concept, however, raises a variety of problems when applied to cultural tangibles and intangibles. For example, everyone concerned about the status of cultural tangibles and intangibles would agree that the goal must be the preservation of these components of the cultural heritage for the use, enjoyment, and enrichment of the current and future generations. As Lyndel Prott and Patrick O'Keefe have pointed out, however, "This means not only physical protection but the possibility of access for persons other than the owner. It may involve restrictions on the right of the possessor whether that be an individual, a legal person, a community or a State". Moreover, while tangible cultural property, such as immovable sites and movable artistic objects, as well as those elements of intangible cultural property that are subsumed under the category of intellectual property, might be accommodated within existing property law, many other types of cultural intangibles are not so easily accommodated. As such, Professors Prott and O'Keefe maintain that we would be better served if we moved away from the application of the concept of property, with its inherent "right to exploit, to alienate, to exclude" and focused instead on the concept of "heritage" which "creates a perception of something handed down; something to be cared for and cherished". Thus, they argue for a "coherent system" of "cultural heritage law" that applies "to all cultural manifestations; a system of law which will take account of the peculiar nature and requirements of those manifestations arising from the need to protect them". Prott and O'Keefe, 1992, pp. 309, 311-313, 318-319.

[9] Merryman, 1986, pp. 831-832, 842, 846, 852-853; Williams, 1978, pp. 52-53. See also Merryman, 1983, pp. 757-760.

[10] Merryman, 1986, pp. 831-832; Boylan, 1993, p. 6. Discussing this concept further, Sharon Williams observed that the internationalist perspective views cultural property as being "universal in character". She went on to note that, "It demonstrates man's diversity and artistic nature. Such achievements of creation by man cannot be regarded as 'belonging' exclusively to any one nation, Cultural property is a medium through which the peoples of the world may gain intellectual exchange and thus they have a right to claim access to it". Alternatively, with reference to cultural nationalism, she observed that, "Nationalism has led states to attempt to divide up a civilizations work. . . . The question is posed, however, whether the state which has become the 'owner' of such a work has exclusive rights attached to it? States are responsible to not only their own citizens but on a broader plane to the civilization of which they form an integral part". Williams, 1978, pp. 52-53. Some observers believe that this cosmopolitan, internationalist approach implies and justifies the possible future "establishment of a concrete international cultural heritage, a new sort of property, owned by the international community as such, administered by an international agency (e.g., UNESCO) and made available to all persons for them to enjoy". Indeed, some have argued that the use of the concept of mankind's common heritage as applied to mankind's cultural heritage is somewhat analogous to the concept as applied to outer space, international waters, and the global environment. Discussing the differences in the application of the concept, Sharon Williams observed, "Cultural property . . . in fact stands in a category of its own. The difference lies in the position of the property concerned. Although it is of universal value it is situated not as a *res nullius* as outer space or a *res*

communis as the deep seabed but in the various states themselves. This is the major difference. States can share the benefits by cultural exchanges and this can be regulated by agreements between them. What is of primary concern to mankind is the concept of destruction. Here, as in environmental protection, we are talking of 'death'. If states do not join together in reality to prevent destruction or mutilation there will be no property to be the subject of future agreements as to the sharing of the benefits of the cultural heritage of mankind. Yet, the survival of mankind is possible without cultural property – but not without air or water". Williams, 1978, pp. 53-63, 201-202.

[11] Williams, 1978, p. 201; Prott and O'Keefe, 1992, pp. 310-311.

[12] The nationalist perspective attributes a national identity to indigenous cultural objects and that, combined with the argument that cultural objects should not be removed from the cultural context from which they originate, as well as recognition of the monetary value of authentic cultural objects on the international market, has led many culturally nationalistic, art-rich states to enact export controls and the pursue efforts to repatriate cultural objects that have previously left the country, either illegally or under dubious legal circumstances. Alternatively, the cosmopolitan, internationalist perspective maintains that since all cultural property, irrespective of current ownership or nation of origin, are part of mankind's cultural heritage, and, consequently, all tangible and intangible components of the common human cultural heritage should be accessible to all the peoples of the global community. As such, the cultural cosmopolitan, internationalists charge that the cultural nationalist perspective often not only leads to the hoarding of cultural objects by art-rich states, it often leads to the gross neglect of valuable cultural objects by those art-rich states that lack the resources to properly document, store, and preserve those objects. Moreover, ironically, protective national legislation often only encourages precisely the type of "black marketeering" in cultural objects that it seeks to curtail. Elaborating on this notion, John Merryman has pointed out that, "such legislation guarantees: (1) that excavation and export will be carried on covertly, callously and anonymously, with no resulting documentation, with serious loss of archaeological and ethnographic information, and with irreparable damage to sites and objects; (2) that the income from trade in such objects will go to the wrong people; (3) that any opportunity to pursue a rational policy of representation of the national culture in foreign museums and collections is foregone; (4) that national scholars, museum personnel, police and customs officials will be frustrated, demoralized and corrupted; (5) that the most valuable works are the most likely to leave the country". Merryman, 1983, pp. 758-759. Thus, in addition to encouraging both corruption and the illicit trade in cultural objects, as well as depriving responsible museums and legitimate collectors the opportunity to legally acquire and display particular, valuable components of mankind's common cultural heritage, export "restrictions, typically justified as 'protection of the national cultural heritage,'" often create a situation where "the object becomes and orphan, and the contextual information it might have provided is lost forever". Merryman and Elsen, 2002, p. xviii. See also: Williams, 1978, pp. 5-202; Merryman, 1986, pp. 831-853.

[13] For example, the informal rules governing the conduct of warfare among the classical Greek city-states between 700 and 450 B.C. regarded religiously and/or ceremonially sacred temples, monuments, and shrines to be inviolable in times of war. This admonition, as well as other customary rules, however, only applied in conflicts among Greeks and not to conflicts between Greeks and non-Hellenic peoples. Ober, 1994, pp. 12-14, 18.

[14] Alexandrov, 1979, p. 19; Toman, 1996, pp. 4-6.

[15] Belligerents sought to capture urban centers for a variety of reasons. For example, in addition to depriving the enemy the use of the town as a base of operations for his field forces, a belligerent might seek to acquire the urban center so as to use it as a base for his own field operations against the enemy's armies. A belligerent might opt to exact a

particularly harsh punishment against a resisting town and its people in an effort to placate his own troops who would be rewarded with the spoils of the town. Finally, a belligerent might also hope to make the town's fate a frightening example to other urban centers that might consider resisting the belligerent's will. Parker, 1994, p. 49.

[16] Stacey, 1994, p. 38; Parker, 1994, pp. 48-48; Rothenberg, 1994, p. 93. Summarizing these norms as applied during the late medieval period in Europe, Robert Stacey observed, "A siege began when a herald went forward to demand that a town or castle admit the besieging lord. If the town agreed, this constituted a surrender, and the lives and property of the townspeople would be protected. If the town refused to surrender, however, this was regarded by the besieging lord as treason, and from the moment the besieger's guns were fired, the lives and property of all the town's inhabitants were therefore forfeit". Stacey, 1994, p. 38. In applying this general norm to the situation that he confronted immediately after the Dutch revolt broke out in 1572, the Commander of the Spanish forces in the Netherlands, the Duke of Alba, observed that there were six separate types of situational contexts in which an army might lay siege to a town. Summarizing this typology, Geoffrey Parker wrote, "First, those that had been taken by the enemy after a siege; second, those that had held out until the enemy brought up its artillery and could therefore resist with impunity no longer; third, those that had admitted the enemy because they had no alternative; and fourth those that had requested a royalist garrison but had been threatened by the enemy before help could arrive. All such towns, according to Alba, deserved leniency when recaptured. Quite different were his fifth category – those that had surrendered before need arose – and his sixth – those that had refused government troops when offered them, choosing instead to admit the enemy". Parker, 1994, p. 49. According to custom, however, the violence associated with the storming and sacking of a city was generally limited to "actions committed in the sudden flush of total victory," after which time these excesses should be suspended. Parker, 1994, p. 48. These customary norms extended into the Napoleonic period. Discussing sieges during this period, Gunther Rothenberg noted, "Military customs made a clear distinction between towns that capitulated and those taken by assault. Many cities surrendered with little or no resistance – Vienna, for example, in 1805 and again in 1809, and here at least the population and the conquerors got along very well. But if an investment or siege was prolonged, civilians most likely would be left to starve before the garrison. . . . Another issue was bombardments, often calculated to set civilian housing on fire, panic the population, and pressure the governor to surrender. Even when there were instructions to limit civilian damage, for example at Copenhagen in 1807, such collateral damage could not be avoided, especially when notoriously inaccurate Congreve rockets were used. After three days of bombardment much of Copenhagen was in flames with several thousand civilian casualties". As in earlier period, when a town was stormed, "during the brutal and confused fighting in the confined space of fortifications and streets, atrocities occurred frequently". Finally, in accord with custom, Professor Rothenberg pointed out, "even when a town was abandoned to pillage, this was limited to twenty-four hours," although this admonition "often did not hold" in practice. Rothenberg, 1994, pp. 92-93. See also Garner, 1920, pp. 435-437.

[17] Examples of the seizure of enemy cultural objects prior to the mid nineteenth century are too numerous to list, but the acquisitions of the Romans during the Republican and Imperial periods and, more recently, the French during the period of the French Revolution and the Napoleonic Wars are particularly egregious. For example, with respect to the latter, the collection in the Louvre, opened in 1793 and originally drawn from the cultural and historical objects amassed by the Bourbons and the Catholic Church, was greatly expanded as a result of trophies captured by the victorious armies of France. Moreover, the four golden horses that are the symbol of Venice and that were, themselves, said to have been

taken by the Venetians following the looting of Constantinople in 1204, were removed to Paris by Napoleon in 1798. Similarly, as pointed out by Professors Merryman and Elsen, "the winged lion from St. Marks in Venice had been placed on a fountain in the Esplanade des Invalids" in Paris. In accord with the peace arrangements that concluded the Napoleonic Wars in 1815, however, much to the resentment of the French, a large portion of the cultural objects amassed by the armies of France were returned to their previous owners. Thus, the golden horses were returned to Venice under the terms of the peace arrangements in 1815. In many cases, however, the objects in question were lost, damaged, or destroyed. Indeed, in their attempt to remove the Venetian winged lion of St. Marks the workmen dropped it, thus breaking it, "much to the delight of the jeering mob" of French observers. Visscher, 1949, pp. 822-827; Williams, 1978, pp. 6-9; Boylan, 1993, p. 23; Merryman and Elsen, 2002, pp. 2-10; Garner, 1920, pp. 435-437.

[18] Boylan, 1993, pp. 23-24; Alexandrov, 1979, pp. 19-20. See also Garner, 1920, pp. 435-437.

[19] With reference to the widespread practice of pillaging the defeated enemy's wealth, Polybius stated, "One may perhaps have some reason for amassing gold and silver; in fact, it would be impossible to attain universal domination without appropriating these resources from other peoples, in order to weaken them. In the case of every other form of wealth, however, it is more glorious to leave it where it was, together with the envy which it inspired, and to base our country's glory, not on the abundance and beauty of its paintings and statues, but on its sober customs and noble sentiments. Moreover, I hope that future conquerors will learn from these thoughts not to plunder the cities subjugated by them, and not to make the misfortunes of other peoples the adornments of their own country". Quoted in Visscher, 1949, p. 823; Merryman, 1986, p. 833. In another context he observed, "The laws and rights of war oblige the victor to ruin and destroy fortresses, forts, towns, people, ships, resources and all other such like things belonging to the enemy in order to undermine his strength while increasing the victor's own. But although some advantage may be derived from that, no one can deny that to abandon oneself to the pointless destruction of temples, statues and other sacred objects is the action of a madman". Quoted in Toman, 1996, p. 4.

[20] Brierly, 1955, pp. 26-35; Alexandrov, 1979, p. 21; Toman, 1996, p. 5.

[21] With respect to legitimate targets, Vattel wrote, "We have a right to deprive our enemy of his possessions, of every thing that may augment his strength and enable him to make war. This every one endeavours to accomplish in the manner most suitable to him. Whenever we have an opportunity, we seize on the enemy's property, and concert it to our own use: and thus, besides diminishing the enemy's power, we augment our own, and obtain at least a partial indemnification or equivalent, either for what constitutes the subject of the war, or for the expenses and losses incurred in its prosecution: – in a word, we do ourselves justice. The right to security often authorizes us to punish injustice or violence. It is an additional plea for depriving the enemy of some part of his possession. This manner of chastising a nation is more humane than making the penalty to fall on the persons of the citizens. With that view, things of value may be taken from her, such as rights, cities, provinces. . . . If it is lawful to take away the property of an unjust enemy in order to weaken or punish him, the same motives justify us in destroying what we cannot conveniently carry away. Thus, we waste a country, and destroy the provinces and forage, that the enemy may not find subsistence there: we sink his ship when we cannot take them or bring them off. All this tends to promote the main object of the war; but such measures are only to be pursued with moderation, and according to the exigency of the case". Quoted in Williams, 1978, p. 5.

[22] Vattel wrote, "For whatever cause a country is ravaged, we ought to spare those edifices which do honour to human society, and do not contribute to increase the enemy's strength, – such as temples, tombs, public buildings, and all works of remarkable beauty. What

advantage is obtained by destroying them? It is declaring one's self an enemy to mankind, thus wantonly to deprive them of these monuments of art and models of taste; . . . We still detest those barbarians who destroyed so many wonders of art, when they overran the Roman empire. However just the resentment with which the great Gustavus was animated against Maximilian duke of Bavaria, he rejected with indignation the advise of those who wished him to demolish the stately palace of Munich, and took particular care to preserve that admirable structure. Nevertheless, if we find it necessary to destroy edifices of that nature, in order to carry on the operations of war, or to advance the works of a siege, we have an undoubted right to take such a step. The sovereign of the country, or his general, makes no scruple to destroy them, when necessity or the maxims of war require it. The governor of a besieged town sets fire to the suburbs, that they may not afford a lodgment to the besiegers. Nobody presumed to blame a general who lays waste gardens, vineyards, or orchards, for the purpose of encamping on the ground, and throwing up an entrenchment. If any beautiful production of art be thereby destroyed, it is an accident, an unhappy consequence of the war; and the general will not be blamed, except in those cases when he might have pitched his camp elsewhere without the smallest inconvenience to himself. In bombarding towns, it is difficult to spare the finest edifices". Quoted in Williams, 1978, pp. 5-6.

[23] Indeed, post 1648 European acceptance of moderation in war was reflected in the virtually universal condemnation of the devastation of the Rhenish Palatinate by the French armies in 1688. Howard, 1994, p. 4; Parker, 1994, p. 54; Rothenberg, 1994, p. 87.

[24] The scope and intensity of hostilities during the wars of the French Revolution and the Napoleonic Era, combined with the systematic pillage of cultural objects by the French during this period, joined to create an intensified awareness of the need to place constraints on the conduct of warfare. Similarly, the burning of Washington by the British in 1814 was condemned, not just in the United States, but also by members of the British Parliament. Nahlik, 1976, p. 1071; Alexandrov, 1979, p. 21; Rogers, 1996, p. 85.

[25] Hartigan, 1983; Schindler and Toman, 1981, p. 3; Williams, 1978, pp. 15-16; Merryman, 1986, p. 833; Boylan, 1993, p. 25; Parks, 1990, pp. 7-8; Toman, 1996, p. 7.

[26] Schindler and Toman, 1981, p. 7.

[27] Schindler and Toman, 1981, p. 7.

[28] Schindler and Toman, 1981, p. 6.

[29] Schindler and Toman, 1981, pp. 8-9.

[30] Schindler and Toman, 1981, p. 10.

[31] Schindler and Toman, 1981, p. 6.

[32] Schindler and Toman, 1981, p. 6.

[33] Williams, 1978, p. 17; Schindler and Toman, 1981, p. 3; Merryman, 1986, p. 834; Parks, 1990, p. 8; Boylan, 1993, p. 25; Toman, 1996, pp. 7-8.

[34] Visscher, 1949, p. 827; Williams, 1978, pp. 16-17; Schindler and Toman, 1981, p. 25; Merryman, 1986, p. 834; Boylan, 1993, pp. 25-26; Toman, 1996, p. 9; Merryman and Elsen, 2002, p. 25. Earlier international community efforts to codify international law and the law of armed conflict began with the 1856 Declaration Respecting Maritime Law and continued with the establishment of the Red Cross and the conclusion of the 1864 Geneva Convention for the Amelioration of the Condition of the Wounded in War, as well as the additional articles signed in Geneva in 1868, and the 1868 St. Petersburg Declaration. Schindler and Toman, 1981, pp. v, 95, 209, 213, 217, 699.

[35] Schindler and Toman, 1981, p. 28.

[36] Schindler and Toman, 1981, p. 29.

[37] Schindler and Toman, 1981, p. 29.

[38] Schindler and Toman, 1981, p. 29.

[39] Schindler and Toman, 1981, p. 32.
[40] Schindler and Toman, 1981, p. 25; Merryman, 1986, p. 834.
[41] Visscher, 1949, p. 827; Schindler and Toman, 1981, pp. 25, 35; Merryman, 1986, p. 834; Boylan, 1993, p. 26; Toman, 1996, pp. 9-10; Merryman and Elsen, 2002, pp. 25-26.
[42] Schindler and Toman, 1981, p. 41.
[43] Schindler and Toman, 1981, pp. 42, 44. In addition to these provisions, Article 54 stated, "Private property, whether belonging to individuals or corporations, must be respected, and can be confiscated only under the limitations contained in the following articles" (Articles 54-60). Schindler and Toman, 1981, p. 44.
[44] Nahlik, 1976, p. 1072; Williams, 1978, p. 17; Schindler and Toman, 1981, p. 25; Roberts, 1994, p. 121.
[45] Visscher, 1949, pp. 827-828, 837-838; Bailey, 1972, pp. 62-65; Nahlik, 1976, pp. 1072-1075; Williams, 1978, p. 17; Alexandrov, 1979, pp. 24-29; Schindler and Toman, 1981, p. 57; Merryman, 1986, pp. 834-835; Parks, 1990, pp. 8-19; Roberts, 1994, pp. 121-122; Biddle, 1994, pp. 141-144; Rogers, 1996, pp. 85-86; Toman, 1996, pp. 10-13; Merryman and Elsen, 2002, p. 26.
[46] Schindler and Toman, 1981, pp. 76-77. For an excellent analysis of this article in historical contexts, see Baker and Crocker, 1919, pp. 149-168.
[47] Biddle, 1994, pp. 141-144.
[48] Schindler and Toman, 1981, pp. 77-78; Nahlik, 1976, p. 1073; Parks, 1990, p. 17; Biddle, 1994, p. 142. See also Baker and Crocker for a historical analysis of Article 25, Baker and Crocker, 1918, pp. 198-203.
[49] Schindler and Toman, 1981, p. 78. See also Baker and Crocker for a historical analysis of Article 26, Baker and Crocker, 1918, pp. 204-208.
[50] Schindler and Toman, 1981, p. 78.
[51] Schindler and Toman, 1981, p. 78. See also Baker and Crocker for a historical analysis of Article 27, Baker and Crocker, 1918, pp. 209-213.
[52] Nahlik, 1976, p. 1073; Alexandrov, 1979, pp. 28-29.
[53] Schindler and Toman, 1981, p. 78. See also Baker and Crocker for a historical analysis of Article 28, Baker and Crocker, 1918, pp. 214-217.
[54] Schindler and Toman, 1981, p. 724.
[55] Schindler and Toman, 1981, p. 725.
[56] Schindler and Toman, 1981, p. 725.
[57] Biddle, 1994, p. 143. See also Parks, 1990, pp. 14-15, 17-18.
[58] For an excellent analysis of the 1907 Convention IV regulations concerning occupation in historical contexts, see Baker and Crocker, 1919, pp. 292-420.
[59] Although minor stylistic changes were made in the wording of these articles in the 1907 version, as compared to the 1899 Convention II, the meaning of the provisions did not change. Schindler and Toman, 1981, pp. 82, 83, 85, 86.
[60] Schindler and Toman, 1981, pp. 82, 83, 85, 86.
[61] Schindler and Toman, 1981, p. 64. The exact wording of the 1899 Convention is slightly different from that of the 1907 Convention.
[62] Bailey, 1972, p. 63. See also Nahlik, 1976, pp. 1074-1075; Howard, 1994, pp. 7-8.
[63] Wright, 1947, pp. 644-645; Bailey, 1972, p. 65; Schindler and Toman, 1981, p. 57; Nahlik, 1976, p. 1072; Roberts, 1994, p. 134; Toman, 1996, p. 10.
[64] Visscher, 1949, p. 838; Parks, 1990, pp. 20-23; Roberts, 1994, pp. 123-126; Biddle, 1994, pp. 144-146.
[65] Garner, 1920, p. 434.
[66] Visscher, 1949, p. 838, Williams, 1978, p. 18; Boylan, 1993, p. 27; Rogers, 1996, p. 86; Garner, 1920, pp. 437-457.

[67] Garner, 1920, p. 437.

[68] The University of Louvain was founded in the early fifteenth century, and was one of Europe's leading universities. By 1914, the university was said to be "the most famous Catholic university in the world". Garner, 1920, pp. 437-441.

[69] Garner, 1920, pp. 441-446.

[70] Garner, 1920, pp. 448-449.

[71] Garner, 1920, pp. 446-451, 453-457.

[72] Garner, 1920, pp. 451-452.

[73] Garner, 1920, p. 452. The peace treaties concluded at the end of World War I contained provisions for the repatriation of works of art. In addition to the repatriation of works of art taken by Germany and its allies during World War I, Germany was also required to repatriate cultural objects taken from France during the Franco-Prussian War. Moreover, the Central Powers were required to compensate the victorious powers for the destruction of cultural properties. For example, see Articles 245, 246, and 247 of the Treaty of Versailles. Visscher, 1949, pp. 829-837; Williams, 1978, p. 19; Merryman and Elsen, 2002, pp. 64-65.

[74] Visscher, 1949, p. 838, Williams, 1978, p. 18; Boylan, 1993, p. 27; Rogers, 1996, p. 86.

[75] Watt, 1979, pp. 62-63.

[76] Visscher, 1949, p. 838; Toman, 1996, p. 14.

[77] Visscher, 1949, pp. 838-839; Toman, 1996, p. 14.

[78] For example, on June 17, 1925, thirty-eight states signed the Geneva Gas Protocol. Schindler and Toman, 1981, pp. 109-119; Boylan, 1993, p. 27; Roberts, 1994, p. 127.

[79] Schindler and Toman, 1981, pp. 147-157; Visscher, 1949, pp. 839-843; Watt, 1979, p. 66; Merryman, 1986, p. 835; Parks, 1990, pp. 25-36; Boylan, 1993, pp. 27-28; Biddle, 1994, p. 148; Rogers, 1996, pp. 86-87; Toman, 1996, pp. 14-16.

[80] Visscher, 1949, pp. 839-840.

[81] Visscher, 1949, p. 840.

[82] Schindler and Toman, 1981, pp. 150-151.

[83] Schindler and Toman, 1981, p. 147; Visscher, 1949, pp. 839-843; Merryman, 1986, p. 835; Boylan, 1993, pp. 27-28; Biddle, 1994, p. 148; Rogers, 1996, pp. 86-87.

[84] For example, on June 8, 1934, the Disarmament Conference adopted a resolution that stated, "The Conference, deeply impressed with the danger overhanging civilization from bombardment from the air in the event of future conflict, and determined to take all practicable measures to provide against this danger, records at this stage of its work the following conclusions: (1) Air attack against the civilian populations shall be absolutely prohibited; (2) The High Contracting Parties shall agree as between themselves that all bombardment from the air shall be abolished, subject to agreement with regard to measures to be adopted for purpose of rendering effective the observance of this rule". Visscher, 1949, p. 843. See also Watt, 1979, pp. 67-75.

[85] Schindler and Toman, 1981, pp. 653-655; Nahlik, 1976, p. 1075; Alexandrov, 1978, pp. 5-27; Alexandrov, 1979, pp. 31-33, 87-102; Merryman, 1986, p. 835; Boylan, 1993, pp. 28-30; Toman, 1996, pp. 16-18.

[86] Schindler and Toman, 1981, p. 654.

[87] Schindler and Toman, 1981, p. 654.

[88] Parks, 1990, p. 36; see also Rogers, 1996, p. 10.

[89] Schindler and Toman, 1981, pp. 163-169.

[90] Visscher, 1949, pp, 843, 859-865; Alexandrov, 1979, p. 32; Boylan, 1993, pp. 30-31; Merryman, 1986, p. 835; Toman, 1996, pp. 18-19.

[91] Visscher, 1949, pp. 859-860; Toman, 1996, p. 19.

[92] Visscher, 1949, p. 861.

[93] Visscher, 1949, p. 861.

[94] Visscher, 1949, p. 861.
[95] Visscher, 1949, pp. 861-862.
[96] Boylan, 1993, p. 31; Rogers, 1996, p. 87; Toman, 1996, p. 19.
[97] Boylan, 1993, pp. 32-33; Parks, 1990, pp. 36-37.
[98] On September 1, Germany's Chancellor, Adolf Hitler stated, "the views expressed in the message of President Roosevelt, namely to refrain in all circumstances from bombing non-military targets . . . is a humanitarian principle, corresponding exactly to my own views, as I have already declared. . . . For my part, I presume that you have noted that, in my speech given today in the Reichstag, I announced that the German air force have received the order to limit their operations to military objectives. One obvious condition for the continuation of these instructions is that the air forces opposing us observe the same rules." Speaking for Great Britain, the British Foreign Secretary, Lord Halifax stated on September 1, "His Majesty's Government welcomes the important and moving appeal of the President of the United States of America against the aerial bombing of civilian populations or undefended towns. . . . His Majesty's government has, in advance, declared that its policy . . . will be . . . to refrain from acts of this nature, and to strictly limit bombing to military targets, it being understood that the enemy scrupulously observes the same rules". At the outbreak of hostilities on September 3, the British and French governments issued a Joint Declaration that stated, "The Governments of France and of the United Kingdom, solemnly and publicly affirm, their intention to conduct the hostilities which have been imposed upon them, with the firm desire to protect the civilian population and to preserve, with every possible measure, monuments of human civilization. In this spirit they have welcomed with profound satisfaction the appeal of President Roosevelt, on the subject of aerial bombing. Therefore, they have already sent express instructions to the commanders of their armed forces, under which they shall only bombard, by aerial or maritime means or by terrestrial artillery, strictly military targets, in the strictest meaning of the term. So far as bombardment by terrestrial artillery is concerned . . . to avoid destruction of areas and buildings presenting an interest for civilization. A request will be addressed to the German Government to know if it will give corresponding assurances. It goes without saying that if the enemy does not observe certain of these restrictions to which the Governments of France and the United Kingdom have placed on their armed forces, these governments reserve the right to undertake any action that they consider appropriate". The Joint Declaration went on to state that bombardment by artillery "will exclude objectives which do not present a clearly defined military objective, in particular, the large urban areas situated outside the battlefield and, similarly, will strive to avoid the destruction of areas and buildings of interest for civilization". Boylan, 1993, p. 33-34.
[99] Sherry, 1987, pp. 120, 145, 147-166, 176, 251; Parks, 1990, pp. 44-47; Boylan, 1993, pp. 34-36; Biddle, 1994, pp. 151-153; Rogers, 1996, p. 12.
[100] Sherry, 1987, pp. 147-166; Biddle, 1994, pp. 152-154.
[101] Boylan, 1993, pp. 34-36; Roberts, 1994, p. 131; Biddle, 1994, pp. 153-154; Rogers, 1996, pp. 88-89. For detailed histories of aerial bombardment during the Second World War, see, Hansell, 1972, Overy, 1980, pp. 26-84; and Report of the American Commission, 1946. For a discussion of air operations from a legal perspective, see Parks, 1990, pp. 44-55.
[102] Report of the American Commission, 1946, pp. 98-99; Merryman and Elsen, 2002, p. 76.
[103] Sherry, 1987, pp. 166-173; Biddle, 1994, p. 154. See also, Hansell, 1980, Overy, 1980, pp. 85-101; and Report of the American Commission, 1946, pp. 157-159.
[104] Werth, 1964; Erickson, 1975; Erickson, 1983; Goure, 1962; Salisbury, 1969; Howard, 1994, p. 8; Parker, 1994, p. 56; Roberts, 1994, p. 132; Merryman and Elsen, 2002, p. 29.
[105] Merryman and Elsen, 2002, p. 29; Tung, 2001, pp. 77-83.
[106] Williams, 1978, pp. 19-20; Merryman, 1986, pp. 835-836; Simpson, 1997; Merryman

and Elsen, 2002, pp. 26-33.

[107] President Roosevelt made General Eisenhower's directive public at a press conference on February 15, 1944. Report of the American Commission, 1946, pp. 48-49; Merryman, 1986, p. 839; Merryman and Elsen, 2002, p. 75. Similarly, at the outset of the Italian campaign, General Harold Alexander directed " . . . that every officer brings continually to the notice of those serving under him our responsibility and obligation to preserve and protect these objects (art treasures and monuments) to the greatest extent that is possible under operational conditions". Report of the American Commission, 1946, p. 61; Merryman and Elsen, 2002, p. 75.

[108] Report of the American Commission, 1946, p. 102; Merryman, 1986, p. 839; Boylan, 1993, p. 36; Merryman and Elsen, 2002, p. 76.

[109] Boylan, 1993, pp. 36-37; Report of the American Commission, 1946.

[110] One of the most controversial examples of the destruction of a historic site in the war in southern and western Europe was the destruction of the Abbey at Monte Cassino, located near Rome. Report of the American Commission, 1946; Green, 1988, pp. 30-39; Merryman and Elsen, 2002, p. 77; Rogers, 1996, pp. 54-55.

[111] The Declaration stated that the enumerated Allied powers "Hereby issue a formal warning to all concerned, and in particular to persons in neutral countries, that they intend to do their utmost to defeat the methods of dispossession practiced by the Governments with which they are at war against the countries and peoples who have been so wantonly assaulted and despoiled. Accordingly, the Governments making this Declaration and the French National Committee reserve all their rights to declare invalid any transfers of, or dealings with, property, rights and interests of any description whatsoever which are, or have been, situation in the territories which have come under the occupation or control, direct or indirect, of the Governments with which they are at war, or which belong, or have belonged, to persons (including juridical persons) resident in such territories, This warning applies whether such transfers or dealings have taken the form of open looting or plunder, or of transactions, apparently legal in form, even when they purport to be voluntarily effected". Simpson, 1997, p. 287. See also: Toman, 1996, p. 20.

[112] Williams, 1978, pp. 19-20, 22-23; Simpson, 1997; Merryman and Elsen, 2002, pp. 33-70

[113] Schindler and Toman, 1981, pp. 823-843; Williams, 1978, pp. 23-29; Merryman, 1986, pp. 835-836; Boylan, 1993, p. 38; Roberts, 1994, pp. 133-135; Toman, 1996, pp. 21-22; Merryman and Elsen, 2002, pp. 26-33.

[114] Biddle, 1994, p. 155.

[115] Williams, 1978, pp. 23-29; Merryman, 1986, pp. 835-836; Boylan, 1993, p. 38; Roberts, 1994, pp. 133-135; Toman, 1996, pp. 21-22; Merryman and Elsen, 2002, pp. 26-33.

[116] Schindler and Toman, 1981, pp.171-186, 299-529; Boylan, 1993, pp. 38-39; Toman, 1996, p. 21.

[117] Schindler and Toman, 1981, pp. 657-696; Bailey, 1972, pp. 65-66; Nahlik, 1976, pp. 1076-1086; Williams, 1978, pp. 34-51; Alexandrov, 1978, pp. 14-27; Alexandrov, 1979, pp. 35-36, 39-60; Parks, 1990, pp. 59-62; Rogers, 1996, pp. 89-103; Merryman, 1986, pp. 836-838; Boylan, 1993, pp. 39-45, 49-101; Toman, 1996, pp. 21-24; 39-356.

[118] Schindler and Toman, 1981, p. 663; see also Toman, 1996, pp. 39-43.

[119] Toman, 1996, p. 40.

[120] Williams, 1978, p. 53.

[121] Merryman, 1986, p. 837; Toman, 1996, p. 24.

[122] Schindler and Toman, 1981, pp. 663-664; see also Nahlik, 1976, pp. 1078-1079; Boylan, 1993, pp. 49-51; Toman, 1996, pp. 45-56.

[123] Schindler and Toman, 1981, pp. 669-670; see also Nahlik, 1976, p. 1078; Boylan, 1993, pp. 115-126; Toman, 1996, pp. 195-220.

[124] Schindler and Toman, 1981, p. 664. See also Boylan, 1993, p. 53; Toman, 1996, pp. 57-66.
[125] Toman, 1996, p. 59.
[126] Schindler and Toman, 1981, p. 664. See also Nahlik, 1976, pp. 1079-1081; Boylan, 1993, pp. 53-58; Toman, 1996, pp. 59-66.
[127] Toman, 1996, pp. 67-82; Nahlik, 1976, pp. 1079-1081; Boylan, 1993, pp. 53-58.
[128] Schindler and Toman, 1981, pp. 664-665. See also: Nahlik, 1976, pp. 1079-1081. Boylan, 1993, pp. 53-58; Toman, 1996, pp. 67-82.
[129] Schindler and Toman, 1981, pp. 664-665.
[130] Schindler and Toman, 1981, p. 665. See also Nahlik, 1976, pp. 1079-1081; Boylan, 1993, pp. 53-58; Toman, 1996, pp. 83-89.
[131] Toman, 1996, p. 99.
[132] Schindler and Toman, 1981, pp. 665-666. See also Boylan 1993, pp. 75-82; Toman, 1996, pp. 97-137.
[133] Schindler and Toman, 1981, p. 666. See also Toman, 1996, pp. 138-140.
[134] Schindler and Toman, 1981, p. 667. See also Toman, 1996, pp. 143-149.
[135] Toman, 1996, p. 151.
[136] Schindler and Toman, 1981, pp. 667-668. See also Boylan, 1993, p. 81; Toman, 1996, pp. 151-172.
[137] Schindler and Toman, 1981, p. 668. See also Toman 1996, pp. 173-179.
[138] Schindler and Toman, 1981, pp. 668-669. See also Boylan 1996, pp. 84-85; Toman 1996, pp. 177-194.
[139] Schindler and Toman, 1981, pp. 673-674. See also Toman, 1996, pp. 177-180.
[140] Schindler and Toman, 1981, p. 665. See also Boylan, 1993, pp. 91-96.
[141] Schindler and Toman, 1981, p. 672. See also Nahlik, 1976, pp. 1082-1084; Boylan, 1993, pp. 91-98; Toman, 1996, pp. 291-300.
[142] Boylan, 1993, p. 43.
[143] Schindler and Toman, 1981, pp. 670; 676-684. See also Toman, 1996, p. 221.
[144] Schindler and Toman, 1981, pp. 689-694. See also Toman, 1996, pp. 331-351.
[145] Schindler and Toman, 1981, pp. 187-193; Bothe, Partsch, & Solf, 1989, pp. 2, 188.
[146] These appeals include: the 1965 International Conference of the Red Cross Resolution for the Protection of Civilian Populations Against the Dangers of Indiscriminate Warfare, Schindler and Toman, 1981, pp. 195-196; the 1968 Resolution adopted at the Teheran conference on Human Rights, Schindler and Toman, 1981, pp. 197-198; the 1968 U.N. General Assembly Resolution 2444 concerning Respect for Human Rights in Armed Conflicts, Schindler and Toman, 1981, pp. 199-200; the 1969 resolution adopted by the Institute of International Law concerning The Distinction Between Military Objectives and Non-Military Objects in General and Particularly the Problems Associated with Weapons of Mass Destruction, Schindler and Toman, 1981, pp. 201-202; and the 1970 U.N. General Assembly Resolution 2675 concerning Basic Principles for the Protection of Civilian Populations in Armed Conflicts, Schindler and Toman, 1981, pp. 203-204.
[147] Schindler and Toman, 1981, pp. 535-549, 551-617, 619-630, 631-636; Bothe, Partsch, & Solf, 1989; Parks, 1990, pp. 112-224; Boylan, 1993, pp. 45-46; Rogers, 1996, pp. 33-41, 56-63, 65-69, 72-83, 100-103.
[148] Schindler and Toman, 1981, p. 574; Bothe, Partsch, & Solf, 1989, pp. 192, 194-195, 309.
[149] Schindler and Toman, 1981, p. 580; Bothe, Partsch, & Solf, 1989, pp. 185, 276-278, 280-285, 297-301, 318, 320-329, 332-334, 357, 359, 360, 362, 517-520.
[150] Bothe, Partsch, & Solf, 1989, p. 582.
[151] Bothe, Partsch, & Solf, 1989, pp. 306, 323-326, 333, 360. As Bothe, Partsch, & Solf point out, the requirement that military objectives make an "effective contribution to

military action . . . does not require a direct connection with combat operation such as is implied in Art. 51, para. 3, with respect to civilian persons who lose their immunity from direct attack only while they 'take a direct part in hostilities'. Thus a civilian object may become a military objective and thereby lose its immunity from deliberate attack through use which is only indirectly related to combat action, but which nevertheless provides an effect contribution to the military phase of a party's overall war effort". Regarding the phrase "definite military advantage," Bothe, Partsch, & Solf observe that, "whether a definite military advantage would result from an attack must be judged in the context of the military advantage anticipated from the specific military operation of which the attack is a part considered as a whole, and not only from isolated or particular parts of that operation". Finally, the use of the word "definite" suggests "a concrete and perceptible military advantage rather than a hypothetical and speculative one". Bothe, Partsch, & Solf, 1989, pp. 324-326; see also Rogers, 1996, pp. 34-36, 58-61.

[152] Bothe, Partsch, & Solf, 1989, pp. 323-324; see also Rogers, 1996, pp. 34-36, 58-61.

[153] Schindler and Toman, 1981, p. 585; Bothe, Partsch, & Solf, 1989, pp. 358, 360, 365. Bothe, Partsch, & Solf note that "'Concrete' means specific, not general; perceptible to the senses. Its meaning is therefore roughly equivalent to the adjective 'definite' used in the two pronged test prescribed by Art. 52(2). 'Direct', on the other hand, means 'without intervening condition or agency'. Taken together the two words of limitation raise the standard set by Art. 52 in those situations where civilians may be affected by the attack. A remote advantage to be gained at some unknown time in the future would not be a proper consideration to weigh against civilian losses". Bothe, Partsch, & Solf, 1989, p. 365; see also Rogers, 1996, pp. 34-36, 58-61.

[154] See, for example, Articles 41, 42, 44, 45, 51, 75. Schindler and Toman, 1981, pp. 576-579, 580-582, 595-597.

[155] See Article 52. Schindler and Toman, 1981, p. 582; Bothe, Partsch, & Solf, 1989, pp. 278, 296, 299-300, 318-327.

[156] See Articles 53, 54, 55, and 56. Schindler and Toman, 1981, pp. 582-584; Bothe, Partsch, & Solf, 1989, pp. 328-357.

[157] Schindler and Toman, 1981, p. 586; Bothe, Partsch, & Solf, 1989, pp. 379-385.

[158] Schindler and Toman, 1981, p. 582.

[159] Schindler and Toman, 1981, p. 582.

[160] Schindler and Toman, 1981, p. 587; Bothe, Partsch, & Solf, 1989, pp. 385-389.

[161] Schindler and Toman, 1981, p. 587.

[162] Schindler and Toman, 1981, p. 582; Bothe, Partsch, & Solf, 1989, pp. 278, 296, 299-300, 318-327.

[163] Bothe, Partsch, & Solf, 1989, p. 329.

[164] Schindler and Toman, 1981, p. 582; Bothe, Partsch, & Solf, 1989, pp. 328-334, 509, 519-520.

[165] Bothe, Partsch, & Solf, 1989, p. 333.

[166] Bothe, Partsch, & Solf, 1989, pp. 333, 520.

[167] Schindler and Toman, 1981, pp. 601-602.

[168] Bothe, Partsch, & Solf, 1989, pp. 519-520.

[169] Bothe, Partsch, & Solf, 1989, pp. 332-333, 519.

[170] Schindler and Toman, 1981, pp. 584-585; Bothe, Partsch, & Solf, 1989, pp. 362-363.

[171] Schindler and Toman, 1981, pp. 580-582, 584-585; Bothe, Partsch, & Solf, 1989, pp. 276, 282, 296, 297, 299, 318, 320, 322, 328-330, 332, 333, 357, 362, 509.

[172] Schindler and Toman, 1981, p. 581.

[173] Schindler and Toman, 1981, p. 581; Bothe, Partsch, & Solf, 1989, pp. 276, 300, 366.

[174] Bothe, Partsch, & Solf, 1989, pp. 276, 277, 283, 299, 300, 303-304, 309, 310, 321, 359-362, 366, 371; Rogers, 1996, pp. 8, 14, 56.
[175] Schindler and Toman, 1981, pp. 584-585.
[176] Bothe, Partsch, & Solf, 1989, pp. 362-364; Rogers, 1996, p. 59.
[177] Bothe, Partsch, & Solf, 1989, pp. 311, 365; Rogers, 1996, pp. 17, 59.
[178] Bothe, Partsch, & Solf, 1989, pp. 367, 368; Rogers, 1996, p. 59.
[179] Schindler and Toman, 1981, p. 582; Bothe, Partsch, & Solf, 1989, p. 317.
[180] Schindler and Toman, 1981, p. 601.
[181] Bothe, Partsch, & Solf, 1989, pp. 514-517; see also Rogers, 1996, pp. 138-142.
[182] Bothe, Partsch, & Solf, 1989, p. 371; Rogers, 1996, pp. 72-83.
[183] Schindler and Toman, 1981, p. 585; Bothe, Partsch, & Solf, 1989, pp. 283, 284, 297, 299, 315-316, 328-330, 333, 370-375, 383, 388-389; Rogers, 1996, pp. 73-75.
[184] Schindler and Toman, 1981, p. 581; Bothe, Partsch, & Solf, 1989, pp. 299, 316.
[185] Schindler and Toman, 1981, p. 582; Bothe, Partsch, & Solf, 1989, pp. 329-330.
[186] With reference to the protection of cultural property, see Article 6 of Protocol II to the 1980 Convention on Conventional Weapons, as well as the 1993 Declaration of the International Conference for the Protection of War Victims. Boylan, 1993, p. 46; Toman, 1996, pp. 26-30.
[187] Williams, 1978, p. 54.
[188] Williams, 1978, pp. 53-54; Merryman, 1986, pp. 842-843, 845-846.
[189] UNESCO, 1985, p. 61.
[190] Boylan, 1993, p. 45.
[191] UNESCO, 1985, p. 62.
[192] UNESCO, 1985, pp. 63-70.
[193] UNESCO, 1985, pp. 75-98; Boylan, 1993, pp. 45, 109-113.
[194] Williams, 1978, p. 54.
[195] UNESCO, 1985, p. 79.
[196] Boylan, 1993, pp. 45, 109.
[197] Article 2 defines the term "natural heritage" as follows, "natural features consisting of physical and biological formations or groups of such formations, which are of outstanding universal value from the aesthetic or scientific point of view; geological and physiographical formations and precisely delineated areas which constitute the habitat of threatened species of animals and plants of outstanding universal value from the point of view of science or conservation; natural sites or precisely delineated natural areas of outstanding universal value from the point of view of science, conservation or natural beauty". UNESCO, 1985, pp. 80-81.
[198] UNESCO, 1985, p. 81.
[199] UNESCO, 1985, pp. 881-94.
[200] Rogers, 1996, p. 104.
[201] Rogers, 1996, p. 89.
[202] DOD Report, 1992, pp. 605-607, 612-616; Rogers 1996, pp. 100-104.
[203] Boylan, 1993, pp. 202, 204.
[204] DOD Report, 1992, p. 100.
[205] DOD Report, 1992, p. 615.
[206] DOD Report, 1992, p. 615.
[207] Boylan, 1993, p. 105.
[208] Boylan, 1993, pp. 78-79, 95, 117-118, 123, 128. For coverage of the early phases of the bombardment of Dubrovnik, up to mid November, see Hensel, 1992, pp. 2612-2617. For a comprehensive discussion of the damage to Dubrovnik see the February 1993 report by M. Jacques Baumel on the Destruction by War of the Cultural Heritage in Croatia and Bosnia-

The Protection of Cultural Objects During Armed Conflicts 99

Herzegovina to the Parliamentary Assembly of the Council of Europe in Boylan, 1993, pp. 225-234. See also, Meron, 1994; Clement, 1994; Rogers, 1996, p. 84.
[209] Desch, 1999, pp. 63-64; Henckaerts, 1999, pp. 593-594.
[210] Merryman and Elsen, 2002, pp. 1174-1187.
[211] Desch, 1999, pp. 63-70; Henckaerts, 1999, pp. 594-596.
[212] Boylan, 1993, pp. 49-51, 189-197; Merryman and Elsen, 2002, p. 1175; Desch, 1999, p. 71.
[213] Schindler and Toman, 1981, pp. 669-670; Merryman and Elsen, 2002, pp. 1175, 1181; Desch, 1999, pp. 70-71, 82-84; Henckaerts, 1999, pp. 617-619.
[214] Desch, 1999, p. 83.
[215] Desch, 1999, p. 83.
[216] Merryman and Elsen, 2002, pp. 1175-1176; Desch, 1999, pp. 71-72; Henckaerts, 1999, pp. 596-597.
[217] Schindler and Toman, 1981, p. 582; Desch, 1999, pp. 72-75; Henckaerts, 1999, pp. 598-606; Hladik, 1999, pp. 621-630; Nahlik, 1976, pp. 1084-1086; Boylan, 1993, pp. 54-57.
[218] Desch, 1999, p.73.
[219] Desch, 1999, pp. 72-75; Henckaerts, 1999, pp. 598-606.
[220] Merryman and Elsen, 2002, p. 1176.
[221] Merryman and Elsen, 2002, p. 1177.
[222] Merryman and Elsen, 2002, pp. 1177-1179; Desch, 1999, pp. 75-79; Henckaerts, 1999, pp. 606-611. One center containing monuments, Vatican City, and five refuges, one in Austria, three in the Netherlands (down from the six originally listed as refuges under special protection), and one in Germany are listed as cultural properties under special protection. Henckaerts, 1999, p. 607. In 1972, authorities from the Khmer Republic applied for "the entry of centres containing the monuments of Angkor and Roluos and of the sanctuaries situated at Pnom-Bok and Pnom-Krom, together with a refuge situated at Angkor". These properties were, however, never registered by UNESCO because several States asserted that "the application for registration had not been presented by the authority which they considered to be the sole government entitled to represent the Khmer Republic". Toman, 1996, pp 108-109.
[223] Merryman and Elsen, 2002, p. 1177.
[224] Merryman and Elsen, 2002, pp. 1177-1178.
[225] Merryman and Elsen, 2002, p. 1178.
[226] Merryman and Elsen, 2002, p. 1178.
[227] Desch, 1999, p. 79.
[228] Desch, 1999, pp. 79-82; Henckaerts, 1999, pp. 613-617.
[229] Merryman and Elsen, 2002, p. 1179.
[230] Merryman and Elsen, 2002, pp. 1179-1181; Desch, 1999, pp. 79-82; Henckaerts, 1999, pp. 613-617.
[231] Henckaerts, 1999, pp. 615-616.
[232] Henckaerts, 1999, p. 617.
[233] Merryman and Elsen, 2002, pp. 1182-1185; Desch, 1999, pp. 84-87.
[234] Desch, 1999, p. 90; Henckaerts, 1999, p. 619.
[235] Boylan, 1993, pp. 49-51, 189-197; Rogers, 1996, p. 105.
[236] Boylan, 1993, pp. 75-88, 1109-113.
[237] Fehrenbach, 1963, pp. 223-224; also cited in Parks, 1990, p. 148.
[238] Merryman, 1986, p. 840.
[239] Cited in Merryman and Elsen, 2002, pp. 80-81.
[240] Merryman, 1986, p. 841.
[241] Merryman, 1986, p. 840.

[242] Boylan, 1993, pp. 8, 127-139; 201-206; Merryman and Elsen, 2002, pp. 71-72, 74; Colwell-Chanthaphonh and Piper, 2001, pp. 217-245.
[243] Boylan, 1993, pp. 127-142.

References

Alexandrov, Emil *International Legal Protection of Cultural Property* (Sofia: Sofia Press, 1979).

Alexandrov, Emil *The Roerich Pact and the International Protection of Cultural Institutions and Treasures* (Sofia: Sofia Press, 1978).

American Commission for the Protection and Salvage of Artistic and Historic Monuments in War Areas, *Report of the American Commission for the Protection and Salvage of Artistic and Historic Monuments in War Areas* (Washington: U.S. Government Printing Office, 1946).

Bailey, Sydney D. *Prohibitions and Restraints in War* (Oxford: Oxford University Press, 1972).

Baker, Joseph R. and Crocker, Henry G. *The Laws of Land Warfare Concerning the Rights and Duties of Belligerents as Existing on August 1, 1914* (Washington: U.S. Government Printing Office, 1919) reprinted in The Inquiry Handbooks, Vol. 2 (Wilmington, Delaware: Scholarly Resources Inc., 1974).

Best, Geoffrey *Humanity in Warfare* (New York: Columbia University Press, 1980).

Best, Geoffrey "Restraints on War by Land before 1945", in Michael Howard (ed), *Restraints on War* (Oxford: Oxford University Press, 1979), pp. 17-37.

Biddle, Tami Davis "Air Power", in Michael Howard, George J. Andreopoulos, and Mark R. Shulman (eds), *The Laws of War: Constraints on Warfare in the Western World* (New Haven: Yale University Press, 1994), pp. 140-159.

Bothe, Michael, Partsch, Karl Josef, and Solf, Waldemar A. *New Rules for Victims of Armed, Conflicts* (The Hague: Martinus Nijhoff Publishers, 1982).

Boylan, Patrick J. *Review of the Convention for the Protection of Cultural Property in the Event of Armed Conflict* (Paris: UNESCO, 1993).

Brierly, J.L. *The Law of Nations: An Introduction to the International Law of Peace* (Oxford: Oxford University Press, 1960).

Clement, Etienne, "Some Recent Practical Experience in the Implementation of the 1954 Hague Convention", *International Journal of Cultural Property*, Vol. 3, #1, (1994), pp. 11-25.

Colwell-Chanthaphonh and Parker, John "War and Cultural Property: the 1954 Convention and the Status of U.S. Ratification", *International Journal of Cultural Property*, Vol. 10, #2 (2001), pp. 217-245.

Desch, Thomas "The Second Protocol to the 1954 Hague Convention for the Protection of Cultural Property in the Event of Armed Conflict", *Yearbook of International Humanitarian Law*, Vol. 2 (1999), pp. 63-90.

Erickson, John *The Road to Berlin* (Boulder: Westview Press, 1983).

Erickson, John *The Road to Stalingrad* (New York: Harper and Row, 1975).

Fehrenbach, T. R. *This Kind of War* (New York: Macmillan, 1963).
Garner, James Wilford *International Law and the World War* (London: Longmans, Green and Co., 1920).
Goure, L. *The Siege of Leningrad* (Stanford: Stanford University Press, 1962).
Green, J. H. "The Destruction of the Abby of Monte Casino", *British Army Review* (1988), pp. 30-39.
Hansell, Haywood S. *The Air Plan that Defeated Hitler* (Atlanta: Higgins McArthur, Longino & Porter, Inc., 1972).
Hansell, Haywood S. *The Strategic Air War Against Germany and Japan* (Washington: U.S. Government Printing Office, 1986).
Hansell, Haywood S. *Strategic Air War Against Japan* (Washington: U.S. Government Printing Office, 1980).
Hartigan, Richard Shelly *Lieber's Code and the Law of War* (Chicago: Precedent Publishing, Inc., 1983).
Henckaerts, Jean-Marie "New Rules for the Protection of Cultural Property in Armed Conflict", *International Review of the Red Cross*, Vol. 81, #835 (September 1999) pp. 593-620.
Hensel, Howard M. "Theocentric Natural Law and the Norms of the Global Community", in Howard M. Hensel (ed), *Sovereignty and the Global Community* (Aldershot: Ashgate Publishing Ltd., 2004), pp. 1-53.
Hensel, Howard M. "The Yugoslav Army's Shelling of Dubrovnik", in Frank N. Magill (ed), *History of Europe* (Grolier, 1992).
Hladik, Jan, "The 1954 Hague Convention for the Protection of Cultural Property in the Event of Armed Conflict and the Notion of Military Necessity", *International Review of the Red Cross*, Vol. 81, #835 (September 1999), pp. 621-634.
Howard, Michael "Constraints on Warfare", in Michael Howard, George J. Andreopoulos, and Mark R. Shulman (eds), *The Laws of War: Constraints on Warfare in the Western World* (New Haven: Yale University Press, 1994), pp. 1-11.
Howard, Michael *"Temperamenta Belli*: Can War be Controlled"? in Michael Howard (ed), *Restraints on War* (Oxford: Oxford University Press, 1979), pp. 1-15.
Kennedy, Paul and Andreopoulos, George "The Laws of War: Some Concluding Reflections", in Michael Howard, George J. Andreopoulos, and Mark R. Shulman (eds), *The Laws of War: Constraints on Warfare in the Western World* (New Haven: Yale University Press, 1994), pp. 214-225.
Meron, Theodor "War Crimes in Yugoslavia and the Development of International Law", *The American Journal of International Law*, Vol. 88, #1 (January 1994), pp. 78-87.
Merryman, John Henry "International Art Law: From Cultural Nationalism to a Common Cultural Heritage", *Journal of International Law and Politics*, Vol. 15, #4 (Summer 1983), pp. 757-763.

Merryman, John Henry "Two Ways of Thinking About Cultural Property", *The American Journal of International Law*, Vol. 80, #4 (October 1986), pp. 831-853.

Merryman, John Henry and Elsen, Albert E. Law, *Ethics, and the Visual Arts* (London: Kluwer Law International, 2002).

Nahlik, Stanislaw E. "International Law and the Protection of Cultural Property in Armed Conflicts", *The Hastings Law Journal*, Vol. 27, #5 (May 1976), pp. 1069-1087.

Ober, Josiah "Classical Greek Times", in Michael Howard, George J. Andreopoulos, and Mark R. Shulman (eds), *The Laws of War: Constraints on Warfare in the Western World* (New Haven: Yale University Press, 1994), pp. 12-26.

Overy, R. J. *The Air War: 1939-1945* (Chelsea, MI: Scarborough House, 1980).

Parker, Geoffrey, "Early Modern Europe", in Michael Howard, George J. Andreopoulos, and Mark R. Shulman (eds), *The Laws of War: Constraints on Warfare in the Western World* (New Haven: Yale University Press, 1994), pp. 40-58.

Parks, W. Hays "Air War and the Law of War", *Air Force Law Review*, Vol. 32, #1, (1990), pp. 1-225.

Prott, Lyndel V. and O'Keefe, Patrick J. "'Cultural Heritage' or 'Cultural Property'", *International Journal of Cultural Property*, Vol. 1, #1 (1992), pp. 307-320.

Roberts, Adam "Land Warfare: From Hague to Nuremberg", in Michael Howard, George J. Andreopoulos, and Mark R. Shulman (eds), *The Laws of War: Constraints on Warfare in the Western World* (New Haven: Yale University Press, 1994), pp. 116-139.

Rothenberg, Gunther "The Age of Napoleon", in Michael Howard, George J. Andreopoulos, and Mark R. Shulman (eds), *The Laws of War: Constraints on Warfare in the Western World* (New Haven: Yale University Press, 1994), pp. 86-97.

Rogers, A.P.V. *Law on the Battlefield* (Manchester: Manchester University Press, 1996).

Salisbury, H.E. *The Siege of Leningrad* (London: Secker and Warburg, 1969).

Schindler, Dietrich and Toman, Jiri, *The Laws of Armed Conflicts* (Alphen ann den Riji, The Netherlands: Sijtheoff and Noordhoff, 1981).

Selesky, Harold E. "Colonial America", in Michael Howard, George J. Andreopoulos, and Mark R. Shulman (eds), *The Laws of War: Constraints on Warfare in the Western World* (New Haven: Yale University Press, 1994), pp. 59-85.

Sherry, Michael S. *The Rise of American Airpower: The Creation of Armageddon* (New Haven: Yale University Press, 1987).

Simpson, Elizabeth *The Spoils of War* (New York: Harry N. Abrams, Inc., 1997).

Stacey, Robert C., "The Age of Chivalry", in Michael Howard, George J. Andreopoulos, and Mark R. Shulman (eds), *The Laws of War: Constraints on*

Warfare in the Western World (New Haven: Yale University Press, 1994), pp. 27-39.

Toman, Jiri *The Protection of Cultural Property in the Event of Armed Conflict* (Aldershot: Dartmouth Publishing Company/UNESCO Publilshing, 1996).

Tung, Anthony M. *Preserving the World's Great Cities* (New York: Three Rivers Press, 2001).

UNESCO, *Conventions and Recommendations of UNESCO Concerning the Protection of the Cultural Heritage* (Paris: UNESCO, 1983).

United States Department of Defense, *Conduct of the Persian Gulf War* (Washington: U.S. Government Printing Office, 1992).

Visscher, Charles De *International Protection of Works of Art and Historic Monuments* in U.S. Department of State Publication 3590, International Information and Cultural Series 8, Department of State Papers (Washington, U.S. Government Printing Office, 1949).

Watt, Donald Cameron "Restraints on War in the Air Before 1945" in Michael Howard (ed), *Restraints on War* (Oxford: Oxford University Press, 1979), pp. 57-77.

Wright, Quincy "The Law of the Nuremberg Trial", *The American Journal of International Law*, Vol. 41 (1947), pp. 38-72, reprinted in Leo Gross (ed), *International Law in the Twentieth Century* (New York: Appleton Century Crofts, 1969).

Werth, Alexander *Russia at War* (New York: Carroll & Graf Publishers, Inc., 1964).

Williams, Sharon A. *The International and National Protection of Movable Cultural Property: A Comparative Study* (Dobbs Ferry, NY: Oceana Publications, Inc., 1978).

Chapter 4

The Principle of Civilian Protection and Contemporary Armed Conflict

Mika Nishimura Hayashi

Introduction

International law can be viewed from an apologetic perspective or a utopian perspective.[1] From one perspective, the most meaningful evidence of the existence of legal rules is the degree to which they influence behavior of states. Rules that are formulated in this way, however, often appear to be only "apologies" for the behavior of powerful states who are capable of pursuing their own policies without external constraints. In order to avoid being excessively apologetic, rules must, at least to some degree, be disconnected from actual behavior and constructed from ideals and aspirations. Rules conceived in this way, however, are often seen as too "utopian," in the sense that, in reality, few states may actually follow the rule. Thus, each perspective contains its own strength and its own weakness. Disproportionate emphasis on the actual behavior of states tends to lead to an extreme form of realism, negating the binding force of any rule. Alternatively, disproportionate emphasis on aspirations and ideals fails to be convincing because it lacks empirical evidence supporting the rule. A further problem of excessive emphasis on normative ideals is that the rule appears to be arbitrarily asserted. Consequently, international law must not overemphasize either behavior or normative ideals, even though it might "seem[s] possible to defend one's legal argument only by showing either its closeness to, or its distance from, state practice."[2] In order not to succumb to either extreme, international law must maintain both ideals and reality in balance.

In their analysis of the law of armed conflict (also called the law of war, *jus in bello*, or international humanitarian law),[3] international lawyers have often failed to keep reality and ideals in balance. Following the two World Wars, many members of the international legal community tended to emphasize the apologetic perspective, whereas, more recently, there has been a noticeable shift from the apologetic perspective and a realist denial to the idealist and utopian affirmation of one of the most important principles of the law of armed conflict: principle of civilian protection. The principle of civilian protection is also called non-combatant immunity, or principle of distinction between combatants and non-combatants,[4] but the core obligation remains the same: it requires the parties to an armed conflict to distinguish at all times between civilians and combatants and between civilian and military objects, and direct their attacks only against the combatants and military objects. The two World Wars of the last century showed a glaring lack of respect of this principle. In contemporary armed conflicts, especially in internal wars, the principle of civilian protection in its most elementary form continues to be violated. In short, there was, and still is, an undeniable distance between the alleged principle of civilian protection and the actual actions of states. The fact that there are persistent violations, however, affected the academic interpretations very differently in the two periods studied in this chapter.

First, the chapter sketches out how the failure to synchronize the law and the actual behavior of states led a number of influential international lawyers to the negation of the principle of civilian protection. Indeed, in the periods after the two World Wars of the last century, the overall tone of the academic opinion concerning the law of armed conflict was realist, and hence, apologetic: the principle of civilian protection, one of the cornerstones of the law of armed conflict, seemed no longer valid, because there was a gap between the alleged principle and the actual behavior of states. While a number of scholars were not sufficiently realist to succumb to this downright denial of the principle of civilian protection, many nonetheless took an inductive approach in its defense and looked for legal techniques to excuse the wanton behaviors of states. Second, the chapter sketches out how the contemporary literature has come to accept a certain distance between the principle of civilian protection and the actual behavior observed in contemporary armed conflicts. When the two periods are compared, there is almost a complete oscillation from one extreme to the other: utopian affirmation of the principle despite the apparent inconsistency between the law and the actual behaviour of states, as opposed to the apology and the denial of the principle because of this degree of inconsistency between ideals and reality. Today, in ascertaining and discussing the principle of civilian protection, the actual behavior of states is given an apparently diminished place. Thus, the focus of the analysis is two-fold: how the discipline has escaped the specter of apology; how this contemporary acceptance of the inconsistency between the law and practice avoids the criticisms that its assertion of the law is unpersuasive and unrealistic. Since the two contrasting trends are closely related to the development of the law of armed conflict through codification and jurisprudence, the relevant background is also described for each period.

Apologetic Trend in the Two Post-World War Periods

Indifference Towards the Principle of Civilian Protection

The principle of civilian protection had been an ancient and widely accepted rule of the law of armed conflict: Not to attack civilian population or civilian objects *per se*, and not to attack indiscriminately. For instance, these two rules appeared in several treaties prior to the First World War, though in different forms. In both the 1899 Hague Convention No. II[5] and in the 1907 Hague Convention No. IV,[6] the idea of the prohibition of indiscriminate attack in land warfare appeared in the form of the prohibition of attacks directed against undefended or unfortified towns, as opposed to defended or fortified towns.[7] The obligation of belligerents to spare the lives of unoffending non-combatants was also accepted in rules of naval warfare. There was an obligation to provide for safe passage to innocent passengers and crews of merchant ships.[8] Similarly, non-discriminatory damage that certain mines in maritime warfare could cause was held as a ground for their prohibition.[9] The principle of civilian protection, understood as distinction between combatants and non-combatants, was not only provided in treaties, but it also formed a part of customary law.[10] It was deemed an acceptable principle in the military community as well.[11]

As it is generally known, this well-established principle of civilian protection failed to offer an adequate protection to the civilians in the First World War.[12] As a consequence, it was felt that the law of war as a whole, including the rules of civilian protection, "urgently needed to be adapted to take account of new technological developments."[13] The League of Nations, however, was more interested in developing an effective regime outlawing the war itself, backed up by disarmament, than in developing an efficient regime of the law of armed conflict.[14] The lack of interest in the law of armed conflict was also evident outside the League of Nations.[15] In particular, efforts concerning the protection of civilian population against the effects of war met very little enthusiasm. For example, the states that participated in the Washington Naval Conference in 1921-1922 decided to have international lawyers discuss the question of aerial bombardment, one of the causes of civilian casualties in the First World War. As a result, the Commission of Jurists, nominated at the Washington Conference, drew up the rules concerning air warfare (hereinafter referred to as the 1923 Hague Rules).[16] An important component of these rules was the application of the principle of civilian protection to the air warfare. According to the 1923 Hague Rules, "[A]erial bombardment for the purpose of terrorizing the civilian population, of destroying or damaging private property not of a military character, or of injuring non-combatants is prohibited."[17] Article 24 further provided that:

(1) An air bombardment is legitimate only when is directed against a military objective, i.e. an objective whereof the total or partial destruction would constitute an obvious military advantage for the belligerent;
(2) Such bombardment is legitimate only when directed exclusively against the following objectives: military forces, military works, military establishments or depots, manufacturing plants constituting important and well-known centers for the production of arms, ammunition or characterized military supplies, lines of communication or of transport which are used for military purposes.

Some writers believe that this was an accurate application of the principle of distinction between combatants and non-combatants as then interpreted,[18] whereas others believe that it was not.[19] In any case, many states voiced their dissatisfaction concerning the narrow definition of the legitimate target. Without a sufficient support of states, the 1923 Hague Rules never entered into force, and hence, it remained a non-binding document. Moreover, neither British, U.S., nor German

Military Manuals adopted the specific provisions analogous to those contained in the 1923 Hague Rules.[20] Later, in 1938, the International Law Association drew up the Draft Convention for the Protection of Civilian Populations Against New Engines of War. Again, the states demonstrated no interest and took no action. Finally, the International Committee of the Red Cross also drew up drafts on the protection of civilians in the 1920's, but they never found enough support from governments, either.[21]

The indifference of states *vis-à-vis* the principle of civilian protection was also observed in attempts to regulate submarine warfare. For example, a protocol regulating submarine warfare was annexed to the Treaty on the Limitation of Naval Armaments of 1922 (hereinafter referred to as the Submarine Protocol).[22] It reaffirmed that the traditional rules concerning the safety of crew and passengers when attacking merchant vessels were also applicable to submarines. While there was optimism in academic circles concerning the future of the Submarine Protocol,[23] it never came into force. The problem with the Submarine Protocol was that it "tried to restore rules which had for all practical purposes been abandoned during the First World War."[24] The same was true for the London Treaty on the Limitation of Naval Armaments[25] and the Procès-verbal of November 6, 1936, that contained provisions to the same effect. All these agreements were, as far as the principle of distinction was concerned, "of questionable value"[26] for the same reason: they merely repeated the rules that had been ineffective in the earlier war. In sum, in the post-World War I period, there is little evidence to suggest that the states seriously attempted to develop rules that could effectively protect the civilian population from effects of war, including the effects of aerial warfare and submarine warfare.

The overall trend of indifference towards the law of armed conflict generally, and the principle of civilian protection, specifically, was not immediately reversed in the period following the Second World War. In the first session of the International Law Commission of the United Nations in 1949, the Commission decided not to deal with this branch of law, under the pretext that "war having been outlawed, the regulation of its conduct had ceased to be relevant."[27] The four Geneva Conventions adopted in 1949[28] restricted their scope to specific categories of the victims of armed conflict and did not address the question of the protection of the civilian population as a whole. In spite of its full title, the Convention relative to the Protection of Civilian Persons in Time of War does not provide a protection of all civilians in all circumstances in time of war.[29] It does not fully deal with the effects of hostilities on the civilian population, either, except in a handful of provisions,[30] since the battle conduct, including the question of weaponry, targeting and modes of fighting, was considered to be a matter of the Hague law and the Hague law including this aspect was not revised during this period.[31] In addition, "[I]n the years following their adoption, the Geneva Conventions attracted remarkably little interest,"[32] and the situation remained unchanged well into the 1960's.[33]

Violations in Reality and Apologies in the Doctrine

Above all, what most affected the interpretation of the principle of civilian protection as a cornerstone of the law of armed conflict was the actual behavior of states during the two World Wars. The blatant disregard of the principle of civilian protection in the two World Wars and, in particular, the indiscriminate submarine warfare and aerial bombardment in these wars, illustrated the gap between the alleged principle and the actual behavior. Indeed, the principle of protection of the civilian population was regularly violated during the First World War.

> Belligerent merchant ships were sunk by German submarines without warning. New instruments of combat, such as poisonous gasses, were devised; aerial warfare put an end to the rules regulating the bombing of unfortified towns; and intimidation was resorted to as a means of breaking the spirit of the civilian population.[34]

Similarly, examples during the Second World War, such as the raids on London, Dresden and Tokyo, as well as the atomic bomb attacks on Hiroshima and Nagasaki did not add any credibility to the claim that states made serious efforts to distinguish between civilian and military targets.[35] While no state claimed to be legally entitled to bombard civilian populations and civilian objects from the air, one of the important goals of these air raids was to undermine the morale of the enemy civilian population.[36]

These gaps between the alleged principle of civilian protection and the actual behavior required explanation. That explanation, in the view of a number of international lawyers, resided in an apology for such behavior and the denial of the principle. The effort to reconcile the actual behavior of states and the legal principle led these members of the international legal community to the conclusion that the legal principle did not exist. There were two grounds on which the validity of the principle of civilian protection was denied: the principle of civilian protection and the actual actions of the states in past wars appeared to be irreconcilable; the prospect that such a reconciliation could be attained in the future appeared hopeless.

Experience of the Past Wars: Gap between the Principle and the Actual Behavior
From the apologetic point of view, the regular and massive violations by all belligerents in past wars meant that the principle of civilian protection was no longer valid. From the apologetic perspective, taking a position that the principle of civilian protection was still valid "would be bound to ignore, or brand as illegal and criminal, recent practice as generally followed"[37] and that was not acceptable to the apologists. Therefore, the apologists maintained that if the past practice showed a record of consistent violations and very little compliance, the rule in question could not be sustained.

According to this view, practice in the two World Wars altered the legal status of the principle of distinction from a time-honored principle of the law of armed conflict to a legally meaningless expression. For example, assessing the submarine warfare in the Second World War, Hersch Lauterpacht observed that the "principle of immunity of non-combatants remained a dead letter."[38] According to him, this practice of ignoring the principle of distinction, followed by both sides to the conflict, was evidence of the applicable law to submarine warfare as it stood.[39] By considering practice as the primary evidence of law, the apologetic view led to the inevitable conclusion that the states were free to resort to submarine warfare without heeding the safety of non-combatants involved. In other words, legally, the principle of distinction did not exist for the submarine warfare. Since practice was held to be the most important indicator of the principle of distinction, a similar conclusion concerning this principle in land warfare and aerial bombardment was also inevitable: the practice of the First World War in which "[A] town was now a defended town simply because it was located in the enemy country and was within range of attack by airplanes"[40] meant that the principle of distinction was no longer valid in land warfare and aerial attacks for the apologists. By the end of the Second World War, "whether the general recourse to strategic target-bombing had the result of endowing it with a measure of legality and of abolishing ... the principles underlying the Hague Rules of 1923"[41] had become a question which was very difficult to refute without making some kind of apologies for this general recourse. Though without giving a clear answer to this question, Lauterpacht acknowledged that practice followed in the Second World War "reduced to the vanishing point the protection of the civilian population from aerial bombardment."[42] Similarly, Georg Schwarzenburger wrote that "[T]he practice of belligerent States in the Second World War and the trends in the relevant post-1945 treaties suggest that the immunity of the civilian population from intentional attack is reaching vanishing point."[43] Charles Fenwick examined the alleged instances of reprisals involving the bombing of cities in Europe during the Second World War. He also concluded that these acts, allegedly resorted to as reprisals, "reduced the laws of war to the vanishing point."[44] Indeed, in both World Wars, the principle of civilian protection was mainly used "as a tool for blaming the enemy and justifying reprisal raids."[45] It did not function as a restraint. If the purpose of the principle of distinction was to restrain the freedom of action of belligerents, it did not fulfill that purpose.

There was a wide agreement as to the cause of this general breakdown of the principle of civilian protection in the two World Wars: this principle was said to have become inadequate and obsolete in modern wars of aerial and submarine warfare. The foundation of the principle of civilian protection had been destroyed "on the one hand, by submarines and aeroplanes and other new instruments, and on the other hand by the fact that every man, woman or child, whether in uniform or not, can be and is used in the belligerent effort."[46] It was further stated that "[N]ew instruments have come and they will be used" and "[t]he old distinction between combatants and non combatants is gone. The sooner every man, woman and child old enough to think realizes that he will be a party to the next war, the better."[47] In other words, the causes of violations of the principle of distinction were: (1) the use of new weapons that were incapable of discriminate attacks; and (2) the new situation in which the category of "non-combatant," whose activities and daily life had been separate from the war effort and the military outcome in the past, had become militarily meaningless. Of the two, the first was precisely the kind of issue in which the principle of civilian protection was supposed to influence the choice of the states concerned.[48] When new technologies that were potentially useful from a military viewpoint became available, states always had a choice of whether or not to employ them. If the principle of civilian protection had meant anything in such a choice, states might have chosen not to utilize new weapons that were inherently non-discriminatory, or new weapons that could be used in such a way to violate the principle of civilian protection. Such was not, however, what the international lawyers witnessed in the two World Wars. Indeed, the states extensively employed such weapons and technologies. Doctrines concerning what was permissible and what was impermissible in warfare had demonstrated little influence on the actions chosen by states in these wars.[49]

Against this background, the overall academic opinion in the post-World War periods was apologetic about the actual behavior of states concerning the principle of civilian protection. The apologetic perspective was so pervasive that until early 1970's, one could "legitimately ask himself whether the principle existed at all."[50]

Dismal Perspective: Unlikelihood of Closing the Gap The possibility of future compliance is a raison-d'être of the obligations of the law of war or of any law. The corollary of this thread of hope, though, is that if the perspective of future compliance is truly nil, if it possesses no deterring power whatsoever, the raison-d'être of that law also disappears. The international lawyers who adopted an apologetic position concerning the massive violations of the principle of civilian protection in past conflicts also adopted a similar pessimism concerning future conflicts.

To put it mildly, there was a feeling that "[I]n dealing with the laws of war it is no longer possible for any private writer to state rules with any confidence that they will be actually observed when war breaks out."[51] The gap between the principle of civilian protection and what actually occurred was so impressive that a number of writers abandoned the defense of the principle of civilian protection for the future completely. Thus, it was believed that not only "... the submarines made its own atrocious code" in the First World War, but that they would be used "even more effectively if another great maritime war ever comes."[52] After the Second World War, Fenwick stated: "The traditional laws of war are not likely, as such, to exercise any restraint upon military commanders."[53] In other words, "the only laws of war that would be likely to hold in a future war would be the moral instincts and restraints of the individual commanders."[54] The gap between the principle of civilian protection and the reality also led a substantial part of the academic community to deny vigorously the utility of the renewal of the law of war in this regard. For instance, a famous, but anonymous article that appeared in the British Yearbook of International Law in 1921 noted that "[I]t may well be doubted whether any rules which could at present be devised would really be adequate to the conduct of the next war."[55] This perception after the First World War was present in the post-Second World War period as well. Fenwick is categorical in stating that discussions concerning the future law of war made no sense.[56] When the nature of warfare changes further, "no rule which was contrary to the nature of war would be observed, and a rule that is not observed only serves to discredit the law."[57] Even Lauterpacht, Fenwick's contemporary, who was less pessimistic and approved the efforts to renew the law of war, thought it unwise to connect the new law of war to the old one. His position might be summarized as follows: The existing, recognized principle of the immunity of non-combatants proved to be unpersuasive in recent wars, and clearly, it could not ensure the future compliance. Therefore, if the new rules were to be formulated, and more importantly, obeyed, one should not "represent them as being governed by any recognized rules of international law."[58] Any connection with the old principle of distinction in the new law of war was only harmful.[59] The new law of war must be capable of ensuring future compliance, otherwise it would serve no purpose.

In sum, many international lawyers writing in both the post-World War I and post-World War II periods looked for closeness between the alleged principle of civilian protection and the actual behavior of states in the two World Wars, and abandoned the defense of the principle of civilian protection when they witnessed the gap between the principle and the actual behavior of states. They also predicted that the gap was unlikely to close in the future. They maintained that the principle of civilian protection had no normative strength to restrain the conducts of states, so there was no point in discussing its renewal or revision. They argued that what determined the content of the law of war was what the states actually did, and accepting such a view inevitably ended up in an apologetic view of the law. When the actual behavior of the states was taken as the most important indicator in assessing the principle prohibiting the indiscriminate attack on the civilian population or civilian objects, the only possible conclusion was that the principle was no longer valid, since there was no adherence to the principle.

Alternative Apologetic Explanations

Not all international lawyers, however, succumbed to the aforementioned apologetic view. There was also a vigorous defense of the principle of civilian protection in the corresponding periods. What is striking, though, is that their arguments in defense of the principle of civilian protection often equally concentrated on explaining the actual behavior of states: they explained that behavior from a different angle. Their defense of the principle of civilian protection capitalized on legal techniques that qualified the apparent violations differently. These legal techniques, however, operated within a framework that was analogous to that of the apologetic school: what the states actually did was critical in the assessment of a legal principle. As such, they offered little more than better apologies for what states did in these wars *vis-à-vis* civilian population and civilian objects.

First Technique: Distinguishing the Principle of Civilian Protection and its Efficacy The first of such techniques to defend the principle of civilian protection was to distinguish between the existence of the principle and its efficacy. Efficacy was understood as a power to induce compliance or the resulting situation in which the rule in question was being complied with. According to this defense, the contention that the principle of civilian protection was cast aside by violations in the war confused the principle itself and its efficacy.[60] The obligations of the law of war, such as distinguishing the civilian population and civilian objects at all times were not affected by past violations, in the sense that their existence was not identical to their actual efficacy.[61] This is a well accepted argument in the discipline of law, and international lawyers today also concur: "[J]ust as incidents of murder, robbery and rape do occur within national legal orders without destroying the system as such, so analogously assaults upon international legal rules point up the weaknesses of the system without denigrating their validity or their necessity."[62] It is simply less obvious in international law than in national legal systems because of the decentralized environment in which the former operates.[63] In any case, according to this interpretation, indiscriminate attacks on civilian population did not mean the end of its prohibition.[64]

In defending the principle of civilian protection, this technique tried to disconnect the alleged principle and the actual behavior of states in the wars. The suggested disconnection could offer a strong defense for the principle. Nonetheless, this disconnection between the principle and the actual behaviour of states could not be complete, because it lacked a firm ground on which such disconnection was suggested. For that reason, it had to be theoretically conceded that the principle could cease to be valid if all sides taking part in the war consistently violated the obligation in question without exception.[65] As an eminent contemporary of the defenders of the principle of civilian protection wrote, "[I]t is not necessary that all the norms of this order be always and without exception obeyed or applied; but it is necessary that they be on the whole efficacious."[66] Clearly, the defenders of the principle of civilian protection were not entirely free from the apologetic perspective.

Second Technique: Characterization of Violations as Reprisals International lawyers who wanted to defend the principle of civilian protection agreed with the apologists that legal norms must be reflected in the actual behavior of the states, at least to some degree. Consequently, they did not ignore the massive civilian casualties in the First and Second World Wars. They, however, resorted to an argument that characterized the behavior of the states differently, though they appeared at first glance to constitute a violation of the principle of civilian protection. While conceding that some violations were simply violations, other acts, equally derogating from the principle, were not characterized as violations. For example, it was argued that there were many instances in both the First World War and the Second World War, in which parties resorting to indiscriminate attacks qualified these acts as reprisals.[67] In the legal vocabulary, a "belligerent reprisal consists of action which would normally be contrary to the laws governing the conduct of armed conflict (the *jus in bello*) but which is justified because it is taken by one party to an armed conflict against another party in response to the latter's violation of the *jus in bello* - for example, the use of prohibited weapons in retaliation for their prior use by an adversary."[68]

In the First World War, France indicated that its bombardment of Freiburg and Carlsruhe was a reprisal to a similar indiscriminate bombardment that had been carried out by Germany.[69] Italy expressed its view that its indiscriminate attack on Austro-Hungarian Trieste was a reprisal to a similar Austrian attack on Venice.[70] Germany resorted to a similar argument of reprisal concerning their submarine warfare.[71] Whether these allegations were based on facts or not was not a primary concern of those scholars who underlined them. The point was what this attitude of states meant in terms of the contested principle of civilian protection. It, according to this argument, demonstrated the belief of these states that there was, indeed, a valid principle prohibiting an indiscriminate attack.[72] Unless the states thought that this principle was valid, they had no need to justify their actions as reprisals. In each of the cited examples, the principle of civilian protection was violated by

France, by Italy and by Germany, respectively. These violating parties invariably took the position that it was an act of reprisal. In doing so, France and Italy were in fact admitting that there was an obligation to refrain from indiscriminate attacks in aerial warfare. By resorting to the argument of reprisal, Germany also admitted that the maritime rule of assuring the safety for crew and passengers applied to submarine warfare. In all these cases, there was an obligation required by the principle of civilian protection that the acting parties were not fulfilling because of prior violations by other belligerents, but nevertheless an obligation that would have been observed if other belligerents had observed it.

Nonetheless, the legal technique of reprisal also operated within the apologetic perspective, attaching primary importance to what states actually did in assessing the principle of civilian protection. While the defending international lawyers sincerely believed in the values of the principle of civilian protection, they were also trapped in the apologetic view of the law and the inductive approach that it entailed.

Utopian Trend in the Contemporary Law of Armed Conflict

Unchanged Reality – Changed Perspective

The 1977 Additional Protocol I to the Geneva Conventions represented an unprecedented change for the protection of civilians in the law of armed conflict.[73] Unlike other binding documents of the law of armed conflict in the past, Additional Protocol I explicitly stipulated the protection of civilian in a very comprehensive way:[74] Article 48 stated, "[I]n order to ensure respect for and protection of the civilian population and civilian objects, the Parties to the conflict shall at all times distinguish between the civilian population and combatants and between civilian objects and military objectives and accordingly shall direct their operations only against military objectives." Similarly, provisions following Article 48 "spell[s] out unprecedentedly detailed rules relating to discrimination in the conduct of military attacks."[75] They were so detailed and comprehensive that some of their aspects were not without controversies, but the prohibition of targeting the civilian population and civilian objects and the principle of distinction underlying this prohibition were not opposed. In the meantime, the tone of writings on the law of armed conflict also changed accordingly. They gradually left its totally pessimistic view and reopened constructive discussions concerning the principle of civilian protection. The change in the academic circles is described by terms such as "reappearance", "restoration" and "resurrection" of the protection of civilians in the law of armed conflict.[76] Today, no one challenges that the principle of civilian protection is an integral part of the law of armed conflict, whatever its legal status may have been in 1945.[77] In fact, and more strikingly, no one seriously challenges the assertion today that even in non-international armed conflicts, the principle of civilian protection must apply as a matter of international humanitarian law.[78]

These assertions, however, are not easy to accept so long as one adheres to the apologetic view of the law of armed conflict, and emphasizes the importance of compliance in the behavior of the various antagonists in armed conflicts. This is especially true with regard to the principle of civilian protection in conflicts of a non-international character, which are the main form of armed conflict today. Indeed, it is often asserted that in these non-international armed conflicts, direct attacks upon the civilian population have "become a rather common feature of military conduct."[79] The lack of respect for the principle of civilian population in non-international armed conflicts could surely resuscitate the specter of the apologetic view, in spite of the codification efforts that produced two sets of provisions to regulate this type of armed conflicts: common Article 3 of 1949 Geneva Conventions,[80] and 1977 Additional Protocol II to these Conventions.[81] While common Article 3(1) of the Geneva Conventions specifically delineates provisions designed to protect those persons taking no active part in the hostilities, it does not explicitly prohibit indiscriminate attacks.[82] Moreover, it was intended to protect individual civilians rather than the civilian population as a whole,[83] so the content of the provision may not be identical to the principle of civilian protection in international armed conflicts.[84] Even more problematical was the exact meaning of the "armed conflict not of an international character" to which common Article 3 was applicable. In spite of many proposals in the preparatory work in this regard, no detailed criteria were agreed upon, so this became a loophole. The practice revealed that "[S]tates persistently refuse to acknowledge its application in situations where there is little doubt that the threshold requirements for its application have been met."[85] In a few of many examples, the concerned states such as France in Algeria (before 1956), the United Kingdom in the Northern Ireland (from 1971) and Russia in Chechnya (1994-1995) refused to apply common Article 3 to the internal conflict.[86] Furthermore, the practice also revealed that even when the parties to a civil war were willing to abide by Geneva Conventions, or more specifically, at least common Article 3, the violations were widespread, as it was the case in Yemen (1962-1967) and Bosnia (1992).[87]

Later, succinct provisions of common Article 3 were transformed into more detailed obligations by Additional Protocol II of 1977. Article 13(1) of Additional Protocol II provides that "the civilian population and individual civilians shall enjoy general protection against the dangers arising from military operations." Unlike common Article 3 of Geneva Conventions, Article 13(2) explicitly provides that the "civilian population as such, as well as individual civilians, shall not be the object of attack." These provisions of Additional Protocol II undoubtedly express the core obligation of the principle of civilian protection. At the same time, Additional Protocol II suffers from the same defects as common Article 3. First, the states themselves determine whether the requirements of applicability are satisfied or not. A state can always argue that the civil war it is dealing with does not meet these requirements, which are actually more narrowly constructed than common Article 3.[88] Second, even with this safety net for the states who do not wish to be regulated by Additional Protocol II, quite a few states that were involved in internal conflicts since 1977, in which humanitarian restraints appeared to be desperately needed, never joined Additional Protocol II.[89] Third, in recent internal conflicts that occurred in the territories of states that are party to Additional Protocol II, little humanitarian restraint was demonstrated.[90] One author even suggests that "Protocol II appears never to have been applied in a single armed conflict since its entry into force."[91]

Against this background, in spite of the codifications of the essence of the principle of civilian protection in common Article 3 and Additional Protocol II, it would be extremely difficult to contend that the codified norm is supported in practice. Consequently, the contention that the principle of civilian protection in internal wars is a customary principle would also be difficult to sustain. So long as one is bound by an excessively apologetic view of the law, it is expected that exclusive attention will be paid to the actual behaviour of states in battlefields. The question then is why the overwhelming majority of the academic writings today affirm the existence of the principle of civilian protection, even in case of internal wars. Given the unchanged fact that the principle of civilian protection continues to be violated, the change must be due to a shift in the perspectives of those members of the international legal community.

Less Apologetic – More Utopian

The change shows a shift from an apologetic perspective to a utopian perspective. The change of the perspective concerning the question of civilian protection is most visible in international jurisprudence. In examining the principle of civilian protection, international judicial institutions no longer exclusively examine the actual behavior of states in armed conflicts. Though actual behaviour is nominally looked at, much more weight is attached to other factors, not related to what parties to the conflict really do in international and non-international armed conflict. In short, there is a clear refutation of the apologetic approach to the question of the principle of civilian protection.

The International Court of Justice The first series of jurisprudence concerning the principle of civilian protection is produced by the International Court of Justice (referred to hereafter as the I.C.J.). In its 1996 advisory opinion that dealt with the question of the legality of threat and use of nuclear weapons (referred to hereafter as the *Legality of Nuclear Weapons* case),[92] the I.C.J. identified two "cardinal principles contained in texts constituting the fabric of humanitarian law."[93] One of them was the principle of civilian protection which, according to the I.C.J., "is aimed at the protection of civilian population and civilian objects and establishes the distinction between combatants and non-combatants." The principle means that "[S]tates must never make civilians the object of attack and must consequently never use weapons that are incapable of distinguishing between civilian and military targets."[94] In the identification of the principle of civilian protection, not a single reference was made to the actual behavior of states.[95] Moreover, the mention of the fact that the treaties of the law of armed conflict enjoy a broad accession is immediately followed by the statement that fundamental rules of this branch of law "constitute intransgressible principles of international customary law,"[96] always without any precise reference to the custom that is supposed to support these principles. The way the I.C.J. affirmed the principle of civilian protection is not easy to accept if one emphasizes the importance of custom or practice. Undoubtedly, it has "taken a somewhat creative approach to the law and some of its conclusions are not easy to justify by reference to the criteria for the determination of rules of customary international law,"[97] since a constant state practice is one of the criteria in ascertaining a customary rule. A careful reading of the arguments in the *Legality of Nuclear Weapons* case suggests that the force of ethics is at work in the identification of the principle of civilian protection.[98] Of course, the I.C.J. being a court of law, it was impossible for it to base its affirmation of the principle directly upon ethics. Ethics that supports the principle of civilian protection had to be in some way connected to the law in the judicial argument. In the *Legality of Nuclear Weapons* case, this link seems to be offered in either the "elementary considerations of humanity,"[99] or the Martens clause,[100] or possibly both.

Concerning the internal wars, the I.C.J. in the *Military and Paramilitary Activities in and against Nicaragua* case (referred to hereinafter as the *Nicaragua* case)[101] held that common Article 3 of Geneva Conventions was customary in nature, and that it was a minimum requirement relevant for both international and internal armed conflict.[102] As with the *Legality of Nuclear Weapons* case two decades later, this finding was not backed by a detailed inquiry into actual behaviors of states, either.[103] Though the term "customary" was ostensibly employed, certain principles in international humanitarian law were presented without specific examples constituting the custom.[104] From a viewpoint that equates rules and actual behavior, the finding "should be reproached for the virtual absence of discussion of the evidence and reasons supporting this conclusion."[105] The conclusion of the *Nicaragua* case concerning the norms enshrined in common Article 3, however, is largely accepted without criticism[106] or enthusiastically supported.[107]

International Criminal Tribunal for the former Yugoslavia Another series of international jurisprudence emanates from *ad hoc* international criminal tribunals, the International Criminal Tribunal for the former Yugoslavia (hereinafter referred to as the I.C.T.Y.) and the International Criminal Tribunal for Rwanda (hereinafter referred to as the I.C.T.R.). Their mandate is to apply the law set out in respective Statutes, and the law of armed conflict is at the core of such law, whose violations result in crimes with which these Tribunals are concerned. This law in each Statute, however, "leaves much room for constructive interpretation."[108] As a result, through their determinations of constitutive elements of the crimes and of the conditions and modalities of their applications, the I.C.T.Y. and the I.C.T.R. have greatly contributed to the development of the law of armed conflict.[109] The principle of civilian protection as an applicable principle in internal wars was extensively discussed in a well-known judgment by the Appeals Chamber of the I.C.T.Y. on the Defence Motion for Interlocutory Appeal on Jurisdiction rendered on October 2, 1995, in the *Prosecutor v. Dusko Tadic* case (hereinafter the *Tadic* case).[110] According to the judgment, "[T]he first rules that evolved in this area [customary law applicable to the civil wars] were aimed at protecting the civilian population from the hostilities."[111] In the course of this discussion on "formation of general rules or principles designed to protect civilians or civilian objects from the hostilities or, more generally, to protect those who do not (or no longer) take active part in hostilities" in civil wars, the Appeals Chamber declared that "[M]any provisions of this Protocol [Additional Protocol II] can now be regarded as declaratory of existing rules or as having crystallized emerging rules of customary law or else as having been strongly instrumental in their evolution as general principles."[112] Given the poor record of compliance with Additional Protocol II, such a conclusion is only possible by shifting the focus on the actual behavior of parties to internal armed conflicts to something else. In this regard, what the Appeals Chamber did was two-fold. On one hand, it took a very broad understanding of state practice when it discussed the evidence supporting the principle of civilian protection as a legal rule in civil wars. It thus discussed verbal statements by governments rather than their actual conducts,[113] verbal statements by insurgents in civil wars rather than what they actually did,[114] resolutions of the League of Nations and the United Nations calling for the respect of principle of civilian protection in civil wars rather than the concrete situations related to the adoption of such resolutions,[115] national military manuals rather than the examination of what their armed forces actually do,[116] and so on. On the other hand, the argument supporting the principle of civilian protection in civil wars in the *Tadic* case was also based on the general purpose of international humanitarian law and its logic, and not exclusively on state practice. Thus, the question that the Appeals Chamber asked was: "Why protect civilians from belligerent violence, or ban rape, torture or the wanton destruction of hospitals, churches, museums or private property, as well as proscribe weapons causing unnecessary suffering when two sovereign States are engaged in war and yet refrain from enacting the same bans or providing the same protection when armed violence has erupted 'only' within the territory of a sovereign State?"[117] Of course, this is just a rhetorical question that prepares the foreground for its affirmative statement: "If international law, while of course duly safeguarding the legitimate interests of States, must gradually turn to the protection of human beings, it is only natural that the aforementioned dichotomy should gradually lose its weight."[118]

The fact that the Appeals Chamber "relied on such verbal evidence as statements, resolutions and declarations rather than battlefield or operational practice, which it largely ignored"[119] should have invited criticisms from the viewpoint that accords importance to the actual behavior of states in ascertainment of legal rules. There seems to be, however, strong support for both the conclusion drawn and the way it was reached.[120] The approach is defended as legitimate, in that it "helps to compensate for scarcity of supporting practice."[121] Concerning the humanitarian purpose to which an important place is also given in the assessment of the principle of civilian protection, it can also be criticized as "a tendency ... to assume that noble humanitarian principles that deserve recognition as the positive law of the international community have in fact been recognized as such by states."[122] Without a demonstration of such a recognition, the approach would dangerously merge the ethics and the law. In spite of this danger, this argument also found a support in the academic opinion.[123]

Balancing the Two Approaches

In the jurisprudence of the I.C.J. and the I.C.T.Y. concerning the principle of civilian protection in armed conflict, the relationship between the principle of civilian protection and the actual behaviour of states has not been seriously pursued. The change in the perspective is a welcome one. After what the discipline had been through in the two post-World War periods concerning the principle of civilian protection, the danger of the excessively apologetic view in this area of law is clear. There is no way that actual behaviors of states match the ethical expectations, and too much emphasis on the actual behavior has to come to an apologetic conclusion. Contemporary jurisprudence clearly refutes the apologetic approach to the question of principle of civilian protection, whether it is in international or internal armed conflict. Principles that constitute the cornerstones of the law of armed conflict, such as the principle of civilian protection, are, by nature, aspirational and utopian. Indeed, precisely because reality is far from utopia, the principle of civilian protection is needed in situations of armed conflict.

At the same time, a complete shift from the apologetic view to the utopian view would be harmful. A law of armed conflict which is purely aspirational and is not supported by the actors concerned would exert no influence on the parties to the armed conflicts, and would serve no purpose.[124] The principle of civilian protection and other rules of international humanitarian law "need not necessarily be in strict accordance with state practice, which is in some cases quite abhorrent, but it must be structured with some awareness of current military practices and of existing military technology."[125] Moreover, describing aspirations that have no support in practice as legal principles may appear arbitrary unless they are founded on something justifiable. In this light, the efforts in contemporary jurisprudence to frame the debate in terms of state practice and customary law are indispensable, even if they seem to be stretched at times. This is not only because of the competence of these judicial organs that does not include the application of non-law such as ethical aspirations. They must not be dispensed with, since, for the principle of civilian protection to be relevant and purposeful, it must be grounded in reality.

The majority of contemporary writers on this subject seem to be aware of the necessity of maintaining a balance between normative, prescriptive standards and reality. Thus, unlike the international lawyers of two post-World War periods, they try to avoid the excessive apology, but they are not excessively idealist and utopian, either.

On one hand, contemporary writers are generally ready to accept that the law of armed conflict and its principles, such as that of civilian protection, are nonetheless to be violated, even frequently.[126] They are, however, not so inductive as the international lawyers of the post-World War periods and not bothered by phenomena of violations, and they affirm the principle of civilian protection. Their reasoning in affirming the principle is often deductive, at least in part. This is visible, for example, in the way the expressions drawn from Martens clause such as "laws of humanity" and "dictates of public conscience" are employed in defending the principle of civilian protection.[127] Some writers even explicitly admit the influence of ethics as a part of the law of armed conflict.[128]

On the other hand, they do not subscribe to a completely utopian and deductive affirmation of the principle that has no support in reality. The way in which the point of contact with reality is assured by contemporary writers is multiple: state practice as evidence of the principle of civilian protection is widely construed and is not limited to what states actually do in battlefields;[129] military manuals are presented as instruments that create mutual expectations of compliance and, hence, as evidence of the contended principle; expressions of international organizations supporting the principle of civilian protection in concrete cases, such as those of the United Nations Security Council, are emphasized.[130] It suffices to look into the recent study by the International Committee of the Red Cross[131] as the best illustration of this trend. This authoritative work identified the principle of distinction between civilians and combatants as a customary rule, and in its second volume named "Practice", discussed a very wide range of practice, not at all confined to what states actually do in battlefields. In this work, 25 Military Manuals are cited as national practice concerning the principle of distinction in international armed conflicts.[132] National legislation that refers to the corresponding articles of Geneva Conventions and Additional Protocol I is also cited as practice.[133] Other types of national practice such as reports to the national legislative organ are also included.[134] Concerning the same principle for internal armed conflicts, national case-law is also cited. Practice supporting the principle of distinction in this study also includes practice of international organizations, international conferences, and international jurisprudence. What this method of study reveals is the contemporary trend concerning the principle of civilian protection, in which the reality outside the battlefields is also considered in the balancing between reality and the law.

Conclusion

The two periods studied in this chapter showed a striking shift from the apologetic view to the utopian view in assessing the principle of civilian protection in armed conflict. Many international lawyers of the post-World War periods of the last century focused on the actual behavior of states in battlefields in their assessment of the principle of civilian protection. Given massive violations and too few examples of compliance, their perspective inevitably led them to negate the principle itself. They had to find apologies for the violations of the principle of civilian protection in these two World Wars. In contrast, in contemporary jurisprudence and academic writings, much less weight is accorded to what the states actually do to the civilian population and civilian objects in armed conflict. The utopian view stresses the aspirations of the law of armed conflict, thus enabling the affirmation of the principle of civilian protection, applicable even in non-international armed conflicts where violations most probably outnumber compliance.

The shift in the perspective which allowed a disconnection between the principle and the narrowly-construed state practice is a welcome one. For obvious reasons, however, this disconnection must not be complete. The apologetic perspective and utopian perspective may appear to be a set of parallel lines of dilemma that can never meet. But it is not so: only by maintaining both perspectives and retaining them both, can the law of armed conflict preserve itself in a meaningful way, just as the rest of the discipline of public international law has always done.[135]

Notes

[1] Koskenniemi, 1989.

[2] Koskenniemi, 1990, p. 8.

[3] In this chapter, the term "law of war" is mainly used in the discussion pertaining to the inter-war period, according to the common usage then. The term "the law of armed conflict" is used otherwise. For the question of semantic preferences, Dinstein, 2004, pp. 12-14.

[4] Gardam, 1993, p. 2; Henckaerts and Doswald-Beck, 2005, vol 1, p. 6.

[5] Article 25, Convention with respect to the Laws and Customs of War On Land (Hague Convention No. II). "The attack or bombardment of towns, villages, habitations or buildings which are not defended, is prohibited."

[6] Article 25, Convention Respecting the Laws and Customs of War on Land (Hague Convention No. IV). "The attack or bombardment, by whatever means, of towns, villages, dwellings, or buildings which are undefended is prohibited."

[7] Bugnion, 1994, p. 833; Henckaerts and Doswald-Beck, 2005, vol 1, p. 3.

[8] Roach, 2000, p. 70.

[9] Naval War College, 1906, pp. 146-53.

[10] Roach, 2000, p. 70.

[11] See, for instance, Naval War College, 1902, pp. 5-37; Naval War College, 1904, pp. 23-27.

[12] *Infra, "Violations in Reality and Apologies in the Doctrine".*

[13] Grewe, 2000, p. 607.

[14] Garner, 1936, pp. 101-103. For the discussions concerning the aerial bombardment and the civilian immunity in the League of Nations in 1930's, see Sibert, 1955.

[15] Aldrich, 2000, pp. 48-51.

[16] Rules concerning the Control of Wireless Telegraphy in Time of War and Air Warfare, drafted by a Commission of Jurists at the Hague, 1923.

[17] Article 22.

[18] McCoubrey, 1998, p. 220; Greenwood, 1999, p. 21; Bugnion, 1994, p. 836.

[19] Green, 1999, p. 580.

[20] Biddle, 1994, p. 150.

[21] Schindler, 2003, p. 169.

[22] Treaty relating to the Use of Submarines and Noxious Gases in Warfare, 6 Feb. 1922, annexed to the Treaty for the Limitation of Naval Armament.

[23] Diena, 1921, p.468.

[24] Grewe, 2000, p. 607.

[25] Article 22, Treaty for the Limitation and Reduction of Naval Armaments.
"The following are accepted as established rules of international law:
(1) In their action with regard to merchant ships, submarines must conform to the rules of international law to which surface vessels are subject.
(2) In particular, except in the case of persistent refusal to stop on being duly summoned, or of active resistance to visit or search, a warship, whether surface vessel or submarine, may not sink or render incapable of navigation a merchant vessel without having first placed passengers, crew and ship's papers in a place of safety. For this purpose the ship's boats are not regarded as a place of safety unless the safety of the passengers and crew is assured, in the existing sea and weather conditions, by the proximity of land, or the presence of another vessel which is in a position to take them on board."

[26] Grewe, 2000, p. 607.

[27] Cited in Gardam, 1993, pp. 24-25.

[28] Geneva Convention for the Amelioration of the Condition of the Wounded and Sick in Armed Forces in the Field; Geneva Convention for the Amelioration of the Condition of the Wounded, Sick and Shipwrecked Members of the Armed Forces at Sea; Geneva Convention Relative to the Treatment of Prisoners of War; Geneva Convention Relative to the Protection of Civilian Persons in Time of War.

[29] Gutteridge, 1949, p. 319. Greenwood gives concrete examples of persons that fall outside the protection provided by this Convention, Christopher Greenwood, 2003, p. 812.

[30] Sibert, 1955, p. 182.

[31] Draper, 1989, p. 14.

[32] Schindler, 2003, p. 171.

[33] Doswald-Beck, 1989, p. 150.

[34] Fenwick, 1934 (originally in 1924), p. 28.

[35] Jaworski, 2004, pp. 95-97.

[36] Jaworski, 2004, pp. 95-97; Castrén, 1955, p. 133; Blix, 1978, p. 33; Doswald-Beck, 1989, p. 144.

[37] Lauterpacht, 1952, p. 370.

[38] Lauterpacht, 1952, p. 374.

[39] Lauterpacht, 1952, p. 374.

[40] Fenwick, 1952, p. 564.

[41] Oppenheim (Lauterpacht ed.), 1952, vol 2, p. 529.

[42] Oppenheim (Lauterpacht ed.), 1952, vol 2, p. 529.

[43] Schwarzenberger, 1958, p. 19.

[44] Fenwick, 1952, p. 566.

[45] Biddle, 1994, pp. 145-146.

[46] Eagleton, 1941, p. 660.

[47] Fenwick, 1949, p. 110.

[48] Castrén, 1955, p. 132.

[49] "The history of bombardment regulation shows a distinct utilitarian development, in which the idea of military effectiveness dominates, and in which the doctrines of permissible violence and social sanction are of secondary importance as checks or influences." Royse, 1928, p. 147. A similar observation concerning the Second World War is found in Best, 1994, pp. 278-281.

[50] Doswald-Beck, 1989, p. 137.

[51] Smith, 1950 (originally in 1948), p. 74.

[52] Dickinson, 1925, p. 27.

[53] Fenwick, 1952, p. 551.

[54] Fenwick, 1952, p. 551, note 41.

[55] anon., 1920.

[56] Fenwick, 1952, p. 550, note 36. His despair vis-à-vis the law of war is so complete that '[H]is present attitude is expressed by the fact that the chapters on war of the present edition have been put in the past tense.'

[57] Fenwick, 1949, p. 113.

[58] Lauterpacht, 1952, p. 379.

[59] Nurick, 1945, pp. 696-697.

[60] Nippold, 2004 (originally in 1923), pp. 133-134.

[61] Kunz, 1934, p. 32.

[62] Shaw, 2003, p. 7.

[63] Brownlie, 1995, pp. 31-35.

[64] The same argument is offered by Moore, 1987 (originally in 1924), p. 35; Kunz, 1951, p. 45.

[65] Kunz, 1951, p. 51.
[66] Kelsen, 1997 (originally in 1942), p. 15.
[67] In this chapter, the term "reprisal" refers to "belligerent reprisal." The discussion is limited to the reprisals in the law of war, as opposed to reprisals or countermeasures in general international law. For the relation between belligerent reprisals and reprisals in general international law, see Provost, 2002, pp. 182-83.
[68] Greenwood, 1989, p. 38.
[69] Garner, 1920, pp. 462-465.
[70] Garner, 1920, pp. 462-463.
[71] Garner, 1920, p. 377.
[72] Kunz, 1951, p. 45.
[73] Protocol Additional to the Geneva Conventions of 12 August 1949, and Relating to the Protection of Victims of Non-International Armed Conflicts (referred to hereafter as Additional Protocol I).
[74] Detter, 2000, pp. 285, 288.
[75] Roberts and Guelff, 2000, p. 420.
[76] Doswald-Beck, 1989, pp. 150-151.
[77] Rogers, 2004, p. 17.
[78] Shaw, 2003, pp. 1068-1076. See also U.K. Ministry of Defence, 2004, pp. 381-382.
[79] Spieker, 2001, p. 146. The examples cited are conflicts in Sudan, Kosovo and Bosnia-Herzegovina.
[80] For the drafting history of common Article 3, see Moir, 1998, pp. 355-361.
[81] Protocol Additional to the Geneva Conventions of 12 August 1949, and Relating to the Protection of Victims of Non-International Armed Conflicts, 1977 (referred to hereafter as Additional Protocol II).
[82] "In the case of armed conflict not of an international character occurring in the territory of one of the High Contracting Parties, each Party to the conflict shall be bound to apply, as a minimum, the following provisions:

(1) Persons taking no active part in the hostilities, including members of armed forces who have laid down their arms and those placed 'hors de combat' by sickness, wounds, detention, or any other cause, shall in all circumstances be treated humanely, without any adverse distinction founded on race, colour, religion or faith, sex, birth or wealth, or any other similar criteria.

To this end, the following acts are and shall remain prohibited at any time and in any place whatsoever with respect to the above-mentioned persons:

(a) violence to life and person, in particular murder of all kinds, mutilation, cruel treatment and torture;

(b) taking of hostages;

(c) outrages upon personal dignity, in particular humiliating and degrading treatment;
(d) the passing of sentences and the carrying out of executions without previous judgment pronounced by a regularly constituted court, affording all the judicial guarantees which are recognized as indispensable by civilized peoples."
[83] Moir, 2002, pp. 116-117.
[84] Detter, 2000, p. 288.
[85] Gardam, 1993, p. 168.
[86] For more examples, Provost, 2002, p. 268.
[87] Moir, 2002, pp. 83-85.
[88] While common Article 3 is applicable to "armed conflict not of an international character occurring in the territory of one of the High Contracting Parties," Additional Protocol II

only applies to conflicts of certain scale and intensity according to its Article 1, which are not requirements of the applicability of common Article 3.

[89] Moir, 2002, p. 120.
[90] Moir, 2002, pp. 120-132. The cases of attacks upon civilians examined are civil wars of El Salvador, Rwanda, Bosnia-Herzegovina and Chechnya.
[91] Tomuschat, 2003, p. 253.
[92] Legality of the Threat or Use of Nuclear Weapons, 1996 I.C.J. 226 (July 8).
[93] *Legality of Nuclear Weapons* case, para. 78.
[94] *Legality of Nuclear Weapons* case, para. 78.
[95] Dupuy, 1999a, p. 455.
[96] *Legality of Nuclear Weapons* case, para. 79.
[97] Greenwood, 2003, p. 816.
[98] Dominicé, 2003, p. 85; Dupuy, 1999a, pp. 455-456.
[99] *Legality of Nuclear Weapons* case, para. 79. Dupuy, 1999b, p. 127.
[100] *Legality of Nuclear Weapons* case, para. 78. Dupuy, 1999a, p. 454.
[101] Military and Paramilitary Activities in and against Nicaragua (Nicar. v. U.S.), Merits, 1986 ICJ Rep. 14 (June 27).
[102] *Nicaragua* case, para. 218.
[103] Meron, 1987, pp. 357-358.
[104] Dominicé, 2003, p. 85.
[105] Meron, 1987, p. 358.
[106] McCoubrey, 1998, p. 256; Ronzitti, 2001, p. 303.
[107] Gardam, 1993, pp. 167-171.
[108] Abi-Saab, 1999, p. 651.
[109] Abi-Saab, 1999, p. 651.
[110] *Prosecutor v. Dusko Tadic* (Appeal) (Decision on the Defence Motion for Interlocutory Appeal on Jurisdiction), ICTY, Appeals Chamber, Decision of 2 Oct. 1995 (Case No. IT-94-1-AR 72), reprinted in *International Legal Materials*, 36 (1996): 32 [hereinafter *Tadic* case]. For the overall picture of the case, see Greenwood, 1996; Warbrick and Rowe, 1996.
[111] *Tadic* case, para. 100.
[112] *Tadic* case, para. 117.
[113] *Tadic* case, para. 105.
[114] *Tadic* case, para. 106.
[115] *Tadic* case, para. 101 and para. 110-111, 114, respectively.
[116] *Tadic* case, para. 106, 118.
[117] *Tadic* case, para. 97.
[118] *Tadic* case, para. 97.
[119] Meron, 1996, p. 239.
[120] Moir, 2002, p. 144.
[121] Meron, 1996, p. 240.
[122] Fenrick, 1997, p. 40-41.
[123] Meron, 2003, pp. 535-538.
[124] Doswald-Beck, 1998, pp. 39-75.
[125] Fenrick, 1997, p. 27.
[126] Cassese, 2004, p. 432; David, 2002, pp. 851-920.
[127] Bugnion, 1994, p. 847. He defends the principle of civilian protection as applied to internal wars.
[128] Detter, 2000, p. 438.
[129] Meron, 1996 ; Abi-Saab, 2003.

[130] Tomuschat, 2003, p. 261; Abi-Saab, 2003, pp. 28-29.
[131] Henckaerts and Doswald-Beck, 2005.
[132] Henckaerts and Doswald-Beck, 2005, vol 2, pp. 4-7.
[133] Henckaerts and Doswald-Beck, 2005, vol 2, p. 7.
[134] Henckaerts and Doswald-Beck, 2005, vol 2, p. 7-10.
[135] Koskenniemi, 1990, p. 8.

References

Abi-Saab, Georges 'International Criminal Tribunals and the Development of International Humanitarian and Human Rights Law', in E. Yakpo and T. Boumedra (eds.), *Liber Amicorum – Judge Mohammed Bedjaoui* (The Hague: Kluwer Law International, 1999), pp. 649-658.

Abi-Saab Georges, 'Les Protocoles additionnels, 25 ans après', in J.-F. Flauss (ed.), *Les nouvelles frontières du droit international humanitaire* (Bruxelles: Bruylant, 2003), pp. 17-39.

Aldrich, George H. 'The Law of War on Land', *American Journal of International Law*, 94 (2000): 42-63.

anonymous., 'The League of Nations and the Laws of War', *British Yearbook of International Law*, 1 (1920): 109-124.

Best, Geoffrey *War and Law since 1945* (Oxford: Clarendon Press, 1994).

Biddle, Tami Davis 'Air Power', in M. Howard, G. J. Andreopoulos and M. R. Shulman (eds.), *The Laws of War: Constraints on Warfare in the Western World* (New Haven: Yale University Press, 1994), pp. 140-159.

Blix, Hans 'Area Bombardment: Rules and Reasons', *British Yearbook of International Law,* 49 (1978): 31-69.

Brownlie, Ian 'International Law at the Fiftieth Anniversary of the United Nations', *Recueil des cours*, 255 (1995): 9-228.

Bugnion, François *Le Comité international de la Croix-Rouge et la protection des victimes de la guerre* (Genève: Comité international de la Croix-Rouge, 1994).

Cassese, Antonio *International Law*, 2nd edn (Oxford: Oxford University Press, 2004).

Castrén, Erik 'La protection juridique de la population dans la guerre moderne', *Revue générale de droit international public*, 26 (1955): 121-136.

David, Eric *Principes de droit des conflits armés*, 3rd edn (Bruxelles: Bruylant, 2002).

Dickinson, Edwin D. 'The New Law of Nations', *West Virginia Law Quarterly*, 32 (1925): 4-32.

Diena, Giulio 'Il trattato di Washington circa l'uso dei sottomarini e dei gas nocivi in guerra', *Rivista di diritto internazionale*, 14 (1921): 465-478.

Dinstein, Yoram *The Conduct of Hostilities under the Law of International Armed Conflict* (Cambridge: Cambridge University Press, 2004).

Dominicé, Christian 'L'application du droit international humanitaire par la Cour internationale de justice', in J.-F. Flauss (ed.), *Les nouvelles frontières du droit international humanitaire* (Bruxelles: Bruylant, 2003), pp. 81-88.

Doswald-Beck, Louise 'The Value of the 1977 Geneva Protocols for the Protection of Civilians', in M. A. Meyer (ed.), *Armed Conflict and the New Law: Aspects of the 1977 Geneva Protocols and the 1981 Weapons Convention* (London: British Institute of International and Comparative Law, 1989), pp. 137-172.

Doswald-Beck, Louise 'Implementation of International Humanitarian Law in Future Wars', in M. N. Schmitt and L. C. Green (eds.), *The Law of Armed Conflict: Into the Next Millennium* (Newport: Naval War College, 1998), pp. 39-75.

Draper, G. I. A. D. 'Humanitarianism in the Modern Law of Armed Conflicts', in M. A. Meyer (ed.), *Armed Conflict and the New Law: Aspects of the 1977 Geneva Protocols and the 1981 Weapons Convention* (London: British Institute of International and Comparative Law, 1989), pp. 3-21.

Dupuy, Pierre-Marie 'Between the Individual and the State: International Law at a Crossroads?', in L. B. de Chazournes and P. Sands (eds.), *International Law, the International Court of Justice and Nuclear Weapons* (Cambridge: Cambridge University Press, 1999a), pp. 449-461.

Dupuy, Pierre-Marie 'Les "considérations élémentaires d'humanité" dans la jurisprudence de la Cour internationale de justice', in R.-J. Dupuy (ed.), *Mélanges en l'honneur de Nicolas Valticos: Droit et justice* (Paris: Pedone, 1999b), pp. 117-130.

Eagleton, Clyde 'Of the Illusion that War does not Change', *American Journal of International Law*, 35 (1941): 659-662.

Fenrick, W. J. 'Prosecuting International Crimes - An Inside View: International Humanitarian Law and Criminal Trials', *Transnational Law and Contemporary Problems*, 7 (1997): 23-43.

Fenwick, Charles G. *International Law*, 2nd, revised and enlarged edn (New York: D. Appleton-Century Company, 1934 [originally in 1924]).

Fenwick, Charles G. *International Law*, 3rd edn (New York: Appleton-Century-Crofts, Inc., 1952).

Fenwick, Charles G. Discussion of the Fourth Session, Forty-Third Annual Meeting of the American Society of International Law, *Proceedings of the American Society of International Law*, 43 (1949): 109-114.

Gardam, Judith Gail *Non-Combatant Immunity as a Norm of International Humanitarian Law* (Dordrecht: Martinus Nijhoff Publishers, 1993).

Garner, James Wilford *International Law and the World War* (2 vols, London: Longmans, Green & Co., 1920).

Garner, James Wilford 'Les lois de la guerre, leur valeur, leur avenir', *Revue de droit international et de législation comparée*, 17 (1936): 96-117.

Green, Leslie C. *The Contemporary Law of Armed Conflict*, 2nd edn (Manchester: Manchester University Press, 1993).

Green, Leslie C. *Essays on the Modern Law of War* (Ardsley: Transnational Publishers, Inc., 1999).

Greenwood, Christopher 'The Twilight of the Law of Belligerent Reprisals', *Netherlands Yearbook of International Law*, 20 (1989): 35-69.

Greenwood, Christopher 'International Humanitarian Law and the *Tadic* Case', *European Journal of International Law*, 7 (1996): 265-283.

Greenwood, Christopher 'Historical Development and Legal Basis', in D. Fleck

(ed.), *The Handbook of Humanitarian Law in Armed Conflicts* (Oxford: Oxford University Press, 1999), pp. 1-38.
Greenwood, Christopher, 'The Law of War (International Humanitarian Law)', in M. D. Evans (ed.), *International Law* (Oxford: Oxford University Press, 2003), pp. 789-823.
Grewe, Wilhelm G. *The Epochs of International Law*, ed. & trans. M. Byers (Berlin: Walter De Gruyter, 2000).
Gutteridge, Joyce A. 'The Geneva Conventions of 1949', *British Yearbook of International Law*, 26 (1949): 294-326.
Henckaerts, Jean-Marie, and Doswald-Beck, Louise (eds.), *Customary International Humanitarian Law* (2 vols, Cambridge: Cambridge University Press, 2005).
Jaworski, Eric '"Military Necessity" and "Civilian Immunity": Where is the Balance?', in S. Yee (ed.), *International Crime and Punishment, Selected Issues*, vol. 2 (Dallas: University Press of America, 2004), pp. 87-127.
Kelsen, Hans *Law and Peace in International Relations* (Buffalo: Williams S. Hein and Co., Inc., 1997 [originally in Cambridge, Massachusetts: Harvard University Press, 1942]).
Koskenniemi, Martti *From Apology to Utopia: the Structure of International Legal Argument* (Helsinki: Finnish Lawyers' Publishing Company, 1989).
Koskenniemi, Martti 'Politics of International Law', *European Journal of International Law*, 1 (1990): 3-32.
Kunz, Joseph L. 'Plus de lois de la guerre?', *Revue générale de droit international public*, 41 (1934): 22-57.
Kunz, Josef L. 'The Chaotic Status of the Laws of War and the Urgent Necessity for their Revision', *American Journal of International Law*, 45 (1951): 37-61.
Lauterpacht, Hersch 'The Problem of the Law of War', *British Yearbook of International Law*, 29 (1952): 360-382.
McCoubrey, Hilaire, *International Humanitarian Law: Modern Developments in the Limitation of Warfare*, 2nd edn (Aldershot: Ashgate, 1998).
Meron, Theodor 'The Geneva Conventions as Customary Law', *American Journal of International Law*, 81 (1987): 348-369.
Meron, Theodor 'The Continuing Role of Custom in the Formation of International Humanitarian Law', *American Journal of International Law*, 90 (1996): 238-249.
Meron, Theodor 'Cassese's *Tadic* and the Law of Non-International Armed Conflicts', in L. C. Vohrah, F. Pocar, Y. Featherstsone, O. Fourmy, C. Graham, J. Hocking and N. Robson (eds.), *Man's Inhumanity to Man, Essays on International Law in Honour of Antonio Cassese* (The Hague: Kluwer Law International, 2003), pp. 533-538.
Moir, Lindsay 'The Historical Development of the Application of Humanitarian Law in Non-International Armed Conflicts to 1949', *International Comparative Law Quarterly*, 47 (1998): 337-361.
Moir, Lindsay *The Law of Internal Armed Conflict* (Cambridge: Cambridge University Press, 2002).
Moore, John Bassett, 'International Law and Some Current Illusions', in

International Law and Some Current Illusions and Other Essays (Colorado: Fred B. Rothman & Co., 1987 [originally in New York: Macmillan, 1924]), pp. 1-39.

Naval War College, *International Law Situations 1901* (Washington: Government Printing Office, 1902).

Naval War College, *International Law Discussions 1903* (Washington: Government Printing Office, 1904).

Naval War College, *International Law Topics and Discussions 1905* (Washington: Government Printing Office, 1906).

Nippold, Otfried *The Development of International Law After the World War*, trans. A.S. Hershey (Clark: Lawbook Exchange, 2004 [originally in Oxford: Clarendon Press, 1923]).

Nurick, Lester 'The Distinction between Combatant and Noncombatant in the Law of War', *American Journal of International Law*, 39 (1945): 680-697.

Oppenheim, Lassa *International Law: A Treatise (Vol. II, Disputes, War and Neutrality)*, 7th edn, ed. H. Lauterpacht (London: Longmans, Green & Co., 1952).

Provost, René *International Human Rights and Humanitarian Law* (Cambridge: Cambridge University Press, 2002).

Roach, J. Ashley 'The Law of Naval Warfare at the Turn of Two Centuries', *American Journal of International Law*, 94 (2000): 64-77.

Roberts, Adams, and Guelff (eds.), Richard, *Documents on The Laws of War*, 3rd edn (Oxford: Oxford University Press, 2000).

Rogers, A.P.V. *Law on the Battlefield*, 2nd edn (Manchester: Manchester University Press, 2004).

Ronzitti, Natalino *Diritto internazionale dei conflitti armati*, 2nd edn (Turin: Giappichelli, 2001).

Royse, M.W., *Aerial Bombardment and the International Regulation of Warfare* (New York: Harold Vinal, Ltd., 1928).

Schindler, Dietrich 'International Humanitarian Law: Its Remarkable Development and its Persistent Violation', *Journal of the History of International Law*, 5 (2003): 165-188.

Schwarzenberger, Georg *The Legality of Nuclear Weapons* (London: London Institute of World Affairs, 1958).

Shaw, Malcolm N. *International Law*, 5th edn (Cambridge: Cambridge University Press, 2003).

Sibert, Marcel 'Remarques et suggestions sur la protection des populations civiles contre les bombardements aériens', *Revue générale de droit international public*, 26 (1955): 177-192.

Smith, H.A. *The Law and Custom of the Sea*, 2nd edn (London: Stevens & Sons Limited, 1950 [originally in 1948]).

Spieker, Heike 'Twenty-Five Years After the Adoption of Additional Protocol II: Breakthrough or Failure of Humanitarian Legal Protection?', *Yearbook of International Humanitarian Law*, 4 (2001):129-166.

Tomuschat, Christian *Human Rights Between Idealism and Realism* (Oxford: Oxford University Press, 2003).

U.K. Ministry of Defence, *The Manual of the Law of Armed Conflict* (Oxford: Oxford University Press, 2004).

Warbrick, Colin and Rowe, Peter 'The International Criminal Tribunal for Yugoslavia: The Decision of the Appeals Chamber on the Interlocutory Appeal on Jurisdiction in the *Tadic* Case', *International and Comparative Law Quarterly*, 45 (1996): 691-701.

Chapter 5

Detention, the 'War on Terror' and International Law

Françoise J. Hampson

Introduction

Since the attacks on the Twin Towers, the Pentagon and another target on September 11, 2001 and as a result of laws, policies and practices implemented or applied in a novel way since then, a large number of people have been detained.[1] The variety of such detentions is striking. They include citizens detained in their own country as enemy combatants;[2] foreigners detained on account of alleged immigration law irregularities;[3] foreigners subject to indefinite detention in national territory on the grounds that they represent a threat to national security but cannot be returned to their country of origin on account of the risk of ill-treatment[4] and foreigners detained outside national territory, potentially indefinitely.[5] A very wide range of States have transferred persons within their jurisdiction to the authorities of another State, where again they may be held indefinitely and may be subjected to proscribed ill-treatment.[6] Such transfers are usually effected without any form of judicial process. They have even taken place in defiance of the orders of the territorial State's judicial authorities.[7] In certain cases, the detentions have been concealed.[8]

This chapter seeks to examine the international legal rules regulating such detentions and transfers. The focus will be principally on international law and not on domestic law, except where the latter claims to be giving effect to the former. It will also consider the status of the different categories of detainees and the rights flowing from such status. For reasons of space and since the issue has been extensively canvassed elsewhere,[9] this text will not address the conditions in which the detainees are held or the treatment to which they are subjected. In order to establish the relevant rules, it is first necessary to consider the potentially applicable legal regimes and then to determine whether they are, in fact, applicable.

It is necessary to sound a note of caution at the outset. There may be a difference between what certain commentators say the law is and what the law is in fact.[10] This is particularly likely to be the case where a person wishes to be able to set aside an inconvenient norm. If the principle in question is interpreted too broadly, it becomes easy to argue that the law is ridiculous and does not answer to current concerns and that it should therefore be ignored. That can also happen, but is less likely, the other way round. That is to say that a commentator who wishes to show that a legal rule remains relevant may be tempted to shape its interpretation so as to make possible novel applications and to avoid the possibility of the law not allowing States to do what they can plausibly argue they need to do. Both of these phenomena, based on the subservience of legal analysis to political agendas, albeit ones of a different type, must be distinguished from an analysis of state practice that suggests that a norm has been interpreted in practice in a way different from the precise wording of the rule.[11] It should also be remembered that the scope of a principle may be unclear without in any way undermining the core of it. Similarly, the potential applicability of a norm is not prejudiced by a finding that it does not apply to the facts of the particular case. There is a fundamental difference between calling into question the applicability of a particular, or indeed any, legal regime and questioning the applicability of a rule on the facts.

Potentially Applicable International Legal Regimes

Without wishing to enter the controversy as to whether international law is one train with many carriages or many different trains,[12] it is clear that some bodies of rules only apply in certain circumstances. The application of international humanitarian law, for example, is principally confined to situations of armed conflict.[13] This raises the possibility that more than one legal regime may be simultaneously applicable. It is necessary to consider the potential applicability of human rights law, the law of armed conflict (LOAC) and international criminal law.

Human Rights Law

The term human rights law is used to include both the international and regional treaty obligations of States and also those human rights obligations flowing, directly or indirectly from the UN Charter.[14] That said, the principal focus will be on treaty commitments.

There are two separate bases on which the potential applicability of human rights law to post 9/11 operations may be called into question. First, it might be the case that, where the law of armed conflicts is applicable, it displaces the applicability of human rights law. Second, commitments under human rights law might be confined to national territory. These will be examined in turn.

Whether the applicability of human rights law is displaced by the applicability of the law of armed conflict. The language of the International Covenant on Civil and Political Rights (ICCPR),[15] of the European Convention on Human Rights (ECHR)[16] and of the American Convention on Human Rights (ACHR)[17] expressly recognises that some rights remain applicable even during war (ECHR and ACHR only) and serious public emergencies.[18] The treaties envisage that in peace-time all the rights are applicable. In the case of certain rights, the precise scope of the right may be modified when the State is dealing with a situation which is not of sufficient gravity as to enable the State to derogate.[19] In situations of emergency, the State may be able to modify significantly the scope of certain rights, subject to certain procedural and substantive requirements.[20] The State has to show the need for and proportionality of the exceptional measures, which must not be inconsistent with the State's other applicable obligations.[21] This would appear potentially to include the Geneva Conventions of 1949.[22] The treaty texts expressly provide that certain rights, such as the prohibition of torture, arbitrary killings and slavery, are non-derogable.[23] That is to say that they remain applicable even during serious national emergencies. In other words, the terms of the treaties make it clear that at least some of their provisions remain applicable even during situations in which the law of armed conflicts may also be applicable.

It therefore comes as something of a surprise to find that the United States and Israel claim that, where the law of armed conflict is applicable, human rights law ceases to apply and human rights mechanisms no longer have jurisdiction.[24] It should be noted that the criterion they appear to use is whether the law of armed conflicts is applicable, not whether it is, in fact, applied.[25]

That view is opposed by the International Court of Justice,[26] the Human Rights Committee established under the ICCPR,[27] the Committee which monitors the Covenant on Economic, Social and Cultural Rights,[28] other treaty bodies[29] and a range of UN Special Procedures, both thematic mechanisms and country rapporteurs. It is also opposed by the European Court of Human Rights[30] and the Inter-American Commission and Court of Human Rights.[31] The view of the two regional courts is of particular importance since their judgments are legally binding.

States in whose territories there is an armed conflict not of an international character have not claimed that the applicability of the law of armed conflict displaces human rights law. Very commonly, States in fact deny that the situation is one to which the law of armed conflict is applicable, describing the situation rather as internal troubles, organised political violence or "terrorism".[32] There have, however, been situations in which States themselves recognised the applicability of some part of armed conflict law. They have not, however, argued that that displaced human rights law. Examples include the recent Chechen cases before the European Court of Human Rights.[33]

Any argument regarding the alleged mutual exclusivity of the two legal regimes is based on a general principle. There is no scope and no basis in law for an argument of mutual exclusivity based only on the law of armed conflicts applicable in international conflicts.

It is *not* that the human rights bodies regard the applicability of the law of armed conflicts as completely irrelevant to the applicability of human rights law. What they reject is the claim that the applicability of one legal regime automatically and completely displaces the other. The law of armed conflict is a form of *lex specialis* but the ICJ has made clear that that does not displace human rights law.[34] Rather, in interpreting human rights law, the monitoring bodies should take into account the law of armed conflicts in determining whether there is a violation of human rights law. They do not have the competence to determine whether there has been a breach of the law of armed conflict itself.

There is an interplay between this issue and the question of the extra-territorial applicability of human rights law, particularly when a State is involved in an international armed conflict outside national territory.

Extra-territorial applicability of human rights law.[35] Most of the principal treaties require victims to be "within the jurisdiction" of the State alleged to have violated their rights.[36] This obviously raises the question of whether they have to be within the territory of that State or whether there are other circumstances in which they can be said to be "within the jurisdiction". Interestingly, when disputing the competence of human rights mechanisms under the question discussed above, Israel and the United States do not appear to have challenged their competence under this heading.[37] Other States, however, have done so. They include Turkey, which asserted that its obligations under the ECHR were not applicable to the invasion and occupation of northern Cyprus;[38] Russia which maintained that it was not responsible for the act of the Transdniestrian authorities in Moldova[39] and the European members of NATO, which claimed that the civilians killed in the RTS television station in Belgrade were not "within their jurisdiction".[40]

The case-law has not raised all the possible permutations. Nevertheless, it is possible to discern certain principles. Where a State is in occupation of the whole or part of the territory of another State, it will be held responsible for the exercise of governmental functions in that territory, in the same way as it would within national territory.[41] In other words, it is not only responsible for the acts of occupying forces. It is also responsible for the acts of other persons exercising State functions.[42] It is not clear whether the test is based on occupation as understood under the 1907 Hague Regulations or whether the only test is effective control.[43] It has been suggested by the European Court of Human Rights, in an *obiter dicta,* that States may be responsible where they exercise only temporary control of territory.[44] Presumably the scope of any human rights jurisdiction would depend on the extent of the control exercised.

There is consistent case-law that, where an individual is detained by the forces of State A in the territory of State B, that person is within the jurisdiction of State A.[45] That does not preclude the possibility of their also being within the jurisdiction of State B.[46] There would not appear to be any reason in law why the position should vary depending on whether State A is operating with the consent of State B or not.[47] The basis of the analysis appears to be the fact that the victim is subject to the effective control of the forces of State A. Not only is this the approach of human rights bodies but it also represents the position taken by certain States, at least in international fora. The respondent governments in the *Bankovic* case conceded that persons detained outside national territory are "within the jurisdiction" of the detaining authorities.[48] The British government, in its response to the Working Group on Arbitrary Detention, divided detainees in Iraq into three categories: persons protected as prisoners of war under Geneva Convention III;

those protected as security detainees under Geneva Convention IV and others.[49] The first two categories were not protected by human rights law because they were protected by the *lex specialis*, the law of armed conflict. It should be noted that the British were *not* saying that the law of armed conflict was applicable to the *situation* and that detainees were therefore not protected by human rights law, whether or not they were in fact protected by the law of armed conflict. The basis for invoking the law of armed conflict is that that was the legal regime *actually applied* to the detainees in question. Of equal importance is the acceptance by the British government that other detainees, such as those suspected of having committed a criminal offence, *were* protected by human rights law.[50] The British government has not taken the same position in proceedings before domestic courts based on the Human Rights Act, which enables the courts to give effect domestically to most of the UK's obligations under the ECHR.[51]

The European Commission and Court of Human Rights have also found applicants to be "within the jurisdiction" in other situations, notably where they are adversely affected by the acts of diplomatic officials. Those cases suggest that the appropriate test is whether the applicant was foreseeably adversely affected by an act within the control of the respondent government, rather than whether the government controlled the person of the applicant. Such a test would be consistent with the law of state responsibility and with all the case-law on the scope of the extra-territorial applicability of human rights law. Arguably, it would not be consistent with the actual decision in *Bankovic*.[52]

In relation to the issue of concern in this paper – detention – it is clear that the detainee is within the jurisdiction of the detaining forces, even when they act outside national territory. That not only means that such detainees are protected under human rights law. It also means that the detaining State is accountable to human rights monitoring bodies for the way in which it deals with the detainees. What is less clear is precisely how each such body will handle the potential relevance of the law of armed conflict.

There is a range of possibilities. It is possible, but unlikely, that the monitoring body would simply accept that the *situation* is one in which the law of armed conflict is applicable and not enquire as to whether it is, *in fact*, being applied to the particular detainee.[53] Or the monitoring body might hold that, if the law of armed conflict authorises the detention, there is no issue with regard to the *grounds* for detention for it to address itself.[54] That could give rise to two different kinds of grey areas.[55] The detainees might object that they were not in fact people who could be detained and that they had been denied any opportunity to seek review of the lawfulness of the detention. The *lex specialis* character of the law of armed conflict would not appear to preclude the possibility of a human right monitoring body examining that question, provided it did so consistently with the law of armed conflict. If, however, those rules do not provide for such review, could a monitoring body require its introduction, on the grounds that it is required under non-derogable human rights law and is not precluded by the law of armed conflict?[56] Or again, if LOAC provides for a system of review but does not specify the characteristics of the review mechanism, can a human rights monitoring body require that the body have the characteristics of a court, including independence from the executive?[57] What if different human rights bodies reached different conclusions on the policy question? The second grey area concerns the time at which the authority to detain ends. Can a human rights body, taking into account the applicable rule of armed conflict law, reach the conclusion that the detention is no longer authorised? A human rights body might be reluctant to decline jurisdiction when the detainee has no other authority to which to turn.[58]

What is clear is that the apparent consensus, at least amongst the treaty bodies, that the applicability of the law of armed conflicts does not displace human rights law may be the end of one debate but it is also the start of a new one.

The International Law of Armed Conflict (LOAC)

Two separate issues need to be considered. There is first the question of the circumstances in which the law of armed conflict is potentially applicable. The second question is whether it is in fact applicable in a particular conflict. The lawfulness or otherwise of the resort to armed force is irrelevant to that question.[59]

Armed conflict – international The law of armed conflict (LOAC) consists of two main streams: rules on the way in which the fighting can be carried out and rules on the protection of victims of the conflict. Both areas are, to a significant extent, regulated by treaty law, at least in the case of international armed conflicts. Article 2 common to the four Geneva Conventions of 1949 and Article 1 of Protocol I of 1977 determine when the rules contained in those conventions are applicable. On that basis, the law of armed conflict

> ...shall apply to all cases of declared war or of any other armed conflict which may arise between two or more of the High Contracting Parties, even if the state of war is not recognized by one of them. The Convention shall also apply to all cases of partial or total occupation of the territory of a High Contracting Party, even if the said occupation meets with no armed resistance.[60]

The first potential problem is what constitutes an "armed conflict"?[61] Not all activities involving armed forces necessarily constitute armed conflicts. Members of security forces, whether they be members of a gendarmerie or soldiers, may be called upon to perform a variety of functions. The phrase implies a particular type of confrontation, involving a particular type of participant. A further question is the limitations in time and space of the concept of conflict. It is normally clear in an inter-State dispute where the conflict is taking place, when it started and when it ends. Is it possible, however, to speak of a "conflict" where a threat is global but the fighting only occurs at particular places and at particular times? In the case of a conflict with a non-State group capable of acting in a number of places, can a State regard itself as in an "armed conflict" not only globally but also indefinitely? State practice would suggest that the concept of armed conflict is more limited and must involve fighting.[62] That implies that the "war on terror" may involve armed conflicts at certain times and in certain places but whether or not it does so will depend on the existence of fighting. It also implies that not all activities undertaken against non-State groups are to be analysed in terms of LOAC. In that case, they need to be examined in the light of domestic and international criminal law and human rights law.

A second, potentially more serious, difficulty for the applicability of the Geneva Conventions is that the armed conflict has to be between two or more States. Where a conflict takes place in the territory of State A between the armed forces of State B and a non-State group in State A but does not involve the armed forces of State A, the conflict would not appear to come within Article 2.

Most of the provisions of the Geneva Conventions and a significant number of those in Protocol I represent customary international law.[63] What is much less clear is the scope of any customary law rules on the applicability of the customary law of armed conflict. The ICRC study on customary law, which addresses the customary rules in both international and non-international conflicts, does not address the question of when, under customary law, those rules are applicable. It is possible that, under customary law, the situation described in the previous paragraph is one in which the customary rules applicable to international conflicts are *prima facie* applicable. That would not necessarily mean that a fighter with the non-State group would be any more entitled to the *status* of a prisoner of war than he would in a conflict to which the treaty rules are applicable.

Armed conflict – non-international There are separate rules of both treaty and customary law which regulate internal or non-international conflicts. Whilst in many respects, particularly in relation to the protection of victims, they resemble the rules in international conflicts, there are significant differences, especially in relation to the status of the non-State fighters.[64] It is also the case that the provisions dealing with how the fighting is carried out tend to be defined with less precision than the rules applicable in international conflicts. The principal concern in this context is to which armed conflicts these provisions apply? It would be theoretically possible to say that any armed conflict not regulated by the rules applicable in international conflicts must be subject to the rules applicable in non-international conflicts. This type of definition, which has the advantage of ensuring that no situation slips between the cracks of two definitions, is used elsewhere in the law of armed conflicts.[65] It is not, however, the way in which the treaty law determines the applicability of the relevant provisions.

The treaty provisions in question are Article 3 common to the four Geneva Conventions and Article 1 of Protocol II of 1977. According to the former, each of the parties to a conflict is bound to apply, as a minimum, the provisions of common Article 3, "[i]n the case of armed conflict not of an international character occurring in the territory of one of the High Contracting Parties ...".

Again, the activity in question needs to qualify as an armed conflict.[66] The provision does not require the involvement in the fighting of the armed forces of the State in whose territory the fighting occurs. A conflict between two non-State groups could come within the terms of the Article.[67] There is nothing on the face of the Article which would prevent its applicability to a conflict between State B and a non-State group in State A, unless the presence of foreign fighting forces in State A was thought to give any fighting an international character.[68]

That is not the case for the applicability of Protocol II. The Protocol supplements common Article 3. It is applicable to some conflicts which also come within that Article. The Protocol is only applicable where the conflict does not come within Article 1 of Protocol 1 and where it takes

> ... place in the territory of a High Contracting Party between its armed forces and dissident armed forces or other organized armed groups which, under responsible command, exercise such control over a part of its territory as to enable them to carry out sustained and concerted military operations and to implement this Protocol.[69]

In other words, the armed forces of the State in whose territory the conflict occurs have to be involved in the fighting for the Protocol to be applicable. Furthermore, the nature and extent of the control which the non-State forces need to exercise means that there is a much higher threshold for the applicability of the Protocol than for that of common Article 3. Again, it is not clear when, according to customary law, the rules regulating non-international conflicts are applicable. Nor is it clear, however desirable it might be, whether all armed conflicts come within either common Article 2 or common Article 3. It is, however, apparent that the overwhelming majority of conflicts come within one or other provision, on condition that they do, in fact constitute armed conflicts.

The Applicability of the Law of Armed Conflict in the "War on Terror"

The phrase the "war on terror" is of no more intrinsic legal significance than the "war on drugs". What matters is whether operations conducted since 9/11 have been operations to which LOAC was applicable.[70] In relation to detention, there would appear to be four types of operation which need to be considered: detentions on the battlefield or closely associated with military activities in Afghanistan; detentions on the battlefield, or closely associated with military activities during the military occupation or closely associated with military activities since the end of the occupation in Iraq; the transfer of a person suspected of involvement in Al Qaeda or other terrorist activities from one State to another; other detentions allegedly directly or indirectly connected to the attack of 9/11. These will be examined in turn to see whether the law of armed conflicts was applicable to the operation. It should be noted that the Security Council determined, in effect, that the attacks of 9/11 were armed attacks for the purposes of Article 51 of the UN Charter.[71] That is to say that the US was entitled to resort to armed force in self-defence against those responsible for the attacks. Even at that stage, the Security Council was aware of the likelihood that the attacks were the work of non-State actors.

Afghanistan Initially, the US tried to persuade the Taliban to hand over members of Al-Qaeda or to co-operate with the US in terminating their activities.[72] The Taliban eventually refused.[73] The resultant conflict required the US and its allies to fight the Taliban, so as to get such control on the ground as to enable them to pursue operations against Al-Qaeda itself. There was an armed conflict between two or more of the High Contracting Parties to the Geneva Conventions. It is irrelevant whether the Taliban was recognised as the government of Afghanistan or whether the Taliban forces were recognised as the armed forces of the government.[74] It is equally irrelevant to a determination as to the applicability of the Geneva Conventions whether the Taliban forces were entitled to prisoner of war status. That is a different question and one which arises only once it is determined that the Geneva Conventions were applicable to the conflict. It is submitted that the issue of whether the Geneva Conventions were applicable is not one about which reasonable people may disagree. As a matter of both treaty law and practice, the Convention provisions regulating international armed conflict were applicable.[75]

There came a period when the nature of the armed conflict and the rules applicable changed. At some point, the coalition forces were there with the consent of the newly installed government of Hamid Karzai. It is not clear at what point the new Afghan authorities had the competence to request or consent to military assistance. Was it when the government was installed and recognised as a government by the coalition, when the Security Council recognised the changed circumstances,[76] after the holding of the Emergency Loya Jirga or only after the holding of elections? Nor is it clear whether at any point the coalition constituted occupying forces. After the key point, whenever that was, it would appear that the situation in those areas in which fighting continued was a non-international armed conflict. Whilst at the time of the drafting of common Article 3 it was probably not envisaged that the conflicts in question would include the armed forces of one State fighting against a non-State group in the territory of another State, nothing precludes its applicability in such a situation.[77]

The position is different with regard to the ISAF force.[78] That is a UN-mandated force with peace enforcement functions in a very limited geographical area.[79] It is not clear in what circumstances the Geneva Conventions are *de jure* applicable to such a force.[80] If it finds itself involved in fighting of a type associated with armed conflict, the best guidance the forces have as to permitted conduct are the rules contained in the Geneva Conventions and Protocols and customary law. A further difficulty concerns which group of rules they would be expected to apply, those applicable in international or non-international armed conflict? As UN forces, they are bound by the Secretary-General's Bulletin, which requires them to respect the principles of the Geneva Conventions.[81]

Iraq Similar questions arise with regard to operations in Iraq but, in this case, it is clear that there was a period of belligerent occupation. To the best of my knowledge, no one has disputed that initially there was an international armed conflict to which the Geneva Conventions were applicable. In the case of the UK and certain other participants, Protocol I was also applicable. The US was bound by such provisions of Protocol I as represent customary law. At some point, Iraq became occupied territory, triggering the applicability of the relevant provisions of the fourth Geneva Convention and of the annex to the fourth Hague Convention of 1907.[82] It is not clear whether that occurred in a graduated way, as territory became occupied, on May 1, 2003 when President George W. Bush declared the end of "major operations" or at some subsequent point. At some stage, the occupying forces arguably became forces acting with the consent of the national authorities. Again, it is not clear at what point that occurred; was it after the alleged transfer of authority to an interim Iraqi government on June 28, 2004 or only after the holding of elections or not even then?[83] After that point, any fighting involving the coalition forces was/will be presumably subject to the rules applicable to non-international conflicts.[84] Where any persons were detained during the initial fighting or subsequent occupation and have remained in detention since then, they will be protected by the rules applicable in international armed conflicts.[85]

Transfers The problem in analysing the transfers is that they have been effected in an extraordinarily wide range of circumstances. Broadly speaking, where a person is detained on a battlefield or in connection with an armed conflict involving the detaining authorities, the detention will be regulated by the law of armed conflict.[86] The detaining State may have continuing obligations in the event of any subsequent transfer to the authorities of another State.[87]

More difficult questions arise where a person is detained by State authorities not involved in an armed conflict and transferred to a party to the conflict.[88] Generally speaking, it would appear that the initial detention is not subject to the law of armed conflict.[89] Once transferred, if they are held in connection with the conflict, the detention would appear to be subject to that body or rules.[90] A difficulty is what is meant by detention in connection with the conflict? If a person in Pakistan, who is not alleged ever to have set foot in Afghanistan but who is alleged to have had contact with members of Al-Qaeda, is detained and transferred to US custody in Guantanamo Bay, is that person detained on account of the conflict or on account of some part of the "war on terror" to which the law of armed conflict is not applicable? Just because some post 9/11 US actions may be justified under Article 51 of the UN Charter does not mean that all action taken is necessarily part of an armed conflict. To hold that all detentions connected in any way with the "war on terror" are subject to the law of armed conflict would not be consistent with the requirements for the applicability of that body of law.

It would appear that some of those transferred to US custody may have been detained allegedly in connection with an armed conflict but that many of them may have been detained on account of suspected involvement in terrorist activity. The detention of the latter category should not be subject to LOAC but to human rights law.

Other post 9/11 detentions Certain individuals have been detained in the State of which they are a citizen or a long-term resident and held in connection with an armed conflict or with activities threatening national security or on immigration charges prior to deportation. At first sight, the last category has nothing to do with LOAC. In certain circumstances, however, the immigration charges might be a cover to mask the internment of "enemy aliens". The post 9/11 detentions in the US for immigration law violations have not generally attracted such a criticism.[91] The first two categories do, however, pose a potential problem. In what circumstances, if any, is a detention within national territory of a citizen or long-term resident subject to the law of armed conflict? Clearly if a citizen of State A fights for State B in a conflict between A and B, he can expect legal proceedings to be brought against him, if State A is able to detain him. The issue is rather whether such proceedings are regulated entirely by domestic law or whether LOAC applies even in such a situation. Article 75 of Protocol I, which provides fundamental due process guarantees to any person detained on account of an international conflict and who is not entitled to any higher standard of protection, is regarded as customary law, including by the US military.[92] This suggests that the law of armed conflict may even have a relevance in such a situation. It should also be remembered, however, that a State may invoke the LOAC where it is far from clear that it is applicable. Whether or not this is the intention in so doing, the result may be to reduce the legal protections otherwise applicable, as in the case of the deaths in Yemen as a result of an attack from an unmanned Predator, targeted against a suspected member of Al Qaeda.[93]

International Criminal Law

The third potentially relevant legal regime is international criminal law.[94] It is not clear to what extent it can appropriately be described as a regime. International law has traditionally regulated the circumstances in which States can exercise national criminal jurisdiction.[95] That usually requires some connection between the individual and the State. It is common for States to exercise criminal jurisdiction over the perpetrator of a criminal act within national territory, irrespective of the nationality of the offender. Many civil law systems exercise jurisdiction over their nationals for crimes committed outside national territory. International law has also defined those offences in relation to which any State is free to exercise jurisdiction over a person in national territory, irrespective of the place where the offence was committed, the nationality of the perpetrator or the nationality of the victim. For the purposes of this text such offences will be called crimes of universal jurisdiction.[96] Such offences have been defined under customary international law and under treaty law.[97] They include war crimes, in both international and non-international armed conflicts, crimes against humanity and a wide variety of terrorist crimes. Treaties dealing with terrorist offences usually go beyond permitting any State to bring criminal proceedings. They usually impose an obligation on the State where the suspect is located either to try the suspect itself or to surrender them for trial in another State.

States have also entered into bilateral and multilateral arrangements to facilitate international judicial co-operation in the criminal sphere generally, not just in relation to international crimes. This includes but is not limited to extradition arrangements.[98] Extradition applies only to potential criminal proceedings in the requesting State.

There is no doubt that any allegation of involvement in virtually any type of terrorist activity concerns an international crime of universal jurisdiction. If the US wished to bring criminal proceedings against a suspect, it could request his extradition from the State in which he is currently present, subject to there being extradition arrangements in place. The major difficulty is that the process of extradition usually requires the requesting State to establish a *prima facie* case.[99] In many cases, the US is not able to produce that type of evidence.[100] It sometimes appears that they wish a person to be transferred in order that he can be questioned by US authorities, rather than being brought before a court. Extradition is not appropriate in the case of a transfer for questioning.

The issue since 9/11 has not generally been that States have failed to discharge their obligations with regard to such arrangements. On the contrary, many States have acted where they had no obligation to do so. There is no general principle of international law which prevents States co-operating on an *ad hoc* basis.[101] There are, however, rules of international law which impose constraints on the transfer of detainees, whether that transfer would be effected under a treaty arrangement or on an *ad hoc* basis.

The majority of transfers appear to have occurred without any form of process before the domestic courts of the detaining State. The detention prior to transfer would be subject to the detaining State's human rights law obligations. The transfer itself would be subject to the principle that people cannot be sent to a place where there is a well-founded fear that they would be subjected to torture, cruel, inhuman or degrading treatment.[102]

Having identified the situations in which different bodies of rules are or may be applicable, it is possible to turn to an examination of the different categories of detainees and their entitlements under those rules.

Detention under International Law

In this context, it is only necessary to consider the detention requirements under human rights law and LOAC.

International Human Rights Law

Human rights law only binds States. That includes persons exercising State functions. Human rights law is generally silent with regard to how a State chooses to meet its international obligations. The State is free, for example, to privatise prisons. In the case of intrinsic State functions, the State will probably remain directly responsible for the acts of such officials, and not merely responsible for a failure to protect the victim.[103] Officially sanctioned detention is an intrinsic State function. The State is therefore likely to be responsible, under human rights law, for the acts of all officials involved in detention and interrogation, irrespective of their status under domestic law. Even if that were not to be the case, the State would be liable for failing adequately to protect the victim from the violation.

Generally speaking, there are not different categories of detainees under human rights law[104] but there are different grounds of detention. These may give rise to a variety of rights, depending on the ground invoked. In order for detention to be lawful, it must be on a ground recognised in international law and provided for in domestic law. The ICCPR simply prohibits arbitrary detention.[105] It is not clear whether that only permits detention on the grounds listed in the ECHR or whether it allows for a wider range of grounds.[106] In particular, it is not clear whether Article 9 of the ICCPR allows for administrative detention.[107] The reservation made by India at the time of ratification and the derogation of the UK may imply that administrative detention is thought to be not normally lawful.[108] It is not clear whether detention as a prisoner of war or as a civilian internee would be treated as particular manifestations of administrative detention or whether they would be regarded as *sui generis*.

Article 9 of the ICCPR is potentially subject to derogation. Even if administrative detention is not permitted in normal circumstances under that article, it could, in certain circumstances, be lawful on condition that the State complied with the substantive and procedural requirements of derogation. It seems inconceivable that the Human Rights Committee would not recognise grounds of detention recognised in LOAC, at least if the State had derogated and invoked those grounds.[109] It is not clear what other safeguards the Human Rights Committee would require to protect against the risk of arbitrariness.[110] In particular, it is not clear whether there is any limit in the time for which a person can be detained on this basis. The US has not submitted any notification of derogation under the ICCPR.

In the context of due process, the European Court of Human Rights has determined that any criminal proceedings against a civilian before a tribunal one or more of whose members is a serving member of the armed forces cannot be fair or independent.[111] The Inter-American Court of Human Rights appears to take the same position.[112] The view of the Human Rights Committee is less clear.[113] Nor is it clear whether a State can derogate from such a principle, possibly subject to procedural safeguards.[114]

There are no circumstances in which, under human rights law, a detention can be concealed.[115] Whilst "disappearances" usually involve a *denial* of detention, unacknowledged or concealed detentions might also be regarded as coming within the concept. Where there is a widespread of systematic practice of concealing detention, the perpetrators may potentially be subject to proceedings for the commission of a crime against humanity.[116] It has been reported that the US has concealed the detention of certain persons, including hiding them from delegates of the International Committee of the Red Cross (ICRC).[117]

Whilst Article 9 of the ICCPR is potentially derogable, the Human Rights Committee has made it clear that even derogable rights may have a non-derogable core.[118] In particular, it regards the right to challenge the lawfulness of detention (*habeas corpus*) as non-derogable.[119] Wherever a person is detained, whatever the grounds, the detaining authorities need to make available a mechanism which enables the detainee to challenge the lawfulness of the detention. This may be based on the facts (a claim that the detainee is not a person who can be subject to detention on that particular ground) or on the law (domestic or international law rules of substance or procedure do not permit the detention). The US governmental authorities tried to deny any such possibility but have been frustrated by the decision of the US Supreme Court allowing detainees to challenge the basis of their detention.[120] It remains to be seen how wide will be the scope of such review and, in particular, whether it will have an impact on status determination. It also remains to be seen how those detained outside the US and Guantanamo Bay will be able to challenge their detention.[121]

Human rights law requires that any challenge as to the lawfulness of detention be determined by a court. This requires the body to be independent of the executive and its findings to be binding on the executive.[122]

It is a violation of Article 7 of the Covenant to transfer a detainee to a State where they are likely to suffer torture, cruel, inhuman or degrading treatment.[123] If the widespread allegations regarding conditions of detention and ill-treatment in US detention centres outside the US territory are accurate, any State which transfers a person allegedly suspected of involvement in terrorist activity to US custody in such a place can be said to be violating this provision. On the basis of the same type of argument, it may also be a violation of the Covenant to transfer detainees who will not have the benefit of due process in the place to which they are sent. Certain States have said that they request assurances that the person will not be subject to proscribed ill-treatment. It is not clear whether such an assurance can ever be sufficient, at least where the problems include the general conditions of detention and the open-ended nature of the confinement, as opposed to ill-treatment inflicted on particular individuals.[124] Even if such an assurance were capable of meeting the need, a human rights body would presumably require the transferring State to reassure itself that the undertakings were being respected. This would require follow-up visits and confidential interviews with those transferred. The US is itself engaged in transferring detainees to other States but, in this case, the allegation is even more serious. It is not simply that there is a real risk of torture in the States to which they are transferred. It is suggested that they are sent to those places for questioning *in order* that they will be tortured into revealing information. In view of the allegations that inhuman treatment, at the very least, is widespread, one has to consider whether the transferring States can be regarded as complicit in the subsequent ill-treatment.[125]

It is beyond the scope of this article to examine the conduct of interrogation, the conditions of detention or the treatment to which detainees have been subject. It is sufficient to note here that there have been widespread allegations of abuse of detainees in Iraq, Afghanistan and Guantanamo Bay.[126] The evidence available to date strongly suggests that many of the allegations are well-founded. The reason for raising the claims is that, taken together with the issues surrounding detention, they give rise to the concern that the human rights violations are not simply the result of over-zealous adherence to instructions or to the presence of the odd "bad apple". They suggest that the violations are either instigated or condoned at a much higher level. This has potential implications for the characterisation of resultant violations and also for the responsibilities of other States.

The Law of Armed Conflict (LOAC)

This section only concerns detentions in situations in which the law of armed conflict is applicable. The issue of the status of people present in a conflict zone raises a variety of discrete but overlapping problems and is fraught with controversy. The issues include not only disagreement about what the law should be but also disagreement about what the law is. There are disputes as to whether there are only two categories of persons, with sub-categories, or whether there are more than two categories.[127] There is even disagreement as to the meaning of the word combatant; it is used by different authors to mean different things.[128] Some of the difficulties involve the application of the rules to the facts, particularly where the types of situations which arise are thought to be significantly different from those which were envisaged at the time of the drafting of the law.[129] It can be difficult to distinguish between an old problem in a new guise and a new problem. The issues arise in three contexts, only two of which are relevant here. The first is the question of who can be targeted and who must not be targeted. The second is the situation at the moment of capture and, in particular, presumptions based on appearances. The third is the actual situation, in fact, of the detainee. The last two questions are important to this discussion. A further difficulty is that provisions of Protocol I, notably Article 44, are important to the discussion and not only has the US not ratified the Protocol but it has expressly declared that it does not accept that particular provision. LOAC contains provisions on the detention of combatants and of certain civilians. There is also a general provision dealing with the detention of any person not otherwise protected by LOAC.

Combatant status in international conflicts Combatant is a technical term. It does not simply mean a fighter. A combatant is, by definition, a person who has the right to participate in hostilities.[130] Certain consequences flow from characterisation as a combatant, both on the battlefield and subsequently. A combatant can be targeted during an armed conflict day or night and irrespective of what he is doing at the time. He cannot be prosecuted for the fact of fighting but he can be prosecuted if he violates the rules applicable to the conduct of hostilities, for example by intentionally targeting civilians. Upon capture, a combatant is entitled to prisoner of war status.[131]

Combatants are members of the armed forces of a party to the conflict.[132] In certain narrowly defined circumstances, the armed forces can include members of other organised militia, on condition that they belong to a Party to the conflict. The group must satisfy the following conditions

(a) that of being commanded by a person responsible for his subordinates;
(b) that of having a fixed distinctive sign recognizable at a distance;
(c) that of carrying arms openly;
(d) that of conducting their operations in accordance with the laws and customs of war.[133]

The group as a whole must satisfy these conditions.[134] Where an individual is fighting with a group which is entitled to combatant status but that person, for example, fails to distinguish themselves from the civilian population, they may forfeit the privileges of belligerency, including combatant status.[135] Where a person is entitled to combatant status but is alleged to have violated the laws and customs of war, they can be tried for such conduct but will retain their status as combatants.[136]

In the case of Afghanistan, the status of two groups needs to be considered, the Taliban and members of Al Qaeda. In the case of Iraq, there are four such groups, at least during the period of occupation: members of the Iraqi armed forces; Iraqis who took up arms to oppose the occupation; foreigners who entered Iraq in order to fight against the coalition and Iraqis suspected of involvement in "ordinary" criminal activities.

The US has denied that any of those groups is entitled to prisoner of war status, with the exception of members of the Iraqi armed forces.[137] It is submitted that, in addition, members of the Taliban should have been accorded that status, together with possibly certain members of Al Qaeda, if they fought as part of the Taliban forces, and possibly certain Iraqi insurgents, if they either constituted a *levée en masse*[138] or were organised in such a way as to satisfy the requirements of a volunteer corps or militia.

The principal US argument for denying the Taleban combatant status is that they were not wearing a uniform and that they did not conduct their operations in accordance with the laws and customs of war.[139] It is not clear whether the armed forces of a State, as opposed to a militia, have to satisfy the four requirements listed above or whether they are presumed to do so.[140] The practice has generally been to assume that the armed forces of a State are combatants.[141] It has been suggested that the members of the Taliban distinguished themselves by wearing a black turban.[142] That is capable of constituting a uniform.[143] A difficulty with the US argument is that the Northern Alliance forces, alongside whom the US forces were fighting, appeared to have no difficulty in identifying opposing armed forces.[144]

It is alleged that certain members of Al Qaeda fought alongside the Taleban.[145] If they actually constituted part of the Taleban forces, for example by obeying orders issued by those forces, then they too would probably qualify for combatant status. If they were fighting alongside the Taleban but not as part of their forces, they might qualify for combatant status but only if they satisfied the four requirements cited above and only if they belonged to a party to the conflict. If members of Al Qaeda participated in the fighting but not on that basis, they would not appear to be entitled to combatant status. It is not clear whether such a fighter is a civilian unlawfully participating in hostilities or an unprivileged belligerent.[146] Given that some fighters appeared to be entitled to combatant status, the wisest thing to have done would have been for the US to treat all fighters as *prima facie* entitled to prisoner of war status, pending determination by a status determination tribunal.

In the case of Iraq, following the end of active hostilities, the coalition forces found themselves in occupation of Iraq. It is not clear whether the coalition, as such, constituted an occupying power or whether each member of the coalition was an occupying power in relation to such area of territory as was controlled by its own armed forces. The answer to that question has implications for responsibility for any violations of applicable rules. Prior to the occupation, the coalition appears to have taken relatively few prisoners and those it did take were quickly released and sent home.[147] In addition to those who had been detained as prisoners of war and then released, as a result of a controversial decision by the administrator, Paul Bremer, the remaining Iraqi armed forces were disbanded and sent home.[148] In other words, at the start of the occupation there were hundreds of thousands of former members of the Iraqi armed forces unsupervised and free to wander around the country, some of whom presumably knew where weapons caches could be found.

Even after the end of active hostilities, there was fighting. It can be analysed in three ways. In some cases, it may have represented a continuation of the previous fighting by members of the Iraqi armed forces. In others, it may have represented the spontaneous outbreak of fighting by individual Iraqis taking up arms to oppose the occupation. In yet others, it may have represented organised resistance to the occupants, by Iraqis and/or foreigners. Any given incident may have involved a mixture of such fighters. Again, unless it was clear that fighters were neither members of the armed forces nor members of a militia or a *levée en masse*, it would have been wisest to treat detained fighters as entitled to prisoner of war status, pending status determination. It is alleged that some of the fighting has been carried out by foreigners who entered in Iraq in order to fight.[149] Their being foreign has no bearing on their status.[150] What matters is whether they formed part of a volunteer corps satisfying the requirements set out above and whether the group belonged to a party to the conflict.

Where members of the armed forces of a party to the conflict fail to distinguish themselves from the civilian population, they may lose the privileges attaching to combatancy. Such fighters can, appropriately, be termed unprivileged or, less appropriately, illegal combatants. Whilst they may forfeit prisoner of war status, they are entitled to the same *treatment* as prisoners of war.[151] They are not to be confused with members of non-State fighting groups who at no point distinguish themselves from the civilian population, who are not subject to a chain of command and who fail to conduct their operations in accordance with the laws and customs of war. It is submitted that such fighters are not any form of combatant, privileged or otherwise. They are civilians participating in hostilities. As such, they can be prosecuted for fighting. They can also be prosecuted for the commission of war crimes.

It is a matter of controversy whether the population of occupied territory has the right to take up arms against the occupying power.[152] Provisions of Protocol I, to which the US is not a party and which probably do not represent customary law, have relaxed the temporal and geographical conditions which combatants in occupied territory need to satisfy in order to retain combatant status.[153] In certain circumstances, they only need to distinguish themselves from the civilian population and to bear their arms openly during each military engagement and when visible to the adversary whilst deploying prior to launching the attack. The provision does not *grant* combatant status. It merely provides that combatants, previously defined as members of the armed forces of a party to the conflict, do not *forfeit* their status in those circumstances.[154] The provision is therefore no basis for arguing that non-State fighting groups with no connection to a party to the conflict are entitled to combatant status.

At the point of detention, a person is either fighting or not fighting. The law establishes that there is a presumption that a person who takes part in hostilities is entitled to prisoner of war status. If there is any doubt as to the entitlement to that status, it is to be resolved by a status determination tribunal.[155]

Civilian status in international conflicts Those who are not combatants are civilians.[156] The Pictet commentary to the Geneva Conventions makes it clear that people are either protected by the third Geneva Convention or the fourth. They cannot fall between the two. No one is outside the protection of the Conventions.[157] Civilian status is defined negatively. Civilians may forfeit one of the incidents of that status, immunity from direct attack, if they fight.[158] Civilians cannot be made the subject of attack "unless and for such time as they take a direct part in hostilities".[159] There are detailed provisions regulating the detention of foreign civilians in the fourth Geneva Convention.

Potential difficulties of both law and fact arise before, during and after detention. The principal legal problem is the meaning of direct participation in hostilities.[160] Is a person who plans attacks carried out by others taking a direct part in the fighting? What about a person who relays instructions from one person to another, who will carry out the attack? What about a person who funds a particular operation or who funds a group which carries out such operations? Whilst combatants can be attacked at any time, civilians taking a direct part in hostilities can only be attacked at the time when they are so participating. How can you tell whether an alleged planner is engaged in planning or whether he is having a meal with his family? It is not clear whether State practice means that the phrase should be construed widely or whether that constitutes the manipulation of the law to preserve its relevance.[161] Clearly, States need to be able to take effective action against those suspected of involvement in attacks against civilians but when should such action be limited to policing, subject to human rights law, and when, if ever, might it be legitimate to make no attempt to detain but simply to kill?[162] These are genuine legal difficulties but they are not directly relevant to the problem of post 9/11 detentions.

Where a person is detained on a battlefield or in an area in which conflict is taking place, there are three possibilities. First, the person may be a combatant. Second, he may be a civilian unlawfully participating in the hostilities. Third, he may be a civilian not taking any part in the fighting. The law needs to establish presumptions to address the immediate need at the point of detention. It has done so by establishing that those who take part in hostilities should be presumed to be combatants and those not fighting should be presumed to be civilian.[163] It must be possible for the detainee to challenge that presumption.

Where a person is detained away from a conflict zone, there are again three possibilities. There may be evidence that he is a combatant, that is to say a member of the armed forces of a State engaged in an armed conflict with the detaining authorities.[164] Alternatively, he may be suspected of having unlawfully participated in hostilities or as otherwise representing a security threat to the detaining forces. There would appear to be no basis, under LOAC, for the detention of a civilian in other circumstances, unless the civilian were being detained on grounds having nothing to do with the fighting, for example as a person suspected of having committed an ordinary crime.

Where the detention occurs in a State other than the one in which the fighting is occurring, is the only law applicable domestic and international criminal law, subject to human rights law? In some cases, the detaining authorities may have obligations as a neutral or as a co-belligerent.[165] Would that make it lawful to resort to potentially lethal force more readily than in the case of attempted detention of a suspected criminal?

Again, generally speaking, this is not the key question in the post 9/11 detentions. The essential problem has been the basis on which the individuals have been detained and their classification, with consequential effects on aspects of the detention regime. At the root of the problem has been the denial of the applicability of human rights law, because the situation is said to be one of armed conflict, combined with the denial of the applicability of LOAC to the conflict in Afghanistan.

Determining the lawfulness of detention in international conflicts under LOAC If a party to an international armed conflict applies the presumption that those detained fighting are entitled to prisoner of war status, it will be necessary to provide a means definitively to determine status. If a person was not detained whilst fighting, he may wish to establish his entitlement to prisoner of war status. A doubt arises where a person asserts a status other than that being afforded by the detaining authorities.[166] A doubt also arises where the detaining authorities are themselves uncertain as to status. Where there is such a doubt, the law requires that the matter be determined by a tribunal, not by the executive.[167] Such determinations are to be made on a case-by-case basis. It is not open to a Head of State to assert that there is no doubt or to determine status, whether in individual cases or across the board.

In the case of civilians, international law provides for the internment of enemy civilians in the territory of a party to the conflict and in occupied territory.[168] Unlike former combatants, who can be detained simply by virtue of having fought and been captured, there needs to be a reason based on the security of the detaining power for interning civilians.[169] There is a right of periodic review to determine whether the grounds necessitating detention continue to exist.[170] Detailed provisions regulate every aspect of internment, including the bringing of criminal proceedings against internees.

In occupied territory, the occupying authorities also have the responsibility for maintaining law and order.[171] That includes allowing the local authorities to detain, for example, suspected criminals under the law previously in force.

Interrogation of detainees in international conflicts There is nothing in international law which prevents the questioning of prisoners of war but they are only obliged to give their name, rank, number and date of birth and cannot be subjected to coercive interrogation.[172] A prisoner of war can be held until the "cessation of active hostilities", unless criminal proceedings are being brought against him, in which case he can be held until the end of those proceedings or of any sentence imposed.[173] If the conflicts in question are defined as those against the Taleban and Iraqi armed forces under the authority of Saddam Hussein, there would appear to be no continuing basis for the detention of prisoners of war, unless criminal proceedings are being brought against them. In the case of prisoners of war, any such criminal proceedings would have to be before a court martial and not a military commission.[174] If a prisoner of war is transferred from one detaining power to another, the transferring State has to ensure that the State receiving the prisoner is willing and able to treat him in accordance with the third Geneva Convention and it retains certain residual responsibilities towards the prisoner of war.[175] There is nothing in international law which prevents the interrogation of civilian internees but, again, they cannot be subjected to coercive interrogation.[176] When the grounds justifying their internment cease to apply, they must be released.[177] There are similar provisions relating to the transfer of internees as apply to prisoners of war.[178]

Detention in non-international armed conflicts There is no equivalent to combatant status in non-international conflicts, for the obvious reason that no State is going to accept the idea that a resident is legally entitled to resort to armed force against the authorities of the State. This means that some people may be detained who previously took part in hostilities and others may be detained in connection with the conflict but without ever having participated in it. LOAC does not establish *grounds* on which people can be detained in non-international conflicts. It simply articulates the rules relating applicable to those who are detained, notably with regard to conditions of detention and to criminal proceedings brought against them.[179] The grounds of detention are therefore, presumably, a matter for domestic law and human rights law.

The rules in Protocol II, which bear a marked resemblance to non-derogable human rights law, stipulate, in effect, that detainees must be treated humanely.[180] They also provide due process guarantees.

The US and Post 9/11 Detentions

The United States authorities have argued that LOAC displaces the possible applicability of human rights law.[181] They have then gone on to assert that, in the case of the conflict in Afghanistan, LOAC was not applicable.[182] They have denied the applicability of either the third or fourth Geneva Convention to persons detained in Afghanistan. The alleged non-applicability of LOAC also denies the detainees the residuary protection afforded under Article 75 of Protocol I, which applies to persons not otherwise protected. Furthermore, US authorities have sought to argue that the procedural and substantive rights available under domestic US law do not apply to detainees outside national territory, for example in Guantanamo Bay. In other words, the US authorities assert that those detained in connection with the conflict in Afghanistan have no rights at all. There are no rules regulating the grounds on which they can be detained, no rules regulating the conditions of detention or the conduct of interrogation and no rules regulating their release.

As demonstrated above, this view is misconceived. International law permits the detention of any person whom the US might legitimately wish to detain but it provides certain guarantees to ensure that detention is not arbitrary and that the detainees are not ill-treated. It needs to be emphasised that there have been voices raised within the United States which have disputed the official analysis, both as a matter of law and with regard to the facts. They include the State Department and many lawyers with the armed services.[183] Anecdotal evidence suggests that many in the legal profession, including lawyers who do not normally work in the fields of civil liberties or human rights, have also opposed the government position. They have been joined by the US Supreme Court and the US Federal District Court of Columbia.[184]

What is profoundly troubling is that, traditionally, the US was in the forefront of States insisting not only on the applicability of rules in armed conflicts but also on the need for enforcement.[185] The International Criminal Tribunal for the former Yugoslavia and the International Criminal Tribunal for Rwanda would not have been created but for strong US support.

It is not that the law has been tried and found wanting. The law has not been tried at all. There are undoubtedly certain areas in which the scope of the law is uncertain and where it gives rise to difficulties. They do not, however, include the rules regulating the grounds for detention and the treatment of detainees.

In addition to legal reasons for respecting the law, there are strong policy reasons for doing so, as the US found at the time of the Vietnam conflict. The more powerful a State, the more it is vulnerable on account of the global nature of its interests and the presence of its citizens world-wide.[186] To acquire a reputation of disregard of the law runs the real risk of creating opposition and exposing those global interests to increased risk of attack. It exposes members of the US armed forces, in particular, to increased risk of ill-treatment, if they find themselves in the power of opposing forces. It completely undermines the US claims to be seeking to spread democracy, accountability and the rule of law. It is likely also to have an adverse effect on the rule of law within the US. Experience has shown that when States seek to allow limited exceptions to the rule of law, they cannot be contained. The bad practices leak out into areas where they were not supposed to be permitted.[187] The occurrence of torture, to the shock and disgust of the majority of Americans, in US detention centres in Iraq, where rules of international law were acknowledged to apply is an inevitable product of an attempt to deny that rules apply to the treatment of detainees in Guantanamo Bay.

What exacerbates these consequences of US policies is the fact that many of those detained appear to have had no connection at all with Al Qaeda or any other group. It may be inevitable that, in the chaos of a military operation, innocent people are swept up with the guilty. The fact that many such detainees have been released, without criminal proceedings and after long periods of detention, calls into question whether there were ever any grounds for detaining them.[188] They appear to have been in the wrong place at the wrong time. That makes it all the more important to ensure that detainees are able to challenge the grounds of their detention and that they are treated humanely. Innocent detainees may show some understanding of short-term detention during which they are treated well. They are likely to be much less understanding of open-ended incarceration in inhuman conditions and being subjected to torture as part of the interrogation process. In addition, it appears that those inflicting the ill-treatment suffer long-term social and psychological problems.

The violations of human rights law and the law of armed conflict have not occurred on an isolated basis. Indeed they illustrate the pattern which the US has so often criticised in other States. In even the best regulated States, violations of human rights will occasionally occur. Such violations are the result of the acts of individuals. More serious is the situation where, owing to defects in the law and the operation of the legal system, violations are widespread or systematic. The domestic system is not able to correct the wrong. Most serious of all is a situation in which the executive sanctions wrongdoing and seeks to avoid all accountability, whether at the hands of national or international judicial mechanisms. The punishment of individual wrongdoers fails to address the true nature of the problem. It needs to be accompanied by the punishment of those who sanctioned the wrongdoing.

Of equal gravity is the relative silence of other States. Whilst generally themselves seeking to respect their international obligations, they have transferred people to US custody, in the full knowledge of what that would entail for the detainees. There is responsibility for complicity in unlawful acts, as well as for the acts themselves.[189]

The fall-out from the aberrations of Guantanamo Bay, Abu Ghraib and Bagram is likely to last for a long time. It is not yet possible to evaluate the effects. It has been said that "those who fail to learn the lessons of history are doomed to repeat them."[190] The real tragedy is that those lessons were learnt once and found expression in the Geneva Conventions. The US learnt them again during and after the conflict in Vietnam. It is apparently not sufficient to learn the lessons once, or even twice. They need to be continually recalled.

Notes

[1] E.g. reports on the web-sites of reputable non-governmental organisations, such as Human Rights Watch (http://www.hrw.org) and Amnesty International (http://www.amnesty.org).

[2] Padilla, a US citizen, was detained in the US originally in federal criminal custody. Following designation by the President as an "enemy combatant", he was detained in military custody; *Rumsfeld, Secretary of Defense v. Padilla et al*, US Supreme Court, June 28, 2004 Ali Saleh Kahlah al-Marri, a Qatari living in the US, was originally subject to criminal charges. Once he was designated as an enemy combatant, he was transferred to military detention and the charges were dropped; Human Rights Watch, note 1, press release June 23, 2003.

[3] 762 non-US citizens were so detained.; Human Rights Watch, note 1, "Presumption of Guilt", August 2002. A report by the Office of the Inspector General of the Department of Justice, "The September 11 Detainees: A Review of the Treatment of Aliens Held on Immigration Charges in Connection with the Investigation of the September 11 Attacks" (June 2003) confirmed that the detainees were subject to various abuses.

[4] The UK introduced legislation after 9/11 which permitted the detention of foreigners who could not be returned to their country of origin owing to a real risk of torture. The legislation was found to be inconsistent with the Human Rights Act, which gives effect to the UK's obligations under the European Convention on Human Rights, in *A, X & Ors v Secretary of State for the Home Department* [2004] HL56 (16 December 2004).

[5] Those detained in Guantanamo Bay, Cuba and at the Bagram air base, Afghanistan are not being detained under the law of armed conflict and were said to be outside the jurisdiction of US federal courts and therefore denied US domestic legal protection. This argument failed in *Hamdi et al v. Rumsfeld, Secretary of Defense, et al*, US Supreme Court, June 28, 2004; see further below.

[6] States effecting such transfers include Bosnia-Herzegovina, Croatia, Indonesia, Malawi, Pakistan, Sweden, Thailand, the USA and Yemen; see Hampson, intervention under Agenda Item 2, UN Sub-Commission on the Promotion and Protection of Human Rights (2004)

[7] In January 2002, 5 Algerians and a Yemeni were abducted by US forces in Bosnia and flown to Guantanamo Bay in contravention of an injunction by the Bosnian Human Rights Chamber that they remain in the country until their cases were determined; Finn, "Al Qaeda recruiter reportedly tortured", *Washington Post* January 31, 2003, A14.

[8] Human Rights Watch, note 1, "US:Investigate 'Ghost Detainees'", September 10, 2004; "The United States' "Disappeared": The CIA's long-term 'Ghost Detainees'", October 12, 2004; Reed Brody, "Prisoners Who Disappear: Ghost Detainees of the United States", *International Herald Tribune*, October 12, 2004.

[9] Greenberg & Dratel; Danner; Human Rights Watch, note 1; Amnesty International, note 1.

[10] E.g. certain comments in "op-eds" by Rivkin & Casey, such as "Assault on the Geneva Convention", Wall Street Journal, March 9, 2003; they appear to see international law, and not just the law of armed conflict (LOAC), as a threat to American security. Two separate issues have overlapped since 9/11. One group of commentators is hostile to any constraint international law might impose on US policies. Following the election of President George W. Bush, their influence increased significantly, well before 9/11; Sands; Keegan, Ch.5. The other group, whilst professing no hostility to international law itself, was of the view that 9/11 heralded an entirely new world, apparently ignoring the significant levels of terrorist activity with which other States had had to deal, and that certain specific rules of international law were not suited to the new environment. Ruth Wedgwood is an example of commentators coming into the second category.

[11] E.g. State practice has dramatically modified the obligation to repatriate POWs in Art. 118 of the third Geneva Convention, note 22 below. In practice, they are free to refuse to be repatriated if they do not wish to return to their own State.

[12] See the discussion of the fragmentation of international law in the annual reports of the International Law Commission to the UN General Assembly; e.g. A/58/10 (2003).

[13] In order for some of the provisions to be capable of implementation in time of conflict, the necessary arrangements need to be made in peace-time; e.g. locating military objectives, so far as possible, away from civilian population centres; establishing arrangements for evacuation and civil defence etc.

[14] Human rights obligations flowing from the UN Charter include the work of the UN Commission on Human Rights and the special procedures which report to the Commission.

[15] International human right treaty texts are available on the web-site of the Office of the High Commissioner for Human Rights; www.ohchr.org.

[16] text available on www.echr.coe.int. For an example of a military lawyer who has no difficulty in accepting the applicability of the European Convention on Human Rights to military operations, probably because he has had to live with it in relation to operations in Northern Ireland, see Garraway, pp.119-123.

[17] text available on www.oas.org/juridico/english/Treaties/b-32.htm

[18] Art.4 ICCPR; Art.15 ECHR; Art.27 ACHR; See generally, Human Rights Committee, General Comment No. 29 on states of emergency, CCPR/C/21/Rev.1/Add.11, 31 August 2001.

[19] See generally, Siracuse Principles on the Limitation and Derogation Provisions in the International Covenant on Civil and Political Rights, Annex, E/CN.4/1985/4 (1985); General Comment No.29, note 18.

[20] The treaty texts indicate which rights cannot be modified, even in an emergency. *Prima facie*, other rights can be modified; General comment, note 18.

[21] Treaty provisions, note 18.

[22] For LOAC treaty provisions, see Roberts & Guelff; also web-site of the International Committee of the Red Cross, www.icrc.org.

[23] Treaty provisions, note 18; the list of non-derogable treaty provisions varies in each of the texts. It should also be noted that the ICCPR, ECHR and ACHR all contain "best treatment" provisions, according to which provisions of the human rights treaties cannot reduce protections afforded under other treaties to which the State is a party. Those other treaties may obviously include the Geneva Conventions and Protocols.

[24] In relation to the United States, this issue has arisen with the Inter-American Commission on Human Rights, exercising its functions under the OAS Charter and the American Declaration on Human Rights; for example, *Disabled Peoples' International et al v. United States*, Case 9213, Inter-Am. C.H.R. 184, OEA/ser. L/V/II.71, doc. 9 rev. 1 (1987) (Annual Report 1986-1987) ; issue of precautionary measures in relation to detainees in Guantanamo Bay, United States response, www.ccr-ny.org/v2/legal/september_11th/docs/4-15-02GovernmentResponse.pdf and with the UN Working Group on Arbitrary Detention, response to the Opinion in Report of the Working Group on Arbitrary Detention, (E/CN.4/2003/8), December 16, 2002, paras. 61-64 by Letter dated 2 April 2003 from the Permanent Mission of the United States of America to the United Nations Office at Geneva addressed to the secretariat of the Commission on Human Rights, E/CN.4/2003/G/73, 7 April 2003. In the case of Israel, the issue has arisen in relation to its reports to the Human Rights Committee under the ICCPR and the Committee on Economic, Social and Cultural Rights; General Comment, note 18, para.16, note 9; see also Human Rights Committee, Concluding Observations on periodic reports by Israel, UN Doc.CCPR/C/79/Add.93, para.10; and CCPR/CO/78/ISR, para. 11; Committee on Economic, Social and Cultural

Rights, E/C.12/1/Add.90, paras. 15 and 31 and in its dealings with special procedures. This raises the question of whether the principle of the "persistent objector" can apply to treaty interpretation; if so, whether there is any exception in the field of treaties of a humanitarian character (see, by analogy Art.60.5 of the Vienna Convention on the Law of Treaties); if not, whether either State party can claim to be a "persistent objector" given that neither State made a relevant statement, declaration of understanding or reservation at the time of signature and/or ratification and that neither State has objected to General Comment No.29, note 18. The US has previously indicated its disagreement with a General Comment, in the case of General Comment No.24. It appears that it is not enough for the State to object; the doctrine appears to be only applicable where the objection is accepted or acquiesced in. Even if other States parties acquiesced, would that be sufficient? Would it not also be necessary for the treaty body to acquiesce? That the HRC has not done. Even if the US were to be regarded as a "persistent objector" where LOAC is applicable, would it be able to rely on that where there has been a determination that LOAC is not applicable, as in the case of the conflict in Afghanistan in relation to the Taliban and Al Qaeda; see further below.

[25] Response to the Working Group on Arbitrary Detention, note 24; see also Report of the Special Rapporteur on Extrajudicial, Summary and Arbitrary Executions, E/CN.4/2005/7, 22 December 2004, paras.43-54.

[26] *The Legal Consequences of the Construction of a Wall in the Occupied Palestinian Territory*, ICJ, Advisory Opinion, 9 July 2004, para. 106; also see *Legality or Threat of Use of Nuclear Weapons*, ICJ, Advisory Opinion, July 8, 1996, para.25.

[27] General comment, note 18 & concluding observations on reports of Israel, note 24.

[28] Concluding observations on report of Israel, note 24.

[29] See, for example, the reports of the Committee Against Torture (CAT) and the Committee on the Rights of the Child, whose Convention contains a provision and an optional protocol expressly applicable in situations of conflict.

[30] See, for example, *Isayeva, Yusupova and Bazayeva v. Russia*, 57947/00, 57948/00 and 57949/00, judgment of 24 February 2005; *Cyprus v. Turkey*, 25781/94, judgment of 10 May 2001; *Loizidou v. Turkey*, 15318/89, judgment of 18 December 1996.

[31] *Abella v. Argentina*, Case 11.137, Report N° 55/97, Inter-Am.C.H.R., OEA/Ser.L/V/II.95 Doc. 7 rev. at 271 (1997); *Las Palmeras v. Colombia*, Preliminary Objections, Judgment of February 4, 2000; *Bámaca Velásquez Case*, Judgment of November 25, 2000, Inter-Am Ct. H.R. (Ser. C) No. 70 (2000); for examples of the case-law of Inter-American Commission under the American Declaration, see note 24.

[32] E.g. United Kingdom in relation to Northern Ireland and Turkey in relation to south-east Turkey.

[33] *Isayeva et* al, note 30; The Russian Constitutional Court has held that the situation in the Chechen Republic falls within Protocol II to the Geneva Conventions of 1949; Judgment of the Constitutional Court of the Russian Federation of 31 July 1995 on the constitutionality of the Presidential Decrees and the Resolutions of the Federal Government concerning the situation in Chechnya, European Commission for Democracy through Law of the Council of Europe, CDL-INF (96) 1. The respondent governments in the case of *Bankovic & others v. Belgium & 16 other members of NATO*, 52207/99, Admissibility Decision of 12 December 2001, which involved an international armed conflict, did not argue that LOAC displaced the ECHR but that the applicants were not within the jurisdiction of the respondent governments; see following section.

[34] Note 26.

[35] See generally Coomans & Kamminga (eds.).

[36] Notes 15-17.

[37] Within the US, the US Solicitor General did rely on this argument in Case Nos 03-334 and 03-343 *Rasul et al. v. George Bush et al.*, and *Al Odah et al. v. George Bush et al.*, US Supreme Court, Brief for the Respondents, October 2003, cited in Sands, p.145, note 6.

[38] *Cyprus v. Turkey* and *Loizidou*, note 30.

[39] *Ilascu and others v. Moldova & the Russian Federation*, with Romania intervening, 48787/99, Judgment of 8 July 2004.

[40] *Bankovic et al*, note 33.

[41] ICJ, Advisory Opinions, note 26; Human Rights Committee, Concluding Observations, note 24; *Cyprus v. Turkey*, note 30.

[42] *Loizidou*, note 30.

[43] "Territory is considered occupied when it is actually placed under the authority of the hostile army. The occupation extends only to the territory where such authority has been established and can be exercised.", Art.42, Regulations annexed to Hague Convention IV of 1907; Roberts & Guelff. In *Ilascu et* al, note 39, Russia was held responsible for the acts of the Trandniestran authorities.

[44] *Issa & others v. Turkey*, 31821/96, admissibility decision of May 30, 2000; decision of second Chamber, 16 November 2004.

[45] *Lopez Burgos v. Uruguay*, HRC 29 July 1981, UN Doc.A/36/40, 176; Communication No.52/1979, CCPR/C/13/D/52/1979; *Coard and others v. the United States*, IACHR Report No. 109/99, Case No. 10,951, 29 September 1999, Ann. Rep. IACHR 1999; *Ocalan v. Turkey*, 46221/99, judgment of 12 March 2003; the case is currently pending before the Grand Chamber.

[46] *Ilascu et al.*, note 39; the applicants were within the jurisdiction of both Moldova and Russia. Even more clearly, the victim in the case of *Lopez Burgos* was initially within the jurisdiction of both Argentina and Uruguay.

[47] Hampson, "Human Rights Law and the Conduct of Military Operations", forthcoming; contra ECHR in *Ocalan*, note 45.

[48] *Bankovic et al*, note 33, at para.37.

[49] Report of the Working Group on Arbitrary Detention, E/CN.4/2005/6, 1st December 2004, paras.6-9; see also UK Ministry of Defence, Manual, *seriatim*.

[50] *Ibid*; no reference was made to their possible protection under the fourth Geneva Convention, by virtue of the occupying power's obligation to apply previous domestic law to criminal detainees; it was perhaps thought that non-derogable human rights law afforded them greater protection, although this is open to question or, alternatively, that human rights law gave greater specificity to the provisions of the fourth Geneva Convention. According to the latter, the occupying power would be required to apply the criminal law and procedure of the sovereign. They may have had reservations as to the compatibility of that law with human rights law.

[51] *Al-Skeini et al. v.Sec. of State for Defence*, [2004] EWHC 2911; in those proceedings, the government disputed whether any persons in Iraq were "within the jurisdiction" for the purposes of the Human Rights Act. The High Court determined that a detainee was "within the jurisdiction" but that the other applicants were not. Both parties are appealing.

[52] The English courts have stated that they cannot reconcile the decisions in *Bankovic et al*, note 33 and those in *Ocalan*, note 45 and *Issa et al*, note 44; *Al-Skeini et al*, para. paras. 265 & 277; see also *R(B) v. Secretary of State for the Foreign and Commonwealth Office*, [2004] EWCA Civ 1344, para. 59.

[53] That has not been the approach taken by the Human Rights Committee in relation to Israel of the Working Group on Arbitrary Detention in relation to the United States; note 24.

[54] In the first and second applications introduced by Cyprus, the European Commission of Human Rights had to determine whether detention as a POW was lawful under the ECHR.

For technical reasons to do with the drafting of the relevant provision (Art.5 ECHR), it could only be lawful if the Geneva Conventions could be taken into account. Turkey had not derogated. The majority of the Commission disregarded the applicability of the Geneva Conventions and found the detentions unlawful. A minority found that the relevance of the Geneva Conventions was triggered by the situation; they could be taken into account even without derogation. On that basis, they found it lawful to detain prisoners of war under the ECHR; *Cyprus v. Turkey*, 6780/74 & 6950/75, Report of the Commission, adopted on 10 July 1976.

[55] A third issue, not of concern in this paper, is the examination of complaints regarding treatment in detention. LOAC prohibits ill-treatment but does not define the proscribed ill-treatment. Should human rights bodies use the same definitions as have been elaborated in non-derogable human rights law or do different tests apply in the LOAC context? It is submitted that there should only be one definition of torture and probably cruelty. In the case of "inhuman or degrading" treatment, since the characteristics and culture of the victim are relevant, the position may be more complicated. Nudity in front of other people is viewed differently in different cultures. That might result in different results in different contexts. If members of armed forces have received torture-resistance training, it is arguable that something that would be inhuman for a civilian might not be for a person so trained. On the other hand, the danger of escalating ill-treatment might lead human rights bodies, as a policy matter, to exclude such training when evaluating the treatment. Human rights bodies usually evaluate the treatment as a whole and not particular incidents of it.

[56] There is, in fact, provision for challenging status determination in the case of prisoners of war and classification as a serious security risk in the case of enemy civilians; see further below.

[57] See generally, CUDH, Report.

[58] A significant part of the pressure on human rights bodies to address situations in which LOAC is also applicable may well be attributable to the lack of any remedial mechanisms in LOAC available as of right to individual complainants and applying international law.

[59] As Article 2 of the Geneva Conventions of 1949 makes clear, the rules on the conduct of hostilities and the protection of victims apply by virtue of the existence of an armed conflict and apply to all parties, including the aggressor; UK Ministry of Defence, p.34.

[60] See also Article 1.4 of Protocol I, not binding on the US; Roberts & Guelff.

[61] "Any difference arising between two States and leading to the intervention of members of armed forces is an armed conflict within the meaning of Article 2, even if one of the parties denies the existence of a state of war."; Pictet, vol. III, p.23; Sandoz et al., p.40.

[62] A single incident involving armed forces can constitute an armed conflict. Pictet, *ibid*, suggests that fighting is not necessary but, it is submitted, this is in the context of POW status; a combatant may be detained away from any fighting but still entitled to POW status. In order for that status to be an issue, however, some fighting does need to be occurring somewhere. During the Gulf War 1990-1991 the UK detained certain Iraqis in the UK and held them as POWs; Hampson, Public Law. This suggests that where a person is detained anywhere, provided that fighting is being carried out somewhere involving the detaining State and the armed forces to which the detainee belongs or against the State to which the a detained civilian belongs, the individual will be protected under LOAC. The end of an armed conflict is not necessarily defined in the same way for all purposes. Generally speaking, Protocol I Art.3 provides that the applicability not only of the Protocol but also of the Geneva Conventions shall cease "in the territory of Parties to the conflict, on the general close of military operations"; Sandoz et al, pp.65-69; the obligation to repatriate POWs arises at the "cessation of active hostilities"; Art. 118 Geneva Convention III; see generally Lavoyer, pp.39-41.

[63] See generally Henckaerts & Doswald-Beck.

[64] *ibid*; the consensus with regard to the content of the customary rules applicable in non-international conflicts has been transformed as a result of the work of the ICTY and the ICTR. This has been reinforced by the Statute of the International Criminal Court, where the basis for inclusion in the list of war crimes in non-international conflicts was the customary status of the prohibition in question, and the trend in certain areas, notably the prohibition and regulation of weapons and the protection of cultural property, to make treaties applicable to both types of conflict.

[65] e.g. a civilian object is defined as an object which is not a military objective; Art.52.1 of Protocol I.

[66] In practice, determining whether activity constitutes an armed conflict is usually more difficult in non-international armed conflicts than in international armed conflicts; that is not a significant issue in the actual situations with which this chapter is dealing.

[67] Both Art.3 common to the Geneva Conventions and Protocol II claim to be binding on all the parties to the conflict. Whilst, theoretically, there is no completely satisfactory way of explaining how non-State groups can be bound by a provision which they have not ratified or how non-States can be bound by customary law, the fact of their being so bound appears to be generally accepted.

[68] It is not being suggested that this was the understanding of the scope of common Art. 3 at the time of its negotiation and adoption; Pictet, Vol. III, pp. 27-38. Rather, the situation described comes within the wording of the article, whether or not it was originally intended to do so.

[69] Protocol II, Art.1.1; the Protocol provides a partial, excluding, definition of armed conflicts in Art.1.2: it does not apply to "situations of internal disturbances and tensions, such as riots, isolated and sporadic acts of violence and other acts of a similar nature, *as not being* armed conflicts" (emphasis added); Roberts & Guelff. It is not clear whether this modifies the threshold of applicability of common Article 3; Article 1.1 says that it was not intended to do so; Sandoz et al, pp.1347-1356.

[70] ICRC, Challenges, p.17 *et seq.*; Lavoyer, p. 39-41; Pejic.

[71] Sec.Co.Res.1368, (2001), 12th September 2001 and 1373, (2001),28th September 2001 referred to the right of self-defence, in the context of the reaction to the attacks of 9/11; see generally Greenwood; Wolfrum, forum.

[72] Even before 9/11, the Security Council had called upon the Taliban to put an end to the activities of Al Qaeda; S/RES/1214 (1998) of 8 December 1998 and S/RES/1267 (1999) of 15 October 1999.

[73] Mullah Omar, the Taliban leader, convened a conference of Islamic clerics to determine whether Osama Bin Laden should be handed over to the Americans; the Council said that he should be but Mullah Omar overrode that decision; Harding, McCarthy & Borger, "US prepares for long war as Taliban close path to peace", the Guardian, September 20, 2001; Mullah Omar in his own words, the Guardian, September 26, 2001.

[74] *Contra* Memo: Alberto Gonzales to President Bush, January 25, 2002; the distinction between arguing the non-applicability of the Geneva Conventions and arguing that members of Al Qaeda and the Taliban were not entitled to POW status was made clear in the memos of Colin Powell to Alberto Gonzales of January 26, 2002, John Ashcroft to President Bush of February 1, 2002 and William H. Taft IV to Alberto Gonzales of February 2, 2002; all memos referred to are reproduced in Danner, pp.83-95. The Memos suggest that, as a matter of domestic law, the President is allowed to override the application of an otherwise applicable treaty. That has no effect on the violation of international law involved in failing to apply a treaty applicable as a matter of international law. In a statement issued on February 7, 2002, President Bush announced that members of the Taliban were "covered"

by the Geneva Conventions, which assumes the applicability of the Geneva Conventions, whether or not the Taliban were entitled to combatant status; Fact Sheet, White House Press Office, Feb. 7, 2002, available at www.whitehouse.gov/news/releases/2002/02/2002027, see Goldman, & Tittemore, pp.23-5. In *Hamdan v. Rumsfeld*, Civil Action Nr 04-cv-1519, the Federal District Court of Colombia determined that the Geneva Conventions of 1949 were applicable to a person captured in Afghanistan during hostilities. The government filed notice of appeal. See generally, Fitzpatrick J.

[75] "… a decision that the Conventions do apply is consistent with the plain language of the Conventions and the unvaried practice of the United States in introducing its forces into conflict over fifty years. It is consistent with the advice of DOS lawyers and, as far as is known, the position of every other party to the Conventions. It is consistent with UN Security Council Resolution 1193 affirming that "All parties to the conflict (in Afghanistan) are bound to comply with their obligations under international humanitarian law and in particular the Geneva Conventions…"."; Taft, note 74, Danner, p.94.

[76] In implementation of the Agreement on Provisional Arrangements in Afghanistan pending the Re-establishment of Permanent Government Institutions (the Bonn Agreement), December 5, 2001, http://afghanland.com/history/bonn.html

[77] Note 68 and accompanying text; neither Afghanistan nor the USA is a party to Protocol II which could, in any event, not be applicable unless Afghanistan was a party to the ongoing conflict. Both the USA and non-State fighters in Afghanistan were also bound by the rules of customary international law applicable in non-international armed conflicts; see Henckaerts & Doswald-Beck.

[78] International Security Assistance Force; ISAF is not a UN-operation but is a UN-mandated operation; Sec. Co. Res. 1386 (2001), adopted under Ch.VII; the mandate was extended under Sec. Co. Res. 1413 (2002) and 1444 (2002).

[79] The function of ISAF is the maintenance of security in Kabul and the surrounding areas to provide a secure environment for the Afghan Interim Authority and UN personnel.

[80] The UK Ministry of Defence, Manual, Ch.14 suggests that when a peace keeping force finds itself engaged in military operations constituting an armed conflict, LOAC is applicable; there are likely to be difficulties in practice in determining whether the peacekeeping force has become a party to the conflict or whether it has found itself coming between the parties to a different practice.

[81] Bulletin on the Observance by United Nations Forces of International Humanitarian Law, 6 August 1999; Roberts & Guelff, 725. The issue of the lawfulness of detention effected by forces engaged in a peace support operation is currently before the European Court of Human Rights regarding detentions ordered by COMKFOR.

[82] The ICJ in the Advisory Opinion on the Wall, note 26, suggested that once territory is occupied the rules on the conduct of military operations are no longer applicable; see note 84.

[83] On June 28, 2004 Paul Bremer, the senior administrator of the Coalition Provisional Authority, handed a "letter of sovereignty" to the chief judge of the Iraqi Supreme Court; UN Sec. Co. Res. 1546 (2004), however, stipulated that the Interim Government to which any "sovereignty" was allegedly restored had to refrain from "taking any actions affecting Iraq's destiny beyond the limited interim period". That, taken together with the continuing presence of foreign armed forces in a context in which it is not clear that the Interim Government had much, if any, choice about that presence, calls into question whether the Interim Government had the competence to request external military assistance. See generally IHL Workshop on the Beginning and End of Occupation and IHL, 2 February 2005, ICRC, Israel.

[84] A further difficulty concerns the rules applicable to operations such as those in Falluja. The ICJ in the Advisory Opinion on the Wall, note 26, suggested that once territory is occupied the rules on the conduct of international operations are no longer applicable, presumably meaning that they must take place in accordance with the law and order authority of the occupying power. It is submitted that this view was *obiter* and that the issue had not been fully argued. See generally, Lubell, *Israeli Yearbook on Human Rights*, forthcoming.

[85] Third Geneva Convention, Art.142; Fourth Geneva Convention, Art.158.

[86] A person can be detained in connection with a conflict even if originally detained outside the territory in which the conflict is occurring. The extent to which Hague Convention V of 1907 may be relevant in such a situation is not clear.

[87] Third Geneva Convention, Art.12; Fourth Geneva Convention, Art.45.

[88] Human Rights Watch, the NGO which has dealt with rendition most systematically, appears to have analysed the transfers in terms of the risk of ill-treatment, rather than in terms of the LOAC obligations of the transferring States; e.g. Guantanamo: New "Reverse Rendition" Case, press release March 30, 2005.

[89] Three situations need to be distinguished. First, where a person is detained in one State, on account of suspected involvement in terrorist activity, and transferred to the US, LOAC does not appear to be relevant. Second, where a person is detained in one State because that State suspects he is a combatant or, possibly, an escaped internee in an on-going conflict in another territory to which that State is not a party, the State may have obligations under both the Geneva Conventions and Hague Convention V of 1907; notes 86 & 87. Third, where a person is detained in one State at the request of a State involved in an armed conflict and his transfer is sought as a combatant or escaped internee, it would appear that the requested State can invoke its rights under LOAC. It appears that, in the majority of cases of transfer, the US has not claimed that the persons whose transfer has been requested actually participated in hostilities in Afghanistan or Iraq.

[90] It would be necessary to determine whether they were held in connection with an international or non-international armed conflict. Furthermore, in relation to occupied territory, if Art. 49 of the Fourth Geneva Convention is applicable to internees, it would appear to require their internment in the occupied territory itself. On the face of it, Art.49 appears to apply to all protected persons in occupied territory.

[91] Note 3.

[92] E.g. Operational Law Handbook (2003), www.jagcnet.army.mil, p.11; this is of relevance to cases such as that of Padilla, note 2.

[93] Report of the Special Rapporteur on Extrajudicial, Summary and Arbitrary Executions, note 25, paras.41-43; Schmitt, pp. 74-81.

[94] See generally Cassese.

[95] See generally, Brownlie In this area, international law appears to be permissive; in other words, States can exercise jurisdiction on a basis recognised in international law, unless for some reason that is not permitted. They do not need the consent of international law so to act; *the "Lotus" Case, P.C.I.J., Series A, No. 10*, pp. 18-19.

[96] It is necessary to distinguish between the question of jurisdiction and that of trials *in absentia*. This section assumes that the person against whom criminal charges are to be brought is within the territory of the State proposing to exercise jurisdiction. Judges Higgins, Kooijmans & Buergentahl call this "territorial jurisdiction over persons for extraterritorial events"; *Arrest Warrant of 11 April 2000*, (DRC v. Belgium), ICJ, judgment of 14 February 2002, separate opinion, para.42.

[97] See generally *the Arrest Warrant Case*, separate opinion of Higgins, Kooijmans & Buergenthal, note 95.

[98] See generally, Gilbert.

[99] *Ibid*; controversially, that is no longer the case under bilateral UK-US treaty of March 2003 where the US is the requesting State but the UK still has to establish "probable cause" where it is the requesting State; Justice Briefing.

[100] E.g. the case of Lofti Raisi, an Algerian, who was held on remand under the earlier extradition arrangements. Despite the court giving the US authorities repeated opportunities to provide evidence of a link with Al Qaeda, beyond his mere presence at the same flying school as some of the 9/11 perpetrators, the US was unable to provide such evidence. Mr. Raisi was released.

[101] Subject to specific rules of international law and possibly to national rules, such as the non-extradition of nationals.

[102] The principle of non-refoulement, which originated in refugee law, now applies generally to the transfer of any person and not just refugees. It is not confined to extradition cases; Committee Against Torture, General Comment No.1, A/53/44, Annex IX, 21 November 1997; Human Rights Committee, General Comment No.20 on Art.7, 10 March 1992, para.9; General Comment No.31 on the nature of the general legal obligation imposed on states parties to the Covenant, 26 May 2004, para.12. European States also generally refuse to transfer persons with a view to criminal proceedings in a jurisdiction which retains the death penalty for the offence in question; it is not clear how transfers to Guantanamo Bay are reconcilable with the usual practice. There may also be an issue where a person is to be transferred to a jurisdiction in which he will not be accorded anything that resembles due process.

[103] The Committee against Torture and the Human Rights Committee, in their concluding observations on state reports, have implied that the State is responsible for what occurs in privatized prisons; e.g. Conclusion and Recommendations of CAT: Netherlands, 16 May 2000, A/55/44, para.186; Concluding Observations of the Human Rights Committee: New Zealand, 7 August 2002, CCPR/CO/75/NZL, para. 13.

[104] The justice system needs to take account of the special needs of juveniles and States are required to distinguish between those detained on remand and convicted prisoners. Conditions of detention, including the accommodation of the victim with other detainees, may need to take account of youth, age, gender and of medical and other similar factors. The European Court of Human Rights has held that any criminal proceedings against a civilian before a tribunal one or more of whose members is a serving member of the armed forces cannot be fair or independent in the context of due process; see further below.

[105] ICCPR, note 13, Art.9.

[106] The ECHR, note 14, Art.5 lists exhaustively the only permitted grounds of detention, *viz* after conviction by a competent court, non-compliance with the lawful order of a court or to secure the fulfilment of an obligation prescribed by law, reasonable suspicion of having committed an offence or to prevent the commission of an offence or flight after committing an offence, of a minor for educational supervision or to bring the minor before a competent authority, for the prevention of spreading of infectious diseases, those of unsound mind, alcoholics, drug addicts or vagrants, to prevent unauthorised entry into a country or where action is being taken with a view to deportation or extradition.

[107] Human Rights Committee General Comment No. 8 of June 30th, 1982, on Right to Liberty and Security of Persons does not make it clear whether administrative detention can be compatible with Article 9.

[108] Hampson, forthcoming, note 30.

[109] General comment No.29, note 18; an early decision of the European Commission of Human Rights illustrates the problems which arise where a human rights body fails to take

into account the applicability of LOAC; 6780/74 & 6950/75, Report of the Commission, adopted on 10 July 1976, opinion of the majority and minority on ECHR Art.15.

[110] e.g. ability to consult a freely chosen lawyer; safeguards include both provisions regarding detention and also due process requirements; see Report of the Special Rapporteur on the Independence of Judges and Lawyers, E/CN.4/2005/60, Part III and the reports referred to therein. See generally *Lawless v. Ireland*, No.3, 332/57, ECHR judgment of 1 July 1961; *Brogan & others v. UK*, 11209/84, ECHR judgment of 29 November 1988; *Brannigan & McBride v. UK*, 14553/89, ECHR judgment of 26 May 1993.

[111] *İncal v. Turkey*, 22678/93, ECHR judgment of 9 June 1998, paras.67-73; *Çiraklar v. Turkey*,19601/92 ECHR judgment of 28 October 1998, paras.37-41 of 28 October 1998; *Ocalan v. Turkey*, 46221/99, ECHR judgment of 12 March 2003, paras.111-121.

[112] *Durand and Ugarte Case*. Judgment of August 16, 2000. Series C No. 68, para.117; *Cantoral Benavides Case*, Judment of August 18, 2000, Series C No.69, paras.110-115. In the first of these two cases, the IACHR considered derogation in the context of Art.7, arbitrary detention but in neither case did the Court specify whether the principle that civilians could not be subjected to proceedings carried out by the military was subject to derogation or whether it was so fundamental as to be non-derogable. Nor is that clarified in Judicial Guarantees in States of Emergency, Advisory Opinion OC-9/87, October 6, 1987.

[113] "The Committee notes the existence, in many countries, of military or special courts which try civilians. This could present serious problems as far as the equitable, impartial and independent administration of justice is concerned. ... While the Covenant does not prohibit such categories of courts, nevertheless the conditions which it lays down clearly indicate that the trying of civilians by such courts should be very exceptional and take place under conditions which genuinely afford the full guarantees stipulated in article 14."; General Comment No. 13: Equality before the courts and the right to a fair and public hearing by an independent court established by law, 13 April 1984, para.4.

[114] "If States parties decide in circumstances of a public emergency as contemplated by article 4 to derogate from normal procedures required under article 14, they should ensure that such derogations do not exceed those strictly required by the exigencies of the actual situation, and respect the other conditions in paragraph 1 of article 14."; *ibid*. In the cases against Turkey before the European Court of Human Rights, Turkey had submitted a valid notice of derogation but, at the relevant time, only in relation to Art.5.3 of the ECHR, in relation to the time for which a person can be held before being brought before a judicial officer. It had not derogated with regard to the composition of the State Security Court.

115 General comment No.29, note 18, para.13 b.

[116] Statute of the International Criminal Court, Art. 7.1.i and 2.i.

[117] House of Commons, Report of the Intelligence and Security Committee, "The Handling of Detainees by UK Intelligence Personnel in Afghanistan, Guantanamo Bay and Iraq", March 2005, Cm 6469, para. 77; see generally Human Rights Watch and Amnesty International, note 1.

[118] General comment No.29, note 18.

[119] *Ibid*, para.16.

[120] *Hamdi*, note 5; *Hamdan*, note 74; in the latter case, the Federal District Court held that the Combatant Status Review Tribunal established, as a result of the decision in *Hamdi*, to determine whether a person was properly detained as an enemy combatant was not a tribunal to determine entitlement to POW status under the Geneva Conventions, p.18.

[121] A wide range of concerns has been raised by the Independent Expert on the situation of human rights in Afghanistan. They include not only torture and death in detention but also excessive use of force and unlawful detention. His concerns with regard to what takes place in detention is exacerbated by the fact that he and other Special Rapporteurs have been

denied access to detainees and, even more disturbingly, the ICRC is being denied access to a variety of places of detention in Afghanistan. An internal Pentagon investigation remains classified; E/CN.4/2005/112, 11 March 2005, paras. 43-46.

[122] General Comment No.29, note 18, para. 16; it is not clear how this affects tribunals envisaged by LOAC for review of necessity of internment (Geneva Convention IV, Arts. 43 and 48) and status review tribunals for PoWs (Geneva Convention III, Art.5); see generally CUDH.

[123] Note 101.

[124] Human Rights Watch, note 1, Still at Risk: Diplomatic Assurances No Safeguard against Torture, April 15, 2005; House of Commons, Foreign Affairs.

[125] Note 189. An analogous issue arises where a State uses information which is likely to have been obtained under torture in another State in judicial proceedings.

[126] Human Rights Watch, note 1; Amnesty International, note 1; House of Commons, Foreign Affairs; House of Commons, Intelligence and Security; the evidence includes undisputed evidence of unnatural deaths in detention.

[127] It is clear that there are two categories: combatants and civilians. There are difficulties in categorising the following groups: a member of armed forces who for some reason is not in uniform when he participates in hostilities; a non-combatant member of armed forces (e.g. civilian air crew) who takes part in the hostilities; a member of an armed group which does not distinguish itself from civilians when carrying out attacks and does not respect the law of armed conflict; a civilian who feeds or shelters members of a non-State armed group; a civilian who is armed in self-defence. The first two groups appear to be combatants who may have forfeited the privileges of combatant status. They are sometimes called "unprivileged belligerents"; Baxter, Mallinson and Mallinson. In the case of the fourth and fifth groups, the question is whether they are taking a direct part in hostilities or whether they have lost the protection of civilian status for some other reason; Quéguiner. The biggest problem concerns the third group. Are they a type of combatant but not qualifying for the privileges of the status, in other words another category of unprivileged belligerent, or are they civilians who forfeit the protection from attack whilst taking a direct part in the fighting? The answer will in large part determine the rules applicable to their detention; see Garraway; *contra* Dinstein, "Unlawful Combatancy", Dinstein, "*Jus in bello*".

[128] Some use the term to mean a member of a group who fights, whether or not he is entitled to do so. Others only use the word to mean a person who is entitled to fight, in other words a member of the armed forces of a party to the conflict. The difficulty is compounded by the fact that, in some languages, the same word is used for combatant and fighter.

[129] E.g. civilians working with, but not necessarily members of, armed forces and carrying out computer network attacks or computer network exploitation; Watkin.

[130] Combatants are "[m]embers of the armed forces of a Party to a conflict ... that is to say, they have the right to participate directly in hostilities"; Protocol I, Art.43.2 Armed forces include non-combatants (e.g. medical personnel). Combatants are therefore fighting members of armed forces. The effect of Art.43 was to merge two groups, each of which had previously been entitled to POW status, fighting members of armed forces and members of a militia which satisfied the requirements of Art.4A2 of Geneva Convention III. Such militia had previously had to establish their entitlement to POW status, unlike armed forces, where it appears to have been presumed; Watkin; Henckaerts & Doswald-Beck, pp. 14-17.

[131] "Any combatant, as defined in Article 43, who falls into the power of an adverse Party shall be a prisoner of war."; Protocol I, Art.44.1. It would appear that the US accepts that any combatant, as defined before 1977 (i.e. fighting members of armed forces and members of militia which satisfy certain requirements), is entitled to POW status. In addition, certain

[132] other members of armed forces or persons closely associated with armed forces are entitled to POW status; see generally Art.4 of Geneva Convention III.

[132] Note 130.

[133] Art.4A2 of Geneva Convention III; see also Art.1, Annex, Hague Convention IV of 1907.

[134] Armed forces appear to be assumed to fulfil these conditions; note 140 & 141. Where an individual does satisfy the requirements but the group with which he fights does not, he would appear not to be entitled to combatant status. Where the group satisfies the requirements but the individual does not comply with the third and fourth requirements, the individual appears not to be entitled to combatant status; Watkin.

[135] Note 127; Henckaerts & Doswald-Beck, p.389.

[136] Art.85 Geneva Convention III; former Communist States made a reservation to that provision. Western States indicated not only that they rejected the reservation but that they would apply the Convention in their mutual relations without the benefit of the reservation, which appears to be an early form of severance of a reservation; Roberts & Guelff.

[137] With regard to the Taliban & Al Qaeda, see Danner and Greenberg & Dratel. With regard to Iraq, few members of the Iraqi armed forces were detained during the initial hostilities and those who were taken prisoner were rapidly released and sent home; Keegan, p.205.

[138] Art.2, Annex to Hague Convention IV; Henckaerts & Doswald-Beck, pp.386-7.

[139] Goldman & Tittemore; see also note 74.

[140] Watkin; if all members of armed forces were required to satisfy the requirements, including compliance with the laws and customs of war, failing which no member would be entitled to combatant status, this would have very serious implications for any armed force which made use of forces out of uniform or which might contain the occasional "bad apple"; Goldman & Tittemore, p.27. It would, effectively, signal the end of combatant status.

[141] Henckaerts & Doswald-Beck, p.15; Watkin.

[142] Goldman & Tittemore, p.28.

[143] *Ibid*; Dinstein, "*Jus in bello*".

[144] *ibid*. It is also difficult to reconcile Donald Rumsfeld's claim that the Taliban had no identifiable chain of command with reports that the US military had attacked the Taliban's command and control networks; *ibid*, p.29.

[145] *ibid*, pp.29-30.

[146] note 127; see further below; the author agrees with Garraway, pp.113-117 and disagrees with Dinstein, considering that they are civilians unlawfully participating in hostilities.

[147] Note 137. It appears that large numbers of the Iraqi armed forces deserted prior to engaging coalition forces; Keegan; Hiro.

[148] Keegan, p.210; Hiro, p.312.

[149] Hiro, p.413.

[150] Goldman & Tittemore, p.29; Geneva Convention III, Art.16.

[151] Art.44.4, Protocol I.

[152] The special provisions for *levée en masse*, together with Arts.43 & 44 of Protocol I and the statements made by certain States at signature and/or ratification of Protocol I, suggest that those opposing occupation can in certain circumstances be combatants. Given that a combatant has the right to participate in hostilities, this suggests that there is such a right, on condition that those fighting satisfy the requirements for constituting the armed forces of a party to the conflict, i.e. responsible command, subjection to an internal disciplinary system which enforces compliance with LOAC and, subject to Art.44, distinguishing themselves from the civilian population and bearing their arms openly. See generally Henckaerts & Doswald-Beck, pp. 11-19; 384-389.

[153] Art.44.3, Protocol I.

[154] Given the wording of the provision, it seems surprising that commentators appear to think that it *gives* combatant status to members of a group which does not otherwise satisfy the normal requirements for being a member of the armed forces of a party to the conflict. In order to benefit from the provision, a person has to be a combatant. That has been defined in Art.43.2. That description is intended as a definition; Art.44.1. On the face of it, Art.44.43 simply means that where a person otherwise entitled to combatant status does not distinguish himself from the civilian population, he will retain that status if he satisfies the two requirements.

[155] Protocol I, Art. 45; Geneva Convention III, Art.5; see further below.

[156] Protocol, Art.50.1; the US Operational Law Handbook, note 92, indicates that this paragraph is accepted as customary law.

[157] Pictet, Vol.4, p.52; Henckaerts & Doswald-Beck, pp.17-19

[158] Protocol I, Art.51.3; it is significant that that provision is in an article dealing with protection. The provision on status is in a different article.

[159] *Ibid*; this appears to open the way to "revolving combatancy". Where there is evidence that not only has a civilian participated in hostilities but that he intends to carry on doing so, it would appear problematic if he could only be treated as a participant whilst actually fighting. His participation resembles that of a member of armed forces, who can be targeted at any time, irrespective of what he happens to be doing at the time. Schmitt suggests a way round the problem; p.79.

[160] See generally, Quéguiner; ICRC.

[161] Henckaerts & Doswald-Beck, pp.23-4. The very real difficulties in relation to the planning of military operations are, with one exception, of much less importance in relation to detention. If the armed forces detain a person who is not fighting, they can initially classify him as a civilian, subject to the possibility of revising that designation. The exception concerns the process of subjecting someone to detention. The characterisation of a person not yet detained but about to be detained as a combatant of civilian will affect the degree of force that can be used.

[162] E.g. targeted killing in Yemen, note 93 and accompanying text. See also *McCann & others v. United Kingdom*, 18984/91, ECHR judgment of 27 September 1995 (the Gibraltar killings case).

[163] Protocol I, Arts.45.1 and 50.1. Baxter suggests that those who fail to comply with the conditions of Art.4A(2) of the third Geneva Convention are entitled to neither POW nor civilian status; p.328. It is submitted that a distinction has to be drawn between those who belong to the armed forces of a party to the conflict but who forfeit the privilege of belligerency, for example by failing to distinguish themselves from civilians or by not bearing their arms openly, and those who fight on behalf of groups which are not the armed forces of a party to the conflict and which do not qualify for any form of combatant status. Baxter's example only concerned the first group.

[164] *Ibid*.

[165] e.g. If a member of the Taliban or Iraqi armed forces left the territory concerned and went to Sweden (neutral) or Poland (co-belligerent) but was sought by the US armed forces for interrogation with a view to prosecution. Does the political slogan "Those who are not with us are against us" translate into a legal principle; can a State be "neutral" in the "war on terror"? The precedent of the Gulf War in 1990-91, in which Iran invoked, without objection on the part of other States, and adhered to neutrality law, with regard to the detaining of Iraqi aircraft flown into its territory, suggests that a State can be neutral even in relation to a UN authorised operation. It is conceivable that neutrality law may be modified to the extent of not being allowed to frustrate a Security Council endorsed collective security operation,

but that may be subject to the obligations of neutrality. This is most likely to have practical impact in the territorial sea of a neutral State.

[166] It is generally assumed that detainees will want to claim combatant status. That will certainly be the case for anyone who has taken part in hostilities. If they are combatants, they cannot be prosecuted for that participation. Where criminal proceedings are brought against a detainee, his status determines before which kind of tribunal he can be tried. Art.102 of Geneva Convention III requires that a POW can only be tried by the same courts as members of the armed forces of the detaining power. In *Hamdan*, note 74, the petitioner sought POW status so that he could be tried before and according to the rules applicable to a US court martial, rather than before and according to the rules applicable to a military commission. Where a person is not fighting when detained but is thought to be a combatant and is detained on that basis, they may want to claim that they are not prisoners of war. Whilst Art.5 of the third Geneva Convention, which deals with status determination, assumes that the person detained has committed a belligerent act, there would appear to be no reason in principle why status determination should not be able to work both ways. This problem arose in the UK during the Gulf War 1990-91; see Hampson, Public Law.

[167] The US Army Field Manual and the US Air Force Pamphlet suggest that Article 5 of the third Geneva Convention applies where a person has committed a belligerent act and that person does not appear to be entitled to POW status and the detainee asserts such an entitlement; US Dep't of the Army Field Manual 27-10, the Law of Land Warfare, para.71(b); US Dep't of the Air Force, International Law – the Conduct of Armed Conflict and Air Operations, AFP 110-31 at 3-3(2). It is not clear what happens where there is no evidence that a person has committed a belligerent act; in the Gulf War 1990-91, it appears that the US used Art.5 tribunals to determine the status of anyone not obviously a civilian; US Military Judge Advocate General Operational Handbook, Lacey & Bill (ed.s) 2000, Ch.5 at 7. The UK Manual requires that, in case of doubt, a person should be detained as a POW. The doubt should be determined by a competent tribunal. Where a person is not held as a POW but is to be tried for an offence arising out of the hostilities and claims POW status, that claim should be determined by a "judicial tribunal" (i.e. a tribunal different from an Art.5 tribunal), preferably before the trial for the offence; UK Ministry of Defence, 8.21 & 8.22; In *Hamdan*, note 74, the Federal District Court determined " ... the government's position that no doubt has arisen as to Hamdan's status does not withstand scrutiny, and neither does the government's position that, if a hearing is required by Army regulations, "it was provided," 10/25/04 Tr. at 40. There is nothing in this record to suggest that a competent tribunal has determined that Hamdan is not a prisoner-of-war under the Geneva Conventions. Hamdan has appeared before the Combatant Status Review Tribunal, but the CSRT was not established to address detainees' status under the Geneva Conventions. It was established to comply with the Supreme Court's mandate in Hamdi, supra, to decide "whether the detainee is properly detained as an enemy combatant" for purposes of continued detention. Memorandum From Deputy Secretary of Defense, to Secretary of the Navy, Order Establishing Combatant Status Review Tribunal 3 (July 7, 2003), ... The government's legal position is that the CSRT determination that Hamdan was a member of or affiliated with al Qaeda is also determinative of Hamdan's prisoner-of-war status, since the President has already determined that detained al Qaeda members are not prisoners-of-war under the Geneva Conventions, see 10/25/04 Tr. at 37. The President is not a "tribunal," however. The government must convene a competent tribunal (or address a competent tribunal already convened) and seek a specific determination as to Hamdan's status under the Geneva Convention. Until or unless such a tribunal decides otherwise, Hamdan has, and must be accorded, the full protections of a prisoner-of-war.", pp.17-19; Goldman & Tittemore, pp.30-32; CUDH.

[168] It should be noted that those protected by the fourth Geneva Convention are a narrower category than the generality of civilians. The group is defined in Art.4 of the Convention; in effect, they are civilians not otherwise protected. The definition therefore excludes, for example, nationals of co-belligerent or neutral States with which the State in question has diplomatic relations. A British journalist or an American aid worker in Iraq was therefore a civilian for the purposes of military operations but not persons protected by the fourth Geneva Convention. They would be protected by Art.75 of Protocol I. Protected persons outside occupied territory (e.g. Iraqis in the US) can be interned or subjected to internment or assigned residence "if the security of the Detaining Power makes it absolutely necessary"; Geneva Convention IV, Arts. 41 & 42. In occupied territory, protected persons can, if considered necessary "for imperative reasons of security", be subjected to internment or assigned residence; *ibid*, Art. 78.

[169] *Ibid.*

[170] Geneva Convention IV, Arts. 43 & 78.

[171] Geneva Convention IV, Art. 64.; see also Art. 43 of the Annex to Hague Convention IV of 1907.

[172] Geneva Convention III, Arts. 13 & 17; Pejic.

[173] *Ibid*, Arts.118 & 119.

[174] *Ibid*, Art.102; see note 141.

[175] *ibid*, Art.12.

[176] Geneva Convention IV, Art. 27.

[177] *Ibid*, Arts. 43 & 78.

[178] *Ibid*, Art.45.

[179] Art. 3 common to the four Geneva Conventions; the ICJ has found the provision to be not only customary law in non-international conflicts but to be a fundamental norm applicable in all conflicts; *Military and Paramilitary Activities in and against Nicaragua* (Nicaragua v. United States of America), ICJ, judgment of 27 June 1986.

[180] Protocol II, Art. 4.

[181] Note 24 and accompanying text.

[182] Note 74.

[183] *Ibid*. The leaking of certain concerns suggests that those responsible for the leaks were military lawyers, concerned at the harm being done to an excellent system of military justice painstakingly put in place after the Vietnam conflict.

[184] Notes 5 and 74.

[185] In *Hamdan*, note 74, the Federal District Court pointed out that "The government has asserted a position starkly different from the positions and behavior of the United States in previous conflicts, one that can only weaken the United States' own ability to demand application of the Geneva Conventions to Americans captured during armed conflicts abroad. *Amici* remind us of the capture of U.S. Warrant Officer Michael Durant in 1993 by forces loyal to a Somali warlord. The United States demanded assurances that Durant would be treated consistently with protections afforded by the Convention, even though, if the Convention were applied as narrowly as the government now seeks to apply it to Hamdan, "Durant's captors would not be bound to follow the convention because they were not a 'state'".", p. 21.

[186] Sands.

[187] E.g. the experience of Israel with authorised departures from the rules normally applicable to the conduct of interrogation in "exceptional" cases.

[188] Both the US and the UK have experience of detaining large numbers of people who pose no threat; in the Second World War, the US interned large numbers of citizens of Japanese

origin and the UK interned large numbers of Germans, without distinguishing between refugees and those who might pose a risk.

[189] "The condoning of torture is per se a violation of the prohibition of torture."; Report of the Special Rapporteur on Torture and other cruel, inhuman or degrading treatment or punishment, A/59/324, 1 September 2004, para.15.

[190] Santayana G., The Life of Reason (1905)

References

Aldrich G. "Guerilla Combatants and Prisoner of War Status", 31 *Am. U. L. Rev.* (1982) 871.

Baxter R. "So Called Unprivileged Belligerency: Spies, Guerrillas and Saboteurs", 28 *BYIL*, 323 (1951).

Bialke J. "Al-Qaeda and Taliban Unlawful Combatant Detainees, Unlawful Belligerency, and the International Laws of Armed Conflicts", Air Force Law Review, spring 2004.

Bothe, Partsch and Solf, New Rules for the Victims of Armed Conflicts, Nijhoff, 1982.

Brownlie I. *Principles of Public International Law*, 6th Ed., OUP, 2003.

Cassese A. *International Criminal Law*, OUP, 2003.

Coomans & Kamminga (eds.), *Extraterritorial Application of Human Rights Treaties*, Intersentia, 2004.

CUDH, Expert Meeting on the Supervision of the Lawfulness of Detention during Armed Conflict, Geneva, 2005.

Danner M. *Torture and Truth*, Granta, 2004.

Dinstein Y. *The Conduct of Hostilities under the International Law of Armed Conflict*, CUP, 2004.

Dinstein Y. "Unlawful Combatancy" 32 *Israel Yearbook on Human Rights* (2002) 247.

Dinstein Y. "*Jus in bello* issues arising in the hostilities in Iraq", 34 *Israel Yearbook on Human Rights* (2004) 1.

Fitzpatrick J. "Jurisdiction of Military Commissions and the Ambiguous War on Terrorism", 96 *Am. J. Int'l. L.* 345 (2002).

Fleck D. (ed.), The Handbook of Humanitarian Law in Armed Conflict, OUP, 2000.

Garraway C. "Interoperability and the Atlantic Divide", 34 *Israel Yearbook on Human Rights* (2004) 105.

Gilbert G. *Transnational Fugitive Offenders in International Law: Extradition and other Mechanisms*, Nijhoff, 1998.

Goldman R. and Tittemore B., "Unprivileged Combatants and the Hostilities in Afghanistan: Their Status and Rights under International Humanitarian and Human Rights Law", American Society of International Law, Task Force on Terrorism, December 2002.

Greenberg K. & Dratel J. *Torture Papers: the road to Abu Ghraib*, CUP, 2005.

Greenwood C. "International Law and the Pre-emptive Use of Force: Afghanistan, Al-Qaida and Iraq", 4 *San Diego Int'l L.J.* 7-37.

Hampson F. "Human Rights Law and the Conduct of Military Operations", Forthcoming.

Hampson F. "The Geneva Conventions and the Detention of Civilians and Alleged Prisoners of War", 1991 *Public Law* 507-522.

Henckaerts J.-M. and Doswald-Beck L., *Customary International Humanitarian Law*, 2 Vols., CUP, 2005.

Hiro D. *Secrets and Lies*, Politico's, 2005.

House of Commons, Foreign Affairs Select Committee, Foreign Policy Aspects of the War against Terrorism, HC 36-I, 5 April 2005.

House of Commons, Report of the Intelligence and Security Committee, "The Handling of Detainees by UK Intelligence Personnel in Afghanistan, Guantanamo Bay and Iraq", March 2005, Cm 6469.

ICRC, International Humanitarian Law and the Challenges of Contemporary Armed Conflicts, Report for 28th International Conference of the Red Cross, December 2003.

Justice, "Briefing on Extradition to the USA: the UK-US Treaty of March 2003 and the EU_US Agreement of June 2003", Justice, July 2003.

Keegan J. *The Iraq War: the 21-Day Conflict and its Aftermath*, Pimlico, 2005.

Lavoyer, J.-P. "International Humanitarian Law: Should it be Re-affirmed, Clarified or Developed?", 34 Israel Yearbook on Human Rights (2004), 35.

Levie H. *Prisoners of War in International Armed Conflicts*, Naval War College International Law Studies, 1978.

Mallison and Mallison "The Juridical Status of Irregular Combatants under the International Humanitarian Law of Armed Conflict", 9 *Case W. Res. J. Int'l. L.* (1977) 39.

Pejic J. "Three Misconceptions about the Laws of War", Crimes of War Project, http://www.crimesofwar.org/onnews/news-miscon.html, October 29, 2004

Pictet J. (ed.) *Commentary to the Geneva Conventions of 1949*, 4 volumes 1952, 1960, 1960 and 1958, ICRC.

Quéguiner J.-F. Direct Participation in Hostilities under International Humanitarian Law, Working Paper for ICRC/TMC Asser Institute meeting, International Humanitarian Law Research Initiative, 2003, Background Paper, http://www.ihlresearch.org/ihl/portalhome.php .

Sandoz, Swinarski Zimmerman et al. (Eds.), *ICRC Commentary on the Additional Protocols of 1977*, Nijhoff and ICRC, 1987.

Schmitt M. "Targeting and Humanitarian Law", 34 *Israel Yearbook on Human Rights* (2004) 59.

Roberts A. and Guelff R., *Documents on the Laws of War*, Oxford, 3rd Ed. (2000).

Rosas A. *The Legal Status of Prisoners of War: A Study in International Humanitarian Law applicable in Armed Conflict*, Helsinki Academia Scientiarum Fennica, 1977.

Sands P. *Lawless World*, Allen Lane, 2005.

UK Ministry of Defence, *The Manual of the Law of Armed Conflict*, Oxford, 2004

Watkin K. Combatants, Unprivileged Belligerents & Conflicts in the 21st Century, International Humanitarian Law Research Initiative, 2004 Background Paper, http://www.ihlresearch.org/ihl/portalhome.php.

Wolfrum R. "The Attack of September 11, 2001, the Wars Against the Taliban and Iraq: Is There a Need to Reconsider International Law on the Recourse to Force and the Rules in Armed Conflict?", Max-Planck-Forum, Berlin, 22 October 2003, www.forum.mpg.de/archiv/20031022/docs/911.

Chapter 6

The Impact of the War on Terror on the Accountability of Armed Groups

George J. Andreopoulos

Introduction*

Few would question the assertion that 9/11 has shifted the tectonic plates. Where most of the discussion seems to focus these days is on the way in which these events have impacted on a whole set of critical issue areas, and the extent to which the responsive actions can be tailored to the challenges at hand, while at the same time remain anchored within the normative parameters of world order.[1]

Human rights and humanitarian norms constitute a critical component of world order. The period after World War II witnessed an unprecedented expansion of human rights and humanitarian norms,[2] the development of international and regional monitoring and enforcement mechanisms,[3] the growth (both in number and role) of non-governmental organizations, as well as the transnational networking of activists involving themselves in issues that were traditionally the "exclusive preserve of governments," or being instrumental in the promotion of new issues onto the agenda of international relations.[4]

While the expansion of normative space[5] has always been a roller-coaster ride of considerable achievements and disturbing setbacks, recent events have posed some unprecedented challenges to its integrity and relevance. One of these challenges relates to non-state actors and their enhanced ability to engage in international, as well as internal conflict situations. This of course is not a new development. Since the end of the cold war, the activity of non-state actors and, more specifically, of non-state armed groups, has attracted considerable attention given their prominent role, and the abusive conduct exhibited in many (primarily internal) conflicts. In 2002, for example, only one out of 67 ongoing conflicts could be classified as interstate (India-Pakistan); 31 were civil wars involving a state and at least one armed group, while the rest (35) were internal conflicts fought among armed groups.[6] However, in this changing landscape of global violence, the war on terror has added another layer of complexity and – in the process – has fuelled the debate on accountability and its prospects.

Accountability, in both its regulatory and voluntary dimensions, has become a major issue in the human rights/humanitarian discourse. It is by definition a relational concept. At the most basic level, an agent is accountable for some act or a failure to act, as well as to someone or some institutional entity. For the purposes of this paper, the notion of accountability refers to the responsibilities incurred by non-state armed groups *vis-à-vis* those entities affected by their conduct in armed conflict situations (for example, civilians, aid providers, and other combatants) to ensure that the conduct in question is consistent with human rights/humanitarian law standards. In the context of modern-day conflicts, it is the deliberate targeting of civilians, rather than the incidental loss of civilian life, and the targeting of IGO and NGO personnel that have placed the humanitarian aspects of protection and the responsibilities of armed groups so prominently on the international agenda.[7] In his first report to the Security Council on *the Protection of Civilians in Armed Conflict,* the UN Secretary-General noted that the "deliberate targeting of non-combatants," is a key characteristic of these conflicts, which results in "civilian casualties and the destruction of civilian infrastructure." Among the perpetrators of this violence, the Report singled out "non-state actors, including irregular forces and privately financed militias."[8]

In addressing the impact of the war on terror on armed group accountability, this essay will briefly examine: (1) the relevant legal framework, and in particular international human rights law (IHRL) and international humanitarian law (IHL); (2) those developments associated with the war on terror that have contributed to the restriction of the relevant normative space and their implications; and (3) in light of the challenges identified, the prospects for promoting accountability among armed groups.

IHRL, IHL and Armed Groups

In dealing with armed groups, the relevant bodies of law are IHRL and IHL.[9] At the outset, it would be useful to point to some key similarities/differences between them.

As bodies concerned with setting standards for humane conduct, IHRL and IHL share a normative commitment to human dignity and well being, irrespective of the status of the person (public official, private individual), and of the situations in which her/his rights and responsibilities are to be exercised (peace, public emergency, war). This commitment has been reaffirmed in recent decisions issued by international tribunals. More specifically, the International Criminal Tribunal for the Former Yugoslavia (ICTY) noted in the Furundzija case that "The general principle of respect for human dignity is the basic underpinning and indeed the very *raison d'etre* of international humanitarian law and human rights law; indeed in modern times it has become of such paramount importance as to permeate the whole body of international law."[10] It is also the driving force behind efforts towards the drafting and adoption of a "minimum humanitarian standards" document, which has been renamed "fundamental standards of humanity." The purpose of such document is "to strengthen protection of all persons in all situations."[11]

Another common characteristic is a traditional emphasis on state-centrism, though different forms of it prevail in each body. The dominant paradigm of IHRL is grounded on the notion of an antagonistic relation between the individual and the state. The rights are held by the individual against the state, and the state must ensure adherence to the relevant human rights norms. The state is the entity that needs to be monitored and constrained, since, in the traditional and still prevailing view, it is the primary source of (potentially) abusive conduct.[12] On the other hand, the protective framework envisaged by IHL was clearly shaped by expectations of reciprocity in inter-state conduct.[13] In such a framework, state interests trumped considerations of individual and group well-being.[14]

The differences are no less pronounced than the similarities. Traditionally, IHL has been concerned with the treatment of combatants and non-combatants by their opponents in wartime (including provisions on the means and methods of warfare), while IHRL has dealt with the relations between states and their own nationals in peacetime and in cases of public emergency. Moreover, IHRL is premised on near-zero tolerance for the loss of human life, while IHL operates within the context of conflict situations that have reached a certain threshold: situations in which the loss of (combatant) life is taken for granted, and allowance is made for the incidental loss of civilian life in the context of lawful military operations.[15]

The division between the areas of applicability of IHRL and IHL has generated serious concerns over possible legal uncertainties and ambiguities in connection with the protection of fundamental rights in situations of internal violence.[16] While this is a multi-faceted issue,[17] it is primarily the accountability of non-state actors that has posed one of the critical, yet least examined challenges to the protective framework.[18]

The international legal framework's growing receptivity to non-state accountability has been shaped by key post-1945 developments that slowly but steadily challenged its state-centric focus.[19] While these developments have been instrumental in articulating a more individual rights/responsibilities-oriented approach, problems persist. While lack of space does not allow for a detailed discussion of all the relevant issues concerning gaps in the protective framework, some of the most important will be highlighted here.

In the context of IHRL, one of the key issues relates to the lack of specificity of some of the most relevant rights and protections in situations of internal violence. In contrast to the greater specificity of IHL, even in situations of non-international conflicts where standards are less well developed than in international conflicts, many human rights provisions, critically important in situations of internal violence, are devoid of any explicit guidance.[20] To be sure, there are some related areas of human rights protection where specific instruments in the form of codes of conduct, or guiding principles, have been adopted to give greater meaning to certain rights, like the United Nations Basic Principles on the Use of Force and Firearms by Law Enforcement Officials.[21] However, and leaving aside for the moment the fact that the principles are not legally binding, this document is applicable in the context of domestic policing, not in the context of a situation of internal violence.[22]

The second relates to the first: while numerous instruments acknowledge the important role of individuals, groups and associations in promoting respect for human rights and fundamental freedoms,[23] the extent to which failure to do so would incur international responsibility, let alone criminal responsibility, save for the commission of the most serious and systematic violations, like genocide, remains unclear.[24] Finally, what are the applicable standards in situations of internal violence that do not reach the threshold required for the applicability of IHL, yet are regarded by public authorities as constituting public emergency and thus justifying derogation from IHRL?[25]

In the context of IHL, a key issue relates to the previously mentioned threshold of applicability. The threshold issue has two aspects: first, governments are traditionally reluctant to apply the relevant humanitarian standards even in situations that qualify as non-international conflicts. Such a move would signal the inability to exercise effective control over their territory and thus, the admission of a credible challenge to governmental authority. Moreover, it can appear, irrespective of declarations to the contrary, as conferring a modicum of legitimacy upon the challenger. In a sense, the very characteristics that dissident groups must possess for the applicability of Additional Protocol II can render the government's legitimacy questionable.[26] Such reluctance is not confined to modern day conflicts. The decolonization process and the concomitant debate over the status of national liberation movements provide ample confirmation to that effect.[27]

The second aspect refers to those cases that fall below the threshold, and are usually characterized as low intensity situations. What are the applicable standards? One obvious answer would be to point to domestic law. This, however, is premised on the idea that the government in question is capable of and willing to enforce the law. What happens in situations of failed or severely weakened states?[28] But even if domestic law was operational, how would states distinguish between "acts of violence" and ordinary crimes, since only the latter "would be under the jurisdiction of domestic criminal law"?[29] In addition, what are the applicable standards in the cases of armed groups that do not meet the criteria established in Protocol II, for example groups that engage in sporadic attacks, do not control any territory, and are unable to meet some of the obligations outlined in the Protocol?[30] These are some of the pertinent issues that merit further examination.

Normative Space after 9/11

The period between the end of the cold war and the events of 9/11 witnessed a series of developments which, arguably, contributed to the mainstreaming of the human rights/humanitarian discourse in a whole set of critical issue areas. Among the most widely debated ones, as to its legal foundations and impact, was the trend towards the identification of human rights/humanitarian law violations as threats to international peace and security.[31] While there were many problems associated with this normative "overstretch," nothing has contributed to the continuing erosion of fundamental standards to the degree that actions and responses associated with the ongoing "war on terror" have done.

The human rights/humanitarian framework is under siege. The following vignettes are indicative of the nature and extent of the problem:[32]

Weakening of Fundamental Norms

The best example here is the prohibition against torture which has been well-established as a peremptory norm of international law occupying thus a unique place within the "normative architecture"[33] of world order.[34] What recent developments have indicated is that the prohibition against torture is being weakened within the "enlightenment zone" of developed democracies. Reports to the effect that US intelligence agencies have been torturing captured terrorist suspects in a number of secret detention centers overseas, and that the US has been "outsourcing" torture-related tasks by handing over suspects to allies known for the brutality of their interrogation methods,[35] have generated troubling questions as to the nature of and commitment to the norm prohibiting such practices. Last, but not least, recent revelations concerning the death and mistreatment of detainees in Abu Ghraib prison, in Guantanamo Bay, and other detention facilities,[36] and the appearance of several memos, like the one written by then White House Counsel Alberto Gonzales on the application of the Geneva Convention on Prisoners of War, and the one written by then Assistant Attorney General Jay Bybee on the standards of conduct for interrogation under the UN Convention Against Torture and Other Cruel, Inhuman and Degrading Treatment or Punishment, are indicative of disturbing setbacks in a previously regarded safe issue area.[37]

Globalizing the Justification of Repressive Measures

Any discussion of this issue will have to address some of the most troubling developments that have occurred in the UN system, the "guardian" of the said human rights standards. Of particular concern are developments that relate to the activities of the United Nations Security Council (UNSC), as evidenced in the work of the Counter-Terrorism Committee (CTC).[38]

In response to the 9/11 attacks, the UNSC adopted resolution 1373 which, among other things, established the CTC which "monitors the implementation of resolution 1373 by all states and tries to increase the capability of states to fight terrorism."[39] Resolution 1373 is an unusual document, since it is the first Chapter VII-based resolution that applies to all the members of the UN system.[40] It constitutes a primary manifestation of UNSC's newly-found legislative activism: the imposition of binding orders on all states regarding counterterrorism, unconstrained by treaty and customary law obligations.[41] The resolution's a la carte treatment of the International Convention for the Suppression of the Financing of Terrorism is particularly telling: it included the treaty's enforcement provisions that suited the counterterrorist agenda, and omitted key constraining provisions such as those relating to the rights of persons accused of terrorism-related offenses, and to the requisites of international humanitarian law.[42]

The CTC has asked all States to report to the Committee "on steps taken or planned to implement resolution 1373." Most member states have submitted reports ranging from a few pages (like Albania and Uzbekistan) to more than a hundred (like Cuba). The eagerness of many countries, with well documented records of massive and systematic violations of human rights, to submit reports cataloguing their concerted efforts to combat terrorism should elicit skepticism.[43] It appears that at this stage the CTC process provides an opening to perennial human rights violators for the international legitimization of repressive criminal laws and procedures under the banner of the anti-terrorist struggle.

There are several developments that lend credibility to such concerns. First, the CTC has consistently refused to address in any serious manner the human rights implications of the campaign against terrorism. The tone was set early on: Sir Jeremy Greenstock, the first chairman of the CTC, noted that it was not the responsibility of the CTC to monitor the human rights obligations of member states.[44]

The second flows from the first: as a result of this attitude, there is a manifest lack of interest on the part of the CTC to challenge specific state laws and regulations whose vague phrasing violates basic criminal law principles, in particular the principle of specificity. The case of Egypt is instructive here. Egypt's definition of terrorism contained in Act no. 97 of 1992 includes, among other things, "any use of force or violence or any threat or intimidation to which the perpetrator resorts in order to....*prevent* or impede the public authorities in the performance of their work." In fact, when the Human Rights Committee (HRC), the monitoring body that oversees implementation of each country's obligations under the International Covenant on Civil and Political Rights (ICCPR), examined Egypt's periodic report in November 2002, it expressed alarm at "the very broad and general definition of terrorism given in Act No. 97..."[45] No such concern was apparently raised by the CTC when it reviewed Egypt's initial report, submitted in December 2001, which contained the very same definition.[46]

Third, this attitude has persisted despite repeated attempts by human rights officials and experts in the United Nations system to suggest quality control mechanisms and greater collaboration between the CTC and various human rights organs. More specifically, the Office of the High Commissioner for Human Rights (OHCHR) submitted, very early on, a note to the Chair of the CTC which included a set of principles that "could guide an analysis of counter-terrorism measures from a human rights perspective."[47] The note reaffirmed the importance of the principles of legality, non-derogability, necessity and proportionality, non-discrimination, due process, and non-refoulement.[48]

Moreover, in addressing the Commission on Human Rights on the issues of human security and terrorism, then High Commissioner Mary Robinson expressed concerns that "counter-terrorism strategies pursued after 11 September have sometimes undermined efforts to enhance respect for human rights."[49] In the same address, she suggested that the Commission might consider establishing "a mechanism to examine from a human rights perspective the counter-terrorism measures taken by states."[50]

In a similar vein, the Vice-Chairperson of the Human Rights Committee (HRC) emphasized, in his briefing of the CTC, the Security Council's "interest in ensuring that the human rights component is not lost sight of."[51] Arguing for a greater CTC involvement in the monitoring of the human rights dimension of state reports, Sir Nigel Rodley urged the Committee to include human rights expertise among its staff.[52]

Last but not least, at a HRC meeting held with the Legal Expert of the CTC, HRC members expressed concern over the post-9/11 focus in states' legislation "on counter-terrorist measures while ignoring human rights."[53] In addition, some committee members voiced concern over instances of legislation, "which empowered the executive to accept as truth the designation made by foreign countries of organizations as terrorist organizations, without examining that designation on its merits,"[54] while one member warned "that some policies, supposedly aimed at combating terrorism, were simply policies of repression."[55]

The response of the CTC to these concerns has been a commitment to ensure a liaison between the recently established Counter-Terrorism Committee Executive Directorate (CTED) and the OHCHR.[56] Even if such interaction were to materialize, however, it would clearly fall well below the minimum requirement of human rights expertise on the CTC. In fact, given the issues at stake, bolder steps are clearly in order: one such step would be the convening of joint CTC and HRC sessions to review counter-terrorist measures for their compliance with human rights standards.

International Humanitarian Law (IHL) vs. Law Enforcement Framework

In previous efforts to promote norm compliance among armed groups, one of the recurring stumbling blocs related to their routine demonization by public authorities as "outlaws," "bandits," or "criminals." The underlying assumption here was that no legitimacy could be attached to these groups and that the law enforcement framework was the only appropriate one for fashioning governmental responses.[57]

The United States' actions on the aftermath of the terrorist attacks of 9/11 are indicative of the attempted fusion of two frameworks: the laws of war, pertaining to armed conflict situations, and the law enforcement, pertaining to a police operation hunting down outlaws. This is reflected in the National Security Strategy document (NSS) and in the National Strategy for Combating Terrorism (NSCT) documents. NSS describes the struggle against global terrorism as "different from any other war in our history. It will be fought on many fronts against a particularly elusive enemy over an extended period of time."[58] At the same time, NSS acknowledges that in the defeat of this global and elusive enemy other tools would be necessary, including the use of the multilateral law enforcement framework (intelligence sharing, police cooperation, joint action against sources of funding for terrorist activities).[59] Likewise, NSCT states that "We must fight terrorist networks…using every instrument of national power-diplomatic, economic, law enforcement, financial, information, intelligence, and military."[60]

This attempted fusion/uneasy coexistence is problematic. It brings to the surface a major tension between two different normative frameworks: the IHL framework, premised on the moral equivalence of the combatants (provided that they satisfy certain criteria to be considered as such),[61] and the criminal law framework, reflective of "claims to unambiguous moral supremacy."[62] Moreover, IHL does not criminalize the taking up of arms and the initiation of military action, provided that certain conditions are met;[63] the law enforcement framework, on the other hand, strictly prohibits these activities and captured dissidents can be prosecuted for sedition and all other violence-related acts.[64]

In many ways, transnational terrorism seems to straddle these two paradigms. First of all, the enormity of the 9/11 and the "very strong international response based on the exercise of the right of self-defense" left little room for doubt as to the relevance of the armed conflict scenario.[65] At the same time, recent trends in warfare have contributed, as several studies have indicated, to the growing relevance of the law enforcement paradigm. For example, in a contribution on armed group adherence to international standards, the ICRC noted that "Amongst armed groups, the distinction between politically-motivated action and organized crime is fading away. All too often, the political objectives are unclear, if not subsidiary to the crimes perpetrated while allegedly waging one's struggle..."[66] It is this very engagement in criminal activity, primarily as a means of financing their operations, that adds to the perception of a paradigmatic overlap.[67]

Subsequent actions by the US administration, and in particular its designation of individuals seized during operations against the Taliban as "unlawful combatants," to whom the protective regime of the Geneva Conventions does not apply, are a testimony to the disturbing implications of this coexistence.[68] To be sure, the Bush administration has said that it would treat the detainees "humanely and, to the extent appropriate and consistent with military necessity, in a manner consistent with the principles of the Third Geneva Convention of 1949."[69] Yet, this selectivity, or what I would call a la carte humanitarianism, subverts both the spirit and the letter of the Geneva Conventions. By a self-proclaimed commitment to humane treatment, a commitment insulated from public scrutiny and judicial review, the fate of hundreds of detainees was –until recently- entrusted to the whims of the executive branch.[70] Moreover, a la carte humanitarianism signals a pathway to the subsumption of jus in bello considerations under jus ad bellum considerations, or, to put it differently, to an understanding that the pursuit of a just cause (defeating terrorism) should not be undermined by constraining international norms.

Any attempts to promote armed group accountability have to confront the unpredictability of the evolving war against terror and the concomitant labeling of certain armed groups as "terrorists" and therefore beyond the pale. Such a posture will adversely impact on any incentives for terrorist/illegal-labeled armed groups to adhere to international standards, incentives that could only be based on a framework (IHRL/IHL) deemed inapplicable under these circumstances.

For example, it is worth raising questions about the prospects for humanitarian negotiations and accountability-promoting initiatives in Colombia when, in the NSS, the US Administration has declared its determination to help the country "defeat illegal armed groups of both the left and right by extending effective sovereignty over the entire national territory and provide basic security to the Colombian people."[71] This problem is acknowledged in the Secretary-General's most recent report on the protection of civilians in armed conflict: "The designation of certain non-State armed groups as terrorist organizations has had an adverse impact on opportunities for humanitarian negotiations. The prohibition on dialogue with armed groups in Colombia...has resulted in severe restrictions on access to populations in need."[72] In the context of our discussion, the designation of illegality indicates a clear shift of emphasis from dealing with, to eliminating these groups. More ominously, though, there is a danger that the "protection agenda" would be shaped not by the enormity of human suffering, irrespective of the labeling of its sources, but on the basis of its central/peripheral relation to the antiterrorist campaign.[73]

The potentially adverse impact of the war on terror on such initiatives is clearly acknowledged by the United Nations Secretary-General in his penultimate report on civilian protection: "The efforts of the United Nations to ensure access to vulnerable populations and to structure appropriate contact with armed actors for this purpose will be vastly more complicated if those armed actors are engaged in terrorist activities or are seen as being so involved…The United Nations will need to formulate clear guidelines for its future work on the protection of civilians in armed conflicts where terrorist organizations are active."[74]

Sustainable Strategies

At this difficult juncture, *any meaningful accountability initiatives must focus on identifying, reaffirming and defending the relevance of the already existing framework.* Such a call to the defense of the framework was issued in a joint statement by the special rapporteurs/representatives, experts and chairpersons of the working groups of the special procedures of the Commission on Human Rights. In their statement, the experts "expressed alarm at the growing threats against human rights, threats that necessitate a renewed resolve to defend and promote these rights."[75]

The emphasis on protecting the already existing framework does not mean that there are no more gaps in the protective regime as envisaged by it. In fact, and more specifically in connection with the accountability of armed groups, there is a gray area between peace and situations of internal violence where it is not clear what the applicable standards of protection are.[76] However, in addition to the war on terror-related restrictions on human rights/humanitarian space, there is another reason for the need to accord primacy to the existing framework: the persistence of abusive conduct by armed groups in conflict situations, despite the fact that the conduct in question clearly falls under the provisions of already existing instruments.

Thus, what are needed now is not more standard-setting; rather, identification and defense of the existing framework from challenges from above (reassertion of hegemonic tendencies), and from below (persistence of abusive conduct in conflict situations). In such a context, a credible strategy will need to focus on more precise identification of already existing rules and more effective use of existing mechanisms and provisions in international legal instruments for improving compliance.

Concerning the rules issue, several recent initiatives point in this direction. To begin with, General Comment 29 on article 4 of the International Covenant on Civil and Political Rights (ICCPR), issued by the Human Rights Committee, constitutes an authoritative interpretation of the protective regime in situations of public emergency.[77] In particular, GC 29 has affirmed the interdependence between derogable and non-derogable provisions, and has stressed the role of other obligations under international law in restricting derogation powers under the

ICCPR. Concerning other bodies of law, GC 29 has highlighted the importance of obligations under IHL (for example on the right to a fair trial) as critical safeguards relating to derogation: "As certain elements of the right to a fair trial are explicitly guaranteed under international humanitarian law during armed conflict, the Committee finds no justification for derogation from these guarantees during other emergency situations. The Committee is of the opinion that the principles of legality and the rule of law require that fundamental requirements of fair trial must be respected during a state of emergency."[78]

In a similar vein, regional human rights mechanisms have emphasized the interrelationship of states' treaty obligations under these two bodies of law. For example, the Inter-American Commission on Human Rights (IACHR) has argued that in combat situations it is necessary to "apply definitional standards and relevant rules of international humanitarian law as sources of authoritative guidance in the assessment of the respect of the Inter-American instruments...It is therefore appropriate, and indeed imperative, for the Commission to consider all relevant international norms, including those of international humanitarian law, while interpreting the international human rights law instruments for which it is responsible."[79]

Moreover, in connection with the applicability of IHL, the ICRC has completed its major study on customary rules which is about to be published.[80] According to the ICRC, "the purpose of this study is to enhance respect for international humanitarian law and thus to offer greater protection to victims of war."[81] The importance of this study lies in the fact that it tries to fill the gaps in the application of treaty law, "gaps due to lack of ratification but also due to lack of substantive coverage,"[82] especially in the cases of non-international armed conflicts.[83]

According to an ICRC Report on this study prepared for the 28th International Conference of the Red Cross and Red Crescent,[84] perhaps the most striking result relates to the number of rules identified as customary in non-international armed conflict. In particular, rules on the conduct of hostilities such as "the principle of distinction, the definition of military objectives, the prohibition of indiscriminate attacks, the principle of proportionality and the duty to take precautions in attack are all part of customary international law" and therefore binding on all parties to the conflict, including armed groups. To this list, the Report includes other rules relating to "the duty to respect and protect medical and religious personnel and objects, together with impartial humanitarian relief personnel and objects used for humanitarian relief operations."

What emerges as a common theme here is the need for identification and better implementation of the already existing normative framework, rather than the need for further codification. In this endeavor, supporting state as well as non-state actor practice is critical. This quest for guidance over standard-setting can materialize in the adoption of a "soft law" document, incorporating the already existing norms, to be used as a frame of reference for engagement initiatives with armed groups.[85] This soft law document would be premised on the growing interdependence between IHRL and IHL rules within the normative architecture of international law.

There are several advantages that such an approach can offer: first, a document, anchored within already existing standards, will reconfirm the validity of the relevant legal framework at a time of unprecedented challenges. Second, a flexible instrument will facilitate the identification of appropriate "entry points" for a dialogue with armed groups.[86] Thus any "principled" interaction with armed groups will be viewed as part of a dynamic, ongoing process whose ultimate goal is the protection of human dignity in all its aspects. The dynamic character of this process would reduce the risks attached to a strategy in which certain standards are singled out during negotiations, creating thus the impression of a hierarchy among standards and normative commitments. In a nutshell, entry points signal the beginning of an ongoing process of normative engagement. Third, and related to the second, the flexibility inherent in a non-legally binding instrument, and its concomitant adaptability in a variety of situational contexts, will facilitate the incorporation of armed groups into the process of implementation. It will thus pave the way for armed groups to be viewed less as "targets" of and more as "stakeholders" in this process. Last, but not least, it will reinforce the need for more proactive protective initiatives, rather than retrospective ones that are favored by an increasingly dominant criminal justice streak within the human rights discourse.

Such a course of action will build on interesting initiatives already underway in the field. Despite numerous obstacles, UN agencies like UNDP, UNHCR and UNICEF, as well as many NGOs engage with armed groups on a regular basis. In the quest for civilian protection, they have negotiated access agreements and arranged ceasefires, even with groups designated as "terrorists" (like the FARC and the Tamil Tigers). In the process, these organizations have experimented with a variety of policy tools to promote compliance among these groups.[87] In this context, it is worth noting that the latest draft of the proposed manual on best practices for engagement with armed groups, being prepared by OCHA in collaboration with member agencies of the Inter-Agency Standing Committee (ISAC), has reaffirmed the commitment to humanitarian protection and assistance under all circumstances: "...if negotiating with an armed group is deemed a humanitarian necessity, then the designation of that group as a "terrorist" group by some states or institutions should not automatically preclude negotiations with the group."[88]

Concerning the more effective use of provisions and existing mechanisms, there are several potential courses of action worth pursuing (the list is by no means exhaustive).

First, a soft law document would be more conducive to the encouragement of "special agreements" between States and armed groups provided for in common article 3 of the Geneva Conventions. There are two reasons for this: (a) a non-legally binding document would assuage states' concerns about the legal status of their opponents; and (b) the flexibility inherent in a soft law document would make it easier to reach a limited agreement on selective provisions of IHL that can appeal to all parties to the conflict.[89] While selectivity can give rise to the previously mentioned issue of the hierarchy of standards, the entry point character of this limited agreement would act as a constraining factor.

Second, the existence of an agreement (even a limited one) can act as a triggering mechanism for the activation of the International Fact Finding Commission provided for by Article 90 of Additional Protocol I. The Commission has repeatedly expressed an interest in investigating alleged violations occurring in the context of non-international conflicts and its mandate includes "the restoration of an attitude of respect for the Conventions and this Protocol." State actors and armed groups should be encouraged to include in all "special agreements" a clause that in cases of violations alleged by one or all sides to a conflict, the Commission will automatically investigate with the ultimate aim of facilitating the restoration of respect for human rights/humanitarian norms. In situations where no such agreement exists, and the violations are massive or systematic, the Security Council should authorize the Commission's investigation with a Chapter VII-based resolution.[90]

Third, more effective use can be made of UN Charter-based and treaty-based organs that have addressed, or can directly address armed groups. For example, the Optional Protocol to the Convention on the Rights of the Child on the involvement of children in armed conflicts expressly forbids armed groups to recruit or use in hostilities persons under the age of 18 years.[91] The treaty's monitoring organ, the Committee on the Rights of the Child, can invite, in conjunction with the Office of the Special Representative of the Secretary-General for Children and Armed Conflict (O/SRSG-CAAC), armed groups to informally submit periodic reports on their compliance with child protection standards. Such an initiative can build on O/SRSG-CAAC's recently launched campaign for an "Era of Application."[92] Particular emphasis should be placed on those armed groups that have been named as having engaged in abusive practices in the Secretary-General's Report to the Security Council on Children and Armed Conflict.

Concluding Remarks

The war on terror has brought into sharper focus the capacity of non-state actors, and in particular that of armed groups, to engage in conflict situations. In the process, this war has also posed unprecedented challenges to the integrity and relevance of the protective framework envisaged by IHRL and IHL. In this context, promoting armed group accountability has emerged as a critical issue of concern, given the persistence of abusive conduct in conflict situations. Despite some gaps and remaining uncertainties in the protective framework, an examination of this problem, in light of recent initiatives, points towards the need for identification/reaffirmation and better implementation of these norms rather than further codification. The creation of a soft-law document with "moral/political weight" would be a step in the right direction. While there is clearly no magic bullet here, the exigencies of the situation demand both defense of and flexibility in the application of these standards. After all, the ultimate test of this framework is the extent to which it provides effective protection to human beings for whose benefit, to slightly paraphrase the ICRC commentary on the Geneva Conventions, it has been drawn up.

Notes

*An earlier version of this chapter was presented at the CISS/ISA Conference in Salzburg, July 7-8, 2004. I would like to thank the participants in our session for their helpful comments.

[1] On World Order, see Falk, 1982.
[2] See the discussion in Lauren, 2003.
[3] For a detailed study of the creation of the most comprehensive regional human rights regime, see Simpson, 2001.
[4] Evangelista, 1999, p. 6; see, more generally, the discussion in pp. 3-21.
[5] In the human rights/humanitarian context, normative space refers to the actors, institutions, rules and processes which contribute to the development, promotion, implementation, and protection of internationally recognized human rights and humanitarian norms.
[6] Capie and Policzer.
[7] The UN Secretary-General has already issued four reports on the protection of civilians: the first in September 1999, the second in March 2001, the third in November 2002 and the fourth in May 2004. Needless to say, the issue of civilian targeting is one of the main reasons, but not the exclusive one, for the recent prominence of accountability-related issues in the human rights discourse.
[8] United Nations Security Council. Report of the Secretary-General to the Security Council on the protection of civilians in armed conflict, 1999.
[9] This section is partly based on my earlier work *On the accountability of non-state armed groups* which will appear in Andreopoulos, Arat and Juviler (eds.), forthcoming.
[10] Prosecutor v. Anto Furundzija, Judgement, IT-95-17/1-T, para. 183.
[11] *Report of the Expert Meeting on Fundamental Standards of Humanity,* 2000.
[12] This view reflects the legacy of the horrors of the second world war, which clearly shaped the debates on the drafting of the foundational document, the Universal Declaration of Human Rights (UDHR). For more on this, see Morsink, 1999, pp. 36-91.
[13] Theodor Meron, 2000.
[14] Having said that, I would argue that a certain form of reciprocity also operated in the early stages of the development of the human rights framework, but of a different kind than the one encountered in IHL. It refers to reciprocal expectations of non-intervention, i.e. mutual understandings as to the non-intrusive (lack of effective monitoring and enforcement mechanisms) nature of human rights instruments. Hence, the declaratory as opposed to the legally binding nature of the UDHR. However, what was originally seen as a sign of weakness proved, eventually, to be a source of strength; on this, see Morsink, 1999, pp. 19-20.
[15] Concerning IHRL, in the case of the death penalty there is a consensus in the human rights community on the need to work towards its eventual abolition. On IHL, and in particular on the issue of the loss of civilian life, see, for example, the precautionary measures provisions of article 57 of Additional Protocol I (1977). The issue of the threshold of applicability is addressed in common article 3 of the 1949 Geneva Conventions, as well as in Additional Protocol II (1977). According to article 1(2) of the Protocol, "situations of internal disturbances and tensions" are excluded, "as not being armed conflicts."
[16] *Report of the Expert Meeting on Fundamental Standards of Humanity,* 2000. There has been a plethora of terms to describe internal conflict situations. The Geneva Conventions and the Additional Protocols refer to *non-international armed conflicts.* Due to disagreements over thresholds of applicability for humanitarian norms, the Secretary-

General has used the term *internal violence* to "describe situations where fighting and conflict, of whatever intensity, is taking place inside countries;" United Nations Economic and Social Council. Commission on Human Rights. Report of the Sub-Commission on Prevention of Discrimination and Protection of Minorities, 1998a.

[17] It includes issues of derogation from internationally guaranteed rights, lack of specificity of existing rules, and ratification of the relevant legal instruments.

[18] United Nations Economic and Social Council, 1998a; and Eide, Rosas and Meron, 1995, pp. 215-223.

[19] I have discussed these developments in *On the accountability of non-state armed groups*, supra note 9.

[20] United Nations Economic and Social Council, 1998a. One example relates to the right to life. While human rights instruments are more specific when it comes to the circumstances under which the application of the death penalty might constitute a violation of the right to life, they are not helpful when it comes to the circumstances under which "certain means or methods of combat" in situations of internal violence "might violate the right to life." This should be contrasted to the more detailed provisions of IHL instruments concerning the illegality of "certain means and methods of warfare," thus shielding the civilian population from the effects of hostilities; ibid.

[21] *Basic Principles on the Use of Force and Firearms by Law Enforcement Officials*, adopted by the Eighth United Nations Congress on the Prevention of Crime and the Treatment of Offenders, Havana Cuba, 1990; see also United Nations Economic and Social Council, 1998a.

[22] Having said that, such a document can offer guidance in developing a similar set of principles for situations of internal violence.

[23] See, for example, United Nations General Assembly, 1999. Article 10 stipulates, "No one shall participate, by act or failure to act where required, in violating human rights and fundamental freedoms…"

[24] This is a separate argument from the one that points to state responsibility for violations perpetrated by non-state actors. To be sure, the state bears responsibility under international law for human rights violations committed by private persons in its territory, and in particular for failure to exercise "due diligence" to prevent the violations in question or to respond to them as required by law, as the Inter-American Court of Human Rights ruled in *Velasquez Rodrigues v. Honduras.* However, this argument is premised on the state's ability to enforce its obligations. In many situations involving armed groups, the state in question has either disintegrated or been severely weakened, hence it lacks capacities of enforcement.

[25] Some of the concerns associated with public emergencies have been addressed in General Comment 29 issued by the Human Rights Committee, which is discussed in my piece *On the accountability of non-state armed groups*, supra note 9.

[26] The characteristics include responsible command, and control over part of the territory so as to carry out sustained and concerted military operations and implement the provisions of Protocol II; see article 1 para.1 of the Protocol.

[27] Firmage, 1971, esp. pp. 414-417.

[28] For similar arguments relating to the applicability of IHRL, see note 24.

[29] This was one of the concerns expressed by the Government of Canada in its comments on the Minimum Humanitarian Standards Report prepared by the Sub-Commission on Prevention of Discrimination and Protection of Minorities; United Nations Economic and Social Council, *Minimum Humanitarian Standards. Analytical Report of the Secretary-*

*General submitted pursuant to Commission on Human Rights resolution 1997/21. Views and information received from States and United Nations bodies. Addendum,*1998b. See also supra, note 16.

[30] For example, obligations pertaining to the protection and care of the wounded, sick and shipwrecked (article 7), or to due process (article 6).

[31] On this trend, see Andreopoulos, 2004, pp. 80-99.

[32] Needless to say, the list is by no means exhaustive.

[33] Expression used by Falk, 2002, p. 23.

[34] A space shared with a few other fundamental norms, including the prohibition against piracy, slavery, the slave trade, genocide, arbitrary deprivation of life, and arbitrary arrest and detention, among others. While there is no consensus as to the exact list of peremptory norms, there is no doubt that the prohibition against torture would be included in any list of such norms. A point of clarification is needed here: declaring that the prohibition against torture is a peremptory norm does not mean that it is not violated; rather, it means that no public authority openly admits to its practice or toleration.

[35] Among the secret detention centers "where U.S. due process does not apply," are one in the U.S.-occupied Bagram air base in Afghanistan, and another in Diego Garcia, an island in the Indian Ocean that the U.S. leases from Britain. The "friendly regimes" to whose intelligence services terrorist suspects are rendered, include Saudi Arabia, Jordan, Egypt and Morocco; Priest and Gellman, 2002; and *The Economist*, 2003, pp. 18-20. However, the U.S. is not the only democracy engaged in such practices. Sweden, a country with a better human rights record than that of the United States, rendered two Egyptian nationals, who had sought political asylum, to their home country; Priest, 2004, p. A01.

[36] For the abuse in Abu Ghraib prison, see Hersh, 2004, pp. 1-72; for the situation in Guantanamo, see Lewis, 2004, p. A1.

[37] Both memos can be found in Greenberg and Dratel (eds.), 2005; pp. 118-121 (Gonzales memo), and pp. 172-217 (Bybee memo).

[38] This is not the only UNSC Committee that has engaged in questionable practices, to say the least. The work of the 1267 Sanctions Committee which was established with the purpose of overseeing the implementation of sanctions imposed on individuals and entities belonging or related to the Taliban, Usama Bin Laden and Al-Qaida, has generated a lot of concern. In particular, critics have pointed to the fact that the process of listing and de-listing institutions and individuals is not subject to any review or appeal, raising thus fundamental questions concerning transparency and accountability. It is instructive to note here that the recent UN report *A more secure world: Our shared responsibility* states that these aspects of the 1267 Committee's work "raise serious accountability issues and possibly violate fundamental human rights norms and conventions." I have discussed the work of the 1267 Committee in Andreopoulos, 2005.

[39] http://www.un.org/Docs/sc/committees/1373/mandate.html

[40] Human Rights Watch Briefing Paper, 2004, p. 4.

[41] Alvarez, 2003, p. 874.

[42] Ibid., p. 875.

[43] Uzbekistan, for example, is highlighting, among other things, provisions of its criminal legislation relating to crimes against public security which include 'the creation or direction of or participation in religious extremist, separatist, fundamentalist or other banned organizations," (art. 244-2). In the 2003 U.S. Department of State Country Reports on Human Rights Practices, Uzbekistan is characterized as "an authoritarian state with limited civil rights." Commenting on the constitutional provisions for an independent judiciary, the

Report notes that "the executive branch heavily influenced the courts in both civil and criminal cases and did not ensure due process;"
http://www.state.gov/g/drl/rls/hrrpt/2003/27873pf.htm

[44] Human Rights Watch Briefing Paper, p. 6.
[45] Ibid., p. 8.
[46] Ibid., pp. 8-9.
[47] Office of the High Commissioner for Human Rights, *Note to the Chair of the Counter-Terrorism Committee: A Human Rights Perspective on Counter-Terrorist Measures,* http://www.un.org/Docs/sc/committees/1373/ohchr1.htm
[48] Ibid.
[49] High Commissioner for Human Rights on human security and terrorism, March 20, 2002; http://www.hrea.org/lists/hr-headlines/markup/msg00274...
[50] Ibid.
[51] United Nations Security Council Counter-Terrorism Committee UN Headquarters, 19 June 2003, Briefing by Sir Nigel Rodley, Vice-Chairperson Human Rights Committee, *Human Rights and Counter-Terrorism Measures,* http://www.unhchr.ch/Huricane/Huricane.nsf/94ec9fed7...
[52] Ibid.
[53] Human Rights Committee Briefed on Work of Counter-Terrorism Committee. Press Release HR/CT/630, 27/03/2003.
[54] Ibid.
[55] Ibid.
[56] United Nations Security Council, 2004, S/2004/642.
[57] The United Nations Secretary-General refers to this problem when, in his penultimate report on the protection of civilians in armed conflict, he cites, as one of the reasons for the difficulties in securing humanitarian access in conflict situations, the unwillingness of states "to engage non-State actors in dialogue, either on the peace process or on their obligations to civilian populations under the Geneva Conventions;" United Nations Security Council. Report of the Secretary-General to the Security Council on the protection of civilians in armed conflict, 2002, p. 6.
[58] *The National Security Strategy of the United States of America.* September 2002, p.5.
[59] Ibid., pp. 6, 10, 11 and 16.
[60] *National Strategy for Combating Terrorism.* February 2003, p. 1.
[61] As provided in 1949 Geneva Convention III, article 4 para. A (2).
[62] See de Torrente, 2002, p. 5.
[63] In particular, those of carrying arms openly, and of having a fixed distinctive sign recognizable at a distance.
[64] Inter-American Commission on Human Rights, 2002.
[65] Watkin, 2004, p. 5.
[66] International Committee of the Red Cross 1999, p. 2.
[67] Watkin, 2004.
[68] The White House claimed that although the Geneva Convention applies to the Taliban detainees as opposed to the Al-Qaida detainees, "neither the Taliban nor al-Qaida detainees are entitled to POW status;" *The White House. Fact Sheet. Status of Detainees at Guantanamo, February 7, 2002;*
http://www.whitehouse.gov/news/releases/2002/02/20020207-13.html
[69] Ibid.

[70] In this context, last year's decision of the US Supreme Court in the Rasul v. Bush and Al Odah v. United States case is a positive development. The Court ruled that the Guantanamo detainees have the right to have their claims relating to wrongful confinement heard in federal court. Although certain issues still remain unclear (for example, whether the Court's ruling applies only to Guantanamo detainees, or to any non-citizen detainees held anywhere in the world), this decision was a major setback for the US administration; see Greenhouse, 2004, p. A1. For excerpts from the decision, see p. A 16.
[71] *The National Security Strategy,* p. 10.
[72] United Nations Security Council, *Report of the Secretary-General to the Security Council on the protection of civilians in armed conflict,* 2004, p. 13.
[73] See also the remarks by de Torrente, 2002, p. 7.
[74] United Nations Security Council. *Report of the Secretary-General on the protection of civilians in armed conflict,* 2002, pp. 15-16.
[75] United Nations Press Release, 2003.
[76] I have discussed this in greater detail in *On the accountability of non-state armed groups,* supra note 9.
[77] United Nations. International covenant on civil and political rights. *General Comment No. 29. States of Emergency (Article 4),* 2001; see also my piece *On the accountability of non-state armed groups,* supra note 9.
[78] Ibid., p. 6.
[79] Inter-American Commission on Human Rights, *Report on Terrorism and Human Rights*, 22 October 2002, http://www.cidh.oas.org/Terrorism/Eng/part.a.htm#A.... see also Inter-American Commission on Human Rights, *Third Report on the Situation of Human Rights in Colombia,* issued in 1999, where the Commission observed that "in order to properly judge the specific claims...(it) has found it necessary at times either to directly apply rules of international humanitarian law,...or to inform its interpretations of relevant provisions of the American Convention by reference to these rules;"
http://www.cidh.oas.org/countryrep/Colom99en/chapter04.htm
[80] Henckaerts and Doswald-Peck (eds.), 2005.
[81] See note 84.
[82] Ibid.
[83] While it is true that the rules covering international conflicts are more comprehensive than the ones covering non-international ones, the number of treaties applying to non-international conflicts is increasing. In addition to common article 3 of the 1949 Geneva Conventions and Additional Protocol II, the following instruments are of relevance here (the list is not exhaustive): the Second Protocol to the Hague Convention of 1954 for the Protection of Cultural Property in the Event of Armed Conflict, the Amended Protocol II (to the 1980 UN convention on Prohibitions or Restrictions on the Use of Certain Conventional Weapons) on Prohibitions or Restrictions on the Use of Mines, Booby-Traps and Other Devices, the Statute of the International Criminal Court, and the Optional Protocol to the Convention on the Rights of the Child on the Involvement of Children in Armed Conflicts; see also note 84.
[84] *Customary International Humanitarian Law. Report prepared by the International Committee of the Red Cross,* 2003. I would like to thank Mr. Daniel Helle, Deputy Head of the ICRC Delegation to the United Nations, for providing me with a copy of this report.
[85] See also the concluding summary of the *Report of the Expert Meeting on Fundamental Standards of Humanity,* 2000; in addition, my piece *On the accountability of non-state armed groups,* supra note 9.

[86] For a discussion of the importance of dialogue as a process, see International Council on Human Rights Policy, 2000, pp. 46-48.
[87] See Capie and Policzer.
[88] UN Office for the Coordination of Humanitarian Affairs, *Humanitarian Negotiations With Armed Groups. A Manual for Practitioners.* Working Draft 3/8, March 2005, p. 47. I would like to thank Manuel Bessler and Gerard Mc Hugh from OCHA for providing me with a copy of this draft.
[89] On special agreements, see also *Improving Compliance with International Humanitarian Law,* 2003.
[90] For the proposal on Security Council involvement, see International Conference of the Red Cross and Red Crescent, 2003.
[91] In article 4(1).
[92] Report to the Special Representative of the Secretary-General for Children and Armed Conflict, 2003.

References

Alvarez, Jose E. "Hegemonic International Law Revisited," *American Journal of International Law,* vol. 97(4), 2003, pp. 873-888.

Andreopoulos, George "Violations of human rights and humanitarian law and threats to international peace and security," in Ramesh Thakur and Peter Malcontent (eds.), *From Sovereign Impunity to International Accountability: The Search for Justice in a World of States.* (United Nations University Press, 2004), pp. 80-99.

Andreopoulos, George *The United Nations and Human Rights Education in the "War on Terror."* Paper presented at the International Studies Association Annual Convention, Honolulu, March 1-5, 2005.

Andreopoulos, George "On the accountability of non-state armed groups," in George Andreopoulos, Zehra Arat and Peter Juviler (eds.), *Center Stage: Non-State Actors in the Human Rights Universe* (Kumarian Press, forthcoming).

Basic Principles on the Use of Force and Firearms by Law Enforcement Officials, adopted by the Eighth United Nations Congress on the Prevention of Crime and the Treatment of Offenders, Havana Cuba, 27 August to 7 September 1990; http://www.unhchr.ch/html/menu3/b/h_comp43.htm

Capie, David and Pablo Policzer *Keeping the Promise of Protection: Holding Armed Groups to the Same Standard as States* (unpublished briefing paper, on file with the author).

De Torrente, Nicolas "Challenges to Humanitarian Action," *Ethics & International Affairs,* vol. 16(2), 2002, pp. 2-8.

Eide, Asbjorn, Allan Rosas and Theodor Meron, "Combating Lawlessness in Gray Zone Conflicts through Minimum Humanitarian Standards," *American Journal of International Law,* vol. 89(1), 1995, pp. 215-223.

Evangelista, Matthew *Unarmed Forces. The Transnational Movement to End the Cold War.* (Cornell University Press, 1999).

Falk, Richard A. *Human Rights and State Sovereignty*. (Holmes and Meier, 1982).
Falk, Richard A. "The Challenges of Humane Governance," in George Andreopoulos (ed.), *Concepts and Strategies in International Human Rights*. (Peter Lang, 2002), pp. 21-50.
Firmage, Edwin Brown "Summary and Interpretation," in Richard A. Falk (ed.), *The International Law of Civil War*. (The John Hopkins Press, 1971), pp. 405-428.
Greenberg, Karen J., and Joshua L. Dratel (eds.) *The Torture Papers. The Road to Abu Ghraib*. (Cambridge University Press, 2005).
Greenhouse, Linda "Access to Courts. Ruling Applies to Those Held Either in U.S. or at Guantanamo," *The New York Times,* June 29, 2004, p. A1
Henckaerts, Jean-Marie, and Louise Doswald-Peck (eds.) *Customary International Humanitarian Law. Volume I: Rules and Volume II: Practice*. (Cambridge University Press, 2005, forthcoming).
Hersh, Seymour M. *Chain of Command. The Road from 9/11 to Abu Ghraib*. (HarperCollins Publishers, 2004).
High Commissioner for Human Rights on human security and terrorism, March 20, 2002; http://www.hrea.org/lists/hr-headlines/markup/msg00274.
Human Rights Committee Press Release, *Human Rights Committee Briefed on Work of Counter-Terrorism Committee*. HR/CT/630, 27/03/2003.\
Human Rights Watch Briefing Paper, *Hear No Evil, See No Evil: The U.N. Security Council's Approach to Human Rights Violations in the Global Counter-Terrorism Effort.* August 10, 2004.
Improving Compliance with International Humanitarian Law. Report prepared by the International Committee of the Red Cross. Geneva, October 2003.
Inter-American Commission on Human Rights, *Third Report on the Situation of Human Rights in Colombia*.
http://www.cidh.oas.org/countryrep/Colom99en/chapter04.htm
Inter-American Commission on Human Rights, *Report on Terrorism and Human Rights,* 22 October 2002, http://www.cidh.oas.org/Terrorism/Eng/part.b.htm
International Committee of the Red Cross, *Holding Armed Groups to International Standards: An ICRC view* (Geneva, 1999); unpublished briefing paper, on file with the author.
International Committee of the Red Cross, *Customary International Humanitarian Law. Report prepared by the International Committee of the Red Cross,* 03/IC/14 (Geneva, 2003); draft, on file with the author.
International Committee of the Red Cross, *Improving Compliance with International Humanitarian Law. Report prepared by the International Committee of the Red Cross* (Geneva, October 2003).
International Council on Human Rights Policy, *Ends&Means: human rights approaches to armed groups* (Geneva, 2000).
International Criminal Tribunal for the Former Yugoslavia, *Prosecutor v. Anto Furundzija,* Judgement, IT-95-17/1-T.

International Humanitarian Law and the Challenges of Contemporary Armed Conflicts (workshop 1), 28th International Conference of the Red Cross and Red Crescent, Geneva, 2 to 6 December 2003,
http://www.icrc.org/web/eng/siteeng0.nsf/iwpList189/4...

Lauren, Paul Gordon *The Evolution of International Human Rights: Visions Seen.* (University of Pennsylvania Press, 2003).

Lewis, Neil A. "Red Cross Finds Detainee Abuse in Guantanamo," *The New York Times*, November 30, 2004.

Meron, Theodor "The Humanization of Humanitarian Law," *American Journal of International Law,* vol. 94(2), 2000, pp. 239-278.

Morsink, Johannes *The Universal Declaration of Human Rights. Origins, Drafting and Intent.* (Philadelphia: University of Pennsylvania Press, 1999).

National Strategy for Combating Terrorism. February, 2003,http://www.whitehouse.gov/news/releases/2003/02/counter_terrorism/counter_terrorism strategy.pdf.

Office of the High Commissioner for Human Rights, *Note to the Chair of the Counter-Terrorism Committee: A Human Rights Perspective on Counter-Terrorist Measures,*
http://www.un.org/Docs/sc/committees/1373/ohchr1.htm

Priest, Dana and Barton Gellman, "U.S. Decries Abuse but Defends Interrogations," *Washington Post,* December 26, 2002.

Priest, Dana "Jet is an Open Secret in Terror War," *The Washington Post,* December 27, 2004.

Report of the Expert Meeting on Fundamental Standards of Humanity, Stockholm 22-24, February 2000 (on file with the author).

Report to the Special Representative of the Secretary-General for Children and Armed Conflict, *Monitoring and Reporting on Children in Armed Conflict. Initiatives to Improve Monitoring and Reporting on the Conduct of Parties to Conflict Relative to Children,* August 22, 2003 (draft, on file with the author).

Security Council Counter-Terrorism Committee UN Headquarters, 19 June 2003. Briefing by Sir Nigel Rodley, Vice-Chairperson Human Rights Committee, *Human Rights and Counter-Terrorism Measures,*
http://www.unhchr.ch/Huricane/Huricane.nsf/94ec9fed7...

Simpson, Brian A.W. *Human Rights and the End of Empire. Britain and the Genesis of the European Convention.* (Oxford University Press, 2001).

The Economist, "Special Report Torture: Ends, means and barbarity,", January 11-17th, 2003, pp. 18-20.

The National Security Strategy of the United States of America. September 2002; http://www.whitehouse.gov/nsc/nss.html

The White House *Fact Sheet. Status of Detainees at Guantanamo, February 7, 2002*; http://www.whitehouse.gov/news/releases/2002/02/20020207-13.html

United Nations Economic and Social Council, Commission on Human Rights. Report of the Sub-Commission on Prevention of Discrimination and Protection of Minorities, *Minimum Humanitarian Standards. Analytical Report of the Secretary-General submitted pursuant to Commission on Human Rights resolution 1997/21,*E/CN.4/1998/87, 5 January 1998(a).

United Nations Economic and Social Council, *Minimum Humanitarian Standards. Analytical Report of the Secretary-General submitted pursuant to Commission on Human Rights resolution 1997/21. Views and information received from States and United Nations bodies. Addendum,* E/CN.4/1998/87/Add.1, 12 January 1998 (b).

United Nations General Assembly. *Declaration on the Right and Responsibility of Individuals, Groups and Organs of Society to Promote and Protect Universally Recognized Human Rights and Fundamental Freedoms,* A/RES/53/144, 8 March 1999.

United Nations. International covenant on civil and political rights. *General Comment No. 29. States of Emergency (Article 4),* CCPR/C/21/Rev. 1/Add. 11, 31 August 2001.

United Nations Office for the Coordination of Humanitarian Affairs, *Humanitarian Negotiations With Armed Groups. A Manual for Practitioners.* Working Draft 2/14, February 2005; draft, on file with the author.

United Nations Press Release, *UN Experts Call for Respect of Liberties in Anti-Terror Measures,* 30 June 2003, http://www.unhchr.ch/huricane/huricane....CDFDCA24DEC1256D550031E966?open document

United Nations Security Council. *Report of the Secretary-General to the Security Council on the protection of civilians in armed conflict,* S/1999/957, 8 September 1999.

United Nations Security Council. *Report of the Secretary-General to the Security Council on the protection of civilians in armed conflict,* S/2002/1300, 26 November 2002.

United Nations Security Council, *Report of the Secretary-General to the Security Council on the protection of civilians in armed conflict,* S/2004/431, 28 May 2004.

United Nations Security Council, *Organizational plan for the Counter-Terrorism Committee Executive Directorate* (Enclosure), S/2004/642, 12 August 2004.

U.S. Department of State Country Reports on Human Rights Practices, 2003; http://www.state.gov/g/drl/rls/hrrpt/2003/27873pf.htm

Watkin, Kenneth, "Controlling the Use of Force: A Role for Human Rights Norms in Contemporary Armed Conflict," *American Journal of International Law,* vol. 98(1), 2004, pp. 1-34.

Chapter 7

The War on Terrorism: Time for a New 'Wise War' Framework?

April Morgan

Introduction

Applying leading legal and ethical standards to evaluate government policy relating to the use of force in the War on Terrorism is problematic.[1] One primary reason for this is that international politics' rules and risks do not conform to one another's contours as closely as they might. Prevailing doctrines currently frame ultimate determinations regarding military operations in dichotomous, mutually exclusive terms of judgment; an action is either legal or illegal, just or unjust. At the same time, 11 September 2001 appears to have awakened in many appreciation for the ambiguity of modern security concerns, the subjectivity of community fears, and the complexity of decision-making under conditions of high stress and significant uncertainty. These abstract variables – especially in combination – are not easily captured by preformulated, dualistic conclusions. Thus, the War on Terrorism presents an opportunity to undertake an overdue endeavor: to realign normative frameworks regarding armed conflict with the contemporary security environment.

The U.S. government began this process through the publication of a new National Security Strategy (NSS 2002), a series of formal and informal statements by administration officials, and the initiation of military campaigns in Afghanistan (2001) and Iraq (2003). This essay presents tentative evidence that the often bristling international response to the revised American security posture can be at least partly explained by clashing cultural predispositions, longstanding normative expectations, and doubts about intentionality. These additional tensions translate into higher social, political, and economic costs of adapting to the post 9-11 world.

All of this raises questions about what constitutes wise – not simply legal or just – war in an era of suicide terrorism embodying what some believe is an ethos of 'apocalyptic nihilism.'[2] On one hand, evidence of potentially devastating threats cannot be ignored simply because it is imperfect. On the other, especially in the absence of clear and complete information, unilateral attempts to alter or infringe on international politics' rules of the game may be perceived as a grave threat by others, whether or not one actually exists.[3]

The essay proceeds in four parts. First, the section below explains how today's security context differs from those Just War Theory and the United Nations (UN) Charter paradigm were designed to address. It concludes that these differences are likely to impede efforts to use Just War Theory and the Charter paradigm to grapple with twenty-first century threats. Second, an evaluation of the so-called Bush Doctrine and the war convention's rules on neutrality and self-defense provides tentative empirical support for the proposition that Americans tend to demonstrate especially low levels of tolerance for ambiguity and contradiction.[4] This can place them at odds with others in world affairs, despite mutual interests, which could otherwise constitute a basis of cooperation.[5] Third, an estimate of partial U.S. costs and consequences flowing from the War on Terrorism reveals potential, adverse spill-over effects; significant expenses of several kinds; and modest international burden-sharing. Thus, a causal sequence may be at work here as cultural variables complicate U.S. attempts to reconcile existing standards with what some have called the era of 'apocalyptic nihilism.'[6] Fourth, the last section proposes a complement to the *jus ad bellum*, designed especially for contemplations of preventive war. This guide to reflective decision-making seeks to minimize the costly divides al-Qaeda has exposed between the strategic, normative, and cultural dimensions of modern international politics and to spur expansion of viable policy options suitable for present and future security needs.

The Post 9-11 World: Not Your Parents' Security Context

The leading legal and ethical frameworks designed to inform decisions regarding the use of force in global politics are Just War Theory and the UN Charter paradigm.[7] However, applying these normative traditions to the War on Terrorism can be perplexing because both were intended to address very different instruments and enemies than those the War on Terrorism spotlights, namely WMD and transnational terrorism. This is to be expected in the case of Just War Theory; Augustine first began working on this doctrine in the 5th century AD to defend Christian participation in Roman wars.[8] Subsequent work by Vitoria, Suarez, and other thinkers on Augustine's original 'cluster of ideas' developed Augustinian principles into a mature theory still in existence, though often modified.[9] The mode of warfare traditional Just War Theory confronted in the 16th and 17th centuries as it came of age was one where:

> Armies lacked the logistical capacity to move quickly and couldn't get far ahead of their baggage trains. Muskets were inaccurate, could fire only a short distance, and were effective only when fired in volleys by highly trained soldiers who stood in mass formations ... Brightly colored uniforms [enabled officers to] keep an eye on soldiers [to prevent desertion].[10]

Even into the next century, battle was a methodical affair where opposing armies were arranged 'according to pattern almost as regularly as chessmen at the beginning of a game.'[11] This type of overt, low-tech, positional warfare is clearly at odds with the prevalence of low-intensity conflict, vastly improved weaponry, and frequent reliance on air power in contemporary military campaigns.

Perhaps less evidently, the security risks the UN Charter authors had in mind sixty years ago were also significantly different from those we face today. The UN's founding, constitutive document was crafted in the spring of 1945 by delegates to an international conference held in San Francisco. By then, chemical weapons had already been used in World War I. They had also played a particularly ugly role against civilians in the Holocaust. Terrorism was not a new phenomenon at that time, either. Although the term was coined in the 1790s in Jacobin France, the behavior significantly pre-dates that period; some trace the first recorded instance of terrorism back to the first century.[12] More recently, the United States government dropped two atomic bombs over Japan at the end of World War II. Thus, neither WMD nor terrorism were unknown when the Charter came into existence.

Yet, this multi-lateral treaty does not explicitly address either WMD or terrorism. There are at least two key reasons for this. First, despite what loomed ahead later that year, '[t]he very idea of nuclear weapons was a closely guarded secret' in the spring of 1945.[13] Charter creators could not have incorporated these weapons into the convention's approach to international security because the concept was not known to them. Second, conference delegates sought to prevent a reoccurrence of the events that precipitated World War II rather than those that ended it. Since their mental images were dominated by the history of combat between European powers, that meant uniformed armies marching *en masse* across internationally recognized borders in order to carry out sustained, overt uses of force against other states with the intention of conquering those territories. They sought to build a legal bulwark against future acts of aggression like Germany's invasion of France. The delegates were focused on conventional state-to-state conflicts.[14] As is often said to be the case, planners were preparing to fight future wars by replaying the last.

What framers of Just War Theory and the UN Charter held in common was a view of war dominated by mechanical, patterned movements of easily spotted troops on the global chessboard of territorial boundaries. Given these earlier threats' relative visibility and predictability, it is perhaps not surprising that both Just War Theory and the UN Charter rely heavily on dualism to shape normative decision-making guidelines. Ultimately, within these paradigms, one occupies either a black or a white square on the chessboard of international politics and maneuvers in ways that can be labeled ethical or unethical, legal or illegal. Both prior security environments stand in stark contrast to the post 9-11 paradigm.

As CIA Director George Tenet testified before Congress, contemporary security concerns extend well beyond Al-Qaeda.[15] Nonetheless, due at least in part to its dramatic and tragic entry into the layperson's vocabulary as a result of criminal behavior culminating on 11 September 2001, this group symbolizes the current security context. With its networks of associated groups and sleeper cells, Al-Qaeda operatives flow undetected across the conventional boundaries and modes of warfare on which applicable normative criteria are based, frustrating counterintelligence officials, international diplomats, and strategic planners in the process.[16]

This prominent terrorist organization is a wealthy, decentralized transnational network 'built upon loosely linked cells that do not rely on' or answer to a single leader or state sponsor.[17] Internet-savvy leaders organizing a particular use of force may 'remain in Pakistan and Iran, while operatives and agents ... travel back and forth coordinating with Al-Qaeda nodes in safe zones such as Yemen, Somalia, Bangladesh, the Philippines, and Chechnya.'[18] Un-uniformed operators dressed in Western garb may circulate unrecognized among civilians in target countries, appearing to live fairly normal lives for months - or longer - as they prepare to strike. The members of these cells do not generally know one another and may never gather together until an attack, if then.[19]

Al-Qaeda's modus operandi takes one of two forms: either stand-alone acts of violence like that of bombing of the USS Cole or waves of coordinated attacks similar to September 11th. After such destructive eruptions onto the public scene, Al-Qaeda typically withdraws from public view for long periods and the violence halts. Indeed, one of Al-Qaeda's defining characteristics is patience.[20] The bombing of the US embassy in Kenya was five years in the making. Plotting the attack on the USS Cole took two years. The cell responsible for the 2001 World Trade Center attack began meeting in 1998. Patient planning punctuated by either mode of violent outburst does not conform to Charter drafters' expectations of sustained military campaigns executed by government-sponsored soldiers in accordance with international legal restrictions on the use of force.

Thus far Al-Qaeda's attacks have not involved WMD. Nevertheless, concerns abound that the state has lost or soon will lose its monopoly on instruments of mass destruction.[21] Bin Laden himself is alleged to have told one interviewer that 'We don't consider it a crime if we tried to have nuclear, chemical, biological weapons.'[22] To another, he promised retaliation in kind should America use nuclear and chemical weapons, 'We have the weapons as deterrent.'[23] Other analysts point to Sheikh Nasr bin Hamid al Fahd's fatwa of May 2003, which sought to legitimize the group's use of chemical, nuclear, radiological, and biological weapons with Koranic justifications.[24] The head of British intelligence (MI5), Eliza Manningham-Buller, is reported to have said that such an attack against a major Western city 'is only a matter of time.'[25] In 2004, al-Qaeda's No. 2 leader - Ayman al-Zawarhi - gave an interview in which he claimed that al-Qaeda has already purchased smart suitcase bombs from disgruntled former Soviet scientists.[26] While many analysts downplay the likelihood that terrorists would actually engage on this scale, others counter that given the high stakes involved and the proliferation of weapons of mass destruction as well as related materiel and expertise after the Soviet Union's collapse, the possibility ought to be reckoned with regardless of how remote it may be.[27]

This level of uncertainty related to Al-Qaeda's motivations and capacity dwarfs that which existed between the United States and the Soviet Union during most of the Cold War. Not only did analysts in each country believe they knew roughly what weapons systems the other side had, but also, despite the lack of perfect transparency, they thought they knew something of the other's likely targets, launch location possibilities, war planning scenarios, and standard operating procedures. Since the Soviet Union's collapse, international security has moved away from the unstable equilibrium of mutually assured destruction between two powerful states with some familiarity of one another's arsenals into a period of disequilibrium marked by extreme asymmetrical interdependence of knowledge and by the increasing potential magnitude of globalized non-state violence.[28] These shifts significantly raise the stakes for everyone – not simply those targeted – because of the potential environmental effects of a WMD event.[29] One analyst has concluded that 'the dimensions of this transnational vulnerability are unprecedented in human history.'[30]

Clearly, the post 9-11 security landscape is not our parents' security landscape. Al-Qaeda's chronic secrecy, periodic invisibility, unknown intentions, and geographic unpredictability make it much harder to see, track, and predict than security threats of earlier eras.[31] Nonetheless, despite the intermittent appearance of these forces and their often fuzzy connections to rogue states, Just War Theory and the UN Charter retain their clear-cut, binary categories defining proper and improper responses. In application, this nonconformity between threats and frames is likely to complicate coordination of actions with rules in the War on Terrorism, making for a fitful transition to the new security environment even under the best of circumstances. The next section indicates that cultural, normative, and moral stakes are also vexing attempts to stymie 'megaterrorism.'[32]

Redefining American Boundaries Around Friendship and Force

U.S. national interests have remained relatively constant over time.[33] As the preamble to the Constitution declares, the people of the United States established their government in order to 'provide for the common defence, promote the general Welfare, and secure the Blessings of Liberty.' Homeland protection, therefore, has been a primary national objective for the United States since its inception as an independent republic through its ascension to superpower status. This truth is continued in the assertion by the G.W. Bush administration that '[d]efending our Nation against its enemies is the first and fundamental commitment of the Federal Government.'[34] The content and prioritization of specific policies intended to promote this good, however, have always been subject to revision in relation to changing domestic and international circumstances. Spreading realization of the magnitude of danger posed by the potency of contemporary terrorism provided one such impetus.

Although scholars disagree as to just how dramatic policy changes in U.S. national security policy have been in the wake of the September 11th attacks, the differences themselves are undeniable. This section explores two. First, President Bush's administration has tightened distinctions it makes between friends and foes, essentially eliminating grey areas between the two camps where threats might lurk undetected or protected. Second, it has re-interpreted international restrictions regarding the use of force in an expansive manner, effectively distancing itself from normative constraints designed to suppress unilateral military responses to perceived threats.

Both policies proclaim the intent and right to take action to stamp out as much ambiguity on the U.S. national security horizon as possible in order to win the War on Terrorism. Efforts such as these to reduce uncertainty and to enhance freedom of action are precisely what one might expect from those whom some cultural psychologists have labeled 'analytic actors'.[35] They are:

> can-do types who assume that people can effectively manipulate their environments in ways that maximize personal objectives. They are solution-oriented. Their negotiation strategies tend to focus on instrumental rationality, linear logic, competition, and dichotomous choices.[36]

Particularly relevant for this essay, they also demonstrate low tolerance for ambiguity, contradiction, and paradox.[37] Their societies are 'built upon clear, explicit, overt rules of behavior which ensure predictability.'[38] Americans are frequently cited as examples of analytic actors in their negotiating styles in business, diplomacy, and interpersonal relations.[39] Hence, efforts by the U.S. government explained in more detail below to reduce uncertainty and to affirm action in the War on Terrorism are not out of character with America's cultural profile. However, at times, these actions may be out of step with other countries' cultural patterns, and thus, American ways of grappling with this global problem may pose an additional source of friction in the War on Terrorism.

Who Goes There? Challenging Neutrality

'Every nation and every region now has a decision to make. Either you are with us, or you are with the terrorists.'[40] With these words, spoken nine days after the attacks of 11 September, President Bush introduced a simple dichotomy between states that defies the right to remain neutral in the War on Terrorism. Developed in detail within international law over the first half of the twentieth century, neutrality refers to the legal status that arises when a state abstains from participating in a war or armed conflict between other states.[41] The 1907 Hague Conventions governing land and sea warfare enunciate the rules of customary international law that bind parties and non-parties alike.[42]

These multi-lateral treaties define particular rights and duties as follows:

1. belligerents are forbidden to move troops, convoys, and munitions across neutral territory; this jurisdiction is 'inviolable'[43]

2. neutrals have a duty to prevent the use of their territory by belligerents and to apply such restrictions consistently and impartially[44]
3. neutrals are forbidden to supply belligerents (directly or indirectly) with war material of any kind.[45]

The conventions encourage a robust defense of their freedoms. Article 10 of Hague Convention V asserts that neutrals retain the right to resist (even by force) attempts to violate their neutrality and Article 26 of Hague Convention XIII declares that a neutral government's exercise of its legal guarantees cannot be construed as 'unfriendly' acts by belligerents. In other words, international law explicitly prompts states to vigorously and forcefully defend neutrality and warns those who would violate it to expect stiff resistance.

Because of the changing nature of warfare and the development of new international institutions, the precise parameters of neutrality's applicability to contemporary conflict are somewhat murky. Nevertheless, the doctrine's essential viability, while conditioned by other legal rules, has been repeatedly upheld in recent state practice, judicial decisions, and scholarly analyses. For example, the system of collective security enshrined in Chapter VII of the UN Charter describes a method of conflict management whereby the Security Council may pass resolutions to identify aggressors and prescribe specific courses of collective action. Under Article 25 of the Charter, when this occurs, member states have a legal obligation to accept and carry out such decisions. This obligation therefore qualifies the right of independent states to choose up sides or to declare themselves impartial bystanders to a particular conflict. They are not legally free to do as they like if directed otherwise by the Security Council.

However, Georgios C. Petrochilos has argued that when the Security Council fails to designate an aggressor or does not require collection action, the right to neutrality stands.[46] Petrochilos uses the 1991 Persian Gulf War to make his case. He argues that Security Council Resolution 678 authorized, but did not require, member states to use all means necessary in support of Kuwait's liberation and the restoration of international peace and security. Without question, this document legalized the actions undertaken by the international coalition to evict Iraqi forces from Kuwait. Simultaneously, by legitimizing rather than compelling the collective use of force, Resolution 678 preserved the freedom of member states to determine their unique levels of involvement - as long as they did nothing to give assistance to Iraq, which would have violated the duty member states have to cooperate fully with the organization under Articles 2(5), 2(7), and 25. Hence, Petrochilos concludes that India, Jordan, and Iran were in 'perfect accord' with the Hague Conventions when their governments refused to grant coalition aircraft permission to enter domestic airspace.[47] Moreover, as these independent, national stances went legally unchallenged by coalition authorities, they appear to have been perceived as falling within the domain of sovereign prerogative.[48] The Persian Gulf War illustrates that the customary legal right to neutrality co-exists with the UN Charter, albeit in a qualified form, and may even subsist in the context of Security Council resolutions authorizing, but not prescribing enforcement actions.[49] The infrequency of Security Council intervention in armed conflicts over the past sixty years further indicates that Charter restrictions on neutrality have not fulfilled their theoretical potential.

Neutrality therefore lingers in international law under the UN Charter paradigm. Its operationalization will likely continue to be worked out on a case-by-case basis given the precise wording of Security Council resolutions and the prioritization of national objectives by member states, among other contextual variables.[50]

While neutrality may be most commonly defined as a legal right, state leaders frequently attach moral judgments to this juridical status and those who claim it. These judgments are often less than complimentary, especially during volatile periods in international relations when policymakers believe they are engaged in a fight for national survival. At such times, there is a tendency to regard neutrals either as 'shirkers neglecting their moral responsibilities or as opportunists waiting to enter the fray at a more advantageous juncture.'[51] John Foster Dulles portrayed this attitude when he declared that neutrality is an immoral notion based on the mistaken belief that 'a nation can buy safety for itself by being indifferent to the fate of others.'[52]

On the other hand, much of Just War Theory appears indifferent to neutrality. The concept is conspicuously absent from the list of criteria to be satisfied if a war is to be determined just. For example, neutrality is of little concern when determining whether or not a particular state possesses sufficient capacity to have a reasonable chance of winning a war. It is irrelevant to ascertaining a ruler's legal basis of authority to lead his or her people. However, the establishment of a just cause, the need to have tried every other means before resorting to force, and possession of a morally pure intention presume an underlying conception of neutrality.[53] Parties who do not attain the standing conferred by the simultaneous existence of these qualities have no moral basis for participating in armed struggle. Even if they are strongly predisposed to join the battle, ethics requires that they stand aside. Alfred P. Rubin has observed, 'Neutrality for them would not be a right but an obligation.'[54] Contrary to much common political rhetoric, this kind of ethical argument holds out an alternative model of neutrality as a condition - almost an infliction - that effectively limits a state's freedom to act in matters of war and peace.

In a different way, Michael Walzer's analysis also counters those who treat neutrality as nothing more than a get-out-of-war-pass. Writing 27 years ago, he posed a simple question to frame the issue: what ethical obligations might be triggered by a statesman who says to a neighbor, in view of troubles which could affect both, 'You're either for me or against me?'[55] He concluded that when the question is asked at the international level, decision-makers retain the ethical right and perhaps the moral obligation to forge national identity and policy according to their countries' particular interests, to remain free of coercive political rhetoric even in the face of collective danger. In a classic communitarian statement, he asserted that:

But the leaders of such a state are not required to calculate as if every human life carried the same moral weight for every decision-maker at every moment in time. Their people's lives are not international resources to be distributed in war so as to balance the risks or reduce the losses of other people ... The leaders of a neutral state are entitled to maintain that immunity; indeed, they may be bound to do so, given the consequences of its loss for their fellow citizens.[56]

More than a mere shield of cowards and free-riders, then, Walzer defends neutrality as consistent with a ruler's paramount duty to protect his or her people. Further, others not necessarily associated with Just War Theory have pointed out that, rather than ignoring international peace and security, neutrality can serve these ends by enabling some actors to rise above the fray where they can function as intermediaries who broker peace and model moderation to enemies locked into 'cut-throat competition.'[57]

Mikael af Malmborg summarizes neutrality's status in contemporary international relations this way: though the idea of a neutral state may not be fashionable in an era characterized by interdependence and globalization because of its isolationist connotations, neutrality must nevertheless be recognized a corollary of state sovereignty.[58] Absent explicit treaty law to the contrary, the norm and its attendant rights to nonparticipation and impartiality survive.

Nevertheless, one of the earliest U.S. government reactions to heightened uncertainty in the War on Terrorism was to define in more stark terms the distinctions the administration makes between friends and foes. This policy addresses Al-Qaeda's slippery quality, its ability to hide within the boundaries of actors U.S. diplomats may have previously labeled allies. Terrorist networks may be transnational and terrorist eruptions may be sporadic, but at specific times and places as they organize and execute plots, portions of these groups are physically located within the territorial borders of sovereign states.[59] Wittingly or unwittingly, then, these states support such individuals at least by acquiescing in their presence. President Bush called this fact to the attention of the international community and made it clear that he expects pro-active support from those who call themselves U.S. allies in the War on Terrorism. In public comments, he further warned that non-allies are subject to hostile action. He also declared in no uncertain terms that his administration will henceforth hold state governments accountable for what terrorist groups do on their soils.

Statements that deny other sovereigns the right to stand 'aloof in the middle' of the War on Terrorism evoke and challenge the spirit of neutrality in two, primary ways.[60] First, the U.S. government maintains that it defines allies and enemies in dualistic terms. For this national security team, no longer is the international system composed of multiple camps such as the first, second, third, and fourth worlds. According to President Bush, there are only two choices: 'Every nation and every region now has a decision to make. Either you are with us, or you are with the terrorists.'[61] He later reiterated this point: 'There is no neutral ground - no neutral ground - in the fight between civilization and terror, because there is no neutral ground between good and evil, freedom and slavery, and life and death.'[62]

This two-dimensional worldview is not compatible with the impartiality component of neutrality because it leaves no space for those who would prefer to remain on the sidelines, at least of the American campaign. Indeed, it flatly denies the possibility of neutral territory.

Second, not only is impartiality not allowed, neither is passivity:

> A coalition partner must do more than just express sympathy, a coalition partner must perform. That means different things for different nations ... Some nations don't want to contribute troops and we understand that. Other nations can contribute intelligence sharing ... But, all nations, if they want to fight terror, must do something ... Over time, it's going to be important for nations to know they will be held accountable for inactivity. You're either with us or against us in the fight against terror.[63]

Former U.S. Secretary of State Colin Powell affirmed this approach when he said, 'We want action, not just statements.'[64] Since these new ground rules identify only two possible categories – doers and non-doers – presumably, those failing the action test are by default automatically relegated to the enemy's camp and in danger of becoming targets. President G. W. Bush affirmed this possibility when he professed that, 'Those who do not hand over the terrorists – like the Taliban – will share in their fate.'[65] Through these warnings, the U.S. government appears to demand active cooperation of various kinds as a fealty test.

This language overlooks the rights expressed in the Hague Conventions for states to refuse to participate in an international conflict, which, in the absence of applicable treaty obligations, continue even until today. It also neglects just war arguments, which hold that neutrality can constitute a moral duty to one's people and take precedence over considerations about the global balance of power. As a result, this effort by U.S. national security decision-makers to adapt to the new global security architecture provides an inhospitable climate for long-standing international expectations of fair play as expressed through the concept of neutrality in international law and Just War Theory.

One could argue that the legal doctrine of neutrality does not apply to the War on Terrorism because it is not a 'real' war. Those pressing this claim might point out that Congress has not issued a formal declaration of war in the War on Terrorism, Afghanistan (2001), or Iraq (2003). Nonetheless, in its early form, *absent overriding treaty qualifications*, key phases of the War on Terrorism have satisfied the prerequisites of the modern neutrality doctrine sufficient to trigger valid claims of nonparticipation and impartiality.[66]

For example, although Hague Conventions V and XIII articulate rules intended to apply during 'war', neither defines it. Moreover, nothing in the Hague Conventions asserts that neutrality provisions apply only when war is formally declared, even if this was assumed to be the lawful way to initiate war in the early twentieth century. There is no evidence that the framers of these conventions did not intend for neutrality to apply when war was 'brought about by means other than a declaration of war or an ultimatum.'[67] This is significant because as long ago as the nineteenth century when the issuance of declarations of war had already fallen into disuse, state practice indicated that war existed when a party 'intended a state of war to exist' as well as when such condition was formally asserted.[68] John Quincy Adams affirmed this interpretation in a speech made before the House of Representatives:

> Nor do I subscribe to it that every nation goes to war only on issuing a declaration or proclamation of war. This is not the fact. Nations often wage war for years, without issuing any declaration of war. The question is not here upon a declaration of war, but acts of war.[69]

The United States has declared war only five times in over two hundred years, despite being engaged in many more, undeclared wars during that period. Thus, a long history of state practice and a close reading of the Hague conventions indicate that declarations of war are irrelevant to neutrality. Today, indications of state intent and the occurrence of a use of force or the existence of generalized hostilities characterized by persistent, organized fighting are typically deemed sufficient for neutrality rules to apply.[70]

Although this may not always be the case, in its early manifestations, the War on Terrorism has satisfied these preconditions of neutrality. As though speaking directly to those who interpret the phrase 'War on Terror' as a mere slogan or rallying cry (which, if so, would presumably not trigger specific rights and responsibilities for other states), President Bush clarified his intention:

> The war on terror is not a figure of speech. It is an inescapable calling of our generation … There can be no separate peace with the terrorist enemy. Any sign of weakness or retreat simply validates terrorist violence, and invites more violence for all nations … The war on terror is our fight.[71]

Backed up by sustained U.S. military action, which lingers on, these stages of the War on Terrorism fulfill the requirements of state intent and armed conflict under which neutrality has traditionally applied.

A more provocative argument against neutrality's application to the War on Terrorism can be made on the basis that up until now, neutrality has been premised upon the existence of a state-to-state battle. Transnational terrorist networks such as Al-Qaeda beg the question: does neutrality apply to third states regarding contests between states and non-state actors? Will state practice, judicial decisions, and political will combine to extend its coverage to third states surrounded by this new kind of international conflict between dissimilar actors? This is an open question. President Bush's admonition that states will be held accountable for what terrorist groups do within their jurisdictions may be telling because it articulates an intention to frame the War on Terrorism as a state-to-state battle, albeit of a new kind where state uses of force may be more geographically dispersed than in previous wars and not necessarily directed at states as targets even though they may occur on sovereign territory. Ironically, if this interpretation stands, it has the potential to satisfy the third prerequisite of neutrality's applicability and validate rights to nonparticipation and nonalignment despite administration efforts to suppress them. If not, and in the absence of armed international conflict, the War on Terrorism could devolve into a virtual war akin to the War on Drugs.

Petrochilos's prediction that the precise parameters of neutrality will continue to be worked out on a case-by-case basis appears to have been prescient. At this point, its applicability to the War on Terrorism does not appear to have been definitively ruled out despite U.S. efforts to suppress it.

When do Threats Begin? Challenging Imminence

A second way in which U.S. decision-makers sought to grapple with the emerging menaces they perceived was through promulgation of a new national security strategy (NSS 2002).[72] Central to this agenda is a claim of the right to pre-emption, i.e., the use of military force prior to a first use of force by another.[73] This stance is akin the belief that the 'best defense is a good offense' and is consistent with George Washington's opinion that, 'Offensive operations, often times, is the surest, if not the only means of defence.'[74] The language explaining the rationale behind this posture sweeps aside all but one normative limitation in a complex system of 18 legal and ethical checks, which together constitute a presumption against state use of force in the post-WW II era.

Article 2(4) of the UN Charter is regarded as the cornerstone of international expectations regarding state use of force. It not only outlaws military force against the territorial integrity and political independence of other states, it also criminalizes threats to use force in these ways.[75] In the 1986 *Nicaragua* case, the International Court of Justice (ICJ) confirmed the prevailing scholarly view that this general prohibition has the character of *jus cogens*.[76] That is, it is a rule so fundamental that states may not deviate from it – it binds all states whether they have explicitly consented to it or not.[77] Only a handful of international legal rules – such as the prohibition of genocide – rise to this level.

Whether or not a correspondingly absolute assumption exists within Just War Theory is the subject of ongoing debate. There are many who assert that one does. For example, Paul Griffiths has argued that the sections of the *Catechism of the Catholic Church*, which deal with the Fifth Commandment construct a 'default assumption that [a] planned use of force is not just…'[78] Unless those who make the case can overcome the burden of proof against this presumption by meeting the theory's criteria for exceptions to this general rule, 'Catholics must rest, happily or otherwise' with the assumption that a lethal use of military force is unjust.[79] This view is often buttressed by the observation that modern conflicts show a tendency toward total wars, which, given present destructive capacity, many deem unacceptably costly, particularly in terms of human life. Others criticize this interpretation for moving too far afield from the classic just war premise that force may be necessary to right wrongs, establish peace, and secure the good society.[80] Nonetheless, even one of the harshest critics of the pacification of Just War Theory acknowledges that the 'widespread nature of this judgment' is one of the likely reasons this conception 'has since 1983 become more broadly accepted as descriptive of the just war idea.'[81]

Jurists and ethicists have thoroughly explored grounds for exceptions to these checks on taking up arms. Pre-eminent among them is self-defense. Both the UN Charter and Just War Theory are overwhelmingly interpreted as supporting the right of self-defense in the event of an armed attack. Article 51 of the UN Charter describes this right as 'inherent.' This sentiment was echoed in the 1996 ICJ advisory opinion on the legality of nuclear weapons. The court ruled that it could not 'lose sight of the fundamental right of every State to survival, and thus its right to resort to self-defense, in accordance with Article 51 of the Charter, when its survival is at stake.'[82] Within the just war tradition, St. Thomas Aquinas and later Scholastic thinkers placed great importance on the state as an essential instrument of human development.[83] Defense of the state therefore was a defense of society more generally. As a result, a strong presumption exists in favor of a right to self-defense in Just War Theory as well.

However, the situation is muddied when a first use of purportedly defensive force occurs prior to an attack. Many international legal publicists flatly deny that the UN Charter permits self-defense in anticipation of an attack.[84] They note that Article 51 recognizes the inherent right to individual or collective self-defense only '*if* an armed attack occurs.'[85] On the other hand, there are those who argue that what is not explicitly prohibited is permitted and thus that self-defense in anticipation of an attack is permitted under the Charter framework.[86]

If anticipatory self-defense is legally permissible, it must meet two criteria, which derive from customary international law. According to the *Caroline* case of 1837, self-defense that occurs prior to an enemy attack must be both necessary and proportionate. In this classic case involving the midnight raid on an American vessel docked at Fort Schlosser along the Canadian-American border, the British government was called upon to demonstrate:

> necessity of self-defense, instant, overwhelming, leaving no doubt of means, and no moment for deliberation .... it must be shown that day-light could not be waited for; that there could be no attempt at discrimination between the innocent and the guilty ... but that there was a necessity, present and inevitable, for attacking her in the darkness of night, while moored to the shore, and while unarmed men were asleep on board ...[87].

The resulting legal standard holds that governments seeking to justify anticipatory force must show that an armed strike by the other was imminent and that nothing but military action would forestall it.[88]

NSS 2002 confronts heightened ambiguity in the contemporary security environment by significantly lowering the *Caroline* threshold of necessity-as-imminence. This shift can be seen in formal U.S. government statements with respect to specific situations as well as in matters of more abstract policy. For example, prior to the 2003 War with Iraq, President Bush spoke of the perceived threat from Iraq this way:

> America must not ignore the threat gathering against us. Facing clear evidence of peril, we cannot wait for the final proof – the smoking gun – that could come in the form of a mushroom cloud ... Understanding the threats of our time, knowing the designs and

deceptions of the Iraqi regime, *we have every reason to assume the worst*, and we have an urgent duty to prevent the worst from occurring ...[89].

The written document, NSS 2002, which reflects this sentiment refers more generally to terrorism.[90] It holds that in response to the new security context, the United States must:

> ... adapt the concept of imminent threat to the capabilities and objectives of today's adversaries ... the greater the threat, the greater is the risk of inaction - and the more compelling the case for taking anticipatory action to defend ourselves, *even if uncertainty remains as to the time and place of the enemy's attack*.[91]

President G. W. Bush was even more forthright in hindsight after the 2003 War with Iraq when, in early 2004, he appeared on the television program *Meet the Press*. Speaking with host Tim Russert, he said: 'Every potential harm to America had to be judged in the context of this war on terror ... I believe it is essential that when we see a threat, we deal with those threats *before they become imminent*. [Otherwise,] [i]t's too late in this new kind of war ...'.[92]

Via such policy statements, U.S. government officials argue that the changing nature of conflict no longer requires them to wait until an actual threat forms, is poised to launch an attack, or has launched an attack because to do so might prove suicidal. Now, U.S. doctrine and government officials proclaim a right to prevent a threat from gathering instead of waiting until one is established. Thus, the U.S. pre-emption policy may be more precisely referred to one of prevention because it amounts to a more liberal scope of action than a 'reflex action', a 'throwing up of one's arms at the very last minute.'[93] Indeed, the initial phase of major hostilities in the 2003 military campaign in Iraq appears to be a textbook example of Walzer's model of preventive war in which '[t]here is often plenty of time for deliberation, agonizing hours, days, even weeks of deliberation, when one doubts that war can be avoided and wonders whether or not to strike first.'[94] Preventive war's amenability to significantly extended decision-making opportunities places additional stress on already strained arguments that anticipatory force is compatible with the Charter paradigm's necessity-as-imminence requirement. Because of this, most legal scholars (some with regret, others with relish) conclude that preventive wars are not compatible with the current legal paradigm nested in the Charter.

Under extraordinary circumstances, some Just War Theory may allow a somewhat wider sphere of action. According to Adam Dolnik, 'even though traditional Just War Theory does not allow states to attack when a threat is not imminent, there are scenarios in which an exception should be made.'[95] Hugo Grotius, for example, flatly denied that preventive wars could be just.[96] In fact, he went so far as to hold that if certainty regarding a neighbor's capacities or intentions were in doubt, war would be unjust:

> First, therefore, the Dread (as we before observed) of our Neighbor's increasing Strength, is not a warrantable Ground for making War upon him. To justify taking up

> Arms in our own Defense, there ought to be a Necessity for so doing, which there is not, *unless we are sure, with a moral Certainty, that he has not only Forces sufficient, but a full Intention to injure us.*[97]

Walzer has identified the 1967 Six Day War between Egypt and Israel as a 'clear case of legitimate anticipation.'[98] In such instances where a state's failure to use force to confront threats of war would seriously risk its territorial integrity and political independence, under this modern interpretation of Just War Theory, states may, in his view, legitimately use force.

Though this exception creates permission in certain situations, restrictions apply. The existence of an actual threat rather than merely a prevalence of fear is key. What does it mean to be threatened? Walzer says,

> Not merely to be afraid ... we also need an objective standard ... that standard must refer to the threatening acts of some neighboring state ... for I can only be threatened by someone who is threatening me, where 'threaten' means what the dictionary says it means: 'to hold out or offer (some injury) by way of a threat, to declare one's intention of inflicting injury.[99]

Without the existence of an actual threat, then, even this modern reformulation of Just War Theory crowds an attack into the category of an unethical preventive war. One difficulty in applying this two-pronged standard to the real world is that the distinction between a fear and a threat lies in the minds of individuals whose perceptions will surely vary. How can the objective conditions called for be standardized in such a way that they consistently means the same thing to everyone? Geography, history, culture, economics, personalities, and intelligence contribute to a highly subjective and variable perception of what constitutes a threatening act. Is not a state such as Israel – historically told by its neighbors that it has no right to exist – more likely to interpret risks as threats than others whose right to exist has been affirmed? In this sense, like the Charter, which did not take account of WMD and terrorism, Just War Theory 'gives very little guidance about how to make decisions in clouded situations like this.'[100]

Perhaps in the spirit of 'who can act, should', U.S. policy-makers have responded to ambiguities within and discontinuities between traditional norms and contemporary risks by taking the lead in streamlining international rules on the use of force. Their makeover denies other states the right to neutrality in the War on Terrorism and claims a unilateral right to act before threats become imminent. In fact, under NSS 2002, the only constraint on its right to use force beyond American borders that the U.S. government has reaffirmed an explicit willingness to be bound by is the administration's perception of the need to defend against possible and future terrorist threats. This corresponds to the 'just cause' criterion of Just War Theory. Just cause identifies an external action committed by another that legitimates a forceful response. In Augustine's words, 'Those wars are generally defined as just which avenge some wrong, when a nation or state is to be punished for having failed to make amends for the wrong done, or to restore what has been taken unjustly.'[101] The classic example is a military strike on homeland territory.

The implied dismissal of all other legal and ethical qualifications, including neutrality and evidence of imminence, has the effect of collapsing numerous constraints in Just War Theory and the Charter paradigm down into a test for this sole, dichotomous variable (see Table 7.1).[102] Questions about legitimate authority, last resort, and Security Council authorization, for example, have been shrugged off with the statement that self-defense does not require a permission slip.[103] This turns the idea of just cause as only the beginning of a multi-step decision-making process on its head; now, just cause is beginning, middle, and end.[104] And, in the end, it either exists or it does not.

Table 7.1 Clearing Normative Obstacles to U.S. Action in the War on Terrorism

Constraints on States' Rights to Use Extraterritorial Force under International Law and Just War Theory	The Constraint Recognized by the United States on its Extraterritorial Use of Force in the War on Terrorism
• Hague rights of neutrals to impartiality & nonparticipation amid armed conflict • U.N. Charter Article 2(4)'s prohibition on the threat or use of force against the territorial integrity and political independence of any state • U.N. Charter Article 51's requirement that self-defense is justified by an armed attack • Security Council authorization of a state's use of force under Ch. VII of the U.N. Charter • The *Caroline*'s proportionality criterion • The *Caroline*'s necessity-as-imminence test • Just War Theory's denial of a general right to preventive war per Grotius and Walzer • Just War Theory's *jus ad bellum* criteria: just cause, legitimate authority, reasonable hope of success, right intention, formal declaration, proportionality, last resort	• Self-defense against existing or possible future threat from WMD/terrorists

Reducing complexities into dichotomies this way is decision-making behavior consistent with analytic cultural actors seeking to eliminate unpredictability and resolve problems in order to (re-)assert control over their environments. This reinterpretation of the war convention is also compatible with the profile of analytic cultural actors as people who, unable to tolerate contradiction (as between desired action and restrictive norm), seek to eliminate it in order to achieve consistency in support of a single truth.[105] The effect is to remove obstacles to action.

It is interesting to note that the European Union's foreign policy chief, or High Representative, has connected the dichotomous nature of U.S. government rhetoric framing strategic choices to a growing rift between the U.S. and Europe. Javier Solana described this rift, which many have commented upon, as a '"cultural phenomenon"… that goes beyond the pattern of U.S. foreign policy swinging between unilateralism and multilateralism.'[106] This time, said Solana, the pendulum is being swung by religion in a way that Europeans find dissonant with their worldviews: 'It is a kind of binary model. It is all or nothing. For us Europeans, it is difficult to deal with because we are secular. We do not see the world in such black and white terms.'[107] Solana believes that this influence is most evident in 'revealing' language such as: with us or against us, rogue states, axis of evil, right and wrong, good and bad.[108] Whereas Americans see the September 11th attacks as an expression of pure evil and an act of war, Europeans are more likely to view them as acts of extreme and criminal political dysfunction stemming from failed states. Where Americans favor the use of force, Europeans prefer to exhaust multilateral institutions and state-building.[109] Public opinion polling in Europe supports this conclusion. For example, in response to a question asked in 2003 about the use of pre-emptive/preventive force, majorities in most countries surveyed said that they believed 'the U.S. use of force against nations that threaten but have not actually attacked one's country is rarely or never justified.'[110] Thus, Solana and others have labeled the U.S. an outlier among other members of the analytic cultural community, its traditional European allies.

However appropriate these adaptations may be from a U.S. security standpoint, they also escalate costs in the fight against terrorism. Other states' policymakers have come to believe that their governments have legal and ethical rights to neutrality and evidence of imminence, among others, which serve them well, and thus defend against policies and actions perceived as promoting their erosion. This expectation has been substantiated over generations through the repeated articulation, elucidation, and application of these rules in numerous treaties, state interactions, and public declarations.

Additionally, because these particular rights are derivatives of the sovereignty norm, disrespecting them may cast doubt on state sovereignty and international order more generally. If one government will not honor another's right to choose its friends and causes, what does it mean to be sovereign? If one country's territory can be legitimately attacked without clear evidence of intent and capacity to harm, what is the value of geographic borders? If these concepts and frontiers are not honored, what will be? Through such spirals of escalating suppositions, a broader and unintended symbolic challenge can emerge from even a localized and exceptional infringement of internationally shared expectations. As D.G. Pruitt has argued, 'The sign from which an intention of threat is inferred consists of *stepping over* a "boundary" on a conceptual dimension.'[111] Those affected by such boundary violations may therefore be expected to reaffirm them in order to prevent a wider unraveling of mutually reinforcing, shared expectations that sustain individual countries and structure international order. To fail to do so could be interpreted as acceding to decay. Hence, even national leaders sympathetic to the need to defend against future terrorist attacks are likely to attach costs to American policies, which they perceive as even potentially corrosive to their conceptual as well as their territorial and political autonomy. The resources the United States puts into absorbing, managing, and paying those costs increases its overall tab in the War on Terrorism.

To demonstrate, the next section undertakes an assessment of some of the actual and potential consequences and costs of the War on Terrorism.

The Running Tab: Consequences and Costs of U.S. Policies in the War on Terrorism

Bewitched By Language? How Words Frame Options

To re-cap, the histories of pre-emption and neutrality in Just War Theory and international law demonstrate that the concept of necessity is elastic in both realms. Choice, cost-benefit ratios, and the subjectivity of information-processing are elements central to practical applications of this concept. However, this elasticity is not adequately captured in ultimately dichotomous normative judgments such as legal or illegal, just or unjust. Thus, on a theoretical level, the realignment of normative guidelines with the current security landscape that the U.S. government has undertaken is appropriate, lest all notions regarding constraints on state use of force wither away. This is a possibility favored by some.

In view of the tension between dualistic normative judgments and amorphous security risks, one might expect U.S. policy-makers to create new, flexible categories of assessment more compatible with the uncertainties of the post 9-11 security paradigm. Yet, official U.S. government rationale for policy choices continues to center around seemingly irreducible dualities. Uses of force are either necessary or unnecessary. Actors on the global stage are either trusted allies or evil-doers. For allies, inaction is not an option. Presumably, government officials make these distinctions because they believe they must in order to ensure national security. Categorical frameworks thus continue to triumph over the conditional.

This overarching framing choice matters because it can skew debate. For example, identifying someone as evil tends to forestall the possibility of redemption. This label suggests that it is not possible to counter the degree of overwhelming – otherwordly, even – psychological dysfunction that engulfs an actor described by this term. Evil amounts to an absolute judgment of an orientation in character, which, once in place, cannot be mediated by mortal intervention. Those overcome by it represent chronic danger because they are marked by an inability to control the externalization of the toxins that circulate within. The only solution in the face of such a menace, therefore, is to destroy it. Peaceful co-existence is not possible.[112]

William Casebeer describes a 'divisional' use of the rhetoric of evil, which he says often constitutes a 'prelude to mobilization',

> By labeling a group of opponents evil, we can pave the way for viewing them as being less than human and not worthy of respect. Indeed, the type of depravity that is called to mind when we picture canonical evil acts sometimes causes us to traffic with a robustly metaphysical picture of evil: those who consort with the devil are evil, and corruption must be rooted out.[113]

Consistent with this use of the concept, the speechwriter credited with creating the 'axis of evil' imagery explained the good government's appropriate reaction to evil this way, 'Goodness in the political arena cannot survive using only the methods of goodness. What do evil governments do? They kill. What do good governments do? They must also kill. In a world where there are evil governments, this is the real moral test.'[114] Thus, evil implies an urgent need to act with lethal force, perhaps in ways perceived as inappropriate when dealing with good actors.

The sense of immediacy implied in the language of evil subtly underlines the necessity component common in many statements by the U.S. government about the War on Terrorism. This focus on necessity also has practical policy implications. According to Gregory A. Raymond,

> [necessity] enjoins one to marshal the wherewithal for defending the state's primary interests, those which cannot be compromised and which must be upheld *at any cost* ... The rhetorical strategy behind the argument from necessity is to frame situations of limited options as situations where no alternatives exist.[115]

If something is deemed to be necessary, or more likely to be necessary than not, a range of policy alternatives is largely foreclosed because it is assumed that they cannot be afforded under present circumstances.[116]

By coupling descriptions of security risks in terms of evil and necessity, a message that urgent, forceful action is mandatory becomes further amplified. In this way, 'moral appeals can be an effective tactic in foreign policy argumentation, swinging the weight of presumption in favor of military intervention ...'.[117] Beyond tilting the immediate decision, other potential complications emerge from this observation. First, continuing to frame the post 9-11 security context in terms of evil and necessity may predispose policymakers to future uses of force, even if other options might successfully resolve new crises. If a reliance on key, value-laden words were to condition planners in analytic cultural communities to take military action to eliminate ambiguity from and to reassert control over their global environments, this would support a linkage between language and culture wherein 'language reflects culture and culture is reproduced by language.'[118]

Raymond has identified a second, likely consequence of constructing policy arguments on the basis of moral appeals, the need to manage questions about intentionality.[119] He predicts that this can be difficult. The next section examines tentative evidence that this general observation applies to international reaction to U.S. policy in the War on Terrorism.

International Questions about Intentionality

Former U.S. Ambassador John Brady Kiesling has asserted that there is an underlying strategic significance to Solana's cultural-linguistic observation, which highlights the effects 'binary' moral judgments may have on other states. As U. S. officials were initiating a military campaign in Iraq, Kiesling resigned, explaining that 'Preventive War has no logical stopping point ... [Even] [o]ur *friends and allies* are afraid of us, afraid of what we'd do. They see us as a rogue elephant and fear us as an aggressive empire.'[120] Secretary of Defense Donald Rumsfeld's prior assurance that the United States could fight and win multiple wars at the same time may have served to inflate this predictable 'logic of exaggeration.'[121]

The Pew Global Attitudes Project has generated quantitative data, which map some of the geography behind Kiesling's thesis. (See Table 7.2.) Based on public opinion polling in 21 countries conducted in 2003, these researchers found that significant segments of various countries were indeed worried about a potential military threat from the United States.[122]

Table 7. 2   Percent of Respondents Worried about a Potential U.S. Military Threat (2003)[123]

Country	Very Worried	Somewhat Worried	Worried to Any Degree
Indonesia	36	38	74
Nigeria	54	18	72
Pakistan	47	25	72
Russia	43	28	71
Turkey	35	36	71
Lebanon	26	32	58
Jordan	21	35	56
Kuwait	35	18	53
Morocco	24	22	46

The Pew analysis described the reaction among Muslims to the new U.S. security stance as particularly acute. Its authors noted that majorities in seven of eight Muslim populations surveyed expressed concerns that the U.S. might become a military threat to their countries. Even in Kuwait, which the United States largely liberated from Iraq in 1991, 53 percent voiced at least some degree of anxiety that the U.S. could constitute a threat to Kuwait. Pew analysts concluded that 'the bottom has fallen out of support for America in most of the Muslim world. Negative views of the U.S. among Muslims, which had been largely limited to countries in the Middle East, have spread to Muslim populations in Indonesia and Nigeria.'[124] Within one year, favorable ratings for the U.S. dropped from 61 percent to 15 percent in Indonesia and from 71 to 38 percent among Muslims in Nigeria.[125] While anti-American attitudes pre-date the Bush Doctrine, the timing as well as degree of these fluctuations and the survey's use of items inquiring specifically about U.S. foreign policy are worthy of note.

Further anecdotal evidence may illuminate some of what drove these worries. An article in Beirut's *Daily Star* specified Lebanese concerns about future U.S. targets for pre-emptive/preventive action.[126] In it, Adib F. Farha cited a report, which claimed that the United States government may have been planning to strike Hezbollah bases in Lebanon. Farha predicted that if U.S. decision-makers were to execute this plan, they would use the 'pretext' that Hezbollah is a terrorist organization and poses a threat to U.S. national security (although Farha described Hezbollah's goal as limited to countering 'Israeli aggression').[127] Setting aside the merits of this particular accusation, Farha's inference that the War on Terrorism is a pre-text for hidden U.S. government motives remains a pervasive one - inside as well as outside the United States.[128] David Hastings Dunn, has summarized the list of usual, suspected motives for the 2003 War with Iraq as: oil, revenge for the President's father, support for Israel, hegemonic control of the Middle East, hubris, and elections.[129]

Whether they know it or not, those who distrust American motivations this way are mobilizing the traditional just war criterion of right intention. Right intention is often an unappreciated dimension of Just War Theory. Disagreement on its meaning and importance is significant. One classic formulation of the concept comes from St. Thomas Aquinas:

> ... So it can happen that even when war is declared by legitimate authority and there is just cause, it is nevertheless made unjust through evil intention. St. Augustine says in *Contra Faustum* (LXXIV): "The desire to hurt, the cruelty of vendetta, the stern and implacable spirit, arrogance in victory, the thirst for power, and all that is similar, all these are justly condemned in war."[130]

Johnson characterizes this aspect of right intention as focused on 'the state of mind' of rulers and soldiers.[131] It requires those who authorize and fight wars to maintain moral control over decisions by suppressing animosity and hatred, which can injure the moral and psychological health of belligerents as well as pervert statecraft.[132] Mastery of this capacity bars the pursuit of otherwise just causes when secretly driven by moral impurities. Just cause cannot make up for a lack of right intention, but the absence of right intention may convert a just war into an unjust war.

Alongside this negative duty, Augustine describes a second, positive requirement of right intention – desire to secure the peace and uplift the good: 'For the true followers of God even wars are peaceful, not being made for greed or out of cruelty, but from desire of peace, to restrain the evil and assist the good.'[133] This aspect of right intention requires that wars be undertaken to establish or restore the peace 'that comes only with a justly ordered community.'[134] Moreover, this high standard compels even when a people may have good reason for feeling that the enemy deserves the worst. This is so because a just and lasting peace can be built only on charity, not on vengeance.[135]

The uneasiness many feel toward the American government as it seeks to address rising security risks speaks to doubts they harbor about right intention, perhaps especially in the first sense, the exploitation of a just cause for ignoble aims. Thus, it should come as no surprise that the same Pew study cited above found that in most countries friendly to the United States, 'only modest percentages have confidence that President Bush will *do the right thing* in international affairs.'[136] These findings affirm Raymond's prediction that policies constructed on the basis of moral appeals tend to raise questions about intentionality, which are difficult to manage.

Other actual and potential costs associated with the new U.S. security stance and international reaction to it are explored below.

Other Costs

The poll numbers, anecdotal analyses, and simple speculations cited above point toward the possibility that the international community has not warmly received the U.S. government's efforts to adapt its national security posture to the post 9-11 landscape. Further systematic and cross-national research on this question at both the mass and elite levels of international relations would be helpful. Assuming that this is the case, however, so what? If U.S. government officials deem these policies to be necessary responses to perceived threats, why should they bother with the perception that the U.S. is a 'rogue colossus?'[137] After all, according to Raymond, decisions taken on the basis of necessity are predisposed to defend a state's primary interests *at any cost* – presumably including international unpopularity.[138] That said, if national security can be had at a lower price, why pay more?

A few of the actual and potential costs to the United States associated with its new offensive security posture are as follows:

1. *Financial costs*: In the three budget years directly following 11 September 2001, the U.S. government added approximately $340 billion in new money to its military, homeland security, and international affairs budgets.[139] That is, in these three categories, the combined federal budget in 2002, 2003, and 2004 was $340 billion higher than annual adjustments to account for inflation would require.[140] This represents a real (inflation-adjusted) increase of more than 40 percent in three years.[141] Because much of this money is borrowed, the War on Terrorism contributes to record-high U.S. budget deficits – $422 billion in 2004 – when measured in dollar terms.[142] Further projections are clouded by significant uncertainties such as the overall cost of coalition actions in Iraq. Nonetheless, with such uncertainties very much in mind, in late 2002, one analyst estimated total costs (direct military spending + follow-on costs

including reconstruction) of a war with Iraq as likely to fall between a low of $99 billion (given favorable conditions) and a high of $1.9 trillion ('given a string of bad luck or misjudgments during or after the war').[143] With merely marginal offsets from international donor conferences and Iraqi oil revenues, Americans are paying the bulk of this bill (unlike the 1991 Persian Gulf War, where the opposite was true).[144] Joshua Goldstein has calculated that for American families whose household incomes are between $50,000-100,000 a year, their monthly shares of war-related spending in the War on Terrorism comes to about $500.[145]

2. *Weakened credibility of U.S. intelligence*: Former U.S. National Security Advisor Zbigniew Brzezinksi has described the loss of American intelligence community credibility around the world as a result of the gap between prewar[146] and postwar[147] estimates of Iraqi WMD:

> The fact is that prior to what has happened, people tended to believe when the United States spoke authoritatively. If the president said that something was so, others, whether they liked it or not, believed it. Today, I think there's widespread international mistrust of what we say, and a great deal of mistrust regarding the reliability of our intelligence. ... The fact is that most of the world thought that there were weapons of mass destruction in Iraq largely because we told them so. And, until recently, they tended to believe us.[148]

Brzezinski has speculated that many U.S. coalition partners such as Poland and Argentina in the 2003 War with Iraq were persuaded to support the military campaign because they trusted U.S. intelligence reports, not because they had their own active intelligence investigations into Iraq's WMD program. He has expressed doubt that they would so readily place their faith in U.S. intelligence estimates in future crises, even though such estimates might be accurate the next time around.[149]

3. *Lack of cooperation with the U.S. in international organizations*: Some members of the international diplomatic community have characterized statements by American officials in presentations made to the international community regarding intelligence findings that Iraq posed a threat to neighbors near and far in 2002 and 2003 as dishonest rather than as inaccurate or as imprecise.[150] Some have also held that officials in various international organizations were as offended by what they described as bullying[151] behavior by American diplomats in international negotiations as by the content of U.S. policy itself.[152] These statesmen and women have relayed an international perception that '[r]eal diplomacy has been replaced with demands that other countries follow U.S. directives or get out of the way.'[153] Thus, many have predicted a 'passive-aggressive' attitude toward cooperation with the United States government for the foreseeable future simply because of a lack of enthusiasm to work with American officials.[154] They point to the U.S.'s

majority share of the cost of current coalition operations in Iraq versus the minority share the U.S. paid in the 1991 Gulf War as evidence of the price of 'the suspicion and disdain' the U.S. government is perceived as showing toward virtually 'the entire architecture of international treaties and norms painstakingly built since World War II.'[155]

4. *The possibility that first uses of force in the absence of impending attacks will spread to other countries*: If American leadership in creating regimes that support a presumption against force was a necessary condition of their widespread adoption, how will U.S. rejection of these norms now affect their sustainability?[156] Will other states such as Russia and France adopt their own pre-emptive/preventive force policies? Have they already signaled that they are doing so?[157] Emulation of U.S. policy expressed in NSS 2002 could lower the international threshold for first uses of interstate force, while at the same time reducing external leverage to prevent them. As one group of scholars has hypothesized,

> Of course, no country will embark suddenly on a war of aggression simply because the United States provides it with a quasi-legal justification to do so. But countries already on the brink of war, and leaning strongly towards war, might use the doctrine to justify an action they already wished to take, and the effect of the U.S. posture may make it harder for the international community in general, and the U.S. in particular, to counsel delay and diplomacy.[158]

Moreover, if other countries perceive such first uses of force to be aggressive rather than defensive, would their own prior actions be warranted? If the U.S. is perceived as an aggressor, would this make Americans less safe? These questions point toward the possibility that international politics could stand at the brink of – or just beyond – a new Security Dilemma.[159]

5. *The loss of life*: According to the U.S. Department of Defense, from the onset of major combat operations in Iraq in March 2003 through December 2004, approximately 1300 American soldiers died in Operation Iraqi Freedom. Eighty-nine percent of these deaths occurred after the declared conclusion of major hostilities on 30 April 2003.[160] One independent initiative, which seeks to record other countries' fatalities in Iraq during the same period, counted about 15,000 Iraqi civilian deaths directly associated 'with the military intervention and occupation of the country.'[161] Just under half were categorized as the result of major combat operations in March and April 2003. The rest were described as 'resulting from the breakdown in law and order' and included deaths resulting from 'inadequate health care or sanitation.'[162] These estimates of Iraqi civilian casualties were challenged by a 2004 article published in the medical journal *The Lancet*.[163] Its researchers indicated that about 100,000 'excess' Iraqi deaths occurred between March 2003 and September 2004.[164] Although part of the variation in Iraqi casualty estimates

was explained by the inclusion of some military personnel and the use of statistical projections by the medical researchers, remaining discrepancies have yet to be reconciled.[165]

6. *Military opportunity costs*: In May 2004, the United States government announced that it would redeploy 3,700 troops from South Korea to Iraq, reigniting concerns that the U.S. military was overextended. On the international plane, the transfer prompted a South Korean newspaper to declare 'a major security gap' on the Korean peninsula at a time when nuclear tensions were running high between North and South Korea.[166] The South Koreans pointed out that their alliance with the United States was the only significant barrier standing between them, a North Korean military of over a million troops and a desperate, isolated regime's efforts to sustain itself - a regime which has announced possession of nuclear weapons.

7. *Increased resentment toward the United States*: Continued deployment of 140,000 troops in Iraq may fuel the impression that the operation is an occupation by an oppressor rather than a liberation by a friend. Even before the Abu Ghraib[167] prison scandal involving abuses of Iraqi prisoners became public, Egyptian President Hosni Mubarak, long viewed as a major Arab ally of the United States, told the French newspaper *Le Monde* that: 'Today there is hatred of the Americans like never before in the region. At the start, some considered the Americans were helping them. There was no hatred of the Americans. After what has happened in Iraq, there is an unprecedented hatred and the Americans know it.'[168] Some U.S. officials have worried that such hatred would translate into more terrorist attacks.[169] Their logic is reminiscent of Niccolo Machiavelli's counsel in *The Prince* that the ideal ruler should seek to be loved and feared,[170] but should never allow himself to be 'hated or despised.'[171] Hatred, Macchiavelli argued, increases the number of enemies one has, and therefore necessarily increases the likelihood of ultimate failure in statecraft.

Given the unbounded nature of the War on Terrorism, these costs could simply constitute the down-payment on a much larger bill yet to come.[172] From this, some conclude that the bill – in all its dimensions, not just the financial – is intolerably high as well as potentially unsustainable on this scale. Others argue that although this is an admittedly expensive policy, given the high stakes involved and the unacceptable consequences of failure, additional resources should be dedicated to ensure victory. Somewhere in the middle are those who advocate increased international burden-sharing.

This chapter provides support for the proposition that deviations from shared expectations of what constitutes right conduct in specific situations can cost dearly. This may be especially true when military action turns out to be preventive rather than preemptive because the international community may be unforgiving of what it perceives to be the unnecessary violation of rules correlated with sovereignty, one conceptual foundation of state independence and international order.[173] Moreover, antagonism may be amplified where widespread support exists for the notion that force was used with false intentions, even if this is not the case. Effectively addressing and incorporating such concerns, which can often be predicted through reference to normative frameworks and inquiry into others' stakes, can help minimize the costs of even the most unpopular policy. Robert Kagan suggests that because of its disproportionate wealth and power, this is something the United States can easily afford to do.[174] What international goodwill, military materiel, human lives, intelligence credibility, and institutional cooperation the United States saves in the process of paying its respects to international norms may be banked for a rainy day when 'multilateralism is impossible and unilateral action unavoidable.'[175]

In the meantime, Secretary of Defense Donald Rumsfeld allegedly wondered in a leaked memo if current U.S. investments in the War on Terrorism are producing the desired return:

> Today, we lack the metrics to know if we are winning the global war on terror. Are we capturing, killing or deterring and dissuading more terrorists every day than the madrassas and the radical clerics are recruiting, training and deploying against us? ... *The cost-benefit-ratio is against us!* Our cost is billions against the terrorists' costs of millions ... *What else should we be considering?*[176]

Early reflection on this point has the potential to move decision-making beyond the seemingly incommensurable and polarizing conclusions that a forcible action is just or unjust, legal or illegal toward a more capacity-oriented notion of what constitutes prudent policy.[177]

The next section seeks to carve out fresh thinking space in support of that process.

'Wise War' Decision-Making Criteria for the 21st Century

If a focus on outgrown dichotomous choices emphasizing necessity predisposes planners to a high-cost use of force policy, what decision-making criteria might promote exploration of a wider range of efficient as well as effective policy options? How should new decision-making criteria be designed to grapple with the indeterminate risks prevalent in the post-September 11th era? If America's national security posture is predicated upon analytic cultural lenses, what might the source of new decision-making criteria be?

Holistic cultures provide a panoply of principles that might apply. These actors are typically:

> relationship and situation-oriented. Social context and social harmony are paramount; negotiations are but one step along the path of any relationship. Moreover, to those who hold this perspective, the world is too complicated and ambiguous a place to mold to one's wishes. The wise person adjusts to the environment and develops an adaptive

personality in order to live comfortably within irresolvable differences. Communication in these cultures tends to emphasize politeness, tact, indirectness, and building strong interpersonal relationships.[178]

For the purposes of this essay, perhaps their most salient characteristic is the tendency to be more accepting of contradictions, paradox, and ambiguity.[179] As the term implies, people in these cultures are more likely than analytic actors to take a holistic approach to problems, to focus on background as well as foreground, long-term as well as short-term.[180] Eastern cultures such as those associated with China, Korea, and Japan present classic examples of this worldview. The proposition presented here is not for Americans to exchange their *weltanschauung* for another. Government planners might, however, consider whether a few holistic principles could be selectively employed to maximize national security at the lowest cost possible.

For example, 'Mao Dun Lu' is a Taoist principle, which asserts that 'reality is not precise or cut-and-dried, but is full of contradictions. Because change is constant, contradiction is constant. Old and new, good and bad, strong and weak, and so on coexist in everything.'[181] The existence of one opposing force depends upon the existence of another to bring it into being. For Taoists, the dialectic between the two propels life forward. *The Book of Lao Zi* offers a classic expression of this belief:

> When all people in the world know the beautiful as beauty,
> There appears ugliness;
> When they know goodness as good,
> There appears evil.
> Therefore, by opposing each other,
> Existence and nonexistence come into being,
> Difficult and easy form themselves,
> Long and short are distinct,
> High and low contrast,
> Sound and voice harmonize,
> Front and back emerge.[182]

Some analysts believe that the Taoist theme of dualism has a special connection to warfare.[183] For example, the relationship between warring opposites is a recurring theme of Sun Tzu's *Art of War* as in this chapter on 'Forms of the Earth':

> And so it is said –
> Know the other and know oneself,
> Then victory is not in danger.
> Know earth and know heaven,
> Then victory can be complete.[184]

While on the spiritual plane, contradictions are passively observed as part of the constant process that 'brings things round and round', for earthly strategists, 'opposition is to be exploited for an end.'[185] Understanding organic power begets efficiency. The superior planner is not 'depleted because he gains energy by moving with the forms of earth, the larger patterns of his world.'[186] This implies that those who discover and work with the natural laws of duality will more readily achieve their goals than those who are unaware of them or swim against their tides.

How might Mao Dun Lu apply to the War on Terrorism? It suggests that in some situations it may be more productive to live within and take advantage of clashes between powerful, antagonistic forces than to eradicate an enemy. Where this is so, contrast is to be embraced for its ability to shape and re-shape the world. However, the key, underlying qualification to this approach in security matters is that contrast is to be embraced. That requires acknowledging, naming, and pointing directly to that which is deemed to define the other; there is no descent into nihilism here. Reasoned assessments across competing paradigms are a must.

Application of this concept to the most high-risk matters of international peace and security may not be as out-of-place as might appear to be the case at first blush. In fact, some compatibility exists between Mao Dun Lu and the philosophy of mutually assured destruction, which informed U.S. national security for decades. As the United States government was strategizing to determine how best to address the threat it perceived from the Soviet state, decision-makers sifted through a series of tactical options: surgical decapitation strikes, counterforce first strikes, missile defense, bomber defense, civil (homeland) defense, covert operations to assassinate foreign leaders – even preemptive and preventive war.[187] In the end, U.S. policymakers found that:

> None of the multitude of options being pursued could prevent either side from destroying the other in a nuclear war. Mutual vulnerability, despite intermittent attempts to remove it through Star Wars defenses or some other scheme, was a constant of the Cold War confrontation. But, instead of despairing, both countries discovered salvation in this predicament. They were forced to rationalize mutual vulnerability as a virtue and learn to live in mutual deterrence as the centerpiece of national security, and eventually they celebrated this newfound source of security.[188]

Because the post 9-11 world is 'not our parents' security context', this is an imperfect analogy at best. Still, it serves to make the point that even when confronted by the most high-risk security threats posed by 'evil' others, safety may not always come from their destruction. Evidence in support of this notion may lie in the observation that since the Soviet Union has collapsed, control over WMD may have decreased rather than increased. The world may be less safe now - when many believe the West has won[189] – than it was when these two forces were at the apogee of their opposition to one another.

The idea that safety may be found within a balance of opposing forces can be translated into three wise war decision-making criteria for the War on Terrorism as follows (see Table 7.3).

Table 7.3 'Wise War' Decision-Making Criteria

---

1. Explain the positives and negatives in the existing situation and how their co-existence can complement one another, excluding neither.

2. Explain how negatives can be turned into positives.

3. Calculate the estimated cost of failure to accept positives and negatives as complementary.

If any of these cannot be done, the use of force is wise.

Taken together, these criteria reaffirm the normative presumption against force by requiring actors to live within the possibility that co-existence with a diametrically opposed and potentially threatening other can be tolerated without sacrificing survival. At the same time, this framework retains the classic just war assumption that some uses of force may be in order. If planners cannot craft a genuinely satisfactory response to any of the three challenges – if complementarity can't be established, if negatives can't be transformed into positives, or if the costs of embracing complementarity are unaffordable – force is not only permitted, it can be prudent.

In situations of impending attack – that is, in clearly preemptive situations - such abstract questions may well be irrelevant. However, when decision-makers are contemplating truly preventive wars and have days, weeks, and months to consider the wisdom of using force, these criteria support the collection and analysis of multiple rounds of intelligence as well as the consideration of a wide range of policy alternatives without causing harm because of an already extended decision-making timeframe. How might they be applied in practice? A brief historical analysis of the early Cold War period shows these principles at work under different circumstances, which provide a basis for future adaptation to the contemporary security environment. Although this explanation draws on the Cold War, this essay does not argue that containment, mutually assured destruction, or deterrence suit the aims of the War on Terrorism. The substance of these policies is not the focus here. Rather, the intent is to demonstrate how these decision-making criteria have been successfully employed to support wise choices about the use of force in another era also characterized by high stakes and great animosities as a basis for thinking about the future.

The first step's requirement that neither force is to be excluded prioritizes national survival. Hence, the primacy of state security is taken as given. Yet, this first criterion does not assume the inevitability of war between opposing forces. Instead, it prompts planners to assess the positive and negative aspects of a conflict and to consider the possibility that they can complement one another.

For example, the international stage was set for a clash between competing archetypal powers in the second half of the 1940s. During that time, American and Soviet decision-makers increasingly saw themselves as standing on separate sides of an 'irreconcilable chasm' between socialism and capitalism, police states and democratic governments.[190] Without a common foe to unite them, the utter incompatibility between the Soviet and American ideologies prompted President Truman to declare that the world was 'divided between two ways of life', one touting 'the will of the majority' and the other the 'will of a minority forcibly imposed upon the majority.'[191] Many assumed that the ultimate socialist intention was to overthrow capitalist governments, an interpretation Soviet words and deeds often supported. With the experience of World War II fresh in their minds, it didn't take much to convince many Americans in particular of a connection between domestic repression and international expansionism.[192] Whether accurate or not, in 1948 the perception of a Soviet threat was so great that the British Foreign Office described the conflict between the U.S. and U.S.S.R. as nothing less than 'the defence of western civilization.'[193]

This widespread interpretation of the ideological origins of the Cold War highlights one obvious 'negative' in a world where the Soviet government presented itself as the vanguard of a global revolution, the threat of annihilation the Soviet Union posed to non-socialist governments. However, by providing a strong foil of nearly world-wide significance, the Soviet model of government also increased the salience of American-style democracy, domestically as well as internationally. Soviet control of elections at home as well as in Poland, Romania, and Bulgaria imbued the U.S.'s two-party competitions with new meaning. While democracy in the U.S. was more than 160 years old in the late 1940s, in part because of its relative geographic isolation, its opportunities to 'know itself and know the other' in relation to it had been somewhat limited. Thus, Lao Zi and Sun Tzu might agree that sustained, though conflictual, engagement with the Soviet Union was positive in that it helped Americans and others vested in the conflict complete their understanding of themselves as political beings whose choices create very different experiences. Without this dangerous conflict, many might have missed an opportunity to know democracy as an alternative to a far less desirable state. In this way, Soviet authoritarianism and totalitarianism complemented American democracy.

The second step in the wise war trilogy nudges decision-makers to be creative in thinking about how they can turn negatives into positives. This approach can also be seen in early postwar conflict management between the U.S. and U.S.S.R. As George Kennan noted in 1947, in the absence of an impending military strike, the perception of an unnecessary or frivolous use of force to roll back communism – whether in the U.S.S.R. or elsewhere – had the potential to pollute the moral basis of the American exemplar; the long-term campaign could thus be lost before a war was over.[194] Instead, even as they prepared contingency plans to fight and win if necessary, American policy-makers relied on the sharp contrast between the two halves of the divided world to fuel their goals. As one presidential advisor said, the United States needed to 'have something positive and attractive to offer, and not just anti-communism.' Thus, in keeping with Truman's belief that communism could succeed only 'where there is weakness, misery, or despair', the Marshall Plan was launched to 'create positive alternatives to communism without generating sympathy for that ideology by opposing it directly.'[195] Similarly, as the Soviet government was actively limiting the self-determination of its satellite states and suppressing the civil and political rights of its citizens, Eleanor Roosevelt assumed a leading role in successfully advocating for the passage of the Universal Declaration of Human Rights in the United Nations.

Through these and other international pro-capitalist, pro-democratic campaigns, the U.S. government sought to universalize the Western idea of liberal democracy as 'the final form of human government', and thus to effectively undermine the legitimacy of the Soviet state.[196] In addition to hopefully denying the creation of new environments in which communism would thrive, even before these plans were implemented, many historians argue that the United States was *invited* to expand its influence throughout Western Europe and Iran in order to provide a counterweight to Soviet power.[197] As a result, over the coming years, the United States was able to parlay its conflict with the Soviet Union into increased global reach without having to incur the human, financial, and other costs of direct military combat with the U.S.S.R. A negative thus became a positive.

The third step asks whether failure to live within the paradox of opposing forces is cost-prohibitive. The advent of nuclear weapons had a profound effect on such use of force calculations. As many have noted, once both sides developed this unprecedented destructive capacity, the threat of retaliation for any first use tended to bestow a 'sobering' or 'stabilizing' effect on statesmen by discouraging the initiation of any action that could result in an escalation leading to war.[198] General MacArthur's warning that total war in the nuclear era would result in an 'incalculable disaster' resonated widely as a cautionary note.[199]

However, even when the United States enjoyed a nuclear monopoly, prior to the first Soviet atomic test in 1949 and prior to the Soviet development of delivery capacity around 1954, the United States heeded a policy of restraint. Thus, the American government's decision to forego preventive war in the early postwar years had to be based on something other than fear of immediate nuclear retaliation. Given the ongoing global struggle for power between the U.S. and U.S.S.R., lack of opportunity to use military force was also an unlikely reason for this restraint.[200] Among the most significant reasons for U.S. planners' reluctant decision to rest within the paradox of co-existence was a new-found wariness of the alternative's potential costs. According to John Lewis Gaddis,

> It quickly became clear to American policymakers, after World War II, that insistence on the total defeat of Germany and Japan had profoundly de-stabilized the postwar balance of power. Only by assuming responsibility for the rehabilitation of these former enemies as well as the countries they had ravaged had the United States been able to restore equilibrium, and even then it had been clear that the American role in this regard would have to be a continuing one. It was no accident that the doctrine of 'unconditional surrender' came under severe criticism, after 1945, from a new school of

'realist' geopoliticians *given to viewing international stability in terms of the wary toleration of adversaries rather than, as a point of principle, their annihilation.*[201]

Thus, concerns about the long-term costs to international stability of failing to tolerate the Soviet state may have provided a psychological constraint that preceded the fear of mutually assured destruction and effectively suppressed the realization of the preventive war option. As a result, not only did the Soviet and American models of governance co-exist without direct military combat for years, in some scholars' eyes, so, too, did 'paranoia and prudence.'[202]

This brief analysis of the tensions between the Soviet Union and the United States during the latter half of the 1940's reveals an interpretation of history consistent with the three-step calculation that a preventive war would have been unwise at that juncture. In that situation, none of the three wise war criteria was satisfied: a complementarity of Soviet and American forces existed, U.S. planners were able to efficiently transform some negative consequences stemming from the Soviet threat into positive international support for American values, and the costs of failing to tolerate the Soviet state were deemed to be unacceptably high to justify a preventive war. Whether or not these decision-making criteria may help chart a successful route around and through contemporary security concerns in the War on Terrorism remains to be seen.

Writing about Pearl Harbor in 1962, Thomas Schelling sought to explain the difficulty and importance of looking beyond one's worldview: 'There is a tendency in our planning to confuse the unfamiliar with the improbable. The contingency we have not considered looks strange; what looks strange is thought improbable; what is improbable needs to be considered seriously.'[203] Successfully managing today's risks requires 'much more agility and flexibility' than yesterday's either/or structures provide.[204] From scenario to scenario, the quest now is to identify anew in each situation the best possible fit between security needs, mental maps, and national resources in a chronically insecure world so as not to back policy into a decision-making corner. In one or more of these future conflicts, wise war criteria may be worth considering.

Notes

[1] The author thanks Edmund F. Byrne and Helena Meyer-Knapp for their professional feedback on an earlier version of this chapter. I also appreciate Rachel Pearsall's able assistance.

[2] Michael Ignatieff, 'It's War, But It Doesn't Have to be Dirty', *The Guardian*, 1 October 2001, <www.ksg.harvard.edu/news/opeds/2001/ignatieff_war_guardian_gd_100101.htm>. *See* Chip Bertlet, 'Apocalyptic Nihilism', 1999, paper written for Boston University's Center for Millennial Studies, <www.mille.org/scholarship/papers/bertletnihilism.html>.

[3] Cohen, 1981, p. 141.

[4] 'War convention' refers to the overarching set of 'norms, customs, professional codes, legal precepts, religious and philosophical principles, and reciprocal arrangements that shape our judgments of military conduct.' Walzer 1977, p. 44.

[5] Peng and Nisbett, 1999. Nisbett, Peng, Choi, Norenzayan, 2001.
[6] Michael Ignatieff, 'It's War, But It Doesn't Have to be Dirty', *The Guardian* 1 October 2001, <www.ksg.harvard.edu/news/opeds/2001/ignatieff_war_gd_100101.htm>.
[7] Here, Just War Theory refers to the Catholic tradition. For other approaches, *see* Nardin, 1996. For an overview of the evolution of Just War Theory and its moral bases, *see* Johnson, 1981. On the UN Charter paradigm, *see* Damrosch, Henkin, Pugh, Schachter, Smit, 2001, pp. 920-1087 and Arend and Beck, 1993.
[8] O'Brien, 1981, p. 4.
[9] Russell, 1975, p. 24.
[10] Mansbach, 2000, p. 303.
[11] Palmer, 1986, p. 99.
[12] Laqueur, 1978, pp. 7-8.
[13] Arend, 2003, p. 97.
[14] Ibid.
[15] Pfleger, 2004. Tenet said, 'The steady growth of Osama bin Laden's anti-U.S. sentiment through the wider Sunni (Islamic) extremist movement, and the broad dissemination of al Qaida's destructive expertise, ensure that a serious threat will remain for the foreseeable future – with or without al Qaida in the picture.'
[16] Gunaratna, 2004, p. 25, note 3.
[17] Murphy, 2002, p. 9a. Cited in Howard and Sawyer, p. ix.
[18] Gunaratna, p. 4.
[19] Howard and Sawyer, p. x. *See also* Gunaratna, 2002, p. 76.
[20] Berger, 2002, p. 242.
[21] Gertz, 2004. Tenet said that 'in addition to Al-Qaeda, more than two dozen terrorist groups are seeking chemical, biological, radiological, and nuclear materials.'
[22] Berger, p. 243.
[23] Hamid Mir, 'Osama Claims He Has Nukes; If U.S. Uses N-arms it will Get Same Response,' *The Dawn of Pakistan,* 10 November 2001. <www.dawn.com/2001/11/10/top1.htm>.
[24] Gunaratna, pp. 4-5.
[25] Gunaratna, p. 5 and p. 25, footnote 12.
[26] *The Associated Press*, 2004, p. 1A.
[27] Combs, 2000, pp. 214-231.
[28] Keohane, 2002, pp. 176-189.
[29] Sagan and Turco, 1993, pp. 369-373. *See also* Sagan, 1983.
[30] Hensel, 2002, p. 19.
[31] This is so even though occasional, surprise sneak attacks which initiate a chronic, sustained violent conflict are not new, as the Japanese attack on Pearl Harbor demonstrated.
[32] Falk, 2003, p. viii.
[33] Hensel, pp. 20 and 42, notes 7 and 8.
[34] National Security Strategy of the United States, October 2002, <www.whitehouse.gov/nsc/nssintro.html>. All references to President Bush refer to the forty-third President of the United States.
[35] Nisbett, Peng, Choi, Norenzayan, 2001. Labels of these two cultural types vary across disciplines. See Cohen, 2002, especially pp. 25-43.
[36] Meyer-Knapp and Peach, 2004.
[37] Peng and Nisbett, 1999. Nisbett, Peng, Choi, Norenzayan, 2001. *See also* Nisbett, 2003.
[38] Hall, 1976.
[39] This is an aggregate portrait; individual Americans may fit the 'holistic profile'. For example, some have suggested that former President Jimmy Carter's success in facilitating

negotiations between Prime Minister Menachem Begin of Israel and President Anwar Sadat of Egypt – two holistic cultures – was due in part to his upbringing in rural Georgia, also a holistic culture. In addition, in specific instances, holistic actors can be analytical and analytic actors can be holistic.

[40] Address by President Bush to a Joint Session of Congress and the American People, 20 September 2001, <www.whitehouse.gov/news/releases/2001/09/20010920-8.html>.

[41] Raymond, 1997a, p. 125. Petrochilos, 1998, p. 613.

[42] Boyle, 1986, p. 61.

[43] Articles 1 and 2, Hague Convention V, Respecting the Rights and Duties of Neutral Powers and Persons in Case of War on Land, <www.yale.edu/lawweb/avalon/lawofwar/hague05.htm>.

[44] Article 9 of Hague Convention V.

[45] Article 6 of Hague Convention XIII.

[46] Petrochilos, p. 581.

[47] Petrochilos, p. 582.

[48] Ibid.

[49] Petrochilos, pp. 580-581.

[50] Petrochilos, p. 583.

[51] Raymond, 1997a, p. 124.

[52] Cited in Raymond, 1997a, p. 124.

[53] Rubin, 1988, p. 14.

[54] Ibid.

[55] Walzer, p. 235.

[56] Walzer, p. 237.

[57] Raymond, 1997a, p. 127.

[58] Mikael af Malmborg, 2001.

[59] *See* Kissinger, 2002.

[60] Herodotus, quoted in Raymond, 1997a, p. 123.

[61] Address by President Bush to a Joint Session of Congress and the American People, 20 September 2001, <www.whitehouse.gov/news/releases/2001/09/20010920-8.html>.

[62] From a speech President Bush delivered at the White House, 19 March 2004, < www.whitehouse.gov/news/releases/2004/03/20040319-3.html>.

[63] 'President Bush Welcomes President Chirac to White House,' 6 November 2001 in a joint news conference with French President Jacques Chirac, <www.whitehouse.gov/news/releases/2001/11/20011106-4.html>. *See also* 'President Bush Speaks to UN,' 10 November 2001, <www.whitehouse.gov/news/releases/2001/11/20011110-3.html>.

[64] Scott Fornek, 'You're with US or Against US, Bush Says,' 21 September 2001, <www.suntimes.com/terror/stories/cst-nws-main21.html>.

[65] Fornek.

[66] One could argue that UN Security Council resolutions such as 1368, passed on 12 September 2001, activate sovereign limitations that override the right to neutrality in the War on Terrorism. It calls upon states to prevent and suppress terrorism and warns that those who do not 'will be held accountable.' However, this particular resolution does not invoke Ch. VII and thus might fall into the very lacuna Petrochilos identified in the Persian Gulf War, which may legitimate the claim that neutrality subsists even in the event of Security Council Resolutions. Moreover, other anti-terrorist treaty provisions may impose obligations for states to take action to prevent and suppress terrorism, yet simultaneously allow them to decline to participate in the War on Terrorism per se. (S/RES/1368) Thus, his

prediction that future applications of neutrality will continue to be determined on an ad hoc basis appears to be on target.

[67] Petrochilos, p.579.
[68] Damrosch, p. 925.
[69] Quoted in Moore, 1906, p. 413.
[70] Petrochilos, p. 605.
[71] From a speech President Bush delivered at the White House 19 March 2004, <www.whitehouse.gov/news/releases/2004/03/20040319-3.html>.
[72] The National Security Strategy of the United States, September 2002, <www.whitehouse.gov/nsc/nss.html>.
[73] Arend, 'International Law and the Preemptive Use of Military Force', p. 89. As explained below, however, many scholars dispute the use of the word pre-emption to describe U.S. actions in Afghanistan and Iraq. They contend that Michael Walzer's phrase 'preventive war' is more appropriate because of the lack of an imminent threat. Walzer, pp.76-85.
[74] William Saffire, 2003.
[75] Exceptions to this rule include inherent rights to individual and collective self-defense per Article 51 of the Charter and actions authorized under Ch. VII of the UN Charter by the UN Security Council.
[76] In fact, the court described this presumption against the use of force as a 'conspicuous example of a rule of international law having the character of *jus cogens*.' Cited in Damrosch, p. 106.
[77] McClain, p. 240.
[78] Griffiths, 2002, p. 31.
[79] Griffiths, p. 31.
[80] Weigel, April 2002, pp. 33-35.
[81] James Turner Johnson, 'Just War, As It Was and Is', *First Things* (January 2005): 18-19.
[82] 8 July 1996 Advisory Opinion on *the Legality of the Threat or Use of Nuclear Weapons*. International Court of Justice 226 Par. 96.
[83] O'Brien, pp. 21-22.
[84] Dinstein, 2001, p. 168, note 182.
[85] Italics mine. Moreover, such self-defense is characterized as provisional; it is legal only 'until the Security Council has taken measures necessary to maintain international peace and security.'
[86] The Permanent Court of International Justice (PCIJ) noted in the *Lotus* case that, 'Restrictions upon the independence of States cannot ... be presumed.' *The S.S. Lotus (France v. Turkey)*, PCIJ 1927, Ser. A, no. 10.
[87] Letter from U.S. Secretary of State Webster to his British counterpart Lord Ashburton, 6 August 1842 quoted in Jennings, 1938, p. 89.
[88] Arend, 'International Law and the Preemptive Use of Military Force', p. 91.
[89] Remarks by President Bush on Iraq at the Cincinnati Museum Center – Cincinnati Union Terminal in Cincinnati, Ohio on 7 October 2002. <www.whitehouse.gov/news/releases/2002/10/print/20021007-8.html>.
[90] While other commentators have focused on the formal justifications the U.S. government has presented to defend its use of force in the War on Terrorism and Iraq, (NSS 2002 and UN Doc S/2003/351), the evidence presented in this chapter indicates that the administration's less formal communications, backed up by military action, may have been at least as salient to many in the international community.
<www.un.int/usa/s2003_351.pdf>.

[91] The National Security Strategy of the United States of America <www.whitehouse.gov/nsc/nssall.html>.
[92] *Meet the Press* transcript for 8 February 2004, <www.msnbc.msn.com/id/4179618/>.
[93] Ibid., p. 75.
[94] Ibid.
[95] Adam Dolnik, 2002, p. 23.
[96] 'But I can by no Means approve of what some Authors have advanced, that by the Law of Nations it is permitted to take up Arms to reduce the growing Power of a Prince or State, which if too much augmented, may possibly injure us ... [T]o pretend to have a Right to injure another, merely from a Possibility that he may injure me, is repugnant to all the Justice in the World: For such is the Condition of the present Life, that we can never be in perfect Security. It is not in the Way of Force, but in the Protection of Providence, and in innocent Precautions, that we are to seek for Relief against uncertain Fear.' Grotius, 1738, Bk. 2, Ch. 1, note 17, p. 141.
[97] Grotius, Bk 2, Ch. 22, note V (1.), p. 477. The title of Ch. 22 is 'On the Unjust Causes of War.' Note V addresses and defines one of the unjust causes of war as 'uncertain Fear.'
[98] Walzer, p. 85. Walzer cites the 'asymmetry in the structure of forces' as a key factor in this determination.
[99] Ibid, p. 78.
[100] Langan, 1992, pp. 6-7. Langan refers here more generally to the indeterminacy of the just cause criterion.
[101] Reference to St. Augustine by St. Thomas Aquinas, *Summa Theologica, Secunda Secundae*, Q. 40 (Article 1) cited in D'Entreves, 1948, p. 159.
[102] Morgan, 2004. *See also* Brunnee and Toope, 2004.
[103] President Bush said in public comments, 'America will never seek a permission slip to defend the security of our country.' Leigh Sales, 'Bush Defends Iraq Invasion', 21 January 2004 <www.abc.net.au/news/newsitems/s1029067.htm>.
[104] O'Brien, p. 20.
[105] Peng and Nisbett, 1999.
[106] 'Solana Fears Widening Gulf Between Europe and U.S.', 8 January 2003, *The Financial Times*, <www.kubik.org/pt/030111pt.htm>.
[107] 'Solana Fears Widening Gulf Between Europe and U.S.'
[108] Ibid.
[109] Ibid.
[110] The Pew Global Attitudes Project, 'War with Iraq Divides World', (Washington, DC, 2003) <http://people-press.org/reports/pdf/185.pdf>.
[111] Cited in Cohen, *International Politics: The Rules of the Game*, p. 142.
[112] Abdel-Nour, 2004, pp. 430-433.
[113] Casebeer, 2004, p. 448.
[114] The speechwriter quoted is David Frum. Abley, 2003, p. A4.
[115] Raymond, 1998-99, p. 679. Italics mine.
[116] Relatedly, to focus on threats as opposed to risks or concerns casts policy options in a moral light, which makes a use of force instinctively ethically understandable.
[117] Raymond, 2002, p. 92.
[118] Cohen, 2001, p. 29.
[119] Raymond, 2002, p. 89.
[120] Speech by Former U.S. Ambassador John Brady Kiesling at the University of California Berkeley 20 March 2003. See also Kiesling's Letter of Resignation published in *The New York Times* 27 February 2003, <www.nytimes.com/2003/02/27/international/27WEB-TNAT.html>.

[121] Cohen, 1981, p. 143. Kenneth Bazinet, 'Multiple Wars Do-able', *New York Daily News* 9 September 2002 <www.nydailynews.com>. Secretary Rumsfeld said, 'We will have, and do have, a capability in the United States to provide for homeland defense, to undertake a major regional conflict and win decisively – including occupying a country and changing the regime if necessary – and simultaneously swiftly defeat another aggressor in another theater ... [In addition, the U.S.] would have the capability of conducting a number of lesser contingencies, such as Bosnia or Kosovo.' The following week, he reiterated this declaration in more succinct terms, 'We can fight all elements of the global war on terrorism simultaneously.' See also Prepared Testimony of U.S. Secretary of Defense Donald H. Rumsfeld before the House and Senate Armed Services Committees regarding Iraq, 18-19 September 2002, <www.defenselink.mil/speeches/2002/s20020918-secdef.html>.

[122] The Pew Global Attitudes Project.

[123] Ibid.

[124] Ibid.

[125] Ibid.

[126] Adib F. Farha, 'And the United States Wonders: 'Why do They Hate Us?'' *The Daily Star*, 28 January 2004, <www.dailystar.com.lb/printable.asp?art_ID=3696&cat_ID=5>.

[127] Ibid.

[128] President Bush addressed this concern in his tour of Southeast Asia in late 2003 when he said that one of his goals was to 'make sure that people who are suspicious of our country finally understand that our motivation is pure.' Ben Terrall, 'Bush in Bali', 6 April 2004 *Indonesia Alert*, <www.indonesialaert.org/print_article.php?&id=27>.

[129] Dunn, 2003, p. 279.

[130] St. Thomas Aquinas, *Summa Theologica, Secunda Secundae*, No. 15, Q. 40 (Article 1) cited in D'Entreves, p. 161.

[131] Johnson, p. 18.

[132] O'Brien, p. 34.

[133] Cited in D'Entreves, pp. 159-161.

[134] Johnson, p. 18.

[135] O'Brien, pp. 34-35.

[136] The Pew Global Attitudes Project.

[137] Kagan, <www.policyreview.org/JUN02/kagan_print.html>, p. 19.

[138] Raymond, 1998-99, p. 679.

[139] Cindy Williams, 'Paying for the War on Terrorism: U.S. Security Choices Since 9/11' paper prepared for presentation at a panel on 'Real Homeland Security' of the ASSA Meetings in San Diego, California, 5 January 2004, <www.ecaar.org/Articles/williams.pdf>.

[140] Williams, p. 10. *See also* Steven Kosiak, 'Funding for Defense, Homeland Security, and Related Activities Since 9/11', Center for Strategic and Budgetary Assessments, 25 June 2004, <www.csbaonline.org/4Publications/Archive/U.20041020.FundingGWAR ON TERRORISM/U.20041020.FundingGWAR ON TERRORISM.pdf>, p. 6.

[141] Williams, p. 10.

[142] Congressional Budget Office. 'Economic and Budget Outlook: An Update', Washington, September 2004, < www.cbo.gov/showdoc.cfm?index=5773&sequence=2>. However, when measured as a percentage of GDP- 3.6% in 2004, according to the CBO - this debt level is lower than those recorded in the mid-1980s and early 1990s. Ibid.

[143] William D. Nordhaus, 'The Economic Consequences of a War With Iraq' in *War with Iraq: Costs, Consequences, and Alternatives*, pp. 73-74. American Academy of Arts and Sciences, Committee on International Security Studies, 2002, <www.amacad.org/publications/monographs/War_with_Iraq.pdf>.

[144] Hepburn, 2003; King and Cummins, 2003.

[145] Goldstein, 2004, pp. 13-22.

[146] See 'Remarks to the U.N. Security Council' by U.S. Secretary of State Colin L. Powell in New York City, 5 February 2003, <www.state.gov/secretary/rm/2003/17300.htm>; 'The Report in Connection with Presidential Determination Under Public Law 107-243', reprinted in *The Congressional. Record* H1958, H1959; and 'President Bush Outlines Iraqi Threat: Remarks by the President on Iraq at the Cincinnati Museum Center', 7 October 2002, <www.whitehouse.gov/news/releases/2002/10/print/20021007-8.html>.

[147] See the Deulfer Report, <www.cia.gov/cia/reports/iraq_wmd_2004/Comp_Report_Key_Findings.pdf> and Associated Press, 'White House Says Search for WMDs in Iraq is Over', 12 January 2005.

[148] 'Interview: Zbigniew Brzezinksi Discusses Comments He Made in *The Washington Post* Regarding US Intelligence and Credibility', National Public Radio 2 February 2004. *See also* Brzezinski, 2004, p. A17.

[149] In a public discussion at New York University on 15 March 2004, Hans Blix pointed out that framing Secretary Powell's presentation to the UNSC of the existence of WMD in Iraq as a certainty without ambiguity served another purpose: to make more likely the desired UNSC authorization for the use of force in Iraq.

[150] Wilson, 2003 and 2004. See also the Letter from French Ambassador to the United States Jean-David Levitte sent to U.S. Congress members, administration officials, and media representatives dated 15 May 2003, <www.cbsnews.com/stories/2003/05/15/world/printable554134.shtml>. In a conference at Rice University in Houston, Ambassador Levitte added that, 'the problem was also that these lies were printed on the basis of information provided by "anonymous sources" within the U.S. administration.' 22 May 2003, <www.info-france-usa.org/printfriendly/statmnts2003/levitte_us052203_pf.asp>.

[151] Kessler, 2003, p. A26. In this article, an unnamed diplomat from a country in support of the U.S. position on Iraq is quoted as saying, 'The U.S. team often acts like thugs. People feel bullied, and that can affect the way you respond when someone makes a request.'

[152] Examples of international cooperation in support of other U.S. goals in the war on terror also exist, such as multi-state cooperation in freezing suspected terrorist assets pursuant to UN Security Resolution 1373, S/RES/1373 (2001).

[153] Foreign Policy in Focus/Center for Defense Information Task Force on 'A Unified Security Budget for the United States' (Washington, DC, 2004) <www.cdi.org/news/mrp/Unified-Budget.rtf>, p. 7.

[154] Kiesling, UC Berkeley speech.

[155] 'A Unified Security Budget for the United States,' p. 7.

[156] Gilpin, 1981; Keohane, 1984.

[157] *See*, for example, the article by Russian Defense Minister Sergey Ivanov, 'The Armed Forces of Russia and Its Geopolitical Priorities', *Russia in Global Politics* 1 (January-February 2004), <www.ln.mid.ru/Bl.nsf/arh/AD300DA29D3E73FDC3256E3E00343564?OpenDocument>. Asked by a reporter about Ivanov's assertions, Russian President Vladimir Putin responded, 'We intend to adhere to these rules in the future and call upon everyone to act in a similar way. But if in international practice, in the practice of international life the principle of the preventive use of force is going to be asserted, then Russia reserves the right to act similarly to defend its national interests.' The Kremlin, 3 November 2003, <www.ln.mid.ru/Bl.nsf/arh/5012941CFB69E89243256DD4005BAB13?OpenDocument>.

[158] Michael E. O'Hanlon, Susan E. Rice, and James B. Steinberg, 'The New National Security Strategy and Preemption', *Global Politics* brief # 113, December 2002, <www.brookings.edu/comm/policybriefs/pb113.htm>.

[159] Betts 2003, pp. 34-35.

[160] Another 150 U.S. military casualties are attributed to Operation Enduring Freedom, most in Afghanistan. <www.defenselink.mil/news/casualty.pdf>.

[161] On Iraqi casualty estimates, see <www.iraqbodycount.net>. This organization, which bases its numbers on witnessed deaths reported by the media, hospitals, morgues, and non-governmental organizations, asserts that total coalition deaths in Iraq from March 2003-December 2004 topped 1400.

[162] <www.iraqbodycount.net/press>.

[163] Les Roberts, Riyadh Lafta, Richard Garfield, Jamal Khudhairi, Gilbert Burnham, 'Mortality Before and After the 2003 Invasion of Iraq: Cluster Sample Survey', *The Lancet*, 29 October 2004, <http://image.thelancet.com/extras/04art10342web.pdf>.

[164] Roberts et al, p.1.

[165] Lila Guterman, 'Researchers Who Rushed Into Print a Study of Iraqi Civilian Deaths Now Wonder Why It Was Ignored,' *The Chronicle of Higher Education* 27 January 2005, <http://chronicle.com/free/2005/01/200501270n.htm>.

[166] 'How They See Us: South Korean Alliance Grows Shaky', *The Week* 4 June 2004, 16 citing an editorial in the Seoul, South Korean newspaper *Chosun Ilbo*.

[167] After Abu Ghraib, claims of false intentions on the part of the United States resurfaced in the Muslim and Arab press. Iraqi journalist Iyad Abu Shaqra said in the pan-Arab *Al-Sharq al-Awsat* that this scandal demonstrated that U.S. leaders 'exploited the deep psychological scar of 9/11' for their own 'hideous' ends. Accounts in Baghdad's *Al-Dawah* and *Al-Ittijah al-Akhar* indicated that the prison abuses revealed the 'falseness' of America's promise to liberate Iraqis. Cited in 'How They See Us: Iraq Was Betrayed', 28 May 2004 *The Week*, p. 14.

[168] Jonathan Karl, 'Increased Tension, Recent Events Stoke Anti-U.S. Sentiments Among Arabs', ABC News, <http://abcnews.go.com/sections/WNT/World/arabs_US_040420-2.html>.

[169] Referring specifically to the prison abuse scandal in an interview on Al-Arabiya television President Bush said, 'I think people in the Middle East who want to dislike America will use this as an excuse to remind people about their dislike.' <www.nytimes.com/2004/05/05/international/06BUSH-FULLTXT.htm>.

[170] 'At this point, a question arises: is it better to be loved than feared, or to be feared than loved? The answer is that a prince would like to be both. But since it is difficult to reconcile these two, it is much safer to be feared than loved-if one must cede to the other.' Machiavelli, 1985, p.271. 'Nevertheless, a prince should make himself feared in such a way that, if he does not gain love, he does avoid hatred: being feared and not being hated are sentiments that readily go together.' Machiavelli, p. 273.

[171] Machiavelli, p. 287.

[172] William D. Hartung, 'The Hidden Costs of War', 14 February 2003, <www.fourthfreedom.org/php/t-si-index.php?hinc+Hartung_report.hinc>. See also Jeffrey Record, 'Bounding the Global War on Terrorism', December 2003, <www.carlisle.army.mil/ssi/pubs/2003/bounding/bounding.pdf>.

[173] This is consistent with Mervyn Frost's identification of state sovereignty as a 'settled' norm. Frost, 1996, pp. 105-110.

[174] Kagan, <www.policyreview.org/JUN02/kagan_print.html>, p. 19. Robert Kagan is also co-founder (with William Kristol) of the Project for the New American Century.

[175] Kagan, p. 20.

[176] 'Rumsfeld's war-on-terror memo', 16 October 2003, <www.usatoday.com/news/washington/executive/rumsfeld-memo.htm>. Italics mine.

[177] On such seemingly incommensurable, dichotomous claims see: Institute for American Values, 'What We're Fighting For: A Letter from America', February 2002 <www.americanvalues.org/html/wwff.html> versus 'Letter from United States Citizens to Friends in Europe' also at <www.americanvalues.org>. See also Vol. 9 (2004) of *Nexus: a Journal of Opinion* published by the Chapman University School of Law in which scholarly articles on the 2003 war with Iraq are divided into two sections, 'A Just War or Just A War? Iraq a Year Later.'
[178] Meyer-Knapp and Peach.
[179] Peng and Nisbett, 1999.
[180] Nisbett, Peng, Choi, Norenzayan, 2001.
[181] Peng and Nisbett p. 4.
[182] Lao Zi, 1993, p. 16.
[183] Roberts, 2001, p. 31.
[184] Sun-tzu, 2001, p. 43.
[185] Moss, p. 31.
[186] Sun-tzu, commentary, p. 196.
[187] Blair, 2003, p. 4
[188] Blair, p. 4.
[189] Fukuyama, 1989 and 1992.
[190] Gaddis, 1987, p. 37.
[191] Quoted in Gaddis, p. 36.
[192] Gaddis, p. 35.
[193] Gaddis, p. 46.
[194] Gaddis, p. 154.
[195] Gaddis, p. 154.
[196] Fukuyama, 1989, p.4.
[197] Gaddis, pp. 46 and 59. *See also* Lundestat, 1986, pp. 263-277; Kuniholm, 1980; Anderson, 1981; and Hathaway, 1981.
[198] *See,* for example, Jervis, 1984, p. 12; Gilpin, 1981, p. 218; and Blecker, 1987, p. 46.
[199] Quoted in Gaddis, p. 134.
[200] The first National Security Council study of this matter in 1948 asserted that the United States military 'must be ready to utilize promptly and effectively all appropriate means available, including nuclear weapons.' NSC 30, 'The United States Policy on Atomic Weapons', 10 September 1948, quoted in Gaddis, pp. 107-108.
[201] Gaddis, p. 237. Italics mine.
[202] Gaddis, p. 229.
[203] Schelling, 1962, p. vii.
[204] 'Joe Galloway: An Interview with General Peter J. Schoomaker, Army Chief of Staff' in *Military.com*, <www.military.com/NewContent/0,13190,Galloway_012104,00.html>.

References

Abdel-Nour, Farid 'An International Ethics of Evil?' *International Relations* 18 (2004): 425-439.

af Malmborg, Mikael *Neutrality and State-Building in Sweden* (Basingstoke: Palgrave Macmillan, 2001).

Ambrose, Stephen E. *Eisenhower: The President* (NY: Simon and Schuster, 1984).

Anderson, Terry H. *The United States, Great Britain, and the Cold War, 1944-1947* (Columbia, Missouri: University of Missouri Press, 1981).
Arend, Anthony Clark and Beck, Robert J. *International Law and the Use of Force* (London: Routledge, 1993).
Arend, Anthony Clark 'International Law and the Preemptive Use of Military Force', *The Washington Quarterly*, 26/2 (Spring 2003): 97.
Bazinet, Kenneth 'Multiple Wars Do-able', *New York Daily News* 9 September 2002 <www.nydailynews.com>.
Berger, Peter *Holy War, Inc. Inside the Secret World of Osama bin Laden* (New York: Free Press, 2002).
Bertlet, Chip 'Apocalyptic Nihilism', 1999, paper written for Boston University's Center for Millennial Studies,
<www.mille.org/scholarship/papers/bertletnihilism.html>.
Betts, Richard K. 'Suicide From Fear of Death?' *Foreign Affairs* (January/February 2003): 34-35.
Blair, Bruce 'The Logic of Intelligence Hype and Blindness', Paper presented at the 10th International Castiglione Conference, 'Unilateral Actions and Military Interventions: the Future of Non-Proliferation', 18-21 September 2003 in Castiglione, Italy. Paper updated 30 December 2003.
Blecker, Coit D. *Reluctant Warriors* (NY: Freeman, 1987).
Blix, Hans, comments in a public discussion/interview at New York University, 15 March 2004.
Boyle, Francis A. 'International Crisis and Neutrality: U.S. Foreign Policy Toward the Iraq-Iran War' in Alan T. Leonhard, (ed) *Neutrality: Changing Concepts and Practices* (Lanham, MD: University Press of America), pp.59-96.
Brunnee, Jutta and Toope, Stephen J. 'Slouching Towards New "Just" Wars: The Hegemon After September 11th', *International Relations* 18 (2004): 405-423.
Brzezinski, Zbigniew 'Restoring Trust in America,' *The Washington Post* 2 February 2004, p. A17.
Bush, George W. Address to a Joint Session of Congress and the American People, 20 September 2001,
<http://www.whitehouse.gov/news/releases/2001/09/20010920-8.html>.
___, Address to the Nation, 11 September 2001,
<http://www.whitehouse.gov/news/releases/2001/09/20010911-16.html>.
___, comments on Al-Arabiya television
<http://www.nytimes.com/2004/05/05/international/06BUSH-FULLTXT.html>.
___, Interview with Sheryl Henderson Blunt in *Christianity Today*, week of 24 May 2004, http://www.christianitytoday.com/ct/2004/121/51.0.html
___, Remarks on Iraq at the Cincinnati Museum Center – Cincinnati Union Terminal in Cincinnati, Ohio on 7 October 2002,
<http://www.whitehouse.gov/news/releases/2002/10/print/20021007-8.html>.
___, Speech delivered at the White House, 19 March 2004,
<www.whitehouse.gov/news/releases/2004/03/20040319-3.html>.
___, The President's State of the Union Address 29 January 2002,
<http://www.whitehouse.gov/news/releases/2002/01/print/20020129-11.html>.

Casebeer, William D. 'Knowing Evil When You See It: Uses for the Rhetoric of Evil in International Relations', *International Relations* 18 (2004): 441-451.

Chhor, Khatya 'Western Press Review: European Defense, Israeli 'Preemption,' and the Heading Rush to Iraqi Economic Reform', 8 October 2003 <http://www.rferl.org/nca/features/2003/10/08102003163711.asp.>

Cohen, Raymond *International Politics: The Rules of the Game* (NY: Longman 1981).

___, 'Language and Conflict Resolution: The Limits of English', *International Studies Review* 3/1 (Spring 2001): 25-51.

___, *Negotiating Across Cultures: International Communication in an Interdependent World,* 3rd edn. (Washington, DC: United States Institute of Peace Press, 2002).

Combs, Cindy C. *Terrorism in the Twenty-first Century*, 2nd edn. (Upper Saddle River: Prentice Hall, 2000).

Damrosch, Lori F., Henkin, Louis, Pugh, Richard Crawford, Schachter, Oscar, Smit, Hans *International Law: Cases and Materials*, 4th edn. (St. Paul, MN: West Group Publishing, 2001).

Dinstein, Yoram *War, Aggression and Self-Defence* 3rd edn. (New York: Cambridge University Press, 2001).

Dolnik, Adam 'Justice Beyond Question? Military Responses to International Terrorism and Just War Theory', *Perspectives* 18 (2002): 21-39.

Falk, Richard, *The Great Terror War* (NY: Olive Branch Press, 2003).

Farha, Adib F. 'And the United States Wonders: "Why do They Hate Us?"' *The Daily Star*, 28 January 2004, <http://www.dailystar.com.lb/printable.asp?art_ID=3696&cat_ID=5>.

Foreign Policy in Focus/Center for Defense Information Task Force on 'A Unified Security Budget for the United States' (Washington, DC, 2004) <http://www.cdi.org/news/mrp/Unified-Budget.rtf>.

Fornek, Scott 'You're with US or Against US, Bush Says,' 21 September 2001, <http://www.suntimes.com/terror/stories/cst-nws-main21.html>.

Frost, Mervyn *Ethics in International Relations: A Constitutive Theory* (Cambridge: Cambridge University Press, 1996).

Fukuyama, Francis 'The End of History?' *The National Interest* (Summer 1989): 3-18.

___, *The End of History and the Last Man* (New York: Free Press, 1992).

Gaddis, John Lewis, *The Long Peace. Inquiries into the History of the Cold War* (NY: Oxford University Press, 1987).

Gertz, Bill, 'Tenet Warns of al Qaeda's 'Spectacular Attacks' Plans', *The Washington Times,* 10 March 2004,<www.washtimes.com/national/20040921-121158-2444r.htm>.

Gilpin, Robert *War and Change in World Politics* (Cambridge: Cambridge University Press, 1981).

Gray, Christine *International Law and the Use of Force* (Oxford: Oxford Press, 2001).

Grotius, Hugo *The Rights of War and Peace, in three books, wherein are explained, The Law of Nature and Nations, and the Principal Points relating to*

Government J. Barbeyrac, notes (London: W. Innys and R. Manby, J. and P. Knapton, D. Brown, T. Osborn, and E. Wicksteeed, 1738).

Gunaratna, Rohan 'Defeating Al Qaeda – The Pioneering Vanguard of the Islamic Movements' in Russell Howard and Reid Sawyer (eds.), *Defeating Terrorism. Shaping the New Security Environment* (Guilford: McGraw-Hill, 2004), pp. 1-28.

___, *Inside Al-Qaeda: Global Network of Terror* (New York: Columbia University Press, 2002).

Guterman, Lila 'Researchers Who Rushed Into Print a Study of Iraqi Civilian Deaths Now Wonder Why It Was Ignored,' *The Chronicle of Higher Education* 27 January 2005, <http://chronicle.com/free/2005/01/200501270n.htm>.

Hall, Edward T. *Beyond Culture* (Garden City, NY: Anchor Press, 1976).

Hallett, Brian *The Lost Art of Declaring War* (Urbana, IL: University of Illinois Press, 1998).

Hartung, William D. 'The Hidden Costs of War', 14 February 2003, <http://www.fourthfreedom.org/php/t-si-index.php?hinc+Hartung_report.hinc>.

Hathaway, Robert M. *Ambiguous Partnership: Britain and America, 1944-1947* (NY: Columbia University Press, 1981).

Hensel, Howard M. 'American National Interests and Objectives' in Howard M. Hensel (ed), *The United States and Europe: Policy Imperatives in a Globalizing World* (Burlington, VT: Ashgate Publishing Co., 2002), pp.1-54.

Hepburn, Donald 'Nice War. Here's the Bill', *The New York Times*, 3 September 2003, <www.nytimes.com/2003/09/03/opinion/03HEPB.htm>.

Hopper, D. Ian 'Computers used by Al-Qaeda Could Be Treasure Trove of Intelligence Data' *Associated Press*, 31 December 2001.

'How They See Us: Iraq Was Betrayed', *The Week*, 28 May 2004, p. 14.

'How They See Us: South Korean Alliance Grows Shaky', *The Week*, 4 June 2004, 16.

Hulse, Carl and Shanker, Thom, 'White House Asks G.O.P. in Congress to add $25 Billion', *The New York Times*, 5 May 2004.
<http://www.nytimes.com/2004/05/06/politics/06SPEN.html>.

Ignatieff, Michael 'It's War, But It Doesn't Have to be Dirty', *The Guardian*, 1 October 2001,<http://www.ksg.harvard.edu/news/opeds/2001/ignatieff_war_guardian_gd_100101.htm>.

Institute for American Values 'What We're Fighting For: A Letter from America', February 2002, <http://www.americanvalues.org/html/wwff.html>.

International Court of Justice, 8 July 1996 Advisory Opinion on *the Legality of the Threat or Use of Nuclear Weapons* 226 Par. 96.

'Interview: Zbigniew Brzezinksi Discusses Comments He Made in *The Washington Post* Regarding US Intelligence and Credibility', National Public Radio, 2 February 2004.

Iraq Body Count, <http://www.iraqbodycount.net/press>.

Ivanov, Sergey 'The Armed Forces of Russia and Its Geopolitical Priorities', *Russia in Global Politics* 1 (January-February 2004),

<http://www.ln.mid.ru/Bl.nsf/arh/AD300DA29D3E73FDC3256E3E00343564?OpenDocument>.
Jelinek, Pauline 'Bush Keeps War Costs Under Hat,' *The Knoxville News-Sentinel*, 11 March 2004, pp. A1 and A11.
Jennings, R.Y. 'The Caroline and McLeod Cases', 32 (1938) *The American Journal of International Law*: 82-99.
Jervis, Robert *The Illogic of American Nuclear Strategy* (Ithaca: Cornell University Press, 1984).
'Joe Galloway: An Interview with General Peter J. Schoomaker, Army Chief of Staff' in *Military.com* 21 January 2004,
<www.military.com/NewContent/0,13190,Galloway_012104,00.html>.
Johnson, James Turner *Just War Tradition and the Restraint of War: A Moral and Historical Inquiry* (Princeton: Princeton University Press, 1981).
Joint Resolution Authorizing the Use of Military Force Against Iraq, H.J. Res. 114/S.J. Res. 45, 10 October 2002.
Kagan, Robert 'Power and Weakness,' *Policy Review* 113 (June 2002).
<www.policyreview.org/JUN02/kagan_print.html>.
Karl, Jonathan 'Increased Tension, Recent Events Stoke Anti-U.S. Sentiments Among Arabs', *ABC News*, 4 April. 2004,
<http://abcnews.go.com/sections/WNT/World/arabs_US_040420-2.html>.
Keohane, Robert O. 'The Globalization of Informal Violence, Theories of World Politics, and the 'Liberalism of Fear'' in Marc A. Genest (ed.), *Conflict and Cooperation. Evolving Theories of International Relations,* 2nd ed (Belmont, CA, 2002), pp. 176-189.
Kiesling, John Brady Letter of Resignation published in *The New York Times*, 27 February 2003, <www.nytimes.com/2003/02/ 27/international/27WEB-TNAT.html>.
___, Speech at the University of California Berkeley, 20 March 2003.
King, Neil, Jr. and Cummins, Chip 'The Postwar Bill for Iraq Surges Past Projections', *The Wall Street Journal*, 5 September 2003, p. A1.
Kuniholm, Bruce R. *The Origins of the Cold War in the Near East: Great Power Conflict and Diplomacy in Iran, Turkey, and Greece.* (Princeton: Princeton University Press, 1981).
Langan, John P. 'The Just War Theory After the Gulf War', *Theological Studies* 53/1 (March 1992): 122-135.
Lao-Zi *The Book of Lao Zi* (Beijing: Foreign Languages Press, 1993).
Laqueur, Walter *Terrorism* (London: Weidenfeld and Nicolson, 1978).
Laws of War: Rights and Duties of Neutral Powers and Persons in Case of War on Land (Hague V) 18 October 1907,
<www.yale.edu/lawweb/avalon/lawofwar/hague05.htm>.
Laws of War: Rights and Duties of Neutral Powers in Naval War (Hague XIII), 18 October 1907, <www.yale.edu/lawweb/avalon/lawofwar/hague13.htm>.
'Letter from United States Citizens to Friends in Europe' also at
<www.americanvalues.org>.
Levitte, Jean-David Letter. 15 May 2003,
<www.cbsnews.com/stories/2003/05/15/world/printable554134.shtml>.

___, Press Conference at Rice University in Houston, Texas, 22 May 2003, <www.info-france usa.org/printfriendly/statmnts2003/levitte_us052203_pf.asp>.
Lieber, Robert J. *No Common Power. Understanding International Relations*, 4th edn. (Upper Saddle River, NJ: Prentice Hall, 2001).
Lundestat, Geir 'Empire By Invitation? The United States and Western Europe, 1945-1952', *Journal of Peace Research* XXIII (1986): 154-184.
Machiavelli, Niccolo *The Prince* James B. Atkinson (ed.), (NY: MacMillan Publishing Co, 1985).
Malmborg, Mikael af, *Neutrality and State-Building in Sweden* (Basingstoke: Palgrave Macmillan, 2001).
Mansbach, Richard W. *The Global Puzzle: Issues and Actors in World Politics*, 3rd edn. (Boston: Houghton Mifflin, 2000).
Meet the Press transcript for 8 February 2004, <www.msnbc.msn.com/id/4179618>.
Meyer-Knapp, Helena and Peach, Lucinda 'Toolkit 3: The U.S. Is Not the Globe', in April Morgan, Lucinda Peach, and Colette Mazzucelli (eds), *Ethics and Global Politics: The Active Learning Sourcebook* (Bloomfield, CT: Kumarian Press, 2004), pp. 67-95.
Mir, Hamid 'Osama Claims He Has Nukes; If U.S. Uses N-arms it will Get Same Response,' *The Dawn of Pakistan*, 10 November 2001, <www.dawn/2001/11/10/top1.htm>.
Moore, John Bassett 'The Destruction of the Caroline', *A Digest of International Law* 2 (Washington, DC: Government Printing Office, 1906): 409-414.
Morgan, April 'The War on Terror: Time for a New Just War Framework?' Paper presented at the International Studies Association Convention, Montreal Quebec, Canada, 17-20 March 2004.
Murphy, Brian 'The Shape of Terrorism Changes,' *Fayetteville Observer*, 21 August 2002, p. 9a.
Nardin, Terry (ed.), *The Ethics of War and Peace: Religious and Secular Perspectives* (Princeton: Princeton University Press, 1996).
Negroponte, John, Press Release SC/7564, 8 November 2002, <www.un.org/News/Press/archives.htm>.
Nexus: a Journal of Opinion, Chapman University School of Law, 9 (2004).
Nisbett, Richard E., Peng, Kaiping, Choi, Incheol, and Norenzayan, Ara 'Culture and Systems of Thought: Holistic Versus Analytic Cognition', *Psychological Review* 108/2 (April 2001): 291-310.
Nisbett, Richard E. *The Geography of Thought: How Asian and Westerners Think Differently...and Why* (NY: Free Press, 2003).
Nordhaus, William 'The Economic Consequences of a War with Iraq' in *War With Iraq. Costs, Consequences, and Alternatives* 51-82. (American Academy of Arts and Sciences, Committee on International Security Studies, 2002) <www.amacad.org/publications/monographs/War_with_Iraq.pdf>.
O'Brien, William V. *The Conduct of Just and Limited War* (NY: Praeger, 1981).
O'Hanlon, Michael E. Susan E. Rice, and James B. Steinberg 'The New National Security Strategy and Preemption', *Global Politics* brief # 113 (December 2002), <www.brookings.edu/comm/policybriefs/pb113.htm>.

'Operation Iraqi Freedom (OIF) U.S. Casualty Status' and 'Operation Enduring Freedom (OEF) U.S> Casualty Status' at,
<www.defenselink.mil/news/casualty.pdf>.

Palmer, R.R. 'Frederick the Great, Guibert, Bulow: From Dynastic to National War' in Peter Paret (ed.), *Makers of Modern Strategy* (Princeton: Princeton University Press, 1986), pp. 91-122.

'Peace in Fallujah, as the U.S. Looks for an Exit', *The Week*, 21 May 2004, p. 4.

Peng, Kaiping and Nisbett, Richard E. 'Culture, Dialectics, and Reasoning About Contradiction,' *American Psychologist* 54/9 (September 1999): 741-754.

Petrochilos, Georgios C. 'The Relevance of the Concepts of War and Armed Conflict to the Law of Neutrality', *Vanderbilt Journal of Transnational Law* 31/3 (May 1998): 575-615.

Pfleger, Katherine 'Tenet Says Danger Extends Beyond Al-Qaeda,' *Associated Press*, 24 February 2004.

'President Bush Speaks to UN,' 10 November 2001,
<www.whitehouse.gov/news/releases/2001/11/20011110-3.html>.

'President Bush Welcomes President Chirac to White House,' 6 November 2001, joint news conference with French President Jacques Chirac,
<www.whitehouse.gov/news/releases/2001/11/20011106-4.html>.

Putin, Vladimir Press conference at The Kremlin, 3 November 2003,
<www.ln.mid.ru/Bl.nsf/arh/5012941CFB69E89243256DD4005BAB13?OpenDocument>.

'Putin Says Russia Will Do What It Must to Protect Its Citizens From Terror,' *Itar-Tass*, 6 November 2002, <www.cdi.org/russia/johnson/6538-4.cfm>.

Raymond, Gregory A. 'The Moral Pulse of International Relations', in Donald J. Puchala, (ed.), *Visions of International Relations: Assessing an Academic Field* (Columbia: University of South Carolina Press, 2002), pp. 81-100.

___, 'Necessity in Foreign Policy', *Political Science Quarterly* 113/4 (1998-99): 673-688.

___, 'Neutrality Norms and the Balance of Power', *Cooperation and Conflict* 32/2 (June 1997): 123-146.

___, 'Problems and Prospects in the Study of International Norms', 41 (1997) *Mershon International Studies Review*: 205-245.

Record, Jeffrey 'Bounding the Global War on Terrorism', December 2003 <www.carlisle.army.mil/ssi/pubs/2003/bounding/bounding.pdf>.

Roberts, Les, Lafta, Riyadh, Garfield, Richard, Khudhairi, Jamal, Burnham, Gilbert 'Mortality Before and After the 2003 Invasion of Iraq: Cluster Sample Survey', *The Lancet*, 29 October 2004,
<http://image.thelancet.com/extras/04art10342web.pdf>.

Roberts, Moss *DaoDeJing: The Book of the Way/Laozi*, translation and commentary. (Berkeley: University of California Press, 2001).

Rubin, Alfred P. 'The Concept of Neutrality in International Law', in Alan T. Leonhard (ed), *Neutrality: Changing Concepts and Practices* (Lanham, MD: University Press of America, 1988), pp. 9-34.

Rumsfeld, Donald, Prepared Testimony before the House and Senate Armed Services Committees regarding Iraq, September 18-19, 2002, <www.defenselink.mil/speeches/2002/s20020918-secdef.html>.

'Rumsfeld's war-on-terror memo', *USA Today,* 16 October 2003, <www.usatoday.com/news/washington/executive/rumsfeld-memo.htm>.
Russell, F.H. *The Just War in the Middle Ages* (Cambridge: Cambridge University Press, 1975).
Saffire, William 'Pre-emption Proves Itself', *The International Herald Tribune,* 15 April 2003, <www.iht.com/articles/93166.html>.
Sagan, Carl and Turco, Richard 'Nuclear Winter in the post-Cold War Era,' *Journal of Peace Research* 30/4 (November 1993): 369-373.
Sagan, Carl *The Nuclear Winter* (Boston: Council for a Livable World Education Fund, 1983).
Sales, Leigh 'Bush Defends Iraq Invasion', 21 January 2004, <www.abc.net.au/news/newsitems/s1029067.htm>.
Schelling, Thomas 'Forward' in Roberta Wohlstetter, *Pearl Harbor: Warning and Decision* (Stanford, CA: Stanford University Press, 1962).
'Solana Fears Widening Gulf Between Europe and U.S.', 8 January 2003, *The Financial Times*, <www.kubik.org/pt/030111pt.htm>.
Sun-tzu, The Denma Translation Group, translation and commentary, *The Art of War: A New Translation* (Boston: Shambala, 2001).
Terrall, Ben, 'Bush in Bali' 6 April 2004, *Indonesia Alert*, <www.indonesialaert.org/print_article.php?&id=27>.
The Associated Press, 'Al-Qaida No. 2 Claims Terrorists Bought Briefcase Nuclear Bombs,' 22 March 2004, *The Daily Times*, p. 1A.
The National Security Strategy of the United States, September 2002 <www.whitehouse.gov/nsc/nss.html>.
The Pew Global Attitudes Project, 'War with Iraq Divides World', (Washington, DC, 2003) <http://people-press.org/reports/pdf/185.pdf>.
U.S. Congress, Authorization for Use of Military Force in Afghanistan, Pub. L. No. 107-40, 115 Stat. 224, 14 September 2001.
UN Security Council Resolution 1373, S/RES/1373(2001).
UN Doc S/2003/351, Letter delivered to the Security Council by U.S. Ambassador to the U.N. John Negroponte dated 20 March 2003, <www.un.int/usa/s2003_351.pdf>.
Walzer, Michael *Just and Unjust Wars: A Moral Argument with Historical Illustrations* (NY: Basic Books, 1977).
Williams, Cindy, 'Paying for the War on Terrorism: U.S. Security Choices Since 9/11' paper prepared for presentation at a panel on 'Real Homeland Security' of the ASSA Meetings in San Diego, California, 5 January 2004.
Wilson, Joseph C. 'What I Didn't Find in Africa', *The New York Times*, 6 July 2003, sec. 4, p. 9.
___, *The Politics of Truth: Inside the Lies that Led to War and Betrayed My Wife's CIA Identity, A Diplomat's Memoir* (NY: Carroll & Graf Publishers, an imprint of Avalon Books, 2004).
Worth, R.F. 'A Nation Defines Itself by Its Evil Enemies,' *The New York Times*, 24 February 2002.

Conclusion

Amid Normative and Conceptual Crisis

Richard Falk

Such a volume of critical and perceptive essays on the relevance of law to armed conflict is both a tribute to the persistence of free inquiry in democratic societies and a sober recognition that the ongoing war on global terror is challenging our understanding of the always problematic interface between law and war. For almost a century this interface has been in tension as a result of the contradictory effects of the technologies of war mainly eroding the limits on its conduct and the technologies of peace making society increasingly aware that a normally decent society may engage in disturbingly indecent tactics and policies under the pressures of wartime. The 9/11 attacks and the American response have made this tension more acute, partly no doubt because of the elusive nature of the underlying conflict, but also due to the insistence by the leadership on both sides that their adversary represents a dangerous embodiment of evil that deserves to be unconditionally destroyed. If the stakes of conflict are posed on this high terrain of morality and security, the moderating role of law seems beside the point. All that counts is victory, which is almost impossible to discern given the character of the conflict and its antagonists. The Secretary of Defense, Donald Rumsfeld, was certainly correct a couple years back when in internal memo he admitted that "we," that is, the US Government, "lack the metrics" to determine whether we are winning or losing the war against terror. The Iraq War has brought these challenges to our understanding and behavior as a country at war to the surface with an unprecedented and disturbing vividness.

The temptation is to explain the relative silence of law in relation to war by reference to the priority of politics, that is, victory not respect for restraint is what gets written up in the history books. Beyond this, the nationalization of truth does not help. Each side in conflict insists that its cause is unconditionally just and that of its opponent is utterly unjust. This self-righteousness is further reinforced by absolutist notions of security associated with the survival of the sovereign state. The advent of nuclear weaponry made it clear that leaders of major states, whatever their ideology and civilizational background, were willing to risk the utter destruction of their own society and the possible annihilation of much of humanity, to avoid defeat in war. At the same time, the use of atomic bombs against Hiroshima and Nagasaki crossed another threshold with a devastating message: namely, that saving lives on our side justified wholesale indiscriminate and massive killing of enemy civilians. Of course, the messages of technological innovation were mixed. The fear of destruction also elevated reliance on rationality to new heights, counseling restraint, giving rise to cooperation with the enemy to avoid confrontation, and even allowing an ethic of co-existence to offer a long-term alternative to war. Beyond this, the advent of 'smart' weaponry has given renewed vitality to tactics of warfare that limit their destructive impact to military targets.

But in addition there was a parallel intensification of diplomatic efforts to bring law to bear both with respect to recourse to war and its conduct. German and Japanese leaders were held criminally accountable for their violations of international law after World War II, expressing the general view that there now existed a higher law than that of the sovereign state to which individuals owed allegiance. True, these trials at Nuremberg and Tokyo were derided as 'victors' justice' but dramatizing the criminal accountability of individuals who were acting on behalf of the state did permanently escalate the claims of law in relation to armed conflict. This escalation was given formal authority by international law specialists who lent their support to the view that the Nuremberg Principles, as endorsed in the General Assembly of the United Nations, had become expressive of norms that formed part of customary international law. The revival and strengthening of this legal impulse was strongly present in the 1990s with such developments as the establishment of the ad hoc tribunals by the UN Security Council to address crimes associated with the breakup of the former Yugoslavia and with the massacres taking place in Rwanda, as the detention of the former dictator of Chile, Augusto Pinochet, for crimes associated with his regime, and as evidenced by the worldwide movement leading in 2002 to the establishment of the International Criminal Court. These developments manifest a widely shared political consciousness that the restraints of law and personal accountability should be operative, whether in relation to crimes against humanity associated with oppressive government or with respect to war making. The same impulse has explained the willingness of governments to articulate an 'international humanitarian law' by way of the 1949 Geneva Conventions and the 1977 Additional Protocols. It is notable that the World Court, the International Court of Justice, in issuing an Advisory Opinion in 2004 on the legality of the Israeli security wall, unanimously affirmed the unconditional applicability of international humanitarian law to the Israel/Palestine conflict, and by extension to all armed conflict. And so, as several of the essays in this volume argue, there seems to be a collision course between the logic of conflict pressing toward absolute violence and the logic of law pressing toward substantial restraint, especially with regard to recourse to war as an instrument of national policy. It is this collision course that is most responsible for an atmosphere of crisis and uncertainty with respect to this entire enterprise embraced by the label 'the law of armed conflict.'

Against this background, the authors of the various chapters are struggling with the originality of the present situation. To begin with, the conflict is between antagonists that are not normal sovereign states. This is obvious with respect to Al Qaeda, which is a shadowy concealed network of sleeper cells with no acknowledged territorial base and no discernible organizational structure. But it also pertains to the United States, which is essentially a 'global state' with its military spread out around the world, including all five oceans and its special forces' units operating covertly within the territories of foreign countries, sometimes without the permission or even knowledge of the territorial government. So far, our political imagination cannot even grasp how a conflict with these stakes and these protagonists will ever be ended, what victory and defeat might mean, whether diplomacy will at some point find a way to restore peace.

There are additional aspects of the conflict that test the strength and even the viability of legal constraint. Perhaps, the most notable of these is the strategic relevance of information to the success of a military struggle of this nature. Because territory is not a stake in the conflict, success and failure is measured by the degree to which the enemy can be found and its plans discovered before they are carried out. This centrality of information also encourages intrusions on privacy and the suspension of normal liberties at home. The enemy is everywhere and nowhere. It is in this context that prompt rationalizations for torture, and leads government lawyers to grant politicians and military commanders 'freedom' from the constraints of the Geneva Conventions, derided as 'quaint,' embodying restraints that pertain to a different age. Similarly, it is in such an atmosphere that the abuses of Abu Ghraib and Guantanamo come to light, first captured on the digital personal cameras of combat soldiers, and then brought to the world by their visual portrayal on a global media. Such disclosures lead to a furious unresolved debate between those who contend that the abuses are the work of a few 'rotten apples' and those who argue that when legal restraints are made subject to 'exceptions,' the exception almost inevitably becomes the rule. But whether it the issue of torture or the controversial provisions of the Patriot Act, the question at stake is what to do in a struggle that is essentially about information. Information has always been important in wartime, but it has never previously been the essential battleground, and we have yet to adjust to this reality. What makes Abu Ghraib and Guantanamo so discrediting to American claims around the world is the sense that the practices revealed are essentially dysfunctional, giving a worrisome impressions of gratuitous cruelty and religious hatred rather than being practices reluctantly undertaken because of severe threats to security being posed.

There is another dimension to this originality of the present conflict. It is the frustrations associated with the inability to translate military superiority into political outcomes. Already this frustration was evident in the course of the Vietnam War, exerting mounting pressure on the American side to impose more and more harsh punishment on the civilian society of Vietnam so as to find some way to induce the militarily inferior side to surrender. Since the armed forces of the enemy refused to surrender no matter how badly beaten, the only alternative was to treat the people of Vietnam as the enemy, and with that move, the restraints of the law of war were substantially abandoned, and still the war was lost! A similar pattern of frustration is evident in Iraq during the period of occupation that has followed upon the end of battlefield combat on April 30, 2003. When military superiority cannot by itself decide the political outcome of conflicts, the struggle shifts to the civilian arenas. When this happens the fundamental principles of restraint embodied in international humanitarian law give way to a variety of unregulated means to frighten the occupied society into submission. Whether this works or not, the authority of legal restraint is substantially weakened, if not altogether abandoned. And restraint is weakened on both sides. When the society under occupation resists by suicide bombers attacking every target from the Red Cross to the UN, shamelessly beheading journalists and civilians, it is obvious that the restraints of international humanitarian law, and elemental humanitarian ethics, have been repudiated. This same pattern of unrestraint can be seen in the behavior of both sides throughout the long hostile and legally dubious occupation of Palestinian territories by Israel. The collapse of restraint and respect for law almost inevitably follows from the ordeal of occupation giving rise to nationalist struggles of resistance where the conflict is not confined to a military arena but spills over to engulf the entire society.

No aspect of the current situation has generated more criticism and concern than President Bush's expansive views and policies with respect to the altered nature of defensive necessity. In reaction to the continuing vulnerability of the United States to the sort of attack that inflicted such major symbolic and substantive harm as occurred on 9/11, and to the projected danger of weapons of mass destruction falling into terrorist hands, the Bush Doctrine claims a right of preemption to initiate war against a state from which terrorist threats may in the future emerge. The radical nature of this claim is heightened by its vague nature, its explicit refusal to condition recourse to war by the imminence of the threat. The American initiation of the Afghanistan War did not arouse much critical reaction as there appeared to be a plausible basis for the claim of an expanded (beyond the UN Charter) right of defensive necessity. But the Iraq War seemed to shatter the basic frameworks of legal and political restraint that had been brought into being by stages over the course of the prior century, with the US Government insisting that new realities of the post-9/11 world required it to exercise discretion to wage wars wherever and whenever it perceived a present or future threat, and to do so without obtaining 'a permission slip' (from the UN Security Council). The fact that the alleged threat associated with Iraq's supposed possession of WMD turned out to be false gave rise to attitudes of opposition around the world. And then there was the suspicion that Washington's anti-terrorist, pro-democracy rationale for the war was a cover for a wider project associated with a grand strategy to establish regional dominance in the Middle East, with the disguised goal of controlling this major source of global energy reserves. In effect, a strategic war motivated by geopolitical ambition was being waged by the United States under the cover of defensive necessity building on the 9/11 climate of fear and patriotic fervor that prevailed among the American people. Such an interpretation gains further credibility due to the presence of the influential pre-9/11 report of the Project of the New American Century entitled "Repairing America's Defenses" that laid out a vision of American grand strategy centered on regime change for Iraq and the importance of projecting American military power in the Middle East and elsewhere. It has never been made clear whether the United States was claiming the right to wage preemptive and preventive wars only for itself, or whether it was setting a precedent available to other states that felt similarly threatened or expansive.

It is this complex entanglement of issues and that consideration makes it valuable to have this wide-ranging scholarly reflection on the law of armed conflict from a variety of angles. Several issues emerge as dominant: (1) to what extent does the altered nature of the threats posed by global terror vindicate claims of anticipatory self-defense? (2) and if so vindicated, is there any requirement of prior endorsement by the UN Security Council? (3) and if not, is this a law making precedent that alters the international law of self-defense or is it an exception that can be validly claimed only by the United States? (4) and given the premium placed on acquiring information should restraints on methods of interrogation and detention be loosened in relation to terrorist suspects? (5) and since the enemy may be hidden within American society to what extent should the privacy of citizens and residents be encroached upon?

In essence, how do we *rethink* the unthinkable from the perspective of the law of armed conflict? Both international law and the just war doctrine have evolved over time to adapt to changes in the global setting, including accommodating technological innovations in weaponry, tactics, and doctrine, but can these frameworks evolve in the present setting to deal with the new modalities of conflict associated with the War on Global Terror, including the rise to prominence of transnational networks and non-state actors? I think one conclusion emerges: there are restraints embodied in the law of armed conflict that seem as important as ever to maintain, and there is no excuse for discarding the *whole* of international humanitarian law because some *parts* may require and justify adjustment. More specifically, there is no justification for humiliating or cruel treatment of detainees and those captured on the battlefield (whether called 'enemy combatants' or 'prisoners of war'). Similarly, there should be a credible assurance that the grounds for suspicion rest on some reasonable basis when detention or intrusion takes place. It is essential that those who are innocent do not face gratuitous denials of their rights simply because of their religious or ethnic identity. Furthermore, there should be no reason to suspend the carefully developed duties of an occupying power to use due diligence to protect cultural sites and artifacts in the aftermath of war, as well as their more general responsibilities to protect civilians and civilian society. And most important of all, the constraints on discretionary war making, so carefully constructed by the diplomacy of the previous century, should not be cast aside in circumstances where there is no showing of a genuine defensive necessity. The authors of the chapters in this book make a variety of heroic efforts to initiate such dialogues, but valuable as these are they represent no more than the beginning of crucial conversations about the future of the law of armed conflict. Without the continuation and enlargement of such conversations, this noble effort, which the United States has in the past contributed to in such significant ways, is likely to be deeply compromised at a time when a globalizing world is more in need than ever before of a common normative language and supportive practices with respect to political violence.

A final observation. Several of the contributors to this study are Americans approaching the issue with professional integrity, but with an American set of preoccupations and perceptions. As a further stage in adapting and reaffirming the law of armed conflict we need to further widen the dialogue to include more participants from different parts of the world, as well as representatives of civil society actors engaged in armed struggle. A new normative consensus that combines legal, ethical, and religious ideas about right conduct can not be produced on the basis of reason alone, but must be built though the participation of scholars and specialists that represent the various regions and civilizations that together comprise the world, and take due account of the rise of non-state actors as political players in relation to armed conflict.

Index

Abu Ghraib 152, 175, 217, 231n167, 243
Abu Shaqra, Iyad 231n167
accountability xii, 152, 171–91, 242
ACHR *see* American Convention on Human Rights
Adams, John Quincy 3, 203
administrative detention 143
aerial warfare 51–3, 54
af Malmborg, Mikael 201
Afghanistan
    customary law 159n77
    denial of law of armed conflict applicability to 149, 151, 155n24
    detention of prisoners 138, 139, 144, 150, 151, 162n121
    lack of declaration of war 202
    mujahadeen 12
    necessity defense for US attack on 10, 244
    non-POW status of fighters 139, 146–7, 158n74, 186n68
    preventive war 227n73
    US attacks against Al-Qaeda bases 27
    US casualties 231n160
    see also Taliban
Al-Qaeda 1, 141, 194, 195–7, 225n15, n21
    Guantanamo detainees 152
    guerra strategy against 12
    non-combatant/POW status of members 146–7, 158n74, 166n167, 186n68
    Taliban refusal to hand over members 139, 158n73
    transfer of detainees 138, 140
    transnational network 196, 201, 203, 243
    UN Sanctions Committee 185n38
    US missile attacks against Afghanistan bases 27
    see also terrorism
Al-Skeini et al. v. Sec. of State for Defence (2004) 156n51
al-Zawarhi, Ayman 196
Alba, Duke of 89n16
Alexander, Harold 95n107
Alexander I, Tsar of Russia 9
Algeria 115
alien peoples 40, 42, 43, 85
American Convention on Human Rights (ACHR) 132, 154n23
'analytic actors' 198, 208–9, 219, 226n39
Andreopoulos, George J. xii, 171–91
apocalyptic nihilism 193, 194
Aquinas, St. Thomas ix, 205, 213
Aristotle 4
armed groups
    accountability of xii, 171–91
    applicability of Geneva Conventions 137
    applicability of Geneva Protocol II 138, 174
The Art of War (Sun Tzu) 219
art, works of 84–5, 86n6
    Brussels Declaration 46
    Draft International Convention (1938) 54–5

Geneva Protocols (1977) 68, 69, 72
Hague Convention (1954) 60
Hague Rules of Air Warfare 52
Lieber Code 45
Oxford Manual 47
Roerich Pact 53–4
UNESCO Conventions 73, 74
World War I 50
Ashcroft, John 158n74
assassination xii, 21–37
    consequences of 27–32
    definitions of 23, 24
    discrimination 26–7
    history of 22–3
    international law 25–6
    legality of 23–4
    US domestic law 23, 24–5, 27
asymmetric warfare 12
atomic bombs 57, 109, 195, 241–2
Austria 9

Bagram 152, 153n5, 185n35
Bangladesh 196
Bankovic case (1999) 134, 135, 156n52
Battle of Britain 56
Baxter, R. 165n163
Begin, Menachem 226n39
Belgium 50–1, 57
bellum 11
bellum hostile 40
bellum romanum 40
Best, Geoffrey 9
Bethmann-Hollweg, Chancellor von 3
Biddle, Tami Davis 49
Bin Hamid al Fahd, Sheikh Nasr 196
Bin Laden, Osama 12, 27, 158n73, 185n38, 196, 225n15
Blix, Hans 230n149
bombardment 43, 46, 50, 89n16, 122n49

    aerial 51–4, 56–7, 59, 94n98, 107, 109, 110
    Disarmament Conference 93n84
    Hague Conventions (1899/1907) 47–8
    indiscriminate 70
    Lieber Code 44–5
    naval 48–9
Bonaparte, Napoleon 3
The Book of Lao Zi 219
Bosnia 115, 153n7
Bothe, Michael 68, 69, 71, 96n151, 97n153
Boylan, Patrick 41, 65
Bremer, Paul 147, 159n83
Brussels Declaration (1874) 10, 45–6, 47
Brzezinski, Zbigniew 215
Bush Doctrine 194, 213, 244
Bush, George Sr. 22
Bush, George W.
    challenge to neutrality 198, 201, 202, 203
    criticisms of 244
    denial of POW status to Taliban 158n74
    homeland protection 197
    hostility to international law 153n10
    Iraq war 140, 205–6, 228n103
    lack of international confidence in 214
    necessity concept 1, 2, 10, 14
    prison abuse scandals 231n169
    treatment of detainees 178
    US motives 229n128
Bybee, Jay 175
Bynkershoek, Cornelius van ix

Canada 3, 75
capitalism 222, 223
Caroline incident (1837) 8, 205, 208

Carter, Jimmy 23, 24, 225n39
Carthage 43
Casebeer, William 211
Castlereagh, Robert Stewart, Viscount 16n35
Castro, Fidel 22, 24, 32
Central Intelligence Agency (CIA) 22
Chamberlain, Neville 54
charitable institutions
    Brussels Declaration 45–6
    Hague Conventions (1899/1907) 48, 49
    Hague Rules for Air Warfare 52
    Lieber Code 45
    Oxford Manual 46–7
    Roerich Pact 53–4
    World War I 50
chauvinist rivalries 40, 42
Chechnya 115, 133, 155n33, 196
chemical weapons 195
Cheney, Richard B. 14n7, 22
children 182
China 219
Christians 40
Church Committee 22, 24, 31, 32
CIA *see* Central Intelligence Agency
Cicero, Marcus Tullius 5
civil war 40, 115, 118, 171
    see also non-international armed conflicts
civilians
    bombardments 43, 54
    detention of 148–50, 165n161
    Geneva Protocols (1977) 66, 67, 68, 69–72, 114, 115–16
    Hague Rules of Air Warfare 52
    ICRC Draft Rules 65–6
    protection of xii, 105–29, 167n168, 179, 181, 245
    punishment of 243–4

Soviet World War II casualties 57
    targeting of 172
    see also collateral damage
Cold War 22, 27, 30, 197, 220, 221–4
collateral damage x, xi, 28
    cultural property destruction 42, 43, 50, 69
    Geneva Protocols (1977) 70, 71
    Gulf War 75
    World War II 56
collective security x, xi, 33, 199
Colombia 178–9
combatants
    civilian protection 105–6
    discrimination principle x
    international humanitarian law 173
    legitimate killing of 26
    redefinition of xi
    status of 145–8, 149, 163n127, n130, 164n152, 165n154, 166n166
    see also prisoners of war
communism 222–3
communitarianism 200
compensation 52
content analysis 6–7
Convention on Prohibitions or Restrictions on the Use of Certain Conventional Weapons Amended Protocol II 187n83
Convention relative to the Protection of Civilian Persons in Time of War 108
Convention on the Rights of the Child 182, 187n83
Copenhagen bombardment (1807) 8, 89n16
cosmopolitanism 41, 54, 60, 73, 85, 87n10, 88n12

coup d'etats 22, 24, 25
crimes against humanity 141, 143, 242
crimes of universal jurisdiction 141, 142
criminal law 141–2, 156n50, 174, 177, 178
cruel treatment 142, 144, 157n55, 245
cultural property xii, 39–103, 245
   common cultural heritage concept 41–3, 44, 60, 73–4, 85–6, 87n10, 88n12
   cosmopolitan internationalist perspective 41, 54, 60, 73, 85, 87n10, 88n12
   definitions of 60–1, 73, 77, 82, 86n7
   Draft International Convention (1938) 54–6
   early attempts at preservation of 43–50
   emblems designating 48, 52–3, 54, 55, 64–5, 83–4
   Geneva Protocol I (1977) 66–72, 75, 76, 78, 81, 82–3
   Gulf War 74–6
   Hague Convention (1954) 60–5, 68–9, 73, 74–5, 76–9, 82, 83–4
   Hague Convention Second Protocol (1999) 76–82, 83
   Hague Conventions (1899/1907) 47–50
   Hague Rules of Air Warfare (1923) 51–3
   ICRC Draft Rules (1957) 65–6
   interwar years 51–6
   nationalistic perspective 41, 42, 85, 87n10, 88n12
   Roerich Pact 53–4
   special protection of 62–4, 68, 69, 79–80, 81, 83–4
   transport of 63–4
   UNESCO Conventions 72–4, 77
   World War I 50–1, 93n73
   World War II 54, 56–9
   Yugoslavia 76
customary law xii, 137, 242
   civilian protection 72, 107, 116–17, 119, 120
   crimes of universal jurisdiction 141
   cultural property protection 39, 85
   Geneva Protocols (1977) 66, 69, 72, 140, 141
   Hague Conventions 50, 74–5, 198
   non-international armed conflicts 77, 137, 138, 159n77, 180
   see also international law
Cyprus 134, 156n54

death penalty 183n15, 184n20
declaration of war x, 202–3
degrading treatment 142, 144, 157n55
demilitarized zones 67–8, 71
democracy 222, 223
deontological ethics 4–5
Desch, Thomas 77–8
detention xii, 131–70, 245
   abuse of prisoners 144–5, 151–2, 175, 217, 231n167, n169, 243
   administrative 143
   Afghanistan 138, 139, 150
   civilians 148–50
   combatant status 145–8
   human rights law 134–5, 136, 140, 142–5, 149, 150
   international criminal law 141–2
   Iraq 134–5, 138, 140, 147, 150
   law of armed conflict 132, 135, 136–41, 145–50, 151

post-9/11 138, 140–1, 148, 149, 151–2
secret detention centers 175, 185n35
transfers 131, 138, 140, 142, 144, 150, 160n89, 161n102
'war on terror' 138–41, 151–2, 175
see also prisoners of war
deterrence 21, 220, 221
Detter Delupis, Ingrid 6
Diem, Ngo Dinh 22, 24
Disarmament Conference (1934) 93n84
discrimination
  assassination of regime leaders 26–7, 33
  Geneva Protocol I (1977) 66–7, 72, 114
  Hague Rules of Air Warfare 53, 66
  jus in bello x, 13
  military necessity 8
  non-international armed conflicts 180
  state practice 120
  submarine warfare 109–10
distinction *see* discrimination
Dolnik, Adam 206
Draft Convention for the Protection of Civilian Populations Against New Engines of War (1938) 54, 108
Draft International Convention for the Protection of Historic Buildings and Works of Art in Time of War (1938) 54–6, 60, 61, 62, 63
Draft Rules for the Limitation of Dangers Incurred by the Civilian Populations in Time of War (1957) 65–6
dualism 210, 219

due process 141, 150, 176
Dugan, Michael 22
Dulles, John Foster 200
Dunn, David Hastings 213
Durand and Ugarte Case (2000) 162n112
Durant, Michael 167n185

ECHR *see* European Convention on Human Rights
educational institutions
  Brussels Declaration 45–6
  Hague Conventions (1899/1907) 48, 49
  Hague Rules for Air Warfare 52
  Lieber Code 45
  Oxford Manual 47
  Roerich Pact 53–4
  World War I 50
Egypt
  counter-terrorism measures 176
  detention centers 185n35
  Gulf War 75
  holistic culture 226n39
  Six Day War 2, 207
Eisenhower, Dwight 58
Elbe, Joachim von ix
Elsen, Albert E. 90n17
ethics
  civilian protection 117, 118, 119
  deontological 4–5
  see also morality
ethnic conflicts 40, 42
Europe
  military necessity norms 8–10
  rules of warfare 40
  US rift with 209
European Convention on Human Rights (ECHR) 132, 134–5, 143, 153n4, 154n16, n23, 156n54
European Court of Human Rights 133, 134–5, 143, 159n81,

161n104, n106, 162n114
evil 209, 210–11, 241
expediency 4
extra-territoriality 134, 135
extradition 142

Fabricius, Gaius 4–5
fair trial 180
Falk, Richard xii, 241–6
Farha, Adib F. 213
Fehrenbach, T.R. 84
Fenwick, Charles 110, 111, 122n56
First World War *see* World War I
Ford, Gerald R. 23, 24, 25
France
   Algeria conflict 115
   cultural property destruction in 50–1, 57
   Gulf War 75
   Jacobin 195
   military necessity norms 8, 9
   reprisals 113–14
French Revolution (1789) 8, 44, 89n17, 91n24
Frost, Mervyn 231n173

Gaddis, John Lewis 223–4
Garner, James W. 50–1
Geneva Convention (1947) 26
Geneva Conventions (1949) 10, 59, 152, 242, 243
   Afghanistan 139, 151, 158n74
   applicability of convention rules 136, 137, 157n59, 183n15
   binding nature of 158n67
   civilian protection 108, 115, 117, 120, 148, 167n168, 186n57
   detentions 134–5, 150, 156n50, 157n54, 160n89, 178
   engagement with armed groups 181
   human rights law 133
   internments 160n90

non-international armed conflict 137–8
prisoners of war 165n163, 166n166, n167, 175, 186n68
Protocol I (1977)
   applicability of 136, 140, 151
   civilian protection 66, 67, 68, 69–72, 114, 120
   combatant status 148
   cultural property protection 66–72, 75, 76, 78, 81, 82–3
   customary law 137, 140
   due process guarantees 141
   International Fact Finding Commission 181–2
   military necessity 10
   US non-ratification of 145
Protocol II (1977)
   applicability of 137–8, 174
   binding nature of 158n67
   civilian protection 115–16, 117–18, 123n88
   cultural property protection 66, 72
   definition of armed conflict 158n69, 183n15
   detentions 150
   military necessity 10
Geneva Protocol (1925) 10
Geneva Red Cross Conferences (1864/1868) 9–10
genocide 28, 174, 204
Genocide Convention (1948) 59
Gentili, Alberico ix, 31, 43
Germany
   civilian protection 107–8
   criminal responsibility of wartime leaders 242
   cultural property destruction 50–1, 56–8, 93n73, 94n98
   ideological struggle with Soviet Union 40

necessity concept 3, 4
postwar balance of power 223
reprisals 113–14
Goethe, Johann Wolfgang von 14
Goldstein, Joshua 215
Gonzales, Alberto 158n74, 175
Great Britain
    aerial bombardment of Germany 56, 94n98
    burning of Washington 91n24
    civilian protection 107–8
    Cold War 222
    Copenhagen bombardment 8
    cultural property protection 58–9
    detention of Iraqis 134–5
    Gulf War 75
    necessity concept 4, 15n35
    see also United Kingdom
Greeks, ancient 11, 16n41, 88n13
Greenstock, Jeremy 176
Griffiths, Paul 204
Grotius, Hugo ix, 8, 43–4, 206–7, 228n96
Guantanamo Bay 153n5, n7, 175, 187n70, 243
    challenges to lawfulness of detention 144
    denial of detainees' rights 151, 152
    transfer of detainees to 140, 161n102
guerra 11–12
guerre mortelle 40, 57, 59, 86
guerrilla warfare xi, 27
Gulf War (1990-1991)
    cultural property protection 74–6
    financial costs of 215, 216
    neutrality of states 165n165, 199
    prisoners of war 157n62, 166n167
    targeting of Saddam Hussein 23, 26–7

Hague Convention (1899)
    civilian protection 106–7
    cultural property protection 47–50, 51, 53, 58, 65, 82
    Martens Clause 40, 49
    military necessity 10
Hague Convention (1907)
    civilian protection 106–7
    cultural property protection 47–50, 51, 53–4, 58, 65, 74, 82
    detention 160n89
    jus in bello 26
    Martens Clause 40, 49
    military necessity 3, 10
    neutrality 198–9, 202, 203
    occupied territory 134, 140
Hague Convention for the Protection of Cultural Property in the Event of Armed Conflict (1954) 60–5, 68–9, 73, 74–5, 76–9, 82, 83–4
    Second Protocol (1999) 76–82, 83, 187n83
Hague Rules of Air Warfare (1923) 51–3, 66, 107–8, 110
Halifax, Lord 94n98
Hamdan v. Rumsfeld (2004) 159n74, 162n120, 166n166, n167, 167n185
Hamdi v. Rumsfeld (2004) 153n5, 162n120, 166n167
Hampson, Françoise J. xii, 131–70
Hardman incident (1910) 3
Harris, Arthur 56
Hayashi, Mika Nishimura xii, 105–29
Henckaerts, Jean-Marie 81–2
Hensel, Howard M. ix–xiv, 39–103
Hezbollah 213
Hiroshima 57, 109, 241–2
historical monuments
    Brussels Declaration 46

Draft International Convention
(1938) 54–5
Geneva Protocols (1977) 68, 69,
72
Hague Convention (1954) 60
Hague Conventions (1899/1907)
48, 49
Hague Rules of Air Warfare
52–3
Oxford Manual 47
Roerich Pact 53–4
UNESCO Conventions 73, 74
World War I 50
Hitler, Adolf 28, 94n98
Hoffman, Stanley 13
holistic approaches xii,
218–20, 225n39
hospitals 45, 46, 48, 52
HRC *see* Human Rights Committee
Hsiang of Sung, Duke 7
human dignity 172, 181
human rights 40, 41
accountability of armed groups
171, 172
counter-terrorism measures 175,
176–7, 179
state responsibility for
enforcement 184n24
state violations of 175–6
Universal Declaration of Human
Rights 59, 183n12, n14, 223
Human Rights Committee (HRC)
133, 143–4, 156n53, 176–7,
179–80
human rights law 132–6
accountability of armed groups
172–4, 179–82
detention 134–5, 136, 140,
142–5, 149, 150, 152
international humanitarian law
comparison 172–3
Nuremberg verdicts 59
soft law document 180, 181–2

state obligations 180
humanitarian law 10, 79, 132, 171,
242, 245
accountability of armed groups
172, 173–4,
180–2
civilian protection 114, 117, 118,
119
human rights law comparison
172–3
law enforcement framework
177–9
non-international conflicts 77–8
rejection of 244
safeguards against derogation
180
soft law document 180, 181–2
UN Counter-Terrorism
Committee 175
see also law of armed conflict
Hume, David 16n42

ICCPR *see* International Covenant
on Civil and Political Rights
ICJ *see* International Court of Justice
ICRC *see* International Committee
of the Red Cross
ICTR *see* International Criminal
Tribunal for Rwanda
ICTY *see* International Criminal
Tribunal for the former
Yugoslavia
ideological conflict 40, 42
ill-treatment 142, 144, 151–2,
157n55
immediacy 8
India 143, 171, 199
indispensability 8
Indonesia 212, 213
inhuman treatment 142, 144, 157n55
intelligence 33, 75, 215, 243
intentionality 211, 212–14
Inter-American Commission on

Human Rights 162n112, 180, 187n79
Inter-American Court of Human Rights 133, 143, 184n24
internal armed conflicts *see* non-international armed conflicts
International Committee of the Red Cross (ICRC)
  civilian protection 65–6, 108, 120
  commentary on Geneva Conventions 182
  criminal activity 178
  customary law 137
  detainees hidden from 143, 163n121
  international humanitarian law 180
International Court of Justice (ICJ) 6, 7, 204, 242
  advisory opinion on nuclear weapons 205
  civilian protection 116–17, 118
  human rights law 133
  occupied territory 159n82, 160n84
International Covenant on Civil and Political Rights (ICCPR) 132, 133, 143–4, 154n23, 176, 179–80
International Criminal Court 76, 158n64, 242
International Criminal Tribunal for the former Yugoslavia (ICTY) 76, 117–18, 151, 158n64, 172, 242
International Criminal Tribunal for Rwanda (ICTR) 76, 117, 151, 158n64, 242
International Fact Finding Commission 181–2
international law xii, 242, 245
  apologetic perspective 105, 106–14, 116, 119, 120
  assassinations 25–6, 27, 33
  civilian protection 105–20
  compliance with 179
  criminal 141–2
  cultural property protection 39, 50, 60, 65–6, 85–6
  detention 131–52
  efficacy principle 112–13
  Hague Rules of Air Warfare 51–3, 66
human rights 132–6
  accountability of armed groups 172–4, 179–82
  detention 134–5, 136, 140, 142–5, 149, 150, 152
  humanitarian law comparison 172–3
  Nuremberg verdicts 59
  soft law document 180, 181–2
  state obligations 180
humanitarian 10, 79, 132, 171, 242, 245
  accountability of armed groups 172, 173–4, 180–2
  civilian protection 114, 117, 118, 119
  human rights law comparison 172–3
  law enforcement framework 177–9
  non-international conflicts 77–8
  rejection of 244
  safeguards against derogation 180
  soft law document 180, 181–2
  UN Counter-Terrorism Committee 175

jus ad bellum 25–6
military necessity 1, 2, 7–8, 10, 11
neutrality 198–200, 202
non-international armed conflicts 77–8
publicists 5–6
UNESCO Conventions 72–4
utopian perspective 105, 106, 114–8, 119–20
'war convention' 3
war definition 12
see also customary law; Geneva Conventions; Hague Conventions; law of armed conflict
International Law Association 54, 108
international norms 2, 3, 41
content analysis 6–7
definition of 15n12
inclusion/exclusion 16n42
interpretation of 132
necessity concept 5, 6, 7–10
publicists 5–6
internationalism 41, 54, 60, 73, 85–6, 87n10, 88n12
internment 141, 143, 149–50, 160n90, 167n188
interrogation of prisoners 10, 150, 167n87, 245
abuse allegations 144
state responsibility for 142–3
torture 152, 175
US denial of detainees' rights 151
Iran 165n165, 196, 199
Iraq
abuse of prisoners 144, 152
challenges of 241
detention of prisoners 134–5, 138, 140, 144, 147, 150, 164n137
financial costs of war against 214–15, 216
Gulf War 75–6, 157n62, 199
interim government 159n83
Iraqi casualties of war 216–17, 231n161
lack of declaration of war 202
necessity defense for US invasion 10, 244
non-combatant status of fighters 146, 147
occupation of 139–40, 243–4
perceived threat from 205–6
preventive war 2, 227n73
regime change 21, 244–5
targeting of Saddam Hussein 22
US casualties of war 216, 231n161
US motives for war 213, 227n90, 244
WMD claims 21, 215, 230n149, 244
Israel
collapse of restraint 244
holistic culture 226n39
interrogations 167n87
rejection of human rights law 133, 134
security wall 242
Six Day War 2, 207
Italy
cultural property destruction 50–1
reprisals 113–14
Japan
atomic bombs dropped on 57, 109, 195, 241–2

criminal responsibility of
wartime leaders 242
holistic culture 219
postwar balance of power 223
US aerial bombardment of 57
Johnson, James Turner 213
Jordan 185n35, 199, 212
jurisdiction
Hague Convention Second
Protocol 81–2
human rights law 134, 135, 136
international criminal law 141,
142
jus ad bellum ix, xii, 25–6, 178, 194,
208
jus in bello (law of armed conflict)
x, xii, 25, 242, 245–6
apologetic vs utopian perspective
105
assassinations 26
civilian protection 106, 107, 119,
120
detention 132, 135, 136–41,
145–50, 151, 152
Geneva Protocols (1977) 66, 72
Hague Convention (1954) 60
Hague Convention Second
Protocol (1999) 76
human rights law relationship
133–4
Lieber Code 45
military necessity 13
Oxford Manual 47
reprisals 113
selective humanitarianism 178
see also customary law;
international law
just cause ix, x, 178, 207–8, 213
Just War Theory ix, xii,
194–5, 197, 221, 245
constraints on use of force 204,
208
neutrality 200–1, 202, 210

preventive war 206–7
right intention 213–14
self-defense 205

Kagan, Robert 218
Karzai, Hamid 139
Kennan, George 222
Kiesling, John Brady 212
killing of regime leaders *see*
assassination
Kitchener, Lord 3
Kosovo 23
Kriegsraison geht vor Kriegsmanier
7–8
Kuwait 75–6, 199, 212

Lao Zi 219, 222
last resort ix
Lauterpacht, Hersch 109–10, 111
law of armed conflict (LOAC) (*jus
in bello*) x, xii, 25, 242,
245–6
apologetic vs utopian perspective
105
assassinations 26
civilian protection 106, 107, 119,
120
detention 132, 135, 136–41,
145–50, 151, 152
Geneva Protocols (1977) 66, 72
Hague Convention (1954) 60
Hague Convention Second
Protocol (1999) 76
human rights law relationship
133–4
Lieber Code 45
military necessity 13
Oxford Manual 47
reprisals 113
selective humanitarianism 178
see also customary law;
international law
League of Nations x, 54, 107, 118

Lebanon 12, 212, 213
Legality of Nuclear Weapons case (1996) 116–17
legality principle 176
legitimacy ix, 8
legitimate targets xi, 49, 51, 75, 90n21, 107
Leningrad, siege of 57
Levitte, Jean-David 230n150
Libya 26
Lieber Code 44–5
Lieber, Francis 7, 44
life, right to 184n20
Lincoln, Abraham 44
LOAC *see* law of armed conflict
London Treaty on the Limitation of Naval Armaments (1936) 108
Lotrionte, Catherine xii, 21–37
Lumumba, Patrice 22, 24
Luxembourg 57

MacArthur, Douglas 223
Machiavelli, Niccolo 217, 231n170
McKinly, William 3
Manningham-Buller, Eliza 196
'Mao Dun Lu' 219–20
Martens Clause 40, 49, 117, 119
Merryman, John 41, 60, 84, 85, 88n12, 90n17
military courts 162n113
military necessity xi, xii, 1–20, 245
  assassination of regime leaders 33
  asymmetric warfare 12
  counter-terrorism measures 176
  cultural property protection 42, 45–7, 49, 58, 61–3, 78–9, 82–3, 84–5
  elasticity of concept 210
  historical trends in support for 8–10
  imminence test 205, 206, 208
  normative support for appeals to 5–10
  US 'war on terror' 10–11, 12, 13, 211
  'war convention' 2–5
Military and Paramilitary Activities in and against Nicaragua case (1986) 117, 204
Mill, John Stuart 16n35
Milosevic, Slobodan 28
mines 107
Moldova 134
morality
  assassinations 28, 29, 31
  deontological 4–5
  neutrality 200–1
  use of force 228n116
  see also ethics
Morgan, April xii, 193–239
Morocco 185n35, 212
Mubarak, Hosni 217
multilateralism 209, 218
Muslims 43, 212–13
mutually assured destruction 220, 221, 223, 224

Nagasaki 57, 109, 241–2
Napoleonic Wars 8, 44, 89n17, 91n24
national identity 41, 42
national liberation movements 174
nationalism 41, 42, 85, 87n10, 88n12, 244
natural heritage sites 74, 86n7, 98n197
natural law 40
naval bombardments 48–9
naval warfare 107
  see also submarine warfare
necessity xi, xii, 1–20, 245
  assassination of regime leaders 33
  asymmetric warfare 12

counter-terrorism measures 176
cultural property protection 42, 45–7, 49, 58, 61–3, 78–9, 82–3, 84–5
elasticity of concept 210
historical trends in support for 8–10
imminence test 205, 206, 208
normative support for appeals to 5–10
US 'war on terror' 10–11, 12, 13, 211
'war convention' 2–5
Netherlands 51, 57
neutrality 165n165, 194, 198–204, 207, 209, 226n66
Newark 3
NGOs *see* non-governmental organizations
Nicaragua 117, 204
Nicholson, Harold 84–5
Nigeria 212, 213
9/11 terrorist attacks *see* September 11th 2001 terrorist attacks
non-discrimination 176
non-governmental organizations (NGOs) 171, 172, 181
non-international armed conflicts
 accountability of armed groups 179
 Afghanistan 139
 civilian protection 115, 116, 117, 120, 123n82
 customary law 77, 137, 138, 159n77, 180
 detentions 150
 Geneva Conventions 183n16
 Hague Convention Second Protocol 77, 82
 human rights law 173
 International Fact Finding Commission 182
 international humanitarian law 77–8, 174
 law of armed conflict 133, 137–8
 treaties covering 187n83
 see also civil war
non-intervention 183n14
non-refoulement 161n102, 176
norms *see* international norms
North Korea 217
Northern Alliance 146
Northern Ireland 115
nuclear weapons 27, 30, 116, 205, 217, 223, 232n200, 241
 see also weapons of mass destruction
Nuremberg Tribunal (1946) 10, 50, 59, 65, 242

occupied territory
 combatant status in 148
 cultural property protection 49, 62, 79, 83
 definition of 156n43
 human rights law jurisdiction 134
 ICJ Advisory Opinion 159n82, 160n84
 Iraq 139–40
 law of armed conflict 136
Office of the High Commissioner for Human Rights (OHCHR) 176, 177
O'Keefe, Patrick 87n8
Omar, Mullah 158n73
Oxford Manual on the Laws of War on Land (1880) 46–7

Pakistan 140, 171, 196, 212
Palestinian territories 242, 244
Parker, Geoffrey 89n16
Partsch, Karl 68, 69, 71, 96n151, 97n153

peacekeeping 159n80
Pearl Harbor 224, 225n31
Petrochilos, Georgios C. 199, 204, 226n66
Pew Global Attitudes Project 212–13, 214
Philippines 196
pillage 43, 46, 48, 49, 62, 81, 90n19
Pinochet, Augusto 242
Poland 57–8
Polybius 43, 90n19
Portugal 9
Powell, Colin 158n74, 202, 230n149
POWs *see* prisoners of war
Pradier-Fodéré, Paul 8
precautionary measures 70–1, 180
preemptive action 204, 206, 216, 245
   assassination 30
   Bush Doctrine 21, 244
   Cold War 220
   international law 25
   military necessity 1–2, 13
   as self-defense xi
   'wise war' decision-making criteria 221
   see also preventive action
Preliminary Draft International Convention for the Protection of Historic Buildings and Works of Art in Time of War (1938) 54–6, 60, 61, 62, 63
preventive action xi, 194, 206–7, 208, 227n73, 245
   Cold War 220, 223, 224
   costs of 216, 217
   logic of exaggeration 212
   military necessity 1–2, 11, 12, 13, 14
   Russia 230n157
   'wise war' decision-making criteria 221
   see also preemptive action

prisoners of war (POWs) 145, 148, 149, 157n62, 163n131
   administrative detention 143
   Afghanistan 139, 146–7, 158n74, 186n68
   customary law 137
   Cyprus 156n54
   Geneva Convention 165n163, 166n166, n167, 175
   interrogation of 150
   Iraq 134, 147
   militia members 163n130
   redefinition of xi
   repatriation of 154n11, 157n62
   see also combatants
proportionality ix, x, 208
   assassination of regime leaders 33
   counter-terrorism measures 176
   Geneva Protocol I (1977) 66, 70, 71, 72
   Hague Rules of Air Warfare 53, 66
   human rights law 133
   military necessity 8
   non-international armed conflicts 180
   preventive war 13
Prosecutor v. Dusko Tadic case (1995) 117, 118
prospect of victory ix–x
Prott, Lyndel 87n8
Pruitt, D.G. 209–10
Prussia 4, 9
public opinion on the United States 209, 212
publicists 5–6
Pufendorf, Samuel ix
Putin, Vladimir 230n157

Qaddafi, Muammar 26
   Al-Qaeda 1, 141, 194, 195–7, 225n15, n21

Guantanamo detainees 152
guerra strategy against 12
non-combatant/POW status of members 146–7, 158n74, 166n167, 186n68
Taliban refusal to hand over members 139, 158n73
transfer of detainees 138, 140
transnational network 196, 201, 203, 243
UN Sanctions Committee 185n38
US missile attacks against Afghanistan bases 27
see also terrorism

Raisi, Lofti 161n100
Raymond, Gregory A. xii, 1–20, 211, 214
Reagan, Ronald 23, 24, 25
realism 4, 105, 106, 223–4
refugees 161n102
regime change 21, 29, 244–5
see also assassination
regional instability 32
relative justice of cause x
religious conflicts 40, 42
religious institutions
    Brussels Declaration 45–6
    Geneva Protocols (1977) 68, 69, 72
    Hague Convention (1954) 60
    Hague Conventions (1899/1907) 48, 49
    Hague Rules for Air Warfare 52
    Nicholson on 84
    Oxford Manual 46–7
    Roerich Pact 53–4
    UNESCO Convention 73
    World War I 50
reprisals 50, 55, 56, 59, 68, 110, 113–14
responsibility 8

right intention 213–14
right motives ix
Robinson, Mary 176
Rodley, Nigel 176
Roerich Pact (1935) 53–4, 65
rogue states 197, 209
Romans 11–12, 16n41, n44, 43
Roosevelt, Eleanor 223
Roosevelt, Franklin D. 56, 94n98
Root, Elihu 8
Rothenberg, Gunther 89n16
Royse, M.W. 122n49
RTS television studio 134
Rubin, Alfred P. 200
rule of law 151–2, 180
Rumsfeld, Donald 1, 10, 164n144, 212, 218, 229n121, 241
Russia
    Chechnya 115, 155n33
    concern about US military threat 212
    military necessity norms 9
    Moldova 134
    preventive use of force 230n157
    see also Soviet Union
Rwanda 76, 117, 242

Sadat, Anwar 226n39
Saddam Hussein 10, 22, 23, 26–7, 28, 150
St. Ambrose ix
St. Augustine ix, 194, 207–8, 213–14
St. Petersburg Declaration 10, 14
Saudi Arabia 75, 185n35
Schelling, Thomas 224
Schindler, Dietrich 65–6
Schneider, Rene 22, 24
Schultz, George 14n7
Schwarzenburger, Georg 110
scientific institutions
    Brussels Declaration 45–6

Hague Convention (1954) 60
Hague Conventions (1899/1907) 48, 49
Hague Rules for Air Warfare 52
Lieber Code 45
Oxford Manual 46–7
Roerich Pact 53–4
UNESCO Conventions 73, 74
World War I 50
Second Protocol to the Hague Convention for the Protection of Cultural Property in the Event of Armed Conflict (1999) 76–82, 83, 187n83
Second World War *see* World War II
self-defense x–xi, 25, 245
　assassinations 23, 27, 30, 33
　military necessity xii, 2, 11, 13, 14
　regime change 21
　response to 9/11 138, 178
　US security policy 2, 205, 208
　war convention 194
self-preservation 4
Seneca, Lucius Annaeus 16n44
September 11th 2001 terrorist attacks xi, 1, 2, 12, 14, 27
　ambiguity of modern security concerns 193
　detention of suspects 131
　impact of 171
　normative space after 174–9
　planning of 196
　simplistic US view of 209
　US national security policy since 197–8, 241, 244–5
　see also Al-Qaeda; terrorism
Shakespeare, William 14
Shaw, Malcolm 6
Sheridan, P.H. 3
Sherman, William T. 14
sieges 43, 46, 48, 89n16

Six Day War (1967) 2, 207
social harmony 218
soft law 180, 181, 182
Solana, Javier 209, 212
Solf, Waldemar 68, 69, 71, 96n151, 97n153
Somalia 12, 23, 167n185, 196
South Korea 217, 219
sovereignty 41, 201, 209, 217, 231n173
Soviet Union
　Cold War 197, 220, 221–4
　collapse of 196
　cultural property protection 59
　German offensive against 57
　ideological struggle with Germany 40
　see also Russia
Spain
　Civil War 54
　conquest of the Americas 40, 43, 85
　military necessity norms 9
Stacey, Robert 89n16
Stalingrad, battle of 57
state practice
　civilian protection 105, 106, 108–12, 113–14, 116–17, 118–20
　declaration of war 203
　detentions 132
state-centrism 172–3
Statute of the International Criminal Court 76, 158n64, 187n83
Suarez, Francisco ix, 194
submarine warfare 108, 109–10, 111, 113, 114
Sukra 4
Sun Tzu 219, 222
Sweden 185n35

Tadic case (1995) 117, 118

Taft, William H. 158n74
Taliban 10, 150, 158n72, 164n144
   non-combatant/POW status of fighters 139, 146, 158n74, 178, 186n68
   refusal to hand over Al-Qaeda members 139, 158n73, 202
   UN Sanctions Committee 185n38
   see also Afghanistan
Tamil Tigers 181
Taoism 219–20
targeting enemy leaders *see* assassination
Taylor, Telford 13, 59
Tenet, George 195, 225n15, n21
terrorism
   assassination 27
   crimes of universal jurisdiction 141, 142
   detention of suspects 131, 138–41, 151–2
   engagement with armed groups 181
   law enforcement framework 177–9
   military necessity 1, 10–11, 12, 13, 14
   repressive counter-terrorism measures 175–7
   September 11th 2001 attacks xi, 1, 2, 12, 14, 27
      ambiguity of modern security concerns 193
      detention of suspects 131
      impact of 171
      normative space after 174–9
      planning of 196
      simplistic US view of 209
      US national security policy since 197–8, 241, 244–5
   see also Al-Qaeda; 'war on terror'
Themistocles 15n21
Thirty Years War (1618-1648) 44, 51
Thomas, Ward 27
threats xi, xii, 205–7, 209, 228n116
Tokyo Tribunal (1948) 10, 50, 242
Toman, Jiri 65–6
torture 152, 157n55, 168n189
   detainees in Afghanistan 162n121
   non-derogable prohibition against 133
   norm against 175, 185n34
   rationalization of 243
   transfer of detainees 142, 144
   'war on terror' 175
Transnational Rules Indicator Project (TRIP) 7
'treacherous' behavior 26, 27
Treaty on the Limitation of Naval Armaments (1922) 108, 121n25
Treaty on the Protection of Artistic and Scientific Institutions and Historic Monuments (Washington/Roerich Pact, 1935) 53–4, 65
TRIP *see* Transnational Rules Indicator Project
Troy 16n49
Trujillo, Rafael 22, 24
Truman, Harry S. 222, 223
Turkey 134, 157n54, 162n114, 212

UN *see* United Nations
UNESCO *see* United Nations Educational, Scientific and Cultural Organization
unilateralism 193–4, 209, 218
United Kingdom (UK)

detentions 143, 153n4, 157n62
internment of Germans 167n188
Iraq war 139–40
necessity concept 3, 4
Northern Ireland 115
peacekeeping 159n80
prisoners of war 166n167
see also Great Britain
United Nations (UN)
  Afghanistan conflict 159n75
  Basic Principles on the Use of Force and Firearms by Law Enforcement Officials 173
  civilian protection 118, 120, 179, 183n7
  Counter-Terrorism Committee 175–7
  engagement with armed groups 181
  human rights law 41
  ISAF force 139
  necessity concept 10
  Sanctions Committee 185n38
  Security Council x–xi, 138, 175–6, 199–200, 226n66, 245
  support for United States 31
  targeting of civilians 172
United Nations Charter x, 12, 26, 194, 195, 197
  constraints on use of force 204, 208
  engagement with armed groups 182
  human rights law 132, 154n14
  neutrality 199–200
  preventive war 206
  Security Council authorization of force 25
  self-defense 2, 13, 14n10, 25, 205
  US post-9/11 actions 138, 140
United Nations Educational, Scientific and Cultural Organization (UNESCO) 60, 99n222
  Convention Concerning the Protection of World Cultural and National Heritage (1972) 73–4, 76, 77, 83
  Convention on the Means of Prohibiting and Preventing the Illicit Import, Export and Transfer of Ownership of Cultural Property (1970) 72–3, 77
United States (US)
  abuse of prisoners 144–5, 151–2, 175, 217, 231n167, n169, 243
  Afghanistan conflict 139, 146–7, 151, 158n74, 159n77, 164n144, 231n160
  assassinations 22–5, 26–7, 31, 32
  burning of Washington 91n24
  challenge to neutrality 194, 198–204, 207
  civilian protection 107–8
  Cold War 197, 220, 221–4
  combatant definition 163n131
  concealment of detainees 143, 163n121
  cultural property protection 44–5, 58–9, 75–6
  denial of combatant/POW status to enemy fighters 146–7, 158n74, 166n167, 186n68
  detentions 140–1, 143–5, 151–2, 167n185, 185n35, 187n70
  extradition of suspects 142
  as 'global state' 243
  Gulf War 75–6, 215, 216
  holistic approaches 225n39
  hostility to international law 153n10
  international reaction to 209, 212–14, 215–16, 217

internment of Japanese citizens 167n188
Iraq war 140, 146–7, 152, 216–17, 227n90, 244–5
Laws of War 26
National Security Strategy 1–2, 14, 177, 193, 197–8, 204, 205–10
necessity concept 3, 4, 10–11, 12–13
nuclear weapons 232n200
preventive warfare 1, 2, 14, 206, 244, 245
regime change 21
rejection of human rights law 133, 134
torture of prisoners 175
'war on terror' 10–11, 12–13, 138–41, 151–2, 177–9, 193–221, 241
World War II aerial bombardments 56, 57, 94n98
Universal Declaration of Human Rights (1948) 59, 183n12, n14, 223
universalism 40–1
Uzbekistan 185n43

Vattel, Emerich de ix, 44, 90n21, n22
Vienna, Congress of 8, 10
Vietnam War 151, 152, 243
Vitoria, Francisco de ix, 40, 194

Waldock, C.H.M. 8
Walzer, Michael 2, 29, 200–1, 206–7, 227n73, 228n98
'war convention' 2–5, 10, 11, 12, 194, 209, 224n4

war crimes 81–2, 141, 147, 158n64
war definition 12
'war on terror' 193–239, 241, 245
  accountability of armed groups 171–2, 178–9, 182
  armed conflict definition 136–7
  consequences and costs of 194, 210–18
  detention of suspects 138–41, 151–2
  erosion of standards 174
  law enforcement framework 177–9
  'Mao Dun Lu' approach 220
  military necessity 10–11, 12, 13
  neutrality 198, 201–4, 226n66
  repressive measures 175–7
  torture 175
  'wise war' decision-making criteria 220–1, 224
  see also Al-Qaeda; terrorism
Washington, George 204
Washington Naval Conference (1921-1922) 107
Washington (Roerich) Pact (1935) 53–4, 65
weapons of mass destruction (WMD) xi, 11, 194
  Al-Qaeda 196
  assassination and its consequences 27, 28–9, 30, 32
  self-defense against 208
  Soviet Union collapse 220
  UN Charter 195
  US claims about Iraq 21, 215, 230n149, 244

see also nuclear weapons
Webster, Daniel 8
Wedgwood, Ruth 153n10
Williams, Sharon 60, 86n6, 87n10
wise war 193, 220–1, 222, 224
WMD see weapons of mass destruction
Wolff, Christian ix
Wolfowitz, Paul 2
World Heritage List 74, 76, 83
World Trade Center see September 11th 2001 terrorist attacks
World War I
    civilian protection 106, 107, 109, 110, 111, 113
    cultural property destruction 50–1, 93n73
    military necessity 4
World War II
    atomic bombs dropped on Japan 57, 109, 195, 241–2
    civilian protection 106, 109, 110, 111, 113
    cultural property destruction 54, 56–9, 85
    internments 167n188

Yemen 115, 141, 196
Yugoslavia, former 40, 76, 117, 134, 242